MATHEMATICS
FOR
COMPUTER GRAPHICS
AND
GAME PROGRAMMING

MATHEMATICS

FOR

COMPUTER GRAPHICS

AND

GAME PROGRAMMING

A Self-Teaching Introduction

D. P. Kothari, PhD
G. K. Awari, PhD
D. D. Shrimankar, PhD
A. R. Bhende, PhD

MERCURY LEARNING AND INFORMATION

Dulles, Virginia
Boston, Massachusetts
New Delhi

Publisher: David Pallai
MERCURY LEARNING AND INFORMATION
22841 Quicksilver Drive
Dulles, VA 20166
info@merclearning.com
www.merclearning.com
1-800-232-0223

D. P. Kothari, G. K. Awari, D. D. Shrimankar, A. R. Bhende.
Mathematics for Computer Graphics and Game Programming.
ISBN: 978-1-68392-356-5

The publisher recognizes and respects all marks used by companies, manufacturers, and developers as a means to distinguish their products. All brand names and product names mentioned in this book are trademarks or service marks of their respective companies. Any omission or misuse (of any kind) of service marks or trademarks, etc. is not an attempt to infringe on the property of others.

Library of Congress Control Number: 2018964987

192021321   Printed on acid-free paper in the United States of America.

Our titles are available for adoption, license, or bulk purchase by institutions, corporations, etc. For additional information, please contact the Customer Service Dept. at 800-232-0223(toll free).

All of our titles are available in digital format at *authorcloudware.com* and other digital vendors. The sole obligation of MERCURY LEARNING AND INFORMATION to the purchaser is to replace the book, based on defective materials or faulty workmanship, but not based on the operation or functionality of the product.

CONTENTS

PREFACE

In this world of fierce competition, it is absolutely necessary for technocrats to keep updated and upgraded with ever-changing technology. As engineers, it's our duty to adapt to these changing scenarios and pay back to society and the nation. This scenario of ever-changing technology has motivated us to write this book and help others keep up with the pace. This book is written keeping in mind the requirements of engineering students and industry professionals.

Features of the Book
- Concepts are explained with relevant mathematical derivations
- Unsolved examples and multiple choice questions are included at the end of the chapters for practice and self-evaluation
- C programs based on various algorithms
- Numerous solved examples in each chapter

Computer graphics is an interdisciplinary subject which is used by undergraduate and postgraduate students of mechanical engineering, aeronautical engineering, production engineering, computer science, and information technology. Most of the current titles, however, do not cover the mathematical concepts related to these topics. As a result, students often have difficulty understanding these mathematical concepts and their analytical treatment. This book aims to help readers understand all of the major topics of the subject. It focuses on the mathematical concepts involved in computer graphics and computer aided design currently taught or used in industry.

—The Authors

1 Chapter INTRODUCTION TO COMPUTER GRAPHICS

1.1 DEFINITION OF COMPUTER GRAPHICS

Computer graphics involves the display, manipulation, and storage of picture and experiential data for proper visualization using a computer. Typical graphics systems comprise a host computer with the support of a fast processor, large memory, frame buffer, and display devices; output devices as color monitors, liquid crystal display, laser printers, plotters, etc.; and input devices (mouse, keyboard, joystick, touch screen, trackball, etc.).

Computer graphics have many applications:

1. Computer graphics are used in developing the components of a Graphic User Interface (GUI). These GUI components are used to communicate between the software and the user. Examples of GUI components are menus, icons, cursors, dialog boxes, scroll bars, etc.

2. Computer graphics are used in the corporate sector for representing the sales data and economic data using pi-charts, histogram, graphs, etc.

3. Office automation software use GUI components for a researcher's report or thesis.

4. Computer graphics are used in the publication of books, magazines, journals, etc.

5. Computer graphics are used in the advertising field to provide graphic features that make advertisements more impactful.

6. Computer graphics are essential in the entertainment and communication industries worldwide, appearing everwhere from TV monitors to mobile phones.

7. Computer graphics are vital to simulation—the imitation of real world processes in a model over time, such as aircraft and car racing simulations. Aircraft simulations train budding pilots before they get hands-on experience in real aircraft.

8. Computer graphics are used in audiovisual teaching aids in education. They improve teaching outcomes in school and help employees develop skills in profession training.

9. Computer graphics are used in the industry for computer-aided design and computer-aided manufacturing (CAD-CAM).

1.1.1 Definition of Computer Aided Design (CAD)

Computer Aided Design is defined as any use of a computer to assist in the creation, modification, analysis, or optimization of 2-dimensional (2D) and 3-dimensional (3D) designs. Examples of 2D CAD include plan or layout designs, and 3D CAD includes solid and 3D modeling. Some of the common applications of 2D CAD are architectural building plans, layout plans, machine part drawing, electrical circuitry drawing, etc. Animated movies and video games are applications of 3D CAD. Vector representations/ parametric representations of 2D entities (such as lines, circles, conics), 3D entities, and

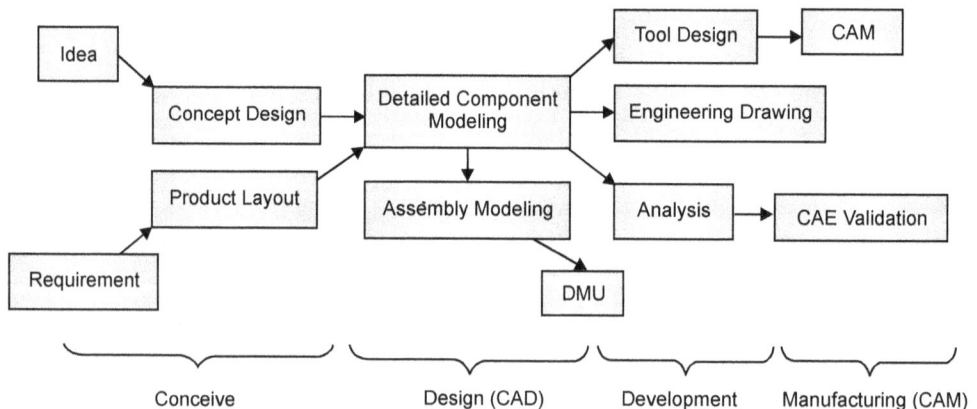

Fig. 1.1 Steps in the engineering process

surfaces are used to develop computer based CAD software. CAD is extensively used throughout the engineering process, as shown in Fig. 1.1. Engineering processes begin as early as conceptual design and layout of product to component modeling, assembly modeling, strength and dynamic analysis of assemblies, to definition of manufacturing methods of components. CAD has become especially important within the scope of Computer Aided Technologies. Benefits of CAD include a greatly shortened design cycle and lower product design and development costs. CAD enables designers to simulate a working model on screen, edit or manipulate the model, maintain the record by saving the files, and generate reports.

1.2 IMAGE GENERATION ON SCREEN

In computer graphics, an image is generated on a display device. Underlying technologies for full-area two-dimensional displays include: cathode ray tube display (CRT), light-emitting diode display (LED), electroluminescent display (ELD), electronic paper, electronic ink, plasma display panel (PDP), liquid crystal display (LCD), organic light-emitting diode display (OLED), laser TV, etc. The multiplexed display technique is used to drive most modern display devices. Earlier cathode ray tube (CRT) based display devices are used in the following display devices:

1. Direct view storage tube (DVST)
2. Calligraphic or random scan display system
3. Raster scan display system

Before moving on to the display device, let us first see the working of the cathode ray tube (CRT).

1.2.1 Working of Cathode Ray Tubes (CRT)

A cathode is a (negatively charged) electron gun that contains a filament. When the filament is heated, the electrons are emitted in a straight beam. When the beam hits a phosphorus-coated CRT screen at a certain velocity, it emits light and a bright spot appears on the screen (Fig. 1.2). The different components of a CRT are:

Cathode: A cathode is made up of a filament which generates electrons on heating. This is also called an electron gun. These negatively charged electrons are directed towards the screen.

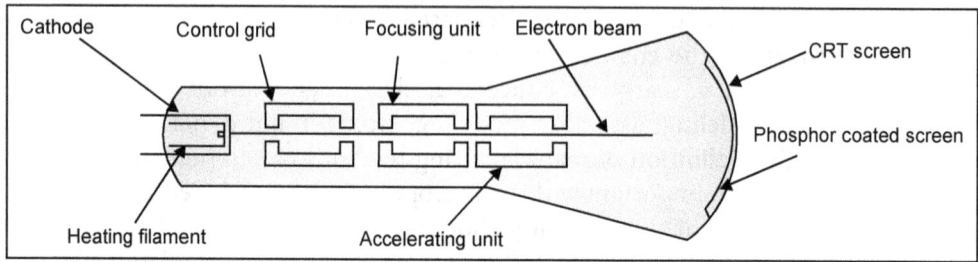

Fig. 1.2 The cathode ray tube

Control Grid: The intensity or brightness of any point on the screen depends upon the intensity of the electron beam coming out from the electron gun. A control grid is used to control the intensity of the electrons emerging from the electron gun according to the intensity of the point required on the screen. The control grid is negatively charged with varying intensity. The intensity of the negative charge is achieved by providing negative voltage to the control grid. If high negative voltage is provided, then a strong negative field is developed, which in turn repels the amount of electrons coming out from the electron gun. On the other hand, if low voltage is supplied to the control grid, this produces a low negative charged field, and that increases the intensity of electrons coming out from the electron gun. In other words, by changing the voltage of the control grid, the brightness of a point on the screen can be changed.

Focusing Anode: The focusing anode is a positively charged field which focuses the electron beam on a particular point on the screen.

Accelerating Anode: The accelerating anode accelerates the velocity of the electrons in an electron beam so that they hit the screen at a high velocity. This ensures that light is emitted and a bright spot appears on the screen.

1.2.2 Design of Deflection Mechanism of CRT

The deflection mechanism deflects the electron beam so that it strikes the screen at the desired location. There are two types of deflection plates: the horizontal deflection plate and the vertical deflection plate. Horizontal deflection plates are basically vertically placed but deflect the electron beam in a horizontal direction, whereas vertical deflection plates are horizontally placed but deflect the electron beam in a vertical direction. These deflection plates are provided with an electric field which deflects the electron beam from its straight path. The deflection mechanism is shown in Fig. 1.3. There are two methods of providing an electric field to the two deflector plates:

1. Electromagnetic field
2. Electrostatic field

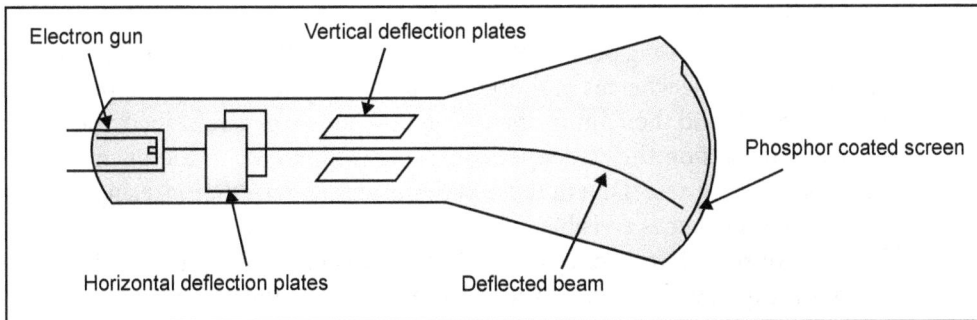

Fig 1.3 Deflection mechanism of CRT

An electromagnetic field is most commonly used in modern display devices such as TV monitors, etc. In this method, a magnetic field is generated in the deflector plates. An electrostatic field is most commonly used in applications such as cathode ray oscilloscopes (CRO). In this method, a static capacitive field is generated in the deflector plates.

1.3 IMAGE GENERATING TECHNIQUES

Image generation techniques are classified on the basis of the use of cathode ray tubes (CRT) in display devices. Devices that use CRT for image generation on screen are called CRT-based display devices. Examples: direct view storage tube (DVST), random scan display devices, and raster scan display devices.

Similarly, display devices that do not use CRT for image generation on the screen are termed non-CRT-based display devices. All modern display devices come under this category. The size of the display device is reduced considerably and it is flatter than a CRT based display device. Non-CRT-based display devices are liquid crystal displays (LCD), light emitting diodes (LED), plasma monitors, etc.

1.3.1 CRT Based Display Devices

As we have discussed earlier, there are three CRT based display devices: direct view storage tubes, calligraphic or random scan display systems and raster scan display systems. These CRT based display devices are further classified into two categories: a line-based system and point-based system as shown in Fig. 1.4. Direct view storage tube and calligraphic or random scan display systems, are examples of line-based system, whereas raster scan display systems are examples of point-based systems. In line-based display devices, any geometric entity on the screen is made up of small lines. Even a curve or circle is also made up of small lines, whereas in point-based systems, it is made up of points. The phosphor coating in CRT is of two types: long persistent phosphor coating and short persistent phosphor coating. In long persistent phosphor coating, the bright spot appears for a long period of time whereas in short persistent phosphor coating it appears for a few milliseconds and then diminishes. When the screen gets refreshed, the bright spot again appears on the screen. This cycle is continued and the phenomenon is called the refresh rate. Due to these cycles of screen refresh, flickering appears on the screen. Flicker is a visible fading between the cycles, especially when the refresh rate or refresh frequency is low. A low refresh rate allows the brightness to drop for time intervals sufficiently long to be noticed by the human eye.

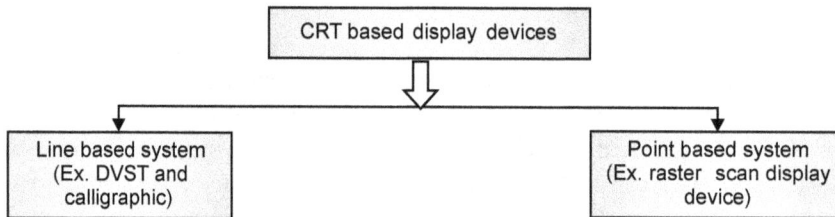

Fig. 1.4 Classification of CRT based display devices

1.3.1.1 Direct View Storage Tube (DVST)

In DVST, the CRT screen is coated with permanent phosphorescence. This permanent phosphorescence coating on the screen ensures the entity drawn on the screen will remain there for long time, say 1 to 2 hours. Because of this permanent phosphorescence, the figure appears on the screen for a long time and changing the entity on the screen becomes difficult. For erasing the entity, the screen must be flooded with a particular voltage. So, if we have to make changes, we have to erase the entire screen by supplying voltage to the screen and then redraw the new entity on the screen. A line in DVST can be drawn from any point to any point on the screen. This property is not shared by other display devices. This is the reason why it is called a line-based system. Any image on the screen of DVST is drawn by using small lines. DVST is a flicker free display device.

The disadvantages of DVST:

1. The process of drawing any entity is slow.
2. No animation is possible.
3. Erasing an entity is difficult.

1.3.1.2 Calligraphic or Random Scan Display System

This is also a line-based system like the DVST, which means we can draw a line from any point to any point on the screen. The drawback of DVST, is that an image appears for a very long time (1 to 2 hours), is eliminated in random scan display systems. Here the picture is refreshed or reappears on the screen about 40 to 50 times in a second. But due to this high frequency of refresh, the refreshing process is not observed by the human eye, but a slight flickering appears on the screen. The main components of random scan display systems are screen, buffer (memory), and controller.

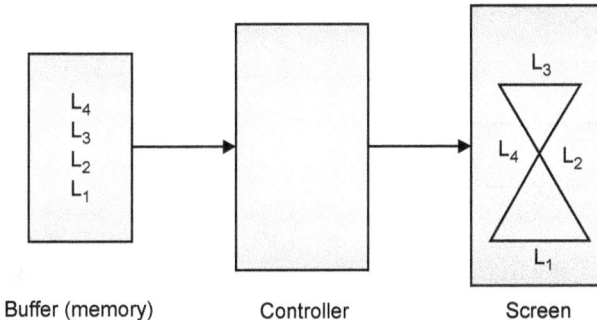

Buffer (memory)   Controller   Screen

Fig. 1.5 Working of a random scan display system

Buffer is memory which stores the information on the entities of the screen. As shown in Fig. 1.5, there are four lines on the screen and the information of these lines is stored in the buffer. The controller controls the flow of data from the buffer to the screen and vice-versa. In every cycle of refresh, it reads the data from the buffer and displays it on the screen. This refresh process is repeated for 40 to 50 times in a second. Erasing the line on the screen means erasing the line from the buffer. This makes changes to the image much easier. The disadvantage of this system is that complex curves are difficult to draw.

1.3.1.3 Raster Scan Display System

In this display system, the entire screen is divided into an array or matrix of points, as shown in Fig. 1.6. These small points are called pixels; hence it is called a point-based system. But a line cannot be drawn from any point to any point on the screen. For monochrome monitors, each pixel can be either black or white. The line on the screen appears by making a particular line of pixels glow. This also uses a refresh display system like a random scan display system, in which the entity on the screen is redisplayed 40 to 50 times in a second. The frame buffer is a memory storage device to store the location of pixels on the screen. The controller's function is to control the display of pixels as per information stored in the frame buffer (this whole cycle is repeated 40 to 50 times in a second).

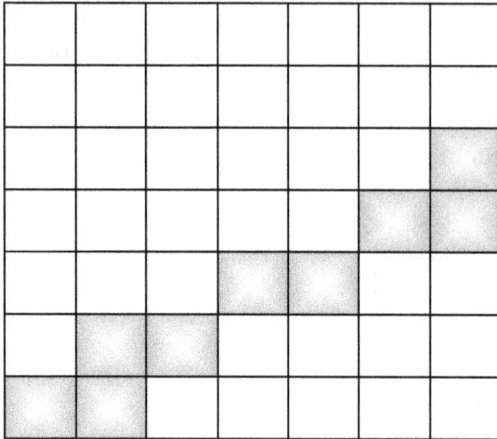

Fig. 1.6. Rasterization

In a raster scan display system, the frame buffer is also called a bit plane or a stroke system, in which an electron beam moves on the entire screen in a zig-zag and gets switched on and switched off during its travel to the entire screen, as shown in Fig. 1.7. Fig. 1.8 shows the frame buffer for a monochrome monitor. Fig. 1.9 shows the frame buffer arrangement with an extended look-up table to increase different color combinations. A color monitor uses a number of frame buffers to represent the various colors on the screen. If a monitor is capable of showing 256, colors, or $2^8 = 256$, there are 8 frame buffers in the display system. Fig. 1.10 shows the frame buffer for a color monitor. Different algorithms are used to decide the sequence of pixels to glow in order to represent a given entity on the screen.

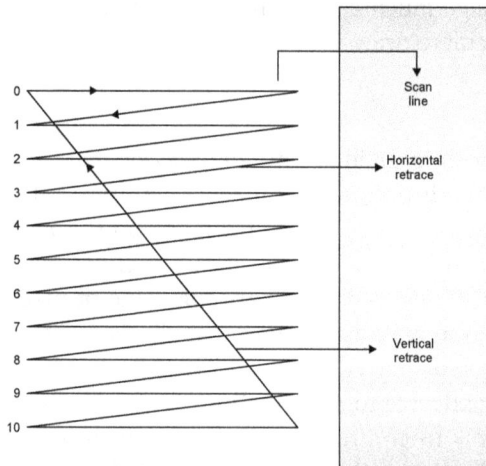

Fig. 1.7 Zigzag strokes of an electron beam

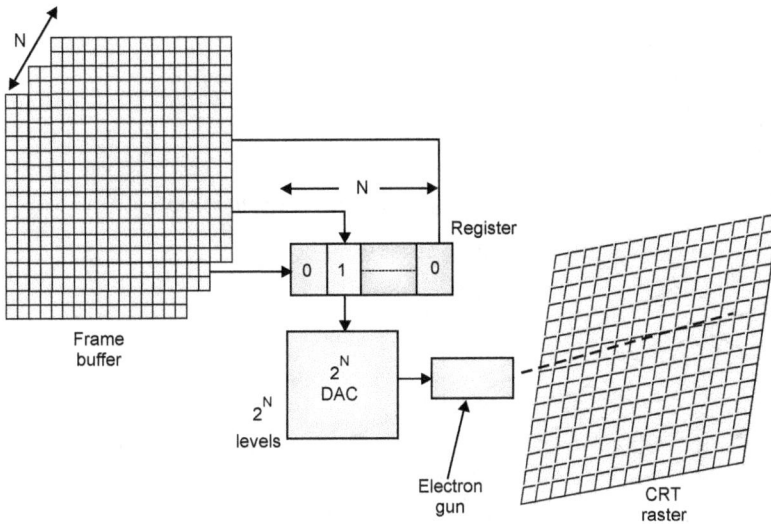

Fig. 1.8 N-bit-plane gray level frame buffers

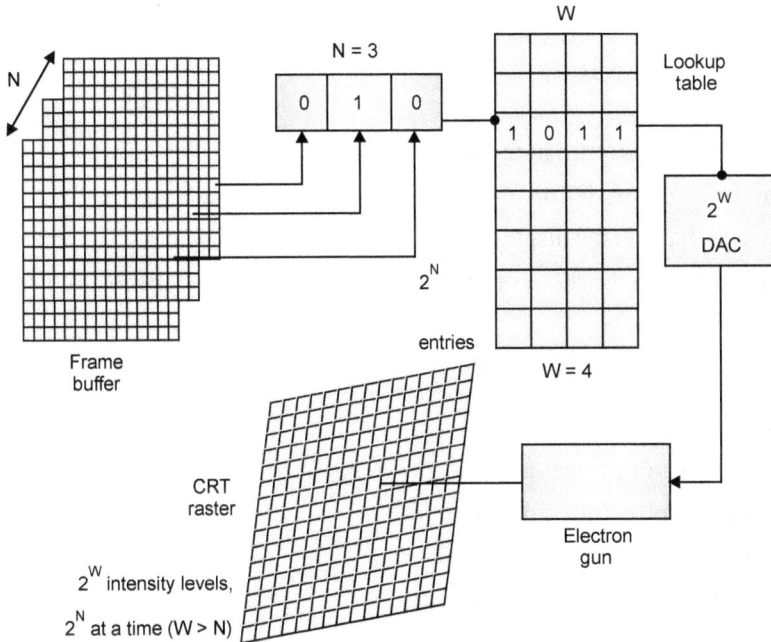

Fig. 1.9 N-bit-plane gray level frame buffer with a W-bit-wide lookup table

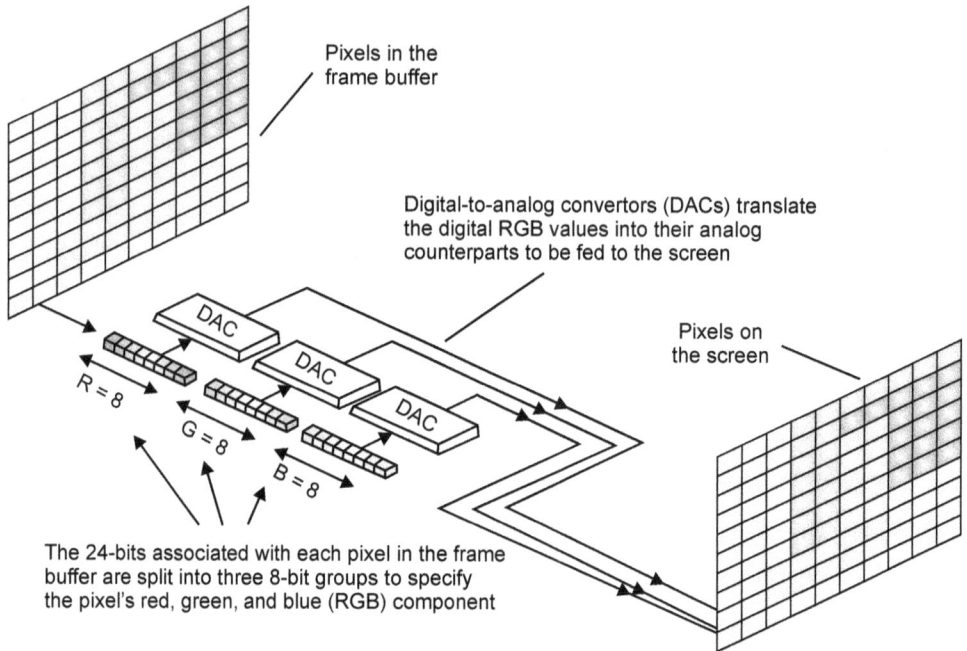

The 24-bits associated with each pixel in the frame buffer are split into three 8-bit groups to specify the pixel's red, green, and blue (RGB) component

Fig. 1.10 A simple color frame buffer

Advantages

- It is possible to add chrominance information to each pixel.
- Position on screen is predefined by the scan progress.
- Less expensive than vector display.
- The DSP (digital signal processor) and graphic processor are cheap and very powerful.
- Very efficient to represent full images.

Disadvantages

- Slow screen update rate, normally 25-120 screen/sec.
- At low resolution, pixels are quite big.
- Non-real time display.
- Improper interpolation of digital samples can produce visual artifacts (aliasing).

1.3.2 Non-CRT based Display Devices

Non-CRT based display devices are also called flat panel displays. CRT based display devices are bulky, heavy, and fragile but flat panel display devices are light and easy to handle. As a result, they have greater demand than CRT based DD. Examples of flat panel display devices are plasma, LCD, LED, etc.

1.3.2.1 Plasma Display

Plasma display consists of a matrix of pixels. Each pixel contains a mechanism which is actuated by voltage. The current emits light and is supplied to the pixel by using a switching device transistor, resistor, etc. The basic technique in plasma is a display consisting of a matrix of cells in a glass envelope, and each cell is filled with gas, like neon. Plasma displays can have an AC dielectric layer placed in between the conductance and the gas, which is bi-stable or DC, or a combined AC/DC hybrid. Large-size plasma has high resolution. Phosphorescent material emits light when excited by either an AC or DC electric field. The material is zinc sulphite doped with manganese. Electroluminescent display has a yellow color. An AC/DC excited thin film electron is mostly used in computer graphics applications. The basic structure is shown in Fig. 1.11.

Cell Structure Comparison

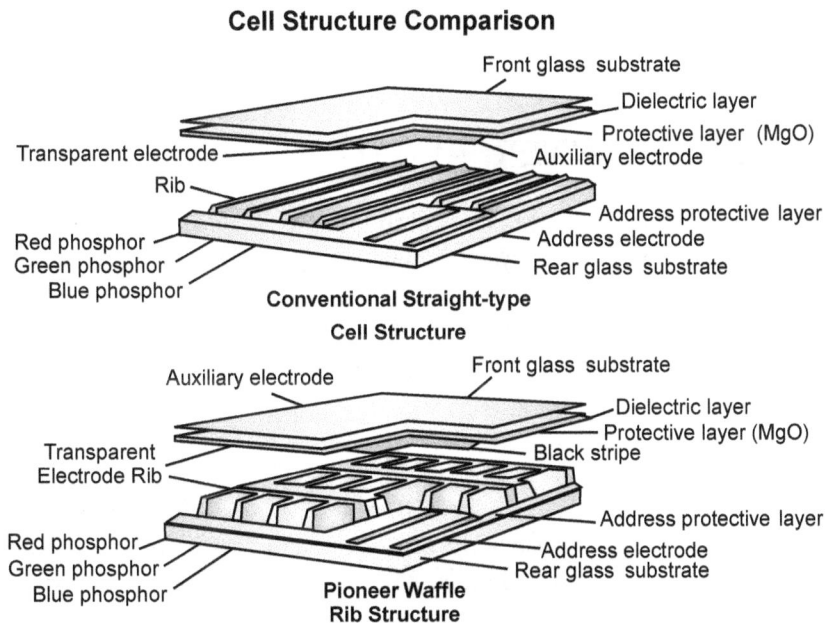

Fig. 1.11 The basic structure of gas discharge plasma display (AC/DC activated)

1.3.2.2 Liquid Crystal Display (LCD)

Liquid crystal display is an example of passive technology. It either transmits or reflects incident which is modified with polarization. The basic principle of polarized light is that transmitted light is passed through the first polarizer and polarized in the xyplane, since the polarized axis of the second polarizer aligns with first one, and vice versa. The ceramic which exists in the mesophase is stable at a temperature between solid and liquid, hence the name liquid crystal. Picture clarity is shown in Fig. 1.12.

Fig. 1.12 Liquid crystal display

1.4 GRAPHIC USER INTERFACE (GUI)

The graphic user interface is used to control the system or a specific application running on the system. Computer systems may have multiple interactive devices to interact with the outside world. Typical examples of interaction with the outside world are visual representation of position, valuator, button, and pick functions. Elements that are used to construct GUI are cursor, radio button, valuators, scroll bars, dialog boxes, menus, icons, etc.

Cursors

Cursors are a very important element of GUI. They are mainly used to indicate location on the screen. Another use of the cursor is the indication of an available operation by clicking the mouse. Cursors come in various types, as shown in Fig. 1.13.

aero_alt	aero_arrow	aero_busy	aero_ew
aero_helpsel	aero_link	aero_move	aero_nesw
aero_ns	aero_nwse	aero_pen	aero_prec
aero_Select	aero_unavai	aero_up	aero_working

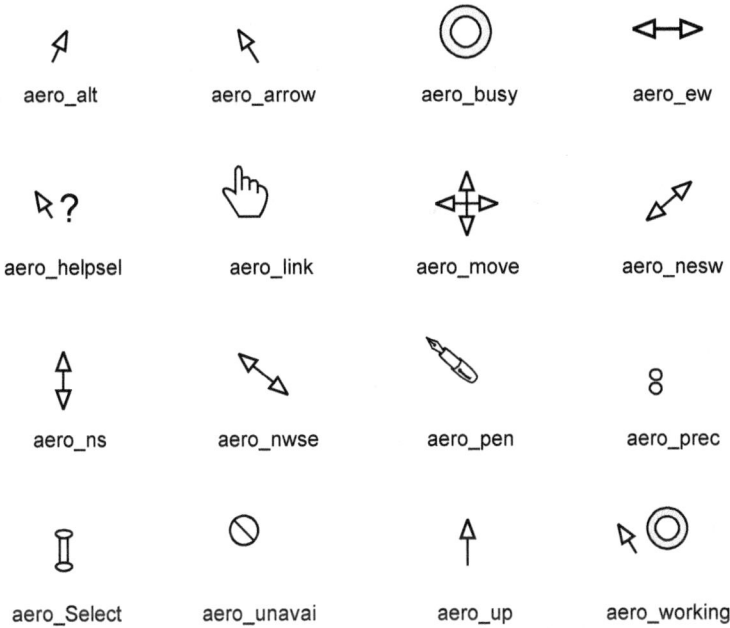

Fig. 1.13 Types of cursors

Radio Buttons

Radio buttons are used to visually implement the choice or button function. Alternatively, the buttons can be used to indicate an on/off status for a particular feature. Fig. 1.14 shows various radio buttons.

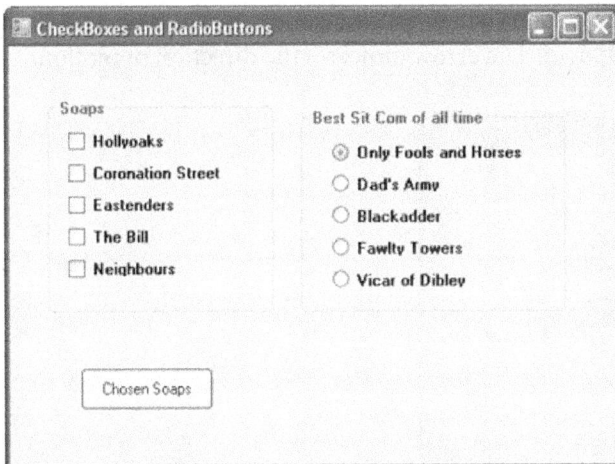

CheckBoxes and RadioButtons

Soaps
- [ ] Hollyoaks
- [ ] Coronation Street
- [ ] Eastenders
- [ ] The Bill
- [ ] Neighbours

Best Sit Com of all time
- (•) Only Fools and Horses
- ( ) Dad's Army
- ( ) Blackadder
- ( ) Fawlty Towers
- ( ) Vicar of Dibley

Chosen Soaps

Fig. 1.14 Radio buttons

Valuators

Valuators, shown in Fig. 1.15, are implemented as either fixed length slider bars or dial pointers. This feature is also available as a numerical value shown under an arrow as additional feedback.

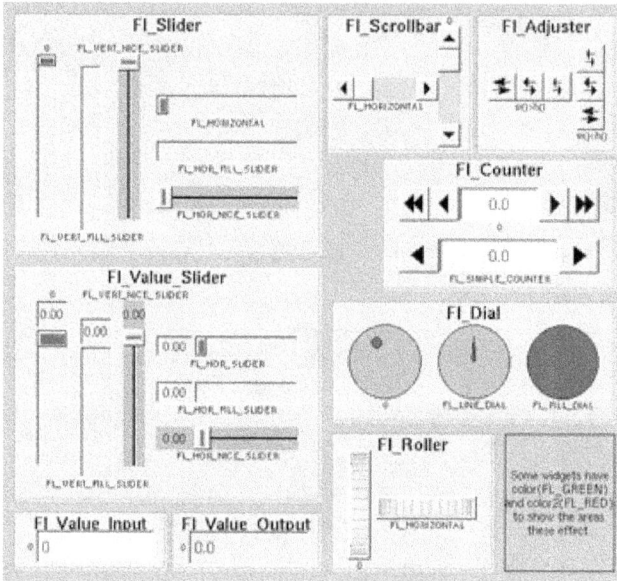

Fig. 1.15 Valuators

Scroll bars

Scroll bars are used to indicate and/or move to a position within a document or other entity as shown in Fig. 1.16. The arrow indicates the direction of motion.

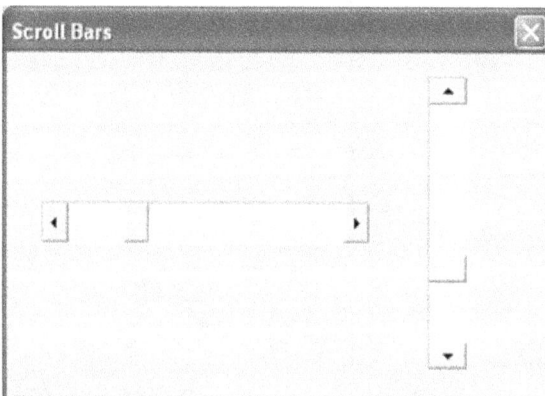

Fig. 1.16 Scroll bars

Dialog boxes

Dialog boxes, shown in Fig. 1.17, are used when multiple inputs are required to specify the desired action in a system. They contain a number of different interactive tools, i.e., radio buttons, valuators, types of boxes, etc.

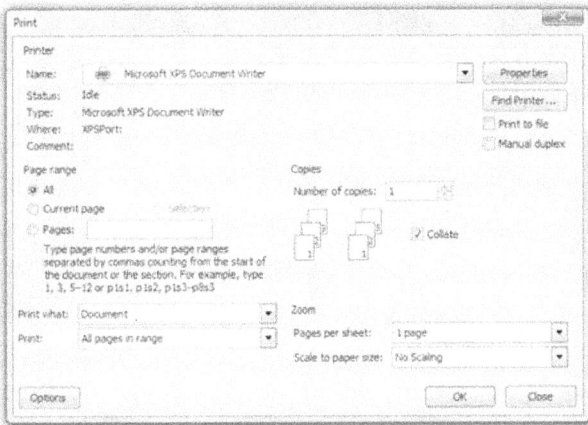

Fig. 1.17 Dialog boxes

Menus

Menus are used to perform functions such as selecting from a set of choices as seen in Fig. 1.18. The most common menus are:

- Pull up
- Pull out
- Tear off, etc.

- Pull down
- Pop up

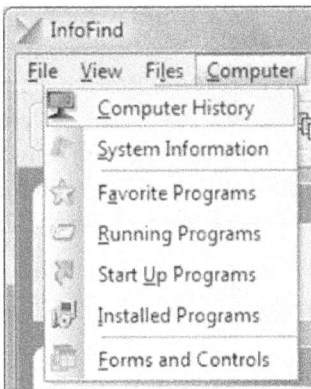

Fig. 1.18 Menus

Icons

Fig. 1.19 shows icons, which provide a pictorial representation of a concept, object, or action.

Fig 1.19 Icons

1.5 REFRESH RATE

A refresh rate depends upon a monitor's horizontal scanning frequency and the number of horizontal lines displayed. The horizontal scanning frequency is the number of lines the electron beam sweeps in one second. It is also known as frame rate, horizontal scan rate, vertical frequency, or frequency. Refresh rate is a CRT monitor measurement in Hz that indicates how many times per second a monitor screen image is renewed. For example, a monitor with a refresh rate of 75 Hz means the screen is going to redraw 75 times per second. Refresh rates below 75 Hz can produce an often-imperceptible flicker that can cause eyestrain after long viewing. While some cards can support as high as 120 Hz, sometimes even higher, it is recommended you run 85-90 Hz; rates beyond 90 Hz add an unnecessary processing burden to the eyes. Finally, LCD does not have a refresh rate. Hence, LCD is a flicker free device.

Problems on refresh rate/monitors

Problem 1

Calculate the different colors obtained with three sets of 8 bit frame buffers.

Solution Different colors obtained can be calculated as follows:

$$[2^n]^m$$

Where,

m = number of frame buffer sets

n = number of frame buffer (bit plane) in each set

here

$m = 3, n = 8$

$[2^8]^3 = 16777216$

Hence, three sets of 8 bit frame buffers can generate 16,777, 216 different colors.

Problem 2

Calculate the refresh rate for a raster screen of 512 × 512 pixels with average access time for each pixel of 200 nanoseconds.

Solution Average access time for each pixel = 200 nanoseconds = 200×10^{-9} sec

Raster screen of 512×512 pixels

$\therefore$ total time to access all pixels = $512 \times 512 \times 200 \times 10^{-9}$ sec

$$= 0.0524 \text{ sec}$$

For one frame to get refreshed, it takes 0.0524 sec. So in 1 sec, the refresh rate would be

$$= \frac{1}{0.0524} = 19 \text{ frames/sec}$$

Problem 3

Calculate the time required to access each pixel, when the refresh rate of 30 frames/second of 4096 × 4096 raster.

Solution Let the time required to access each pixel = X

$\therefore$ total time to access all pixels (each frame) = $(4096 \times 4096 \times X)$ sec

Refresh rate is 30 frames in one second. Hence, time required to access each pixel is calculated as

$$30 = \frac{1}{(4096 \times 4096 \times X)}$$

$$X = \frac{1}{(4096 \times 4096 \times 30)} = 1.98 \times 10^{-9} \text{ sec}$$

$$= 1.98 \text{ nanoseconds}$$

Problem 4

Calculate maximum RAM size for 32 bit and 64 bit operating systems and 1920 × 1080 raster screen.

Solution 32 bit operating system means, for each pixel on the screen, there are 32 frame buffers in the memory.

No. of pixels on the screen = 1920 × 1080 = 2073600 pixels

No. of bits for 32 bit operating system = 2073600 × 32 bits

$$= \frac{66355200}{8} \text{ bytes} = 8294400 \text{ bytes}$$

$$= \frac{8294400}{1024} \text{ kilobytes} = 8100 \text{ kilobytes}$$

$$= \frac{8100}{1024} \text{ megabytes} = 7.91 \text{ megabytes}$$

(It may be noted that to convert bytes to kilobytes, we have to divide by 1024)

No. of bits for 64 bit operating system = 2073600 × 64 bits

$$= \frac{132710400}{8} \text{ bytes} = 16588800 \text{ bytes}$$

$$= \frac{16588800}{1024} \text{ kilobytes} = 16200 \text{ kilobytes}$$

$$= \frac{16200}{1024} \text{ megabytes} = 15.82 \text{ megabytes}$$

RAM sizes required for a given raster screen using 32 bit and 64 bit operating system are 7.91 MB and 15.82 MB respectively.

Problem 5

For a 21.5 inch monitor having a screen resolution of 1920 × 1080, calculate pixels per inch (ppi)

Solution Pixels per inch (ppi) is the number of pixels per square inch

$$ppi = \frac{d_p}{d_i}$$

where,

$$d_p = \sqrt{H_p^2 + V_p^2}$$

d_p = diagonal resolution in pixels

H_p = horizontal resolution in pixels

d_i = diagonal size of monitor in inches

V_p = vertical resolution in pixels

Here,

H_p = 1920,

V_p = 1080

d_i = 21.5 inch

$$ppi = \frac{d_p}{d_i}$$

$$d_p = \sqrt{H_p^2 + V_p^2}$$

$$d_p = \sqrt{(1920)^2 + (1080)^2}$$

$$d_p = 2202.9$$

$$ppi = \frac{2202.9}{21.5} = 102.46 \, ppi$$

Problem 6

Calculate pixels per inch (ppi) for Nokia N 90 mobile having screen resolution 352×416 and 2.1 inch monitor.

Solution

Here,
$$H_p = 352$$
$$V_p = 416$$
$$d_i = 2.1 \text{ inch}$$
$$d_p = \sqrt{H_p^2 + V_p^2}$$
$$d_p = \sqrt{(352)^2 + (416)^2}$$
$$d_p = \sqrt{123904 + 173056}$$
$$d_p = \sqrt{296960}$$
$$d_p = 544.94$$
$$ppi = \frac{d_p}{d_i}$$
$$ppi = \frac{544.94}{2.1} = 259.49 \, ppi$$

1.6 WORKING OF LASER PRINTERS

Laser printing is an electrostatic digital printing process that rapidly produces high quality text and graphics by passing a laser beam over a charged drum to define a differentially charged image. The drum then selectively collects charged toner and transfers the image to paper, which is then heated to permanently fix the image. As with digital photocopiers and multifunction printers (MFPs), laser printers employ a xerographic printing process, but differ from analog photocopiers in that the image is produced by the direct scanning of the medium across the printer's photoreceptor. Hence, it proves to be a much faster process compared to the latter. There are typically seven steps involved in the laser printing process.

Raster image processing

Each horizontal strip of dots across the page is known as a *raster line or scan line*. Creating the image to be printed is done by a raster image processor (RIP), typically built into the laser printer. The raster image processor generates a bitmap of the final page in the raster memory. For fully graphical output using a page description language, a minimum of 1 megabyte of memory is needed to store an entire monochrome letter/A4 sized page of dots at 300 dpi. At 300 dpi, there are 90,000 dots per square inch (300 dots per linear inch). In a color printer, each of the four CYMK toner layers is stored as a separate bitmap, and all four layers are typically preprocessed before printing begins, so a minimum of 4 megabytes is needed for a full-color letter-size page at 300 dpi. Memory requirements increase with the square of the dpi, so 600 dpi requires a minimum of 4 megabytes for monochrome, and 16 megabytes for color at 600 dpi. Printers capable of tabloid and larger size may include memory expansion slots.

Charging

In older printers, a corona wire positioned parallel to the drum, or in more recent printers, a primary charge roller, projects an electrostatic charge onto the photoreceptor (otherwise called the photo conductor unit), a revolving photosensitive drum or belt, which is capable of holding an electrostatic charge on its surface while it is in the dark, as shown in Fig. 1.20.

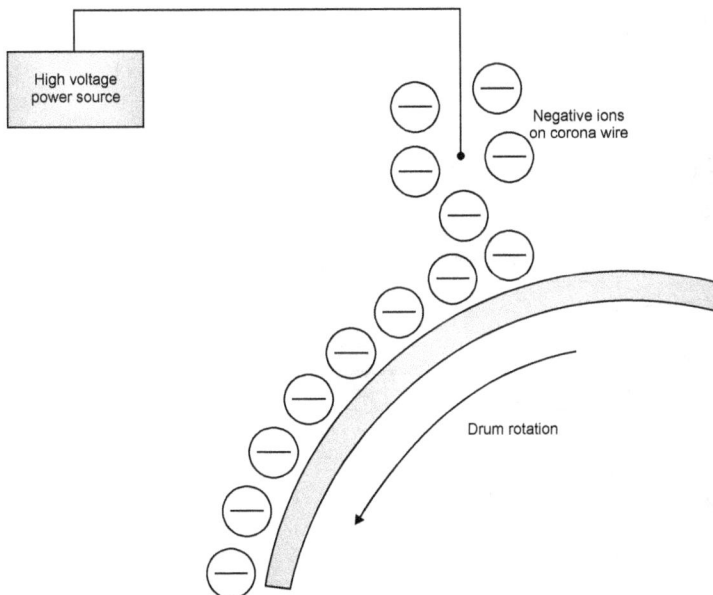

Fig 1.20 Applying a negative charge to the photosensitive drum

An AC bias is applied to the primary charge roller to remove any residual charges left by previous images. The roller will also apply a DC bias on the drum surface to ensure a uniform negative potential. Numerous documents describe the photosensitive drum coating as a silicon sandwich with a photo charging layer, a charge leakage barrier layer, as well as a surface layer. One version uses amorphous silicon containing hydrogen as the light receiving layer, boron nitride as a charge leakage barrier layer, as well as a surface layer of doped silicon, notably silicon with oxygen or nitrogen which at sufficient concentration resembles machining silicon nitride.

Exposing

The laser is aimed at a rotating polygonal mirror, which directs the laser beam through a system of lenses and mirrors onto the photoreceptor. The cylinder continues to rotate during the sweep and the angle of sweep compensates for this motion. The stream of rasterized data held in memory turns the laser on and off to form the dots on the cylinder. Lasers are used because they generate a narrow beam over great distances. The laser beam neutralizes (or reverses) the charge on the black parts of the image, leaving a static electric negative image on the photoreceptor surface to lift the toner particles, as shown in Fig. 1.21.

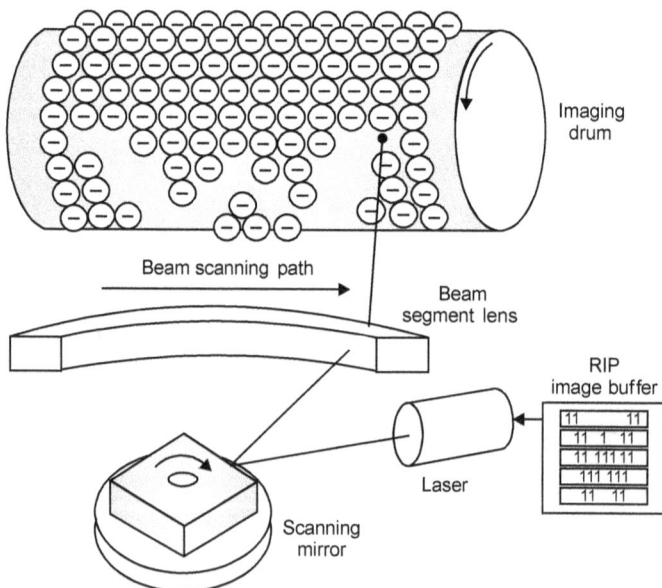

Fig 1.21 The laser neutralizes the negative charge

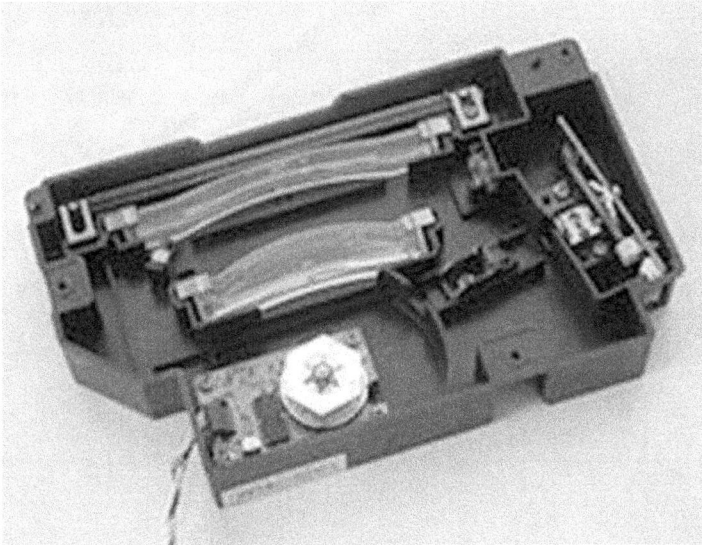

Fig 1.22 An actual laser unit from a Dell P1500

Some non-laser printers expose by an array of light emitting diodes spanning the width of the page, rather than by a laser ("exposing" is also known as "writing" in some documentation). Fig. 1.22 shows the laser unit of a Dell P 1500.

Developing

The surface with the latent image is exposed to toner, fine particles of dry plastic powder mixed with carbon black or coloring agents. The toner particles are given a negative charge and are electrostatically attracted to the photoreceptor's latent image, the areas touched by the laser. Because like charges repel, the negatively charged toner will not touch the drum where the negative charge remains.

Transferring

The photoreceptor is pressed or rolled over paper, transferring the image. Higher-end machines use a positively charged transfer roller on the back side of the paper to pull the toner from the photoreceptor to the paper.

Fusing

The paper passes through rollers in the fuser assembly where heat of up to 200°C (392°F) and pressure bond the plastic powder to the paper as shown in Fig. 1.23. One roller is usually a hollow tube (heat roller) and the other is a rubber backing

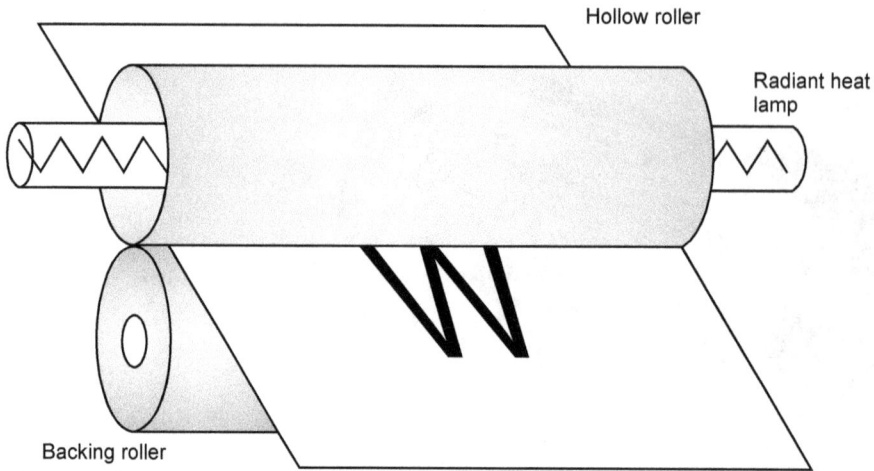

Fig 1.23 Melting toner on paper using heat and pressure

roller (pressure roller). A radiant heat lamp is suspended in the center of the hollow tube, and its infrared energy uniformly heats the roller from the inside. For proper bonding of the toner, the fuser roller must be uniformly hot.

Some printers use a very thin flexible metal fuser roller, so there is less mass to be heated and the fuser can more quickly reach operating temperature. If paper moves through the fuser more slowly, there is more roller contact time for the toner to melt, and the fuser can operate at a lower temperature. Smaller, inexpensive laser printers typically print slowly, due to this energy-saving design, compared to large high speed printers where paper moves more rapidly through a high-temperature fuser with a very short contact time.

Cleaning

When the print is complete, an electrically neutral soft plastic blade cleans any excess toner from the photoreceptor and deposits it into a waste reservoir, and a discharge lamp removes the remaining charge from the photoreceptor. Toner may occasionally be left on the photoreceptor when an unexpected event, such as a paper jam, occurs. The toner is on the photoconductor ready to apply, but the operation failed before it could be applied. The toner must be wiped off and the process restarted. Fig. 1.24 shows a magnified image of color laser printer output, showing individual toner particles comprising 4 dots of an image with a bluish background.

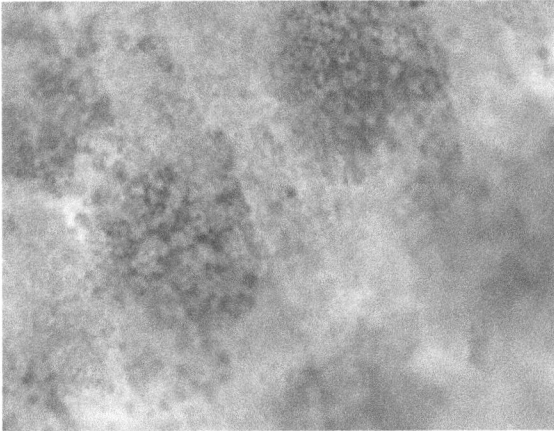

Fig 1.24 A magnified image printed from a color laser printer

Problems on Printers

Problem 7

Assume a computer with 16 bit per word and a transfer rate of 1 million instructions per second. How long would it take to fill the frame buffer for a 600 dpi (dots per inch) laser printer with a page size of $8\frac{1}{2}''$ by 14" inch.

Solution

$$1 \text{ instruction } = 1 \text{ dot} = 1 \text{ bit}$$

$$\therefore \qquad 600 \text{ dots } = 600 \text{ bits}$$

$$\text{page area } = 8.5'' \times 14'' = 119 \text{ inches squared}$$

$$\text{Dots per inch } = \text{printable area} \times \text{dpi area}$$

$$\text{Dots per inch } = \text{page area} \times 600 \text{ dpi} \times 600 \text{ dpi}$$

$$= 119 \times 600 \times 600 \text{ dots or bits}$$

$$= 42840000 \text{ dots or bits}$$

Transfer rate of 1×10^7 bits in 1 sec. So, to transfer 42840000 dots or bits, it takes X sec

$$\text{time require to print one page} = \frac{42840000}{1 \times 10^7}$$

$$= 42.8 \text{ sec}$$

$$\therefore \text{ No. of pages print in 1 min } = \frac{60}{42.8} = 1.4 \text{ page/min}$$

Problem 8

Suppose a printer of 300×300 dpi resolution producing $7\frac{1}{2} \times 10\frac{1}{2}$ inch printed area on an $8\frac{1}{2} \times 11$ inch page. Calculate no. of pages printed per minute, if a sustained data rate to the laser print engine of 1 megabit/sec.

Solution

$$\text{Printable area on page} = 7.5 \times 10.5 = 78.75 \text{ inch}^2$$

$$\therefore \qquad \text{No. of } \frac{dots}{page} = 78.75 \times 300 \times 300$$

$$= 7087500 \text{ dots/page}$$

Data rate of 1 megabit in one sec, so to print 7087500 it takes

$$= \frac{7087500}{1 \times 10^6} \text{sec}$$

$$= 7.08 \text{ sec/page}$$

$$\therefore \qquad \text{so in one minute } = \frac{60}{7.08} = 8.47 \text{ pages/minute}$$

EXERCISES

1. Explain the various applications of computer graphics.
2. What are the benefits of CAD from manufacturing considerations?
3. What are the various hardware requirements in setting up the CAD system?
4. Write short notes on (*i*) icons (*ii*) GUI.
5. Explain the working of random scan display. Why is this not used in modern CAD?
6. Explain any two output devices in a CAD system.
7. Explain the difference between time based systems and point based systems, with examples.
8. What is flickering in display devices?
9. Explain the components of raster scan display devices.
10. Explain the refresh rate.

11. What is a pixel and a frame buffer?

12. What is a bit plane? How are bit planes used to get different color and B and W gray levels?

13. Explain the working of laser printers.

14. How is an image generated on a screen?

15. What are the different parameters for comparing graphic display devices? Compare various display devices on these parameters.

OBJECTIVE QUESTIONS

1.1 In CRT, the control grid is used to control the intensity of electrons coming out from an electron gun, and is charged with
(*a*) negative voltage   (*b*) positive voltage
(*c*) neutral   (*d*) none of the above

1.2 The phenomenon of having a continuous glow on the screen even after it is removed is called
(*a*) fluorescence   (*b*) persistence
(*c*) phosphorescence   (*d*) incandescence

1.3 Aspect ratio is generally defined as the ratio of
(*a*) vertical to horizontal points
(*b*) horizontal to vertical points
(*c*) vertical to (horizontal + vertical) points
(*d*) either (*a*) or (*b*) depending on the convention followed

1.4 Which of the following devices have relative origin?
(*a*) Joystick   (*b*) Track ball
(*c*) Mouse   (*d*) none of the above

1.5 The focusing unit in a cathode ray tube (CRT) is used to
(*a*) accelerate the electron beam
(*b*) control amount of electrons from electron gun
(*c*) control position of electron beam on the screen
(*d*) emit electrons

1.6 Refresh rate below this value results in picture flickering:
(*a*) 85 Hz   (*b*) 35 Hz
(*c*) 50 Hz   (*d*) 25 Hz

1.7 Computer graphics models are now commonly used for making
- (*a*) motion pictures
- (*b*) music videos
- (*c*) television shows
- (*d*) all of above

1.8 Which of the following are CRT based display devices?
- (*a*) Raster scan display device
- (*b*) Direct View Storage Tube (DVST)
- (*c*) Calligraphic or vector based or random scan display device
- (*d*) all of the above

1.9 Which of the following are non CRT based display devices?
- (*a*) LCD
- (*b*) LED
- (*c*) Plasma
- (*d*) all of the above

1.10 The brightness of a spot on the screen depends upon
- (*a*) number of electrons striking the phosphor coating (screen)
- (*b*) distance between cathode and screen
- (*c*) speed of electrons striking the screen
- (*d*) type of phosphor coating

1.11 Which of the following is a point based display system?
- (*a*) DVST
- (*b*) Random scan display device
- (*c*) Raster scan display device
- (*d*) All of the above

1.12 Which of the following is a line based display system?
- (*a*) Random scan display device
- (*b*) Raster scan display device
- (*c*) LCD
- (*d*) LED

ANSWERS

1.1 (*a*)	**1.2** (*b*)	**1.3** (*d*)	**1.4** (*c*)
1.5 (*c*)	**1.6** (*d*)	**1.7** (*d*)	**1.8** (*d*)
1.9 (*d*)	**1.10** (*a*)	**1.11** (*c*)	**1.12** (*a*)

Chapter 2 VECTOR REPRESENTATION OF GEOMETRIC ENTITIES

2.0 INTRODUCTION

The previous chapter was about the evolution of computer hardware and display devices in particular. From this study, one can say that all the modern display devices (screens) are divided into small number of discrete cells called pixels and the screen is called a raster screen. Now, to draw any entity on this screen, one needs to develop the logic which will select the series of pixels on the screen so that the desired entity appears on the screen. This process of selection of pixels is called rasterization. For example, a line is to be drawn on the screen from start point to end point. So, it is necessary to develop a program which will select the intermediate pixels inbetween the start point and the end point so that the desired line appears on the screen.

Algorithm

Before writing any computer program, it is empirical to develop a logic to perform each task and write it out in logical steps. An algorithm is nothing but writing logical steps in a systematic manner. There can be many steps in any algorithm, but the important steps in any graphic algorithm are the declaration of variables, initialization, calculation, and plotting pixels. Steps in an algorithm are shown in Fig. 2.1.

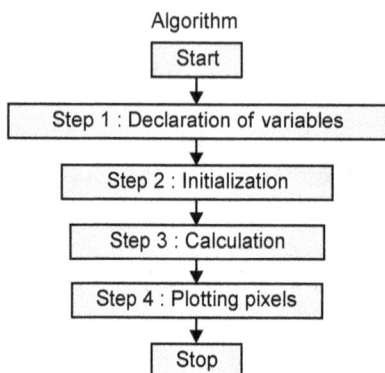

Algorithm

```
        Start
          |
          v
Step 1 : Declaration of variables
          |
          v
   Step 2 : Initialization
          |
          v
   Step 3 : Calculation
          |
          v
   Step 4 : Plotting pixels
          |
          v
        Stop
```

Fig. 2.1 Steps in an algorithm

(*i*) **Declaration of variables:** All variables which are going to be used in the algorithm are declared in this step, along with the types of variables (integer, float, etc.).

(*ii*) **Initialization:** Initialize the variables which the compiler will need to ask at the time of the program is executed.

(*iii*) **Calculation:** What calculations are necessary to perform the algorithm?

(*iv*) **Plotting pixels:** Apply the logic to plotting the points on the raster screen.

In this chapter, algorithms for generating simple two dimensional geometrical entities (such as line, circle, ellipse, arc) will be studied. There will be a total of three algorithms for line generation: equation of line, digital differential analyser (DDA), and Bresenham's line generation algorithm. Circles and ellipses will be generated by using Bresenham's midpoint algorithm. Arcs will be generated by using trigonometric function.

2.1 LINE GENERATION ALGORITHM USING EQUATION OF LINE

A line is a very basic geometrical entity. Fig. 2.2 shows a line having end points A and B.

Line Generation

The line is one of the basic geometrical entities. Vector displays are particularly well suited for the display of lines. An appropriate controlled voltage is supplied to x and y deflection circuitry for vector display to generate a line.

The nature of raster-graphics display, however, only allows us to display a discrete approximation of a line since the process is restricted to turning on only discrete points or pixels. In order to discuss line drawing, first consider the mathematically ideal line.

Mathematical Analysis

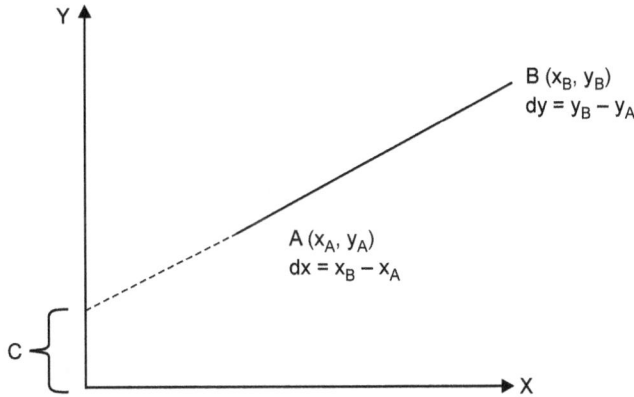

Fig. 2.2 A line

equation of line $y = mx + c$ ...(2.1)

where,

$$m = \text{slope}$$

For line shown in Fig. 2.2,

$$m = \tan\theta = \frac{dy}{dx} = \frac{y_B - y_A}{x_B - x_A}$$

$$c = y \text{ axis intercept}$$

put the start point in the equation (2.1)

$$y_A = mx_A + c$$

$$c = y_A - mx_A \qquad \text{...(2.2)}$$

$$c = y_A - \left(\frac{y_B - y_A}{x_B - x_A}\right)x_A \qquad \text{...(2.3)}$$

Line Algorithm Using Equation of Line for |M|<1

STEP 1:   [DECLARATION OF VARIABLES]

int	(x_A, y_A) & (x_B, y_B)	end point coordinates of line
float	m	slope of line
float	c	y intercept
float	(x, y)	coordinates of current pixel representing line

STEP 2:   [INITIALIZATION]

Read (x_A, y_A) & (x_B, y_B)

STEP 3:   [CALCULATION]

$$m = \frac{y_B - y_A}{x_B - x_A}$$

$$c = y_A - mx_A$$

STEP 4:   [PLOTTING PIXEL FOR LINE]

$$x = x_A$$
$$y = y_A$$

loop,
put pixel (round "x", round "y")

$$x = x + 1$$
$$y = mx + c$$

Continue loop until $(x \leq x_B)$

STEP 5:   [STOP]

Problems on Equation of Line

Problem 2.1

Rasterize a line by using an equation of line having end point coordinates as (5,2) & (15,6)

Solution

End points (5,2) & (15,6)

Slope $\qquad m = \dfrac{y_B - y_A}{x_B - x_A} = \dfrac{6-2}{15-5} = \dfrac{4}{10} = 0.4$

$$c = y_A - mx_A = 2 - (0.4) \times 5 = 2 - 2 = 0$$

Calculation 2. $\quad x_2 = x_1 + 1 = x_2 = 5 + 1 = 6$ and $y_2 = mx_2 + c = 0.4 \times 6 + 0 = 2.4$

Calculation 3. $\quad x_3 = x_2 + 1 = x_3 = 6 + 1 = 7$ and $y_3 = mx_3 + c = 0.4 \times 7 + 0 = 2.8$

Fig. 2.3 shows the rasterization of a line after plotting the pixels.

Sr. No.	x	y	round x	round y
1	5	2	5	2
2	6	2.4	6	2
3	7	2.8	7	3
4	8	3.2	8	3
5	9	3.6	9	4
6	10	4	10	4
7	11	4.4	12	5
8	12	4.8	12	5
9	13	5.2	13	5
10	14	5.6	14	6
11	15	6.0	15	6

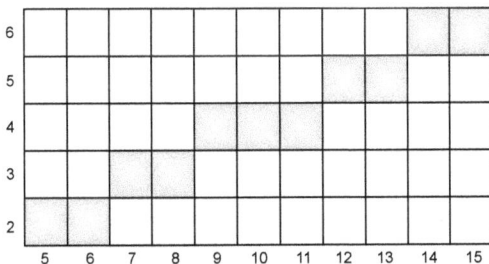

Fig. 2.3 The rasterization of a line

Line Algorithm Using Equation of Line for |M|>1

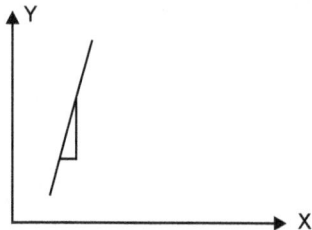

Y = incremented by 1
X = calculated
y = mx + c

$$x = \frac{y - c}{m}$$

Fig. 2.4 Line having slope > 1

STEP 1: [DECLARATION OF VARIABLES]

int	(x_A, y_A) & (x_B, y_B)	end point coordinates of line
float	m	slope of line
float	c	y intercept
float	(x, y)	coordinates of current pixel representing line

STEP 2: [INITIALIZATION]

Read (x_A, y_A) & (x_B, y_B)

STEP 3: [CALCULATION]

$$m = \frac{y_B - y_A}{x_B - x_A}$$

$$c = y_A - mx_A$$

STEP 4: [PLOTTING PIXEL FOR LINE]

$$x = x_A$$
$$y = y_A$$

loop,
put pixel (round "x", round "y")

$$y = y + 1$$

$$x = \frac{y - c}{m}$$

Continue loop until ($y \le y_B$)

STEP 5: [STOP]

Problem 2.2

Rasterize a line by using an equation of line having end point coordinates as (5,2) & (6,7)

Solution

End points (5, 2) & (6, 7)

Slope
$$m = \frac{y_B - y_A}{x_B - x_A} = \frac{7-2}{6-5} = \frac{5}{1} = 5$$

$$c = y_A - mx_A = 2 - (5)\; x\; 5 = 2 - 25 = -23$$

Calculation 2. $y_2 = y_1 + 1 = 2 + 1 = 3$ and $x_2 = \dfrac{y_2 - c}{m} = x_2 = \dfrac{3+23}{5} = 5.2$

Calculation 3. $y_3 = y_2 + 1 = 3 + 1 = 4$ and $x_3 = \dfrac{y_3 - c}{m} = x_2 = \dfrac{4+23}{5} = 5.4$

Fig. 2.5 shows the rasterization of a line after plotting the pixels.

Sr No.	x	Y	round x	round y
1	5	2	5	2
2	5.2	3	5	3
3	5.4	4	5	4
4	5.6	5	6	5
5	5.8	6	6	6
6	6.0	7	6	7

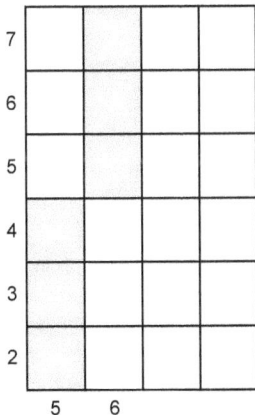

Fig. 2.5 The rasterization of a line

Algorithm for Line Generation Using an Equation of Line for Any Slope

STEP 1:   [DECLARATION OF VARIABLES]

int	(x_A, y_A) & (x_B, y_B)	end point coordinates of line
float	m	slope of line
float	c	y intercept
float	(x, y)	coordinates of current pixel representing line

STEP 2:   [INITIALIZATION]

Read (x_A, y_A) & (x_B, y_B)

STEP 3:   [CALCULATION]

$$m = \frac{y_B - y_A}{x_B - x_A}$$

$$c = y_A - mx_A$$

STEP 4:   [PLOTTING PIXEL FOR LINE]

$$x = x_A$$
$$y = y_A$$

loop,
put pixel (round "x", round "y")
if $|m| < 1$

$$x = x + 1$$
$$y = mx + c$$

Continue loop until $(x \leq x_B)$
else $|m| > 1$

$$y = y + 1$$
$$x = \frac{y - c}{m}$$

Continue loop until $(y \leq y_B)$

STEP 5:   [STOP]

2.2 LINE GENERATION USING DDA ALGORITHM

The digital differential analyser is a line generation algorithm based on the incremental method. In DDA, the calculations at each step are performed using the results from the previous step. In this method, the value of one coordinate is incremented by one in each step and determines the corresponding integer value of the other coordinate.

Mathematical analysis

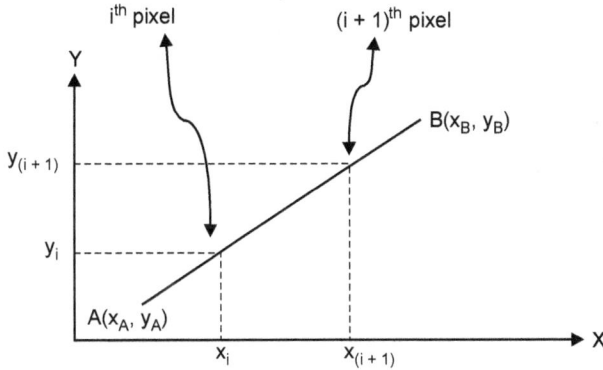

Fig. 2.6

Let i^{th} pixel coordinates be (x_i, y_i) as shown in Fig. 2.6

Equation of line becomes

$$y_i = mx_i + c \qquad \qquad ...(2.4)$$

Let $(i+1)^{th}$ pixel coordinates are $(x_{(i+1)}, y_{(i+1)})$

$$y_{(i+1)} = mx_{(i+1)} + c \qquad \qquad ...(2.5)$$

Subtract eq. (2.4) from eq. (2.5)

$$y_{(i+1)} - y_i = m[x_{(i+1)} - x_i] \qquad \qquad ...(2.6)$$

Apply condition

$$if |m| < 1$$

$$x_{(i+1)} = x_i + 1$$

Put the value of $x_{(i+1)}$ in Eq. (2.6)

$$y(i+1) - y_i = m[x_i + 1 - x_i]$$

$$y_{(i+1)} = y_i + m$$

$$else |m| > 1$$

$$y_{(i+1)} = y_i + 1$$

Put value of $y_{(i+1)}$ in Eq. (2.6)

$$y_i + 1 - y_i = m[x_{(i+1)} - x_i]$$

$$\frac{1}{m} = [x_{(i+1)} - x_i]$$

$$x_{(i+1)} = x_i + \frac{1}{m}$$

Common denominator for increment

$$\text{if } (|\,dy\,| < |\,dx\,|)$$

$$\text{DENO} = |\,dx\,|$$

$$\text{else } (|\,dy\,| \geq |\,dx\,|)$$

$$\text{DENO} = |\,dy\,|$$

$$x_{(i+1)} = x_i + \frac{dy}{DENO}$$

$$y_{(i+1)} = y_i + \frac{dy}{DENO}$$

ALGORITHM

STEP 1:   [DECLARATION OF VARIABLES]

int	(x_A, y_A) & (x_B, y_B)	end point coordinates of line
int	dx, dy	difference of x and y coordinates
int	DENO	common denominator
float	(x_{incr}, y_{incr})	increments in x and y coordinate
float	(x, y)	coordinates of current pixel representing line
int	i	loop counter

STEP 2:   [INITIALIZATION]

Read (x_A, y_A) & (x_B, y_B)

STEP 3:   [CALCULATION]

$$dx = x_B - x_A$$

$$dy = y_B - y_A$$

STEP 4:   [PLOTTING PIXEL FOR LINE]

if $(|\,dy\,| < |\,dx\,|)$

DENO $= |\,dx\,|$

if $(|\,dy\,| \geq |\,dx\,|)$

DENO $= |\,dy\,|$

$$x_{incr} = \frac{dx}{DENO}$$

$$y_{incr} = \frac{dy}{DENO}$$

$$x = x_A$$

$$y = y_A$$

$$i = 0$$

loop

put pixel (round "x", round "y")

$$x = x + x_{incr}$$

$$y = y + y_{incr}$$

$$i\,++$$

Continue loop until $(i \leq DENO)$

STEP 5:   [STOP]

Problems on DDA Algorithms

Problem 2.3

Rasterize a line by using a DDA algorithm having end point coordinates as (5,2) & (10,6)

Solution

End points (5,2) & (10,6)

$$dx = 10 - 5 = 5$$
$$dy = 6 - 2 = 4$$
$$|dx| \geq |dy|$$
$$\text{DENO} = dx$$

$$x_{incr} = \frac{dx}{\text{DENO}} = \frac{dx}{dx} = 1$$

$$y_{incr} = \frac{dy}{\text{DENO}} = \frac{dy}{dx} = m = \frac{4}{5} = 0.8$$

$$x = x + x_{incr} = x + 1$$
$$y = y + y_{incr} = y + 0.8$$

Calculation 2. $\quad y_2 = y_1 + 0.8 = 2 + 0.8 = 2.8$ and $x_2 = x_1 + 1 = 5 + 1 = 6$

Calculation 3. $\quad y_3 = y_2 + 0.8 = 2.8 + 0.8 = 3.6$ and $x_3 = x_2 + 1 = 6 + 1 = 7$

Fig. 2.7 shows the rasterization of a line after plotting the pixels.

i	X	y	round x	round y
0	5	2	5	2
1	6	2.8	6	3
2	7	3.6	7	4
3	8	4.4	8	4
4	9	5.2	9	5
5	10	6	10	6

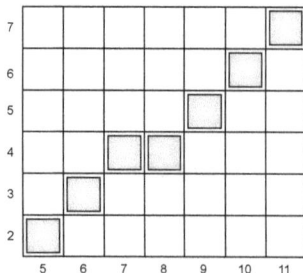

Fig. 2.7 The rasterization of a line

Varieties of Lines Using DDA

$$|M|<1 \qquad\qquad |M|>1$$

$dx = + ve$ $dy = + ve$ $\theta < 45°$ $x_{(i+1)} = x_i + 1$ $y_{(i+1)} = y_i + m$	$dx = + ve$ $dy = + ve$ $\theta > 45°$ $x_{(i+1)} = x_i + \dfrac{1}{m}$ $y_{(i+1)} = y_i + 1$
$dx = + ve$ $dy = - ve$ $\theta < 45°$ $x_{(i+1)} = x_i + 1$ $y_{(i+1)} = y_i - m$	$dx = + ve$ $dy = - ve$ $\theta > 45°$ $x_{(i+1)} = x_i + \dfrac{1}{m}$ $y_{(i+1)} = y_i - 1$
$dx = - ve$ $dy = - ve$ $\theta < 45°$ $x_{(i+1)} = x_i - 1$ $y_{(i+1)} = y_i - m$	$dx = - ve$ $dy = - ve$ $\theta > 45°$ $x_{(i+1)} = x_i + \dfrac{1}{m}$ $y_{(i+1)} = y_i - 1$

$dx = - ve$ $dy = + ve$ $\theta < 45°$ $x_{(i+1)} = x_i - 1$ $y_{(i+1)} = y_i - m$	$dx = - ve$ $dy = + ve$ $\theta > 45°$ $x_{(i+1)} = x_i + \dfrac{1}{m}$ $y_{(i+1)} = y_i + 1$
$dx = + ve$ $dy = 0$ $x_{(i+1)} = x_i - 1$ $y_{(i+1)} = y_i$	$dx = 0$ $dy = + ve$ $x_{(i+1)} = x_i$ $y_{(i+1)} = y_i + 1$

Problem 2.4

Rasterize a line by using a DDA algorithm having the equation "$y = 2x + 6$"

Solution

Equation of Line $\quad\quad\quad y = 2x + 6$

Put $x = 0$ we get $y = 6$

Put $y = 0$ we get $x = -3$

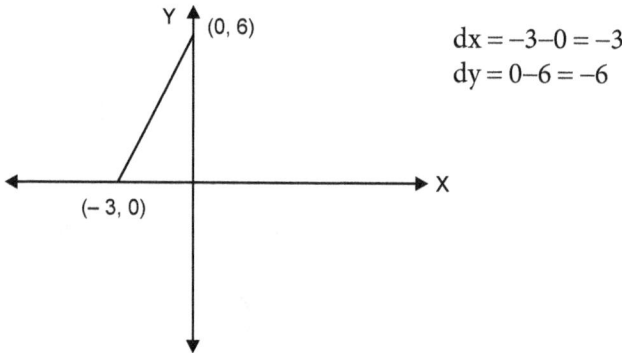

$dx = -3 - 0 = -3$
$dy = 0 - 6 = -6$

Fig. 2.8 Intersection points of a line with x- and y-axis

From Fig. 2.8, $\quad\quad\quad dx = -3 - 0 = -3$

$$dy = 0 - 6 = -6$$

$$|dy| > |dx|$$

$$dx = -ve \text{ and } dy = -ve$$

$$x_{(i+1)} = x_i - \frac{1}{m}$$

$$y_{(i+1)} = y_i - 1$$

Fig. 2.9 shows the rasterization of a line after plotting the pixels.

i	x	Y	Round x	Round y
0	0	6	0	6
1	-0.5	5	-1	5
2	-1	4	-1	4
3	-1.5	3	-2	3
4	-2	2	-2	2
5	-2.5	1	-3	1
6	-3	0	-3	0

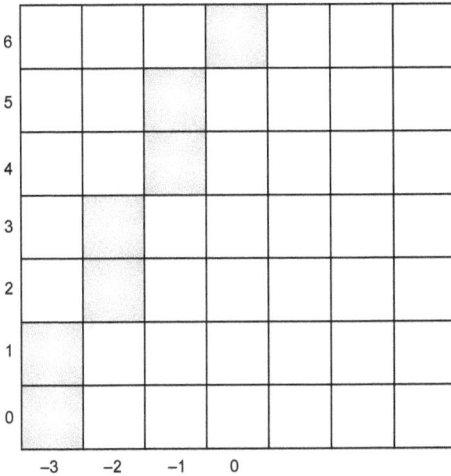

Fig. 2.9 The rasterization of a line

Compare Line Generation Using Equation of Line and DDA

1. The DDA algorithm is faster than the direct method since it involves only addition or subtraction and eliminates the use of multiplication or division.

2. In an equation of line, every value of x and y is calculated on its own, i.e. there is no use of a previous value to calculate the next value, but in the case of DDA the previous value is used to calculate the next value.

2.3 BRESENHAM'S LINE GENERATION ALGORITHM

An accurate and efficient algorithm for generating a line has been developed by Bresenham which uses only incremental calculations. Here the procedure is to test the sign of an integer parameter whose value is proportional to the difference between the separations of the two pixel positions from an actual line.

To understand the working of this method, consider a line with a positive slope of less than 1.

Bresenham's line generation algorithm for $| m | < 1$

Mathematical Analysis

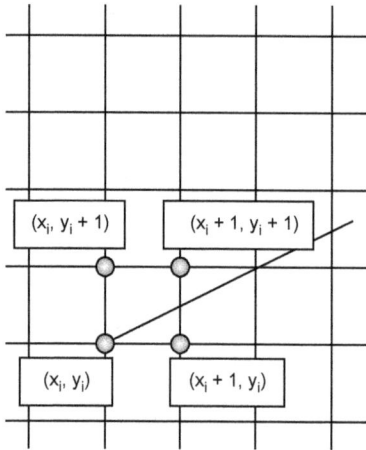

Fig. 2.10 Position of the line on a grid

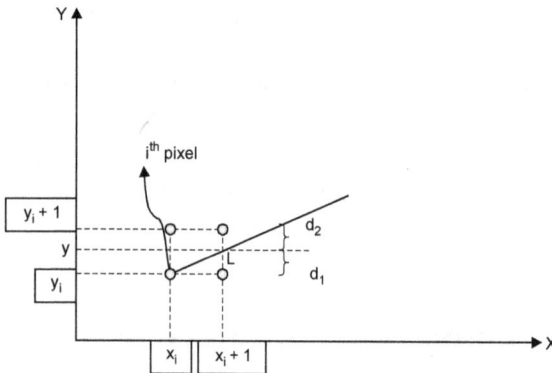

Fig. 2.11

Let (x_i, y_i) be any i^{th} pixel coordinate representing a line having integer coordinates as shown in Fig. 2.10.

Let $(x_{(i+1)}, y_{(i+1)})$ be any $(i+1)^{th}$ pixel coordinate representing a line as shown in Fig. 2.11.

Apply the condition for determining the coordinates of $(i+1)^{th}$ pixel

$$if(d_1 - d_2) < 0 \text{ or } d_1 < d_2$$

$$x_{(i+1)} = x_i + 1$$

$$y_{(i+1)} = y_i$$

$$else(d_1 - d_2) \geq 0 \text{ or } d_1 \geq d_2$$

$$x_{(i+1)} = x_i + 1$$

$$y_{(i+1)} = y_i + 1$$

From Fig. 2.11

$$d_1 = y - y_i \qquad \qquad \text{...(2.7)}$$

$$d_2 = (y_i + 1) - y \qquad \qquad \text{...(2.8)}$$

Subtract Eq. (2.7) from Eq. (2.8)

$$d_1 - d_2 = y - y_i - (y_i + 1) + y$$

$$d_1 - d_2 = 2y - 2y_i - 1 \qquad \qquad \text{...(2.9)}$$

Point L is on the line and satisfies the equation of line.

Coordinates of point $L(x_i + 1, y)$

$$y = mx + c$$

$$y = m(x_i + 1) + c$$

$$y = mx_i + m + c \qquad \qquad \text{...(2.10)}$$

Substitute value from Eq. (2.10) in Eq. (2.9)

$$d_1 - d_2 = 2(mx_i + m + c) - 2y_i - 1$$

$$= 2mx_i + 2m + 2c - 2y_i - 1$$

$$d_1 - d_2 = 2mx_i - 2y_i + 2m + 2c - 1$$

$$d_1 - d_2 = 2mx_i - 2y_i + k$$

Where $k = 2m + 2c - 1$

$$d_1 - d_2 = 2\frac{dy}{dx}x_i - 2y_i + k$$

$$(d_1 - d_2)dx = 2dyx_i - 2dxy_i + k \, . \, dx \qquad \qquad \text{...(2.11)}$$

Where $(d_1 - d_2)dx$ is decision parameter p_i

$$p_i = 2dyx_{i+1} - 2dxy_{i+1} + k. \, dx \qquad \qquad \text{...(2.12)}$$

Where p_i is the decision parameter for i^{th} pixel

Rewrite the condition in terms of p_i

$$\text{if } p_i < 0$$

$$x_{(i+1)} = x_i + 1$$

$$y_{(i+1)} = y_i$$

$$\text{else } p_i \geq 0$$

$$x_{(i+1)} = x_i + 1$$

$$y_{(i+1)} = y_i + 1$$

The decision parameter for $(i+1)^{th}$ pixel

$$p_{(i+1)} = 2dyx_{(i+1)} - 2dxy_{(i+1)} + k.\, dx \qquad \qquad ...(2.13)$$

Therefore, the common difference of the decision parameter between the consecutive pixels is given by Eq. (2.13) − Eq. (2.12)

$$p_{(i+1)} = p_i + 2dyx_{(i+1)} - 2dxy_{(i+1)} + k.\, dx - 2dyx_i + 2dxy_i - k.\, dx$$

$$p_{(i+1)} = p_i + 2dy(x_{(i+1)} - x_i) - 2dx(y_{(i+1)} - y_i) \qquad \qquad ...(2.14)$$

Apply the condition to Eq. (2.14)

if $(p_i < 0)$

$$x_{(i+1)} = x_i + 1$$

$$y_{(i+1)} = y_i$$

Applying these values to Eq. (2.14) we get

$$p_{(i+1)} = p_i + 2dy \qquad \qquad ...(2.15)$$

Else $(pi \geq 0)$

$$\left. \begin{aligned} x_{(i+1)} &= x_i + 1 \\ y_{(i+1)} &= y_i + 1 \end{aligned} \right\} \text{Apply these values to Eq. (2.14)}$$

$$p_{(i+1)} = p_i + 2dy - 2dx \qquad \qquad ...(2.16)$$

Calculate the decision parameter of the first point of the line (x_A, y_A)

$$p_1 = 2dyx_A - 2dxy_A + k.dx \qquad \qquad ...(2.17)$$

Put the values of the starting point coordinates in the equation of line

$$y_A = mx_A + c$$

$$y_A = \frac{dy}{dx} x_A + c$$

$$dx.y_A = dy.x_A + c.dx \qquad \qquad ...(2.18)$$

Put the value of Eq. (2.18) in Eq. (2.17)

$$p_1 = 2dyx_A - 2(dy.x_A + c.dx) + k.dx$$

Put $k = 2m + 2c - 1$

$$p_1 = 2dyx_A - 2dy.x_A - 2c.dx + 2m.dx + 2c.dx - dx$$

$$p_1 = 2\frac{dy}{dx}.dx - dx$$

$$p_1 = 2dy - dx \qquad \qquad ...(2.19)$$

Algorithm for a Line Using Bresenham's for $|m| < 1$

STEP 1:   [DECLARATION OF VARIABLES]

int	(x_A, y_A) & (x_B, y_B)	end point coordinates of line
int	dx, dy	difference of x and y coordinates
int	(x, y)	coordinates of current pixel representing line
int	p	decision parameter
int	i	loop counter

STEP 2:   [INITIALIZATION]

Read (x_A, y_A) & (x_B, y_B)

STEP 3:   [CALCULATION]

$$dx = x_B - x_A$$
$$dy = y_B - y_A$$
$$p = 2dy - dx$$

STEP 4:   [PLOTTING PIXEL FOR LINE]

$$x = x_A$$
$$y = y_A$$
$$p = 2dy - dx$$
$$i = 0$$

loop,

put pixel (x, y)

$$\text{if } p < 0$$
$$x = x + 1$$
$$y = y$$
$$p = p + 2dy$$

Else $p \geq 0$

$$x = x + 1$$
$$y = y + 1$$
$$p = p + 2dy - 2dx$$
$$i++$$

Continue loop until $(i \leq dx)$

STEP 5:   [STOP]

Problem 2.5

Rasterize a line by using Bresenhem's algorithm for slope (m < 1) having end point coordinates as (5,2) & (10,6)

Solution

End points (5,2) & (10,6)

$$dx = 10 - 5 = 5$$
$$dy = 6 - 2 = 4$$

Calculate decision parameter of first point of the line (x_A, y_A) and $i = 0$

$$p = 2dy - dx = 2 \times 4 - 5 = +3$$

Calculation : for $i = 1$

As $p > 0$ then new decision parameter

$$p = p + 2dy - 2dx = 3 + 2 \times 4 - 2 \times 5 = 1$$

I	X	Y	p
0	5	2	+3
1	6	3	+1
2	7	4	-1
3	8	4	+7
4	9	5	+5
5	10	6	+3

Fig. 2.12 shows the rasterization of a line after plotting the pixels.

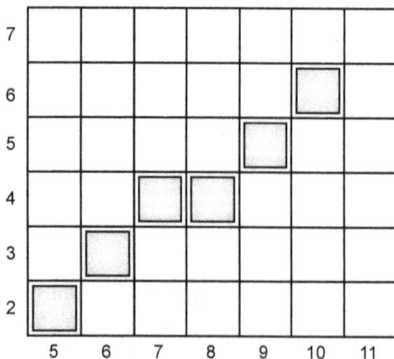

Fig. 2.12 The rasterization of a line

Bresenham's Line Generation Algorithm for $|m| > 1$

Mathematical Analysis

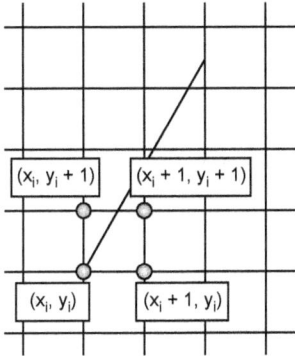

Fig. 2.13 Position of the line on a grid

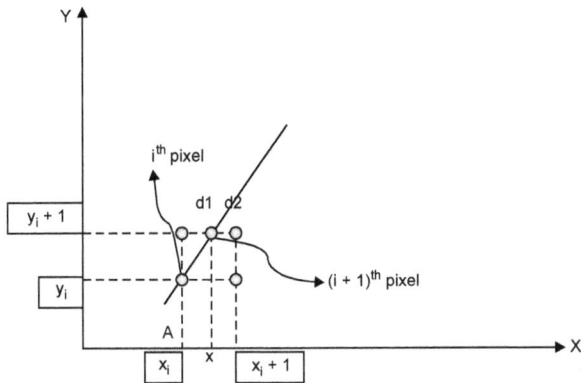

Fig. 2.14

Let (x_i, y_i) be any i^{th} pixel coordinate representing a line having integer coordinates as shown in Fig. 2.13

Let $(x_{(i+1)}, y_{(i+1)})$ be any $(i+1)^{\text{th}}$ pixel coordinate representing a line as shown in Fig. 2.14

Apply the condition for determining the coordinates of $(i+1)^{\text{th}}$ pixel

$$\text{if } (d_1 - d_2) < 0 \text{ or } d_1 < d_2$$

$$x_{(i+1)} = x_i$$

$$y_{(i+1)} = y_i + 1$$

$$\text{else } (d_1 - d_2) \geq 0 \text{ or } d_1 \geq d_2$$

$$x_{(i+1)} = x_i + 1$$

$$y_{(i+1)} = y_i + 1$$

From Fig. 2.14

$$d_1 = x - x_i \qquad \text{...(2.20)}$$
$$d_2 = (x_i + 1) - x \qquad \text{...(2.21)}$$

Subtract Eq. (2.21) from Eq. (2.20)

$$d_1 - d_2 = x - x_i - (x_i + 1) + x$$
$$d_1 - d_2 = 2x - 2x_i - 1 \qquad \text{...(2.22)}$$

Where y represents y-coordinate of $(i + 1)^{th}$ pixel when $y = y_i + 1$

$$y = mx + c$$
$$y_i + 1 = mx + c$$
$$x = \frac{y_i + 1 - c}{m}$$
$$x = \frac{dx}{dy}(y_i + 1 - c) \qquad \text{...(2.23)}$$

Substitute the value from Eq. (2.23) in Eq. (2.22)

$$d_1 - d_2 = \frac{dx}{dy}(y_i + 1 - c) - 2x_i - 1$$

$$(d_1 - d_2)dy = 2dx(y_i + 1 - c) - 2dyx_i - dy$$
$$(d_1 - d_2)dy = 2dxy_i - 2dyx_i + 2dx - 2dx.c - dy$$
$$(d_1 - d_2)dy = 2dxy_i - 2dyx_i + k \qquad \text{...(2.24)}$$

Where $k = 2dx - 2dx.c - dy$

Where $(d_1 - d_2)dx$ is decision parameter p_i

$$p_i = 2dxy_i - 2dyx_i + k \qquad \text{...(2.25)}$$

Where p_i is the decision parameter for $(i + 1)^{th}$ pixel

The decision parameter for $(i + 2)^{th}$ pixel

$$p_{(i+1)} = 2dxy_{(i+1)} - 2dyx_{(i+1)} + k \qquad \text{...(2.26)}$$

Therefore the common difference of the decision parameter between the consecutive pixels is given by

Eq. (2.26) – Eq. (2.25)

$$p_{(i+1)} = p_i + 2dxy_{(i+1)} - 2dyx_{(i+1)} + k - (2dxy_i - 2dyx_i + k)$$
$$p_{(i+1)} = p_i + 2dx(y_{(i+1)} - y_i) - 2dy(x_{(i+1)} - x_i) \qquad \text{...(2.27)}$$

Apply the condition to Eq. (2.27)

$$\text{if } (p_i < 0)$$
$$\left. \begin{array}{l} x_{(i+1)} = x_i \\ y_{(i+1)} = y_i + 1 \end{array} \right\} \text{ Apply these values to Eq. (2.27)}$$

We get

$$p_{(i+1)} = p_i + 2dx \qquad \qquad \dots(2.28)$$

else $(pi \geq 0)$

$$\left.\begin{array}{l} x_{(i+1)} = x_i + 1 \\ y_{(i+1)} = y_i + 1 \end{array}\right\} \text{Apply these values to Eq. (2.27)}$$

$$p_{(i+1)} = p_i + 2dx - 2dy \qquad \qquad \dots(2.29)$$

Calculate the decision parameter of the first point of the line (x_A, y_A)

$$p_1 = 2dxy_A - 2dyx_A + k \qquad \qquad \dots(2.30)$$

Put the values of starting point coordinates in the equation of the line

$$y_A = mx_A + c$$

$$y_A = \frac{dy}{dx}x_A + c$$

$$dx.y_A = dy.x_A + c.dx \qquad \qquad \dots(2.31)$$

Put the value of Eq. (2.31) in Eq. (2.30)

$$p_1 = 2(dy.x_A + c.dx) - 2dyx_A + k$$

Put $k = 2m + 2c - 1$

$$p_1 = 2dx - dy \qquad \qquad \dots(2.32)$$

Algorithm for Line Using Bresenham's for $|m| > 1$

STEP 1: [DECLARATION OF VARIABLES]

int	(x_A, y_A) & (x_B, y_B)	end point coordinates of line
int	dx, dy	difference of x and y coordinates
int	(x, y)	coordinates of current pixel representing line
int	p	decision parameter
int	i	loop counter

STEP 2: [INITIALIZATION]

Read (x_A, y_A) & (x_B, y_B)

STEP 3: [CALCULATION]

$$dx = x_B - x_A$$
$$dy = y_B - y_A$$

STEP 4: [PLOTTING PIXEL FOR LINE]

$$x = x_A$$
$$y = y_A$$
$$p = 2dx - dy$$
$$i = 0$$

loop,

put pixel (x, y)

$$\text{if } p < 0$$
$$x = x$$
$$y = y + 1$$
$$p = p + 2dx$$

else $(p \geq 0)$

$$x = x + 1$$
$$y = y + 1$$
$$p = p + 2dx - 2dy$$
$$i++$$

Continue loop until $(i \leq dy)$

STEP 5: [STOP]

Problem 2.6

Rasterize a line by using Bresenhem's algorithm for slope ($m > 1$) having end point coordinates as (2, 5) & (6, 10)

Solution

End points (2, 5) & (6, 10)

$$dx = 6 - 2 = 4$$
$$dy = 10 - 5 = 5$$

Calculate the decision parameter of the first point of the line (x_A, y_A) and $i = 0$

$$p = 2dx - dy = 2 \times 4 - 5 = +3$$

Calculation: for $i = 1$ As $p > 0$ then new decision parameter

$$p = p + 2dx - 2dy = 3 + 2 \times 4 - 2 \times 5 = +1$$

I	X	Y	p
0	2	5	+ 3
1	3	6	+ 1
2	4	7	− 1
3	4	8	+ 7
4	5	9	+ 5
5	6	10	+ 3

Fig. 2.15 shows the rasterization of a line after plotting the pixels.

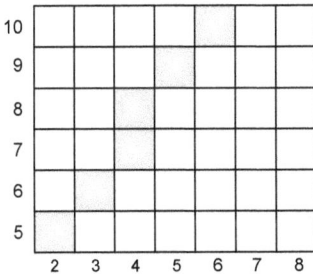

Fig. 2.15 The rasterization of a line

Algorithm for Line Using Bresenham's for Any Slope

STEP 1:   [DECLARATION OF VARIABLES]

int (x_A, y_A) & (x_B, y_B) end point coordinates of line

int dx, dy difference of x and y coordinates

int (x, y) coordinates of current pixel representing line

int p decision parameter

int $(signx, signy)$ sign changing variables

int i loop counter

STEP 2:   [INITIALIZATION]

Read (x_A, y_A) & (x_B, y_B)

STEP 3:   [CALCULATION]

$$dx = x_B - x_A$$
$$dy = y_B - y_A$$

STEP 4:   [PLOTTING PIXEL FOR LINE]

$$x = x_A$$
$$y = y_A$$

if $(dx \geq 0)$

$$\text{sign } x = +1$$

else $(dx < 0)$

$$\text{sign } x = -1$$

if $(dy \geq 0)$

$$\text{sign } y = +1$$

else $(dy < 0)$

$$\text{sign } y = -1$$

if $(|dy| < |dx|)$

$$p = 2dy.\text{sign } y - dx.\text{sign } x$$
$$i = 0$$

loop,

$$\text{put pixel } (x, y)$$

if $(p < 0)$

$$x = x + \text{sign } x$$
$$y = y$$
$$p = p + 2dx.\text{sign } y$$

else $(p \geq 0)$

$$x = x + \text{sign } x$$
$$y = y + \text{sign } y$$
$$p = p + 2dy.\text{sign } y - 2dx.\text{sign } x$$
$$i++$$

Continue loop until $(i \leq dx.\text{sign } x)$
else $(|dy| > |dx|)$

$$p = 2dx.\text{sign } x - dy.\text{sign } y$$
$$i = 0$$

loop,

$$\text{put pixel } (x, y)$$

if $p < 0$

$$x = x$$
$$y = y + \text{sign } y$$
$$p = p + 2dx.\text{sign } x$$

else $(p \geq 0)$

$$x = x + \text{sign } x$$
$$y = y + \text{sign } y$$
$$p = p + 2dx.\text{sign } x - 2dy.\text{sign } y$$
$$i++$$

Continue loop until $(i \leq dy.\text{sign } y)$

STEP 5: [STOP]

2.4 BRESENHAM'S MIDPOINT CIRCLE GENERATION ALGORITHM

The circle is one of the important geometric entities. It is a symmetric entity composed of diameters. Fig. 2.16 shows an origin-centered circle divided into 8 parts. This property of a circle (symmetric about diameters) can be used in the generation of circle with minimum codes. Out of the eight parts shown in Fig. 2.16, only the first part is to be generated; the remaining 7/8ths are generated by using the symmetry of the circle. Generation starts from point (0, R) where R is the radius of the circle.

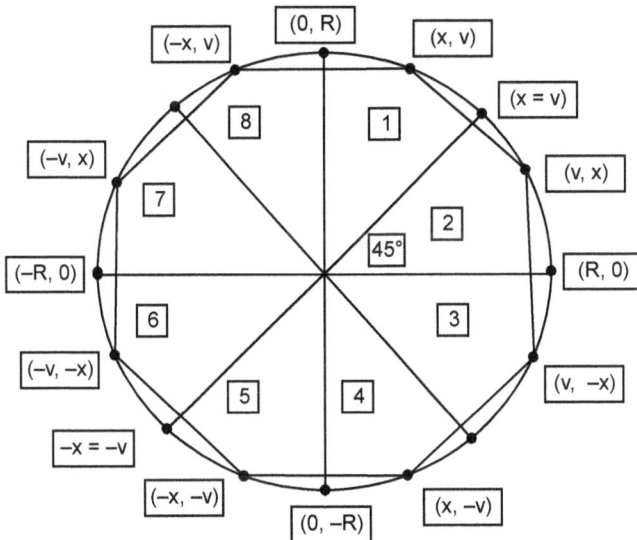

Fig. 2.16 Use of symmetry for a circle generation

Fig. 2.17 shows two equal parts of a quarter circle. If a tangent is drawn to part 1 then the absolute slope of the tangent would be less than one. Similarly if a tangent is drawn to part 2, then the absolute slope of the tangent would be greater than one. This indicates that the arc of part 1 is more horizontal than part 2 whereas the arc of part 2 is more vertical than part 1. But the slope of the tangent will be equal to one at the point where part 1 and part 2 meet. That means x coordinate is equal to y coordinate at that point. Therefore the generation of a circle starts from point (0, R) and ends where x coordinate is equal to y coordinate.

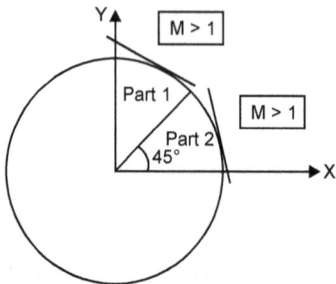

Fig. 2.17 Slope of tangents to circle

Mathematical Analysis

Figure 2.18 shows a one-eighth part of a circle. As discussed in the previous topic, if a tangent is drawn to part 1, then the absolute slope of the tangent would be less than one or the arc of part 1 is more horizontal. So, the value of x coordinate will be incremented by one in every step and the y coordinate needs to be calculated. The value of y coordinate is calculated depending upon the position of the midpoint of two successive vertical points. Two cases are discussed below; Fig. 2.19 shows the position of the midpoint outside the circle and Fig. 2.20 shows the position of the midpoint inside the circle.

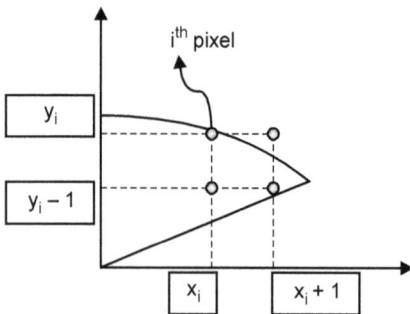

Fig. 2.18 Position of the arc of a circle on a grid

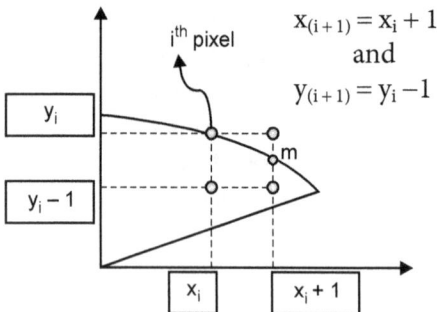

Fig. 2.19 Midpoint outside the circle

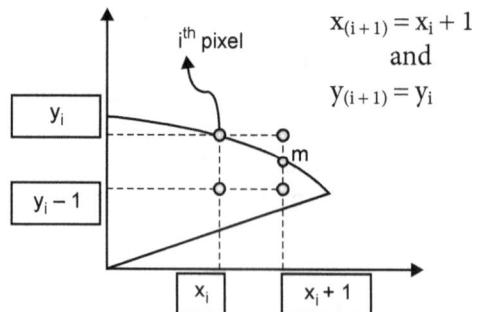

Fig. 2.20 Midpoint inside the circle

The equation of the circle is given by

$$x^2 + y^2 = R^2$$

$$x^2 + y^2 - R^2 = 0 \qquad \qquad \qquad \text{...(2.33)}$$

If $x^2 + y^2 - R^2 < 0$ then point lies inside the circle

And $x^2 + y^2 - R^2 > 0$ then point lies outside the circle

Let p_i be the decision parameter of ith point

$$p_i = x^2 + y^2 - R^2 \qquad \qquad \qquad \text{...(2.33a)}$$

Coordinates of the midpoint $m\left(x_i + 1, y_i - \dfrac{1}{2}\right)$

Put the values in Eq. (2.33a)

$$p_i = (x_i + 1)^2 + \left(y_i - \frac{1}{2}\right)^2 - R^2 \qquad \qquad \text{...(2.34)}$$

The decision parameter of $(i + 1)^{\text{th}}$ pixel is given by

$$p_{(i+1)} = (x_{(i+1)} + 1)^2 + \left(y_{(i+1)} - \frac{1}{2}\right)^2 - R^2 \qquad \qquad \text{...(2.35)}$$

Find the difference of the decision parameters by Eq. (2.35) – Eq. (2.34)

$$p_{(i+1)} - p_i = (x_{(i+1)} + 1)^2 + \left(y_{(i+1)} - \frac{1}{2}\right)^2 - R^2 - \left[(x_i + 1)^2 + \left(y_i - \frac{1}{2}\right)^2 - R^2\right]$$

$$p_{(i+1)} = p_i = (x_{(i+1)} + 1)^2 - (x_i + 1)^2 + \left(y_{(i+1)} - \frac{1}{2}\right)^2 - \left(y_i - \frac{1}{2}\right)^2 - R^2 + R^2$$

$$p_{(i+1)} = p_i = (x_{(i+1)} + 1)^2 - (x_i + 1)^2 + \left(y_{(i+1)} - \frac{1}{2}\right)^2 - \left(y_i - \frac{1}{2}\right)^2 \qquad \text{...(2.36)}$$

If midpoint is inside the circle then

$$\left.\begin{array}{l} x_{(i+1)} = x_i + 1 \\[2mm] y_{(i+1)} = y_i \end{array}\right\} \text{Put these values in Eq. (2.35)}$$

$$p_{(i+1)} = p_i + (x_i + 2)^2 - (x_i + 1)^2 + \left(y_i - \frac{1}{2}\right)^2 - \left(y_i - \frac{1}{2}\right)^2$$

$$p_{(i+1)} = p_i + [x_i^2 + 4x_i + 4 - x_i^2 - 2x_i - 1]$$

$$p(i + 1) = p_i + 2x_i + 3 \qquad \qquad \qquad \text{...(2.37)}$$

Or if midpoint is outside the circle then

$$\left.\begin{array}{l} x_{(i+1)} = x_i + 1 \\ y_{(i+1)} = y_i - 1 \end{array}\right\} \text{ Put these values in Eq. (2.36)}$$

$$P_{(i+1)} = P_i + (x_i + 2)^2 - (x_i + 1)^2 + \left(y_i - \frac{1}{2}\right)^2 - \left(y_i - \frac{1}{2}\right)^2$$

$$P_{(i+1)} = P_i + \left[x_i^2 + 4x_i + 4 - x_i^2 - 2x_i - 1\right] + \left[y_i^2 - 3y_i + \frac{9}{4} - y_i^2 + y_i - \frac{1}{4}\right]$$

$$P_{(i+1)} = P_i + [2x_i + 3] + [-2y_i + 2]$$

$$P_{(i+1)} = P_i + 2x_i - 2y_i + 5 \qquad\qquad ...(2.38)$$

For finding the start point decision parameter

Coordinates of start point $x = 0$, $y = R$, put these values in Eq. (2.33)

$$P_s = (0+1)^2 + \left(R - \frac{1}{2}\right)^2 - R^2$$

$$P_s = 1 + R^2 - R + \frac{1}{4} - R^2$$

$$P_s = 1 - R + \frac{1}{4}$$

$$P_s = \frac{5}{4} - R \text{ (float value)}$$

$$P_s = 1 - R \qquad\qquad ...(2.38a)$$

(converting into integer value)

Midpoint Circle Generation Algorithm

STEP 1: [DECLARATION OF VARIABLES]

int	(x_C, y_C)	center point coordinates of circle
int	(x, y)	coordinates of current pixel representing line
int	R	Radius of circle
int	p	decision parameter

STEP 2: [INITIALIZATION]

Read (x_C, y_C) & R

$$x = 0$$
$$y = R$$
$$p = 1 - R$$

STEP 3: [PLOTTING PIXEL FOR CIRCLE]

loop,

put pixel (x_c, y_c, x, y)

if $(p \leq 0)$

$$x = x + 1$$
$$y = y$$
$$p = p + 2x + 3$$

else $(p > 0)$

$$x = x + 1$$
$$y = y - 1$$
$$p = p + 2x - 2y + 5$$

Continue loop until $(x \leq y)$

STEP 4: [PLOT CIRCLE FUNCTION]

plot circle (x, y, x_c, y_c)

put pixel $(x + x_c, y + y_c)$

put pixel $(-x + x_c, y + y_c)$

put pixel $(-x + x_c, -y + y_c)$

put pixel $(x + x_c, -y + y_c)$

put pixel $(y + x_c, x + y_c)$

put pixel $(-y + x_c, x + y_c)$

put pixel $(-y + x_c, -x + y_c)$

put pixel $(y + x_c, -x + y_c)$

STEP 5: [STOP]

Problem 2.7

Generate 1/8th circle using Bresenham's circle generation algorithm with center of circle (30, 20) & radius 9.

Solution

$x_c = 30, y_c = 20, R = 9$

P	X	$x + x_c$	Y	$y + y_c$	(x_c, y_c)
$1 - 9 = -8$	0	$0 + 30 = 30$	9	$20 + 9 = 29$	(30, 29)
$-8 + 2(1) + 3 = -3$	1	$1 + 30 = 31$	9	$20 + 9 = 29$	(31, 29)
$-3 + 2(2) + 3 = 4$	2	$2 + 30 = 32$	9	$20 + 9 = 29$	(32, 29)
$4 + 2(3) - 2(8) + 5 = -1$	3	$3 + 30 = 33$	8	$20 + 8 = 28$	(33, 28)
$-1 + 2(4) + 3 = 10$	4	$4 + 30 = 34$	8	$20 + 8 = 28$	(34, 28)
$10 + 2(5) - 2(7) + 5 = 11$	5	$5 + 30 = 35$	7	$20 + 7 = 27$	(35, 27)
$11 + 2(6) - 2(6) + 5 = 16$	6	$6 + 30 = 36$	6	$20 + 6 = 26$	(36, 26)

Fig. 2.21 shows the rasterization of a line after plotting the pixels.

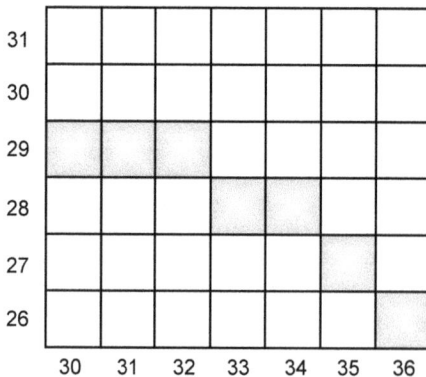

Fig. 2.21 The rasterization of a circle

2.5 BRESENHAM'S MIDPOINT ELLIPSE GENERATION ALGORITHM

Mathematical Analysis

The ellipse is another important geometric entity. It is a symmetric entity about its major axis and minor axis. Fig. 2.22 shows an origin-centered ellipse divided into 4 parts. This property of ellipse (symmetric about its major axis and minor axis) can be used in the generation of an ellipse with minimum codes. Out of the four parts shown in Fig. 2.22, only the first part is to be generated; the remaining three quarter parts are generated by using the symmetry of ellipse. Generation starts from point $(0, Ry)$ where Ry is the semi-minor axis of the ellipse.

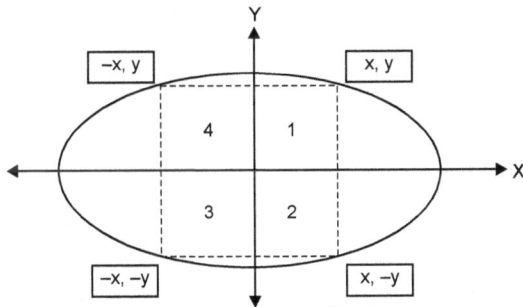

Fig. 2.22 The use of the symmetry of an ellipse for the ellipse generation

Fig. 2.23 shows two parts of a quarter ellipse. If a tangent is drawn to part 1 then the absolute slope of the tangent will be less than one. Similarly, if a tangent is drawn to part 2, then the absolute slope of the tangent will be greater than one. This indicates that the arc of part 1 is more horizontal than part 2, whereas the arc of part 2 is more vertical than part 1. But the slope of the tangent will be equal to one at the point where part 1 and part 2 meet (point m). Therefore the generation of the ellipse starts from point $(0, Ry)$ and ends at point m. The condition at point m is derived in Eq. (2.39a).

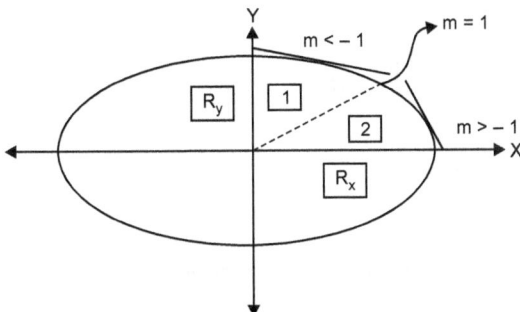

Fig. 2.23 Slope of the tangents to the two parts of an ellipse

$$\frac{x^2}{R_x^2} + \frac{y^2}{R_y^2} = 1$$

or

$$x^2 R_y^2 + y^2 R_x^2 = R_x^2 R_y^2$$

$$x^2 R_y^2 + y^2 R_x^2 - R_x^2 R_y^2 = 0 \qquad \ldots(2.39)$$

Differentiate Eq. (2.39) w. r. t. x and y, we get

$$2x.R_y^2 \, dx + 2yR_x^2.dy = 0$$

$$2x.R_y^2 \, dx = -\, 2yR_x^2.dy$$

$$\frac{dy}{dx} = \frac{-2xR_y^2}{2yR_x^2}$$

$$-1 = \frac{-2xR_y^2}{2yR_x^2}$$

$$2xR_y^2 = 2yR_x^2$$

$$xR_y^2 = yR_x^2$$

or $\qquad \ldots(2.39a)$

Mathematical Analysis for Generation of Ellipse in Part (1)

Fig. 2.24 shows part 1 of a quarter ellipse. As discussed in the previous topic, if a tangent is drawn to part 1 then the absolute slope of the tangent will be less than one or the arc of part 1 is more horizontal. So, the value of the x coordinate will be incremented by one in every step and the y coordinate needs to be calculated. The value of the y coordinate is calculated depending upon the position of the midpoint of two successive vertical points. Two cases are discussed below; Fig. 2.25 shows the position of the midpoint outside the ellipse and Fig. 2.26 shows the position of the midpoint inside the ellipse.

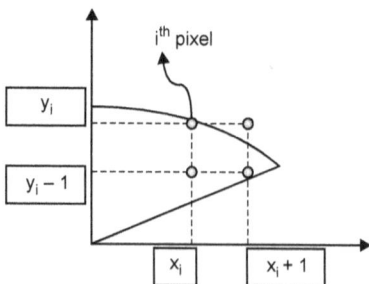

Fig. 2.24 Position of the arc of an ellipse on a grid

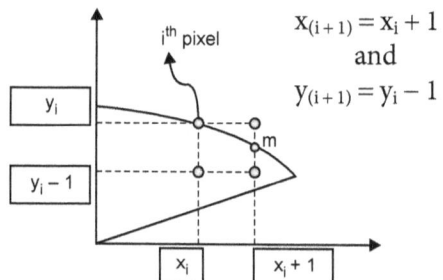

Fig. 2.25 Midpoint outside the ellipse

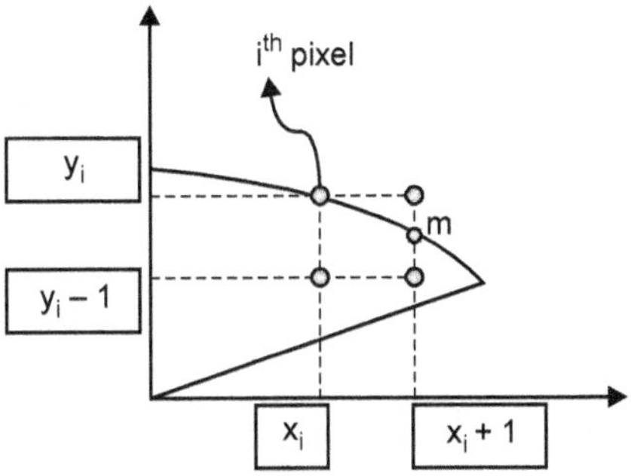

Fig. 2.26 Midpoint inside the ellipse

$$x_{(i+1)} = x_i + 1 \text{ and } y_{(i+1)} = y_i$$

Equation of ellipse

$$x^2 R_y^2 + y^2 R_x^2 - R_x^2 R_y^2 = 0$$

if $(x^2 R_y^2 + y^2 R_x^2 - R_x^2 R_y^2 < 0)$ then point is inside the ellipse

else $(x^2 R_y^2 + y^2 R_x^2 - R_x^2 R_y^2 > 0)$ then point is outside the ellipse

Let p_i be the decision parameter of ith point

$$p_i = x^2 R_y^2 + y^2 R_x^2 - R_x^2 R_y^2 \qquad \qquad \text{...(2.40)}$$

Coordinates of the midpoint $m\left(x_i + 1, y_i - \dfrac{1}{2} \right)$

Put the values in Eq. (2.40)

$$p_i = (x_i + 1)^2 R_y^2 + \left(y_i - \dfrac{1}{2} \right)^2 R_x^2 - R_x^2 R_y^2 \qquad \text{...(2.41)}$$

Decision parameter of $(i + 1)^{th}$ pixel is given by

$$p_{(i+1)} = (x_{(i+1)} + 1)^2 R_y^2 + \left(y_{(i+1)} - \dfrac{1}{2} \right)^2 R_x^2 - R_x^2 R_y^2 \qquad \text{...(2.42)}$$

Find the difference of the decision parameters by Eq. (2.42) – Eq. (2.31)

$$p_{(i+1)} - p_i = (x_{(i+1)} + 1)^2 R_y^2 + \left(y_{(i+1)} - \dfrac{1}{2} \right)^2 R_x^2 - R_x^2 R_y^2$$

$$- \left[(x_i + 1)^2 R_y^2 + \left(y_i - \dfrac{1}{2} \right)^2 R_x^2 - R_x^2 R_y^2 \right]$$

$$p_{(i+1)} - p_i = p_i + (x_{(i+1)} + 1)^2 \cdot R_y^2 - (x_i + 1)^2 \cdot R_y^2$$

$$+ \left(y_{(i+1)} - \dfrac{1}{2} \right)^2 \cdot R_x^2 + \left(y_i - \dfrac{1}{2} \right)^2 R_x^2$$

$$\text{...(2.43)}$$

If midpoint is inside the ellipse then

$$x_{(i+1)} = x_i + 1$$
$$y_{(i+1)} = y_i$$
} Put these values in Eq. (2.43)

$$P_{(i+1)} = P_i + (x_i + 2)^2 \cdot R_y^2 - (x_i + 1)^2 \cdot R_y^2 + \left(y_i - \frac{1}{2}\right)^2$$

$$\cdot R_x^2 - \left(y_i - \frac{1}{2}\right)^2 \cdot R_x^2$$

$$P_{(i+1)} = P_i + [2x_i + 3]R_y^2$$

...(2.44)

Else midpoint is outside the circle then

$$x_{(i+1)} = x_i + 1$$
$$y_{(i+1)} = y_i - 1$$
} Put these values in Eq. (2.43)

$$P_{(i+1)} = P_i + (x_i + 2)^2 R_y^2 - (x_i + 1)^2 R_y^2 + \left(y_i - \frac{1}{2}\right)^2 \cdot R_x^2 - \left(y_i - \frac{1}{2}\right)^2 \cdot R_x^2$$

$$p(i+1) = P_i + [x_i^2 + 4x_i + 4 - x_i^2 - 2x_i - 1]R_y^2 + \left[y_i^2 - 3y_i + \frac{9}{4} - y_i^2 + y_i - \frac{1}{4}\right]R_x^2$$

$$P_{(i+1)} = P_i + [2x_i + 3]R_y^2 + [-2y_i + 2]R_x^2$$

...(2.45)

For finding the start point decision parameter

Coordinates of the start point $x = 0, y = Ry$, put these values in the equation

$$P_s = (0+1)^2 R_y^2 + \left(R - \frac{1}{2}\right)^2 R_x^2 - R_y^2 R_x^2$$

$$P_s = R_y^2 + \left[-R_y + \frac{1}{4}\right]R_x^2$$

$$P_s = R_y^2 - \left[R_y - \frac{1}{4}\right]R_x^2$$

$$R_y \gg \frac{1}{4}$$

$$P_s = R_y^2 - R_y \cdot R_x^2$$

Mathematical Analysis for the Generation of an Ellipse in Part (2)

Fig. 2.27 shows part 2 of a quarter ellipse. As discussed in the previous topic, if a tangent is drawn to part 2 then the absolute slope of the tangent will be greater than one or the arc of part 2 is more vertical. So, the value of the y coordinate will be incremented by one in every step and the x coordinate needs to be calculated. The value of the x coordinate is calculated depending upon the position of the midpoint of two successive horizontal points. Two cases are discussed; Fig. 2.28 shows the position of the midpoint inside the ellipse and Fig. 2.29 shows the position of the midpoint outside the ellipse.

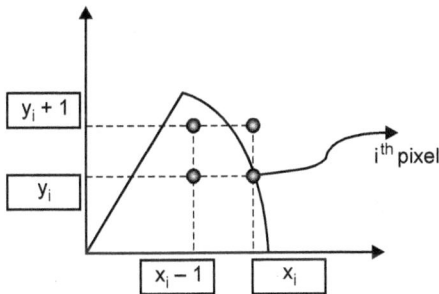

Fig. 2.27 Position of the arc of an ellipse on a grid

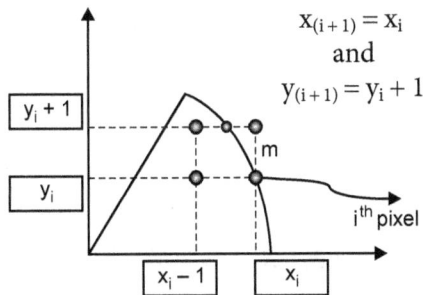

Fig. 2.28 Midpoint inside the ellipse

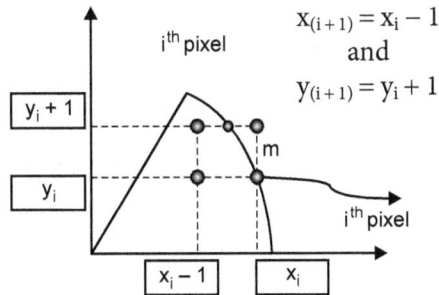

Fig. 2.29 Midpoint outside the ellipse

Equation of an ellipse

$$x^2 R_y^2 + y^2 R_x^2 - R_x^2 R_y^2 = 0 \qquad \qquad ...(2.46)$$

if $x^2 R_y^2 + y^2 R_x^2 - R_x^2 R_y^2 < 0$ then point is inside the ellipse

else $x^2 R_y^2 + y^2 R_x^2 - R_x^2 R_y^2 > 0$ then point is outside the ellipse

Let p_i be the decision parameter of ith point

$$p_i = x^2 R_y^2 + y^2 R_x^2 - R_x^2 R_y^2 \qquad \qquad ...(2.47)$$

Coordinates of the midpoint $m\left(x_i - \dfrac{1}{2}, y_i + 1\right)$

Put the values in Eq. (2.47)

$$p_i = \left(x_i + \frac{1}{2}\right)^2 R_y^2 + (y_i + 1)^2 R_x^2 - R_x^2 R_y^2 \qquad \text{...(2.48)}$$

Decision parameter of $(i+1)^{\text{th}}$ pixel is given by

$$p_{(i+1)} = \left(x_{(i+1)} - \frac{1}{2}\right)^2 R_y^2 + (y_{(i+1)} + 1)^2 R_x^2 - R_x^2 R_y^2 \qquad \text{...(2.49)}$$

Find the difference of the decision parameters by Eq. (2.49) – Eq. (2.48)

$$p_{(i+1)} - p_i = \left(x_{(i+1)} - \frac{1}{2}\right)^2 R_y^2 + (y_{(i+1)} + 1)^2 R_x^2 - R_x^2 R_y^2$$

$$-\left[\left(x_i - \frac{1}{2}\right)^2 R_y^2 + (y_i + 1)^2 R_x^2 + R_x^2 R_y^2\right]$$

$$p_{(i+1)} = p_i + \left(x_{(i+1)} - \frac{1}{2}\right)^2 \cdot R_y^2 - \left(x_i - \frac{1}{2}\right)^2 \cdot R_y^2 + (y_{(i+1)} + 1)^2$$

$$\cdot R_x^2 - (y_i + 1)^2 R_x \qquad \text{...(2.50)}$$

If midpoint is inside the ellipse then

$$\left.\begin{array}{l} x_{(i+1)} = x_i \\ y_{(i+1)} = y_i + 1 \end{array}\right\} \quad \text{Put these values in Eq. (2.50)}$$

$$p_{(i+1)} = p_i + \left(x_i - \frac{1}{2}\right)^2 \cdot R_y^2 - \left(x_i - \frac{1}{2}\right)^2 \cdot R_y^2 + (y_i + 2)^2 \cdot R_x^2 - (y_i + 1)^2 \cdot R_x^2$$

$$p_{(i+1)} = p_i + [2y_i + 3] R_x^2 \qquad \text{...(2.51)}$$

Else midpoint is outside the circle then

$$\left.\begin{array}{l} x_{(i+1)} = x_i - 1 \\ y_{(i+1)} = y_i + 1 \end{array}\right\} \quad \text{Put these values in Eq. (2.50)}$$

$$p_{(i+1)} = p_i + \left(x_i - 1 - \frac{1}{2}\right)^2 R_y^2 - \left(x_i - \frac{1}{2}\right)^2 R_y^2 + (y_i + 1 + 1)^2 R_y^2 - (y_i + 1)^2 R_x^2$$

$$p_{(i+1)} = p_i + [-2x_i + 2] R_y^2 + [2y_i + 3] R_x^2 \qquad \text{...(2.52)}$$

For finding the start point decision parameter
Coordinates of the start point $x = R_x$, $y = 0$, put these values in the equation

$$p_s = \left(R_x - \frac{1}{2}\right)^2 R_y^2 + (0+1)^2 R_x^2 - R_y^2 R_x^2$$

$$p_s = R_x^2 - \left[R_x - \frac{1}{4}\right] R_y^2$$

$$R_x \gg \frac{1}{4}$$

$$p_s = R_x^2 - R_x \cdot R_y^2 \qquad\qquad\qquad ...(2.53)$$

Bresenham's Midpoint Ellipse Generation Algorithm

STEP 1:   [DECLARATION OF VARIABLES]

int	(x_C, y_C)	center point coordinates of ellipse
int	(x_1, y_1) & (x_2, y_2)	coordinates of current pixel for part (1) & part (2)
int	R_x, R_y	semi-major and semi-minor axis of ellipse
int	p_1, p_2	decision parameter for part (1) and part (2)

STEP 2:   [INITIALIZATION]

Read (x_C, y_C)
Read R_x, R_y

STEP 3:   [PLOTTING PIXEL FOR ELLIPSE]
Plotting part (1) of ellipse ($m < 1$)

$$x_1 = 0$$
$$y_1 = R_y$$
$$p_1 = R_y^2 - R_y \cdot R_x^2$$

loop,
put pixel $((x_c, y_c)\, x_1, y_1)$
if $(p_1 \leq 0)$

$$x_1 = x_1 + 1$$
$$y_1 = y_1$$
$$p_1 = p_1 + (2x_1 + 3)R_y^2$$

else $(p_1 > 0)$

$$x_1 = x_1 + 1$$
$$y_1 = y_1 - 1$$
$$p_1 = p_1 + (2x_1 + 3) R_y^2 + (-2y_2 + 2)R_x^2$$

Continue loop until $(R_y^2 . x_1 \le R_x^2 . y_1)$

Plot part (2) of ellipse $(m >= 1)$

$$x_2 = R_x$$
$$y_2 = 0$$
$$p_2 = R_x^2 - R_x . R_y^2$$

loop,

put pixel $((x_c, y_c) x_2, y_2)$

if $(p_2 \le 0)$

$$x_2 = x_2$$
$$y_2 = y_2 + 1$$
$$p_2 = p_2 + (2y_2 + 3)R_x^2$$

else $(p_2 > 0)$

$$x_2 = x_2 - 1$$
$$y_2 = y_2 + 1$$
$$p_2 = p_2 + (2y_2 + 3) R_x^2 + (-2x_2 + 2)R_y^2$$

Continue loop until $(R_x^2 . y_2 \le R_y^2 . x_2)$

STEP 4: [PLOT CIRCLE FUNCTION]

plot ellipse (x_1, y_1, x_c, y_c)

put pixel $(x_1 + x_c, y_1 + y_c)$

put pixel $(-x_1 + x_c, y_1 + y_c)$

put pixel $(-x_1 + x_c, -y_1 + y_c)$

put pixel $(x_1 + x_c, -y_1 + y_c)$

STEP 5: plot ellipse (x_2, y_2, x_c, y_c)

put pixel $(x_2 + x_c, y_2 + y_c)$

put pixel $(-x_2 + x_c, y_2 + y_c)$

put pixel $(-x_2 + x_c, -y_2 + y_c)$

put pixel $(x_2 + x_c, -y_2 + y_c)$

Problem 2.8

Generate an ellipse using Bresenham's midpoint algorithm with the center of the ellipse (15, 17) & $R_x = 9$ and $R_y = 7$.

Solution   Generation of part (1)

$x_c = 15, y_c = 17, R_x = 9$ and $R_y = 7$.

$p_s = R_y^2 - R_y \cdot R_x^2 = 49 - 81 \times 7 = -518$

P	x	$R_y^2 \cdot x$	$x + x_c$	Y	$R_x^2 \cdot y$	$y + y_c$	(x_c, y_c)
− 518	0	0	15	7	518	24	(15, 24)
− 371	1	49	16	7	518	24	(16, 24)
− 28	2	98	17	7	518	24	(17, 24)
413	3	147	18	7	518	24	(18, 24)
142	4	196	19	6	486	23	(19, 23)
131	5	245	20	5	405	22	(20, 22)
380	6	294	21	4	324	21	(21, 21)
	7	**343**	22	3	**243**	20	(22, 20)

Generation of Part (2)

The starting point decision parameter is $p_s = R_x^2 - R_x \cdot R_y^2 = 81 - 9 \times 49 = -360$

	x	$R_y^2 \cdot x$	$x + x_c$	Y	$R_x^2 \cdot y$	$y + y_c$	(x_c, y_c)
− 360	9	441	24	0	0	17	(24, 17)
− 360 + 81 (2 + 3) = 45	9	441	24	1	81	18	(24, 18)
45 + 81 × 7 + 49 × (− 14) = − 74	8	392	23	2	162	19	(23, 19)
− 74 + 81 × 9 = 655	8	392	23	3	243	20	(23, 20)
655 + 81 × 11 + 49 × (− 12) = 958	7	343	22	4	324	21	(22, 21)
	6	**294**	21	5	**405**	22	(21, 22)

Fig. 2.30 shows the rasterization after plotting the pixels.

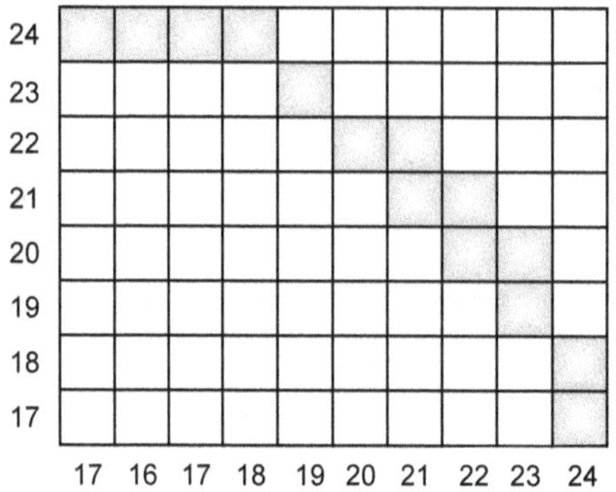

Fig. 2.30 The rasterization of part (1) and part (2) of an ellipse

2.6 ARC GENERATION ALGORITHM USING TRIGONOMETRIC FUNCTION

An arc is a section of a circle. An arc is specified by a start angle, an end angle, and a radius, as shown in Fig. 2.31. An arc can be generated in a clockwise direction and an counterclockwise direction. Both these cases are discussed below.

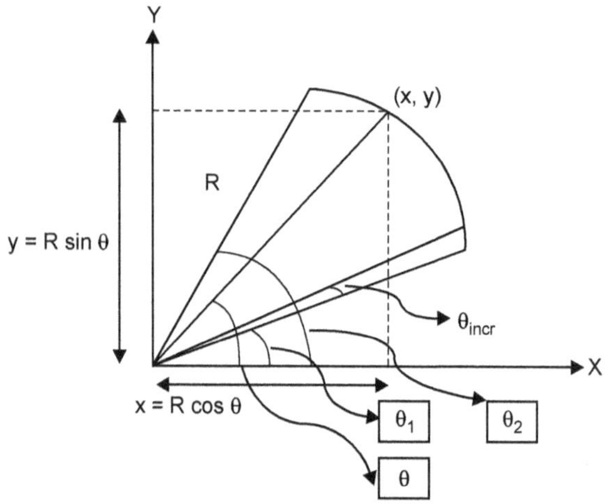

Fig. 2.31 Analysis of an arc in a counterclockwise direction

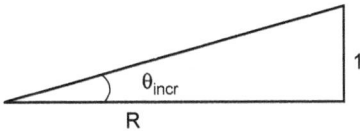

$$\tan(\theta_{incr}) = \frac{1}{R}$$

$$\theta_{incr} >> 1$$

$$\tan(\theta_{incr}) = \theta_{incr}$$

$$\theta_{incr} = \frac{1}{R}$$

Counterclockwise Direction

Fig. 2.32 shows an origin centered arc having radius R, start angle θ_1, end angle θ_2. Here the start angle is less than the end angle and the arc is to be generated in an counterclockwise direction.

Counterclockwise arc generation when $\theta_1 < \theta_2$

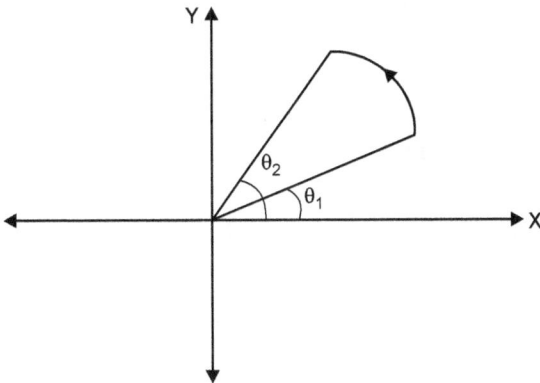

Fig. 2.32 An arc generation in a counterclockwise direction when $\theta_1 < \theta_2$

Counterclockwise arc generation when $\theta_1 > \theta_2$

Fig. 2.33 shows an origin centered arc having radius R, start angle $\theta 1$, and end angle $\theta 2$. Here, the start angle is greater than the end angle and the arc is to be generated in a counterclockwise direction.

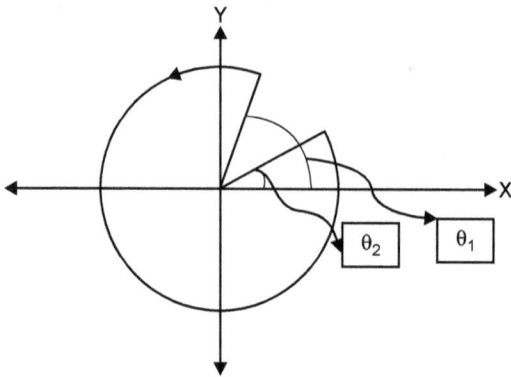

Fig. 2.33 The arc generation in a counterclockwise direction when $\theta_1 > \theta_2$

$$\theta_2 < \theta_1$$
$$\theta_2 = 2\pi + \theta_2$$

Algorithm for the arc generation in a counterclockwise direction

Step 1:   [DECLARATION OF VARIABLES]

int	(x_C, y_C)	center point coordinates of arc
float	(x, y)	coordinates of current pixel representing arc
int	R	radius of arc
float	θ_1 (rads)	start angle of arc
float	θ_2 (rads)	end angle of arc
float	θ(rads)	current point inclination
float	θ_{incr} (rads)	increment of θ

Step 2:   [INITIALIZATION]
Read (x_c, y_c)
Read θ_1, θ_2
Read R

Step 3:   [CALCULATION]

$$\theta_{incr} = \frac{1}{R}$$

Step 4:   [PLOTTING PIXELS]

If
$$\theta_2 < \theta_1$$
$$\theta_2 = 2\pi + \theta_2$$
$$\theta = \theta_1$$

Loop,

Put pixel (round $(x + x_c)$, round $(y + y_c)$)

$$x = R \cos \theta$$

$$y = R \sin \theta$$

$$\theta = \theta + \theta_{incr}$$

Loop continue until $(\theta \leq \theta_2)$

Step 5:   [STOP]

Algorithm for Arc Generation in a Clockwise Direction

When $\theta_1 > \theta_2$

Fig. 2.34 shows an origin centered arc having radius R, start angle θ_1, and end angle θ_2. Here the start angle is greater than the end angle and the arc is to be generated in a clockwise direction.

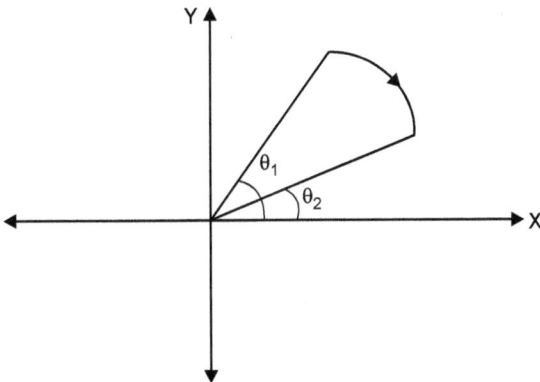

Fig. 2.34 The arc generation in a clockwise direction when $\theta_1 > \theta_2$

When $\theta_1 < \theta_2$

Fig. 2.35 shows an origin centered arc having radius R, start angle θ_1, and end angle θ_2. Here the start angle is less than the end angle and the arc is to be generated in a clockwise direction.

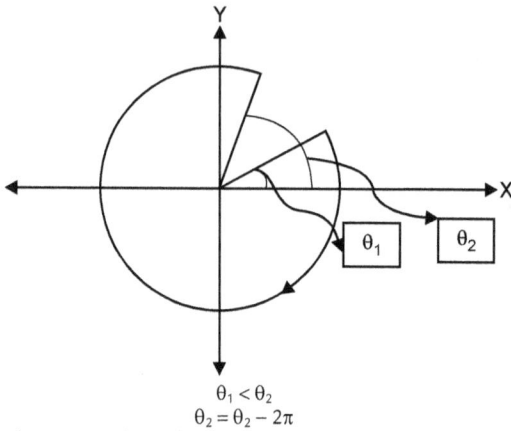

$$\theta_1 < \theta_2$$
$$\theta_2 = \theta_2 - 2\pi$$

Fig. 2.35 Analysis of an arc in a clockwise direction when $\theta_1 < \theta_2$

Step 1: [DECLARATION OF VARIABLES]

int	(x_C, y_C)	center point coordinates of arc
float	(x, y)	coordinates of current pixel representing arc
int	R	radius of arc
float	θ_1 (rads)	start angle of arc
float	θ_2 (rads)	end angle of arc
float	θ(rads)	current point inclination
float	θ_{incr} (rads)	increment of θ

Step 2: [INITIALIZATION]
Read (x_c, y_c)
Read θ_1, θ_2
Read R

Step 3: [CALCULATION]

$$\theta_{incr} = \frac{1}{R}$$

Step 4: [PLOTTING PIXELS]
If
$$\theta_1 < \theta_2$$
$$\theta_2 = \theta_2 - 2\pi$$
$$\theta = \theta_1$$

Loop,

Put pixel (round $(x + x_c)$, round $(y + y_c)$)

$$x = R \cos \theta$$

$$y = R \sin \theta$$

$$\theta = \theta - \theta_{incr}$$

Loop continue until $(\theta \geq \theta_2)$

Step 5:   [STOP]

Problem 2.9

Generate an arc in a counterclockwise direction using a trigonometric function algorithm having center (3, 2), start angle = 30°, end angle = 60°, and radius of arc = 10.

Solution

$$\theta_1 = 30° = 0.523 \text{ rad}$$

$$\theta_2 = 60° = 1.05 \text{ rad}$$

$$x_c = 3, y_c = 2, R = 10$$

$$\theta_{incr} = \frac{1}{R} = \frac{1}{10} = 0.1$$

θ	$x = R \cos \theta$	$x + x_c$	$y = R \sin \theta$	$y + y_c$
0.523	8.66 = 9	9 + 3 = 12	4.99 = 5	5 + 2 = 7
0.623	8.12 = 8	8 + 3 = 11	5.83 = 6	6 + 2 = 8
0.723	7.49 = 7	7 + 3 = 10	6.61 =7	7 + 2 = 9
0.823	6.8 = 7	7 + 3 = 10	7.33 = 7	7 + 2 = 9
0.923	6.08 = 6	6 + 3 = 9	7.97 = 8	8 + 2 = 10
1.023	5.2 = 5	5 + 3 = 8	8.53 = 9	9 + 2 = 11

Fig. 2.36 shows the rasterization after plotting pixels.

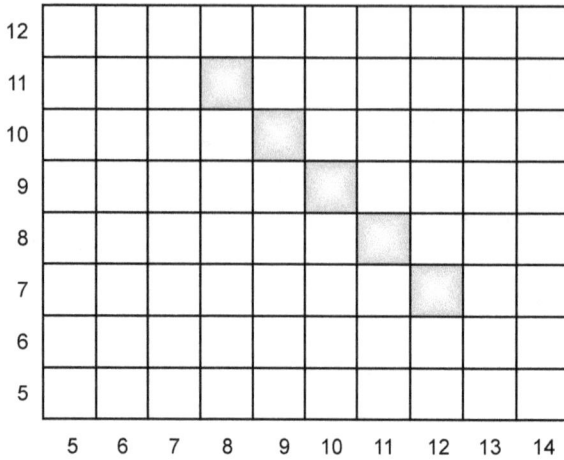

Fig. 2.36 The rasterization of an arc

Problem 2.10

Generate an arc in a counterclockwise direction using a trigonometric function algorithm having center (4, 3), start angle = 350°, end angle = 10°, and radius of arc = 10.

Solution

$$\theta_1 = 350° = 6.109 \text{ rad}$$

$$\theta_2 = 10° = 0.174 \text{ rad}$$

$$x_c = 4, y_c = 3, R = 10$$

As,

$$\theta_2 < \theta_1$$

$$\theta_2 = 2\pi + \theta_2 = 2\theta + 0.174 = 6.45 \text{ rad}$$

$$\theta_{incr} = \frac{1}{R} = \frac{1}{10} = 0.1$$

θ	$x = R \cos \theta$	$x + x_c$	$y = R \sin \theta$	$y + y_c$
6.109	9.85 = 10	10 + 4 = 14	− 1.73 = − 2	− 2 + 3 = 1
6.209	9.97 = 10	10 + 4 = 14	− 0.74 = − 1	− 1 + 3 = 2
6.309	9.99 = 10	10 + 4 = 14	0.25 = 0	0 + 3 = 3
6.409	9.99 = 10	10 + 4 = 14	1.25 = 1	1 + 3 = 4

Fig. 2.37 shows the rasterization after plotting pixels.

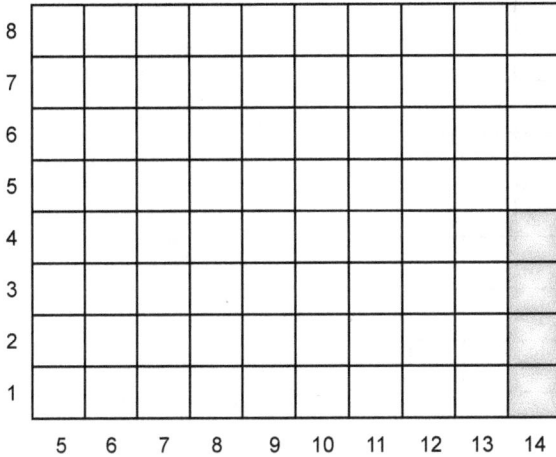

Fig. 2.37 The rasterization of an arc

Problem 2.11

Generate an arc in a clockwise direction using a trigonometric function algorithm having center (5, 3), start angle = 45°, end angle = 15°, and radius of arc = 10.

Solution

$$\theta_1 = 45° = 0.7853 \text{ rad}$$

$$\theta_2 = 15° = 0.261 \text{ rad}$$

$$x_c = 5, y_c = 3, R = 10$$

$$\theta_{incr} = \frac{1}{R} = \frac{1}{10} = 0.1$$

θ	$x = R\cos\theta$	$x + x_c$	$y = R\sin\theta$	$y + y_c$
0.7853	7.07 = 7	7 + 5 = 12	7.07 = 7	7 + 3 = 10
0.6853	7.74 = 8	8 + 5 = 13	6.33 = 6	6 + 3 = 9
0.5853	8.33 = 8	8 + 5 = 13	5.52 = 6	6 + 3 = 9
0.4853	8.84 = 9	9 + 5 = 14	4.66 = 5	5 + 3 = 8
0.3853	9.27 = 9	9 + 5 = 14	3.76 = 4	4 + 3 = 7
0.2853	9.59 = 10	10 + 5 = 15	2.81 = 3	3 + 3 = 6

Fig. 2.38 shows rasterization after plotting pixels.

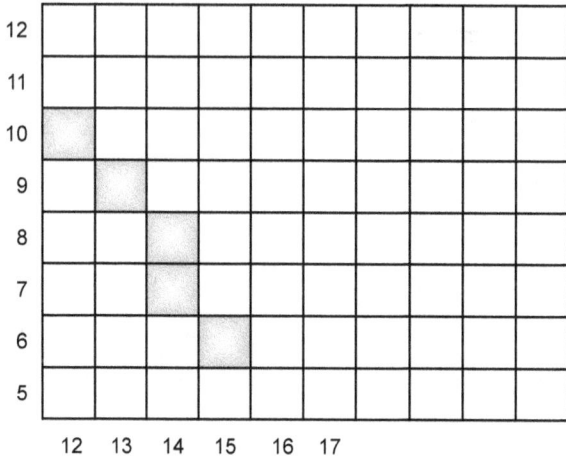

Fig. 2.38 The rasterization of an arc

Problem 2.12

Generate an arc in a clockwise direction using a trigonometric function algorithm having center (7,4), start angle = 15°, end angle = 345°, and radius of arc = 10.

Solution

$$\theta_1 = 15° = 0.261 \text{ rad}$$

$$\theta_2 = 345° = 6.02 \text{ rad}$$

$$x_c = 7, y_c = 4, R = 10$$

As

$$\theta_1 < \theta_2$$

$$\theta_2 = \theta_2 - 2\pi = 6.02 - 2\pi = -0.261 \text{ rad}$$

$$\theta = \theta_1 = 0.261$$

$$\theta_{incr} = \frac{1}{R} = \frac{1}{10} = 0.1$$

θ	$x = R\cos\theta$	$x + x_c$	$y = R\sin\theta$	$y + y_c$
0.261	9.66 = 10	10 + 7 = 17	2.58 = 3	3 + 4 = 7
0.161	9.87 = 10	10 + 7 = 17	1.6 = 2	2 + 4 = 6
0.061	9.98 = 10	10 + 7 = 17	0.6 = 1	1 + 4 = 5
-0.039	9.99 = 10	10 + 7 = 17	− 0.38 = 0	0 + 4 = 4
-0.139	9.99 = 10	10 + 7 = 17	− 1.38 = − 1	− 1 + 4 = 3
-0.239	9.99 = 10	10 + 7 = 17	− 2.36 = − 2	− 2 + 4 = 2

Fig. 2.39 shows the rasterization after plotting pixels.

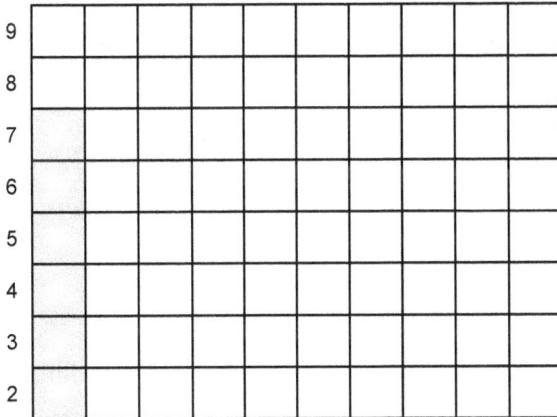

Fig. 2.39 The rasterization of an arc

EXERCISES

1. What is rasterization?
2. Explain the DDA algorithm for rasterizing a line having end points at A (x_1, y_1) and B (x_2, y_2).
3. Explain Bresenham's line algorithm to draw a line between any two end points.
4. Compare the two line generation algorithms using DDA and Bresenham's.
5. Derive decision parameters in Bresenham's midpoint circle generation algorithm.

6. What is the basic concept of line drawing? Write the names of the algorithm used in line drawing.

7. Why is an algorithm required? Explain its steps in any graphics application.

8. What are the advantages and disadvantages of a DDA algorithm?

9. Explain, with a suitable example, why in a DDA for a straight line the value of x is incremented by one in case of a slope less than one.

10. Explain and write Bresenham's midpoint algorithm to draw a circle of radius "R" at center (x_c, y_c).

11. Explain the midpoint subdivision algorithm for the generation of a circle with radius = 5 units and center at (5, 3).

12. Explain how the choices of pixel are done in plotting a circle by Bresenham's ellipse algorithm.

13. The midpoint subdivision algorithm is computationally less intensive than Bresenham's algorithm for circle. Explain.

OBJECTIVE QUESTIONS

2.1 In a DDA algorithm, the common denominator (DENO) is equal to
(a) dx if $(dx \le dy)$
(b) dy if $(dx \ge dy)$
(c) $|dx|$ if $(|dx| \le |dy|)$
(d) $|dy|$ if $(|dx| \ge |dy|)$

2.2 In a DDA algorithm, loop (iterations) continue until the following condition satisfies
(a) loop counter $\le$ DENO
(b) loop counter $\le dx$
(c) loop counter $\le dy$
(d) loop counter $\ge$ DENO

2.3 If the slope of the line is less than 1, then Bresenham's line generation algorithm works on
(a) difference of distance between two successive horizontal points
(b) difference of distance between two successive vertical points
(c) all of the above
(d) none of the above

2.4 If the slope of the line is positive and less than 1, then in Bresenham's line generation algorithm
(a) loop continues until loop counter $\le |dy|$
(b) loop continues until loop counter $\ge |dy|$
(c) loop continues until loop counter $\le |dx|$
(d) loop continues until loop counter $\ge |dx|$

2.5 In Bresenham's midpoint circle generation,
   (*a*) only 1/16th of circle is generated and remaining 15/16th by symmetry
   (*b*) only 1/8th of circle is generated and remaining 7/8th by symmetry
   (*c*) only 1/4th of circle is generated and remaining 3/4th by symmetry
   (*d*) only 1/2th of circle is generated and remaining 1/2th by symmetry

2.6 Bresenham's circle generation algorithm works by checking the position of
   (*a*) midpoint of two successive horizontal points
   (*b*) midpoint of two successive vertical points
   (*c*) midpoint of two successive diagonal points
   (*d*) all of the above
   (*e*) none of the above

2.7 In Bresenham's midpoint ellipse generation algorithm,
   (*a*) only 1/16th of ellipse is generated and remaining 15/16th by symmetry
   (*b*) only 1/8th of ellipse is generated and remaining 7/8th by symmetry
   (*c*) only 1/4th of ellipse is generated and remaining 3/4th by symmetry
   (*d*) only 1/2th of ellipse is generated and remaining 1/2th by symmetry

2.8 In Bresenham's ellipse generation algorithm, 1/4th of ellipse is further divided
   into two parts on the basis of
   (*a*) Major axis and minor axis   (*b*) Radius of ellipse
   (*c*) Center of ellipse   (*d*) Slope of tangents

2.9 In an arc generation algorithm using trigonometric function in a
   counterclockwise generation when $\theta_1 > \theta_2$, then the value of θ_2 is adjusted as
   (*a*) $\theta_2 = \pi + \theta_2$ (*b*) $\theta_2 = 2\pi + \theta_2$
   (*c*) $\theta_2 = 3\pi + \theta_2$ (*d*) $\theta_2 = 4\pi + \theta_2$

2.10 In an arc generation algorithm using trigonometric function in clockwise
   generation when $\theta_1 < \theta_2$, then the value of θ_2 is adjusted as
   (*a*) $\theta_2 = \theta_2 - \pi$ (*b*) $\theta_2 = \theta_2 - 2\pi$
   (*c*) $\theta_2 = \theta_2 - 3\pi$ (*d*) $\theta_2 = \theta_2 - 4\pi$

ANSWERS

2.1 (*c*)	**2.2** (*a*)	**2.3** (*b*)	**2.4** (*c*)
2.5 (*b*)	**2.6** (*a*)	**2.7** (*c*)	**2.8** (*d*)
2.9 (*b*)	**2.10** (*b*)		

Chapter 3 Two-Dimensional Transformation

3.1 INTRODUCTION

In many practical applications, it is necessary to make an entity look better by manipulating its orientation, size, or shape. These mathematical techniques to manipulate or make changes in the entity are called transformations, and transformations of two-dimensional entities such as circles, triangles, etc. are called 2D transformations.

Many engineering problems such as synthesis of mechanisms or analysis of structural elements require a two-dimensional geometric model made up of lines, circles, and rectangles. These models are further analyzed by changing their position, orientation, or size in an organized and efficient way using transformations. Transformations play an integral part in all CAD systems to create and view an object. One of the most common and important tasks in computer graphics is to transform the coordinates (position, orientation, and size) of either an object within the graphical scene or the camera that is viewing the scene. It is also frequently necessary to transform coordinates from one coordinate system to another (e.g., world coordinates to viewpoint coordinates to screen coordinates). All of these transformations can be efficiently handled using simple matrix representations. Further, they can be particularly useful for combining multiple transformations into a single composite transform matrix.

3.2 REPRESENTATION OF 2D GEOMETRY

In computer graphics, the shape and size of 2D objects are represented by 2D numerical descriptions tied to a coordinate system, i.e., in the form of x, y Cartesian coordinate. These geometrical representations are shifted, resized, and reoriented by the application of transformation. The basic building block of any geometry is a point, e.g., a line is made up of two points; planes are made by joining more than two coplanar lines to form a closed loop; solids are made out of planes. Hence a point is considered the basic element of any 2D model. All 2D models can be defined by a set of x, y coordinates or points. For example, a triangle is represented by x, y coordinates of its three vertices $A(x_1, y_1)$, $B(x_2, y_2)$ and $C(x_3, y_3)$ as shown in Fig. 3.1.

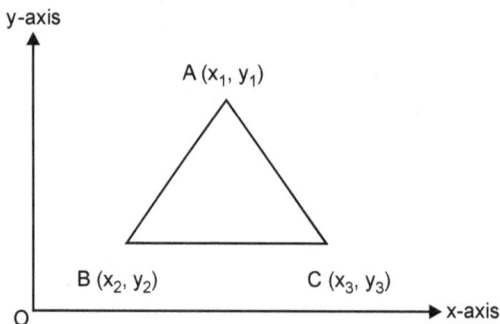

Fig. 3.1 Triangle representation in a Cartesian coordinate system

The vertices ABC of a triangle are represented in matrix form as follows:

$$\begin{bmatrix} A \\ B \\ C \end{bmatrix} = \begin{bmatrix} x_1 & y_1 \\ x_2 & y_2 \\ x_3 & y_3 \end{bmatrix}$$

where each x, y pair is a position vector relative to the specified coordinate system. The matrix representation of a geometric model is useful for manipulation in computer graphics applications. Some geometric transformations are obtained by matrix multiplication and others by matrix addition.

3.3 TYPES OF 2D TRANSFORMATIONS

Transformation involves the calculation of new coordinates (transformed points) from the coordinates of original points. There are three basic types of transformations and two special transformations.

Basic transformations are

1. Scaling
2. Rotation
3. Translation

Special transformations are

1. Reflection
2. Shear

3.3.1 Scaling Transformation

In scaling transformation, the original coordinates of an object are multiplied by the given scale factor. There are two types of scaling transformations: uniform and non-uniform. In uniform scaling, the coordinate values change uniformly along the x, y, and z coordinates, whereas in non-uniform scaling, the change is not necessarily the same in all the coordinate directions.

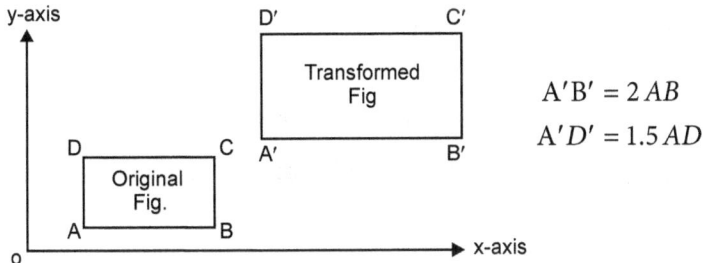

Fig. 3.2 Scaling transformation

$$\text{scaling factor,} = s = \frac{\text{transformed length}}{\text{original length}}$$

$$\text{Scaling factor in the } x \text{ direction} = s_x = \frac{A'B'}{AB} = \frac{2AB}{AB} = 2$$

$$\text{Scaling factor in the } y \text{ direction} = s_y = \frac{A'D'}{AD} = \frac{1.5AD}{AD} = 1.5$$

If scaling factor is greater than "1" it is called enlarging scaling and if scaling; factor is less than "1" it is called reducing scaling.

Mathematical Analysis

Let $p(x, y)$ be the coordinate of the original point.

Let $p(x', y')$ be the coordinate of the final point.

Then the transformation equation for scaling is given by

$$x' = x \cdot s_x \qquad \qquad ...(3.1)$$

$$y' = y \cdot s_y \qquad \qquad ...(3.2)$$

We can write the above equation in matrix form as follows:

$$[x' \, y'] = [x \, y] \begin{bmatrix} s_x & 0 \\ 0 & s_y \end{bmatrix}$$

$$[p'] = [p][s]$$

where

$$s = \begin{bmatrix} s_x & 0 \\ 0 & s_y \end{bmatrix}$$

s = scaling the transformation matrix

p = coordinates of the original figure

p' = coordinates of the final figure

Problem 1

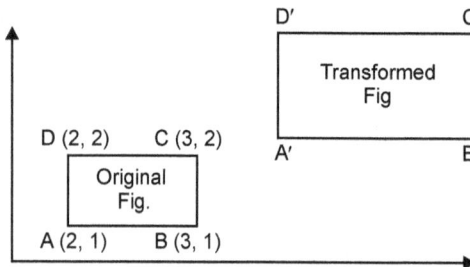

D (2, 2)   C (3, 2)

Original Fig.

A (2, 1)   B (3, 1)

Transformed Fig.

Fig. 3.3

Scale the figure with $s_x = 2$ and $s_y = 1.5$.

Solution

$$[p'] = [p] \cdot [s]$$

$$[p'] = \begin{bmatrix} 2 & 1 \\ 3 & 1 \\ 3 & 2 \\ 2 & 2 \end{bmatrix} \cdot \begin{bmatrix} 2 & 0 \\ 0 & 1.5 \end{bmatrix}$$

$$[p'] = \begin{bmatrix} 4 & 1.5 \\ 6 & 1.5 \\ 6 & 3 \\ 4 & 3 \end{bmatrix}$$

When scaling transformation is carried out, in addition to scaling the figure, the figure also gets shifted. The shift depends on the scaling factors s_x and s_y.

3.3.2 ROTATION TRANSFORMATION

In rotation, the object is rotated by θ angle about the origin. The convention is that the direction of rotation is CCW if θ is a positive angle and CW if θ is a negative angle. The transformation for rotation R_θ is analyzed as follows.

Mathematical analysis

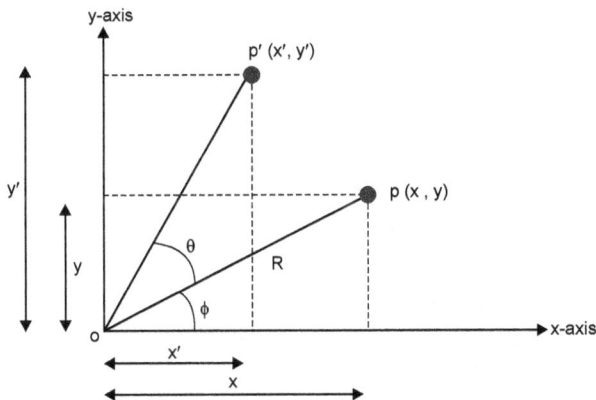

Fig. 3.4 Rotation transformation

$$x = R\cos\phi$$

$$y = R\sin\phi$$

$$x' = R\cos(\theta + \phi)$$

$$y' = R\sin(\theta + \phi)$$

$$x' = R[\cos\theta\,\cos\phi - \sin\theta\,\sin\phi]$$

$$y' = R[\sin\theta\,\cos\phi + \cos\theta\,\sin\phi]$$

$$x' = R\cos\theta\,\cos\phi - R\sin\theta\,\sin\phi \qquad ...(3.3)$$

$$x' = x\cos\theta - y\sin \qquad ...(3.4)$$

$$y' = R\sin\theta\,\cos\phi + R\cos\theta\,\sin\phi \qquad ...(3.5)$$

$$y' = x\sin\theta + y\cos\theta \qquad ...(3.6)$$

We can write the above equation in matrix form as follows:

$$[x'\ y'] = [x\ y]\begin{bmatrix} \cos\theta & \sin\theta \\ -\sin\theta & \cos\theta \end{bmatrix}$$

$$[p'] = [p]\cdot[R]$$

where

$$R = \begin{bmatrix} \cos\theta & \sin\theta \\ -\sin\theta & \cos\theta \end{bmatrix}$$

R = rotation transformation matrix

p = coordinates of the original figure

p' = coordinates of the final figure

Problem 2

Rotate the figure through 90° to CCW about origin. A (2, 1), B (5, 1) C (4, 3).

Solution

$$[p'] = [p] \cdot [R]$$

$$[p'] = \begin{bmatrix} 2 & 1 \\ 5 & 1 \\ 4 & 3 \end{bmatrix} \cdot \begin{bmatrix} \cos 90 & \sin 90 \\ -\sin 90 & \cos 90 \end{bmatrix}$$

$$= \begin{bmatrix} 2 & 1 \\ 5 & 1 \\ 4 & 3 \end{bmatrix} \cdot \begin{bmatrix} 0 & 1 \\ -1 & 0 \end{bmatrix}$$

$$[p'] = \begin{bmatrix} -1 & 2 \\ -1 & 5 \\ -3 & 4 \end{bmatrix}$$

Note: θ = positive for the CCW rotation

θ = negative for the CW rotation

3.3.3 TRANSLATION TRANSFORMATION

In translation, an object is displaced by a given distance and direction from its original position. If displacement is given by vector $v = t_x I + t_y J$, the new object point $P'(x', y')$ can be found by applying translation transformation to $P(x, y)$. See Fig. 3.5.

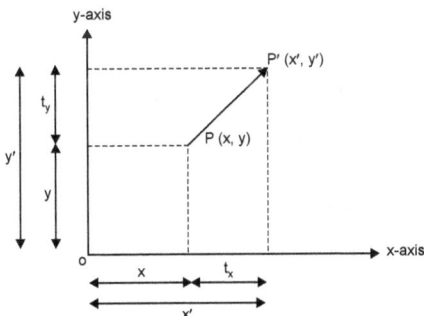

Fig. 3.5 Translation transformation

$$x' = x + t_x$$

$$y' = y + t_y$$

We can write the above equations in matrix form as follows:

$$[x'\, y'] = [x\, y] + [t_x\, t_y]$$

$$[p'] = [p] \cdot [T]$$

where

$$T = [t_x\, t_y]$$

$$[T] = \text{translation transformation matrix}$$

$$p = \text{coordinates of the original figure}$$

$$p' = \text{coordinates of the final figure}$$

3.4 NEED OF HOMOGENEOUS COORDINATES

As mentioned previously, the basic transformations are:

1. Scaling $\qquad [x'\, y'] = [x\, y] \begin{bmatrix} s_x & 0 \\ 0 & s_y \end{bmatrix}$

2. Rotation $\qquad [x'\, y'] = [x\, y] \begin{bmatrix} \cos\theta & \sin\theta \\ -\sin\theta & \cos\theta \end{bmatrix}$

3. Translation $\qquad [x'\, y'] = [x\, y] + [t_x t_y]$

Of these, scaling and rotation transformations are captured by matrix multiplication, whereas translation transformation is captured by matrix addition of two matrices.

Matrix multiplication is easier than matrix addition. This is explained by combine transformation (scaling and rotation).

Example 1

Combine transformation (scaling and rotation).

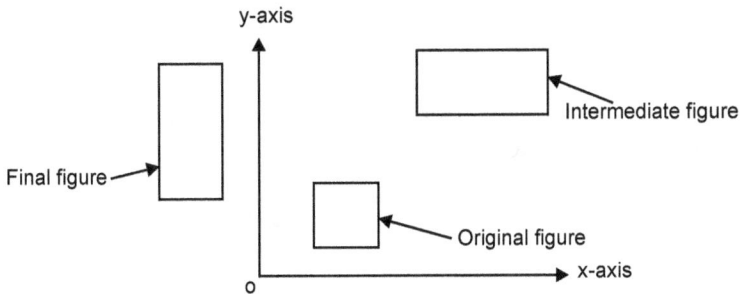

Fig. 3.6 Combine transformation

In this procedure, the figure is scaled and rotated about the origin. The total transformation is carried out in two steps:

Scaling $[p_1] = [p] \cdot [S]$

Rotation $[p'] = [p_1] \cdot [R]$

$[p'] = [p] \cdot [S] \cdot [R]$

$[p'] = [p] \cdot [T_T]$

where

$[T_T]$ = total transformation or resultant transformation matrix

$[T_T]_{2 \times 2} = [S]_{2 \times 2} [R]_{2 \times 2}$

Example 2

Combine transformation (scaling and translation).

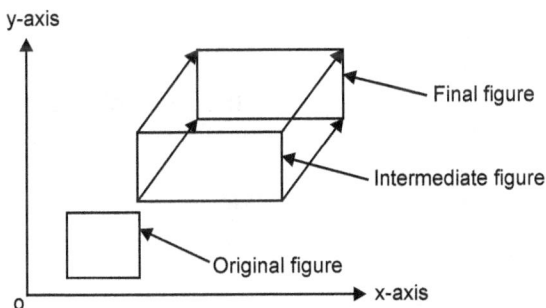

Fig. 3.7 Combine transformation

The total transformation is carried out in two steps:

Scaling $\qquad [p_1] = [p] \cdot [S]$

Translation $\qquad [p'] = [p]\,[S]_{2 \times 2} + [T]_{1 \times 2}$

$\qquad\qquad\qquad [p'] = [p_1]_{1 \times 2} + [T]_{1 \times 2}$

Translation transformation is a 1×2 matrix, i.e., a row matrix, and it is to be added to the matrix in order to achieve the coordinates of the transformation point (Example 2).

Scaling and rotation transformations are both 2×2 matrices and are to be multiplied to matrix p in order to get the coordinates of the transformation point (Example 1).

If a combination of rotation and scaling transformations is carried out, the final transformation can be written as a product of the original transformation (p) and the resultant transformation matrix (T_T) (Example 1). This resultant transformation matrix is a product of respective scaling and rotation transformation matrices. This permits the calculation of final transformation directly without having to calculate the intermediate transformation (Example 1).

When translation is involved in a series of transformations, it is not possible to calculate the resultant transformation matrix T_T because the order of translation transformation matrix 1×2 and the operation of addition is involved. Hence the final transformation can only be achieved by calculating the coordinates of intermediate transformation at each stage. This increases the calculations and hence slows down the transformation process (Example 2).

In order to avoid this difficulty, the transformation matrix needs to be written in the same dimension, i.e., order of scaling and rotation matrix, and also translation is to be carried out by matrix multiplication instead of addition. This is possible by writing the coordinates of the points and matrices in a 3×3 homogeneous form. Coordinates of original point are written as

$$[x \ \ y] = [x \cdot h \ \ y \cdot h \ \ h]$$
$$[2 \ 3] = [2 \ 3 \ 1] \left.\begin{array}{l} \\ = [4 \ 6 \ 1] \\ = \begin{bmatrix} 1 & 1.5 & 0.5 \end{bmatrix} \end{array}\right\} \text{all these represent the same point } [2 \ 3]$$

Advantage of homogeneous coordinates in case of translation

$$[x' \ y'] = [x \ y] + [t_x \ t_y]$$

Using homogeneous coordinates

$$[x'\ y'\ h] = [x\ y\ 1]\begin{bmatrix} 1 & 0 & 0 \\ 0 & 1 & 0 \\ t_x & t_y & 1 \end{bmatrix}$$

$$x' = x + t_x$$
$$y' = y + t_y$$
$$h = 1$$

Thus translation transformation can be captured in matrix multiplication using homogeneous coordinates.

In the other two operations, the basic matrix will remain the same, only 0 and 1 are added to the third row and third column.

Scaling

$$[x'\ y'\ h] = [x\ y\ 1]\begin{bmatrix} s_x & 0 & 0 \\ 0 & s_y & 0 \\ 0 & 0 & 1 \end{bmatrix}$$

Rotation

$$[x'\ y'\ h] = [x\ y\ 1]\begin{bmatrix} \cos\theta & \sin\theta & 0 \\ -\sin\theta & \cos\theta & 0 \\ 0 & 0 & 1 \end{bmatrix}$$

Thus, using homogeneous coordinates, we can capture translation by matrix multiplication similar to rotation and scaling, which are also captured as matrix multiplication.

Problem 1

Find the 3 × 3 transformation matrix for the figure shown in Fig. 3.8.

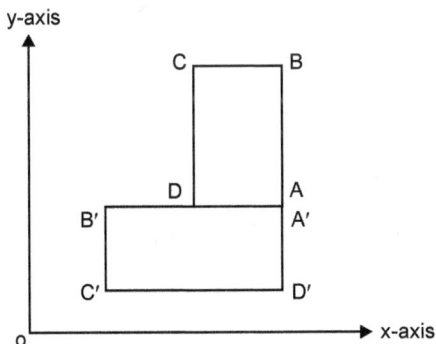

Fig. 3.8

Solution

The total transformation is carried out in the following steps:

Step 1: Translate figure to the origin about point A.

$$t_x = -x_A \text{ and } t_y = -y_A$$

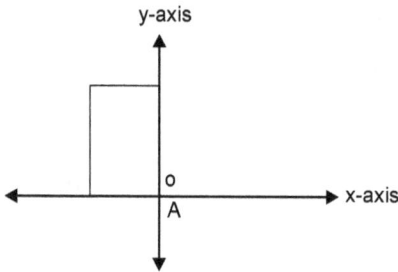

Fig. 3.9 Position of a rectangle after translation

$$T_1 = \begin{bmatrix} 1 & 0 & 0 \\ 0 & 1 & 0 \\ -x_A & -y_A & 1 \end{bmatrix}$$

Step 2: Rotate figure about the origin through 90° in the CCW direction.

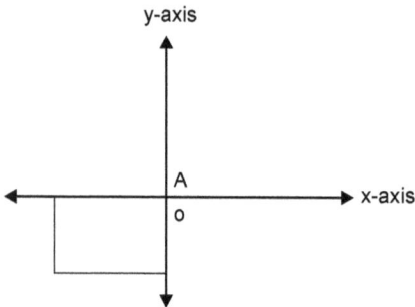

Fig. 3.10 Position of a rectangle after rotation

$$R = \begin{bmatrix} \cos 90 & \sin 90 & 0 \\ -\sin 90 & \cos 90 & 0 \\ 0 & 0 & 1 \end{bmatrix} = \begin{bmatrix} 0 & 1 & 0 \\ -1 & 0 & 0 \\ 0 & 0 & 1 \end{bmatrix}$$

Step 3: Translate point A from the origin to its original position.

$$t_x = x_A \text{ and } t_y = y_A$$

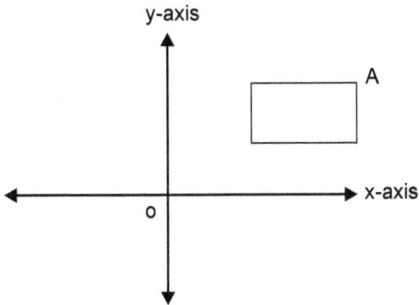

Fig. 3.11 Position of a rectangle after back translation

$$T_2 = \begin{bmatrix} 1 & 0 & 0 \\ 0 & 1 & 0 \\ x_A & y_A & 1 \end{bmatrix}$$

The final transformation matrix equation is given by

$$[p'] = [p] \cdot [T_T]$$

where T_T = total transformation matrix

$$T_T = \begin{bmatrix} 1 & 0 & 0 \\ 0 & 1 & 0 \\ -x_A & -y_A & 1 \end{bmatrix} \begin{bmatrix} 0 & 1 & 0 \\ -1 & 0 & 0 \\ 0 & 0 & 1 \end{bmatrix} \begin{bmatrix} 1 & 0 & 0 \\ 0 & 1 & 0 \\ x_A & y_A & 1 \end{bmatrix}$$

$$T_T = \begin{bmatrix} 0 & 1 & 0 \\ -1 & 0 & 0 \\ y_A & -x_A & 1 \end{bmatrix} \begin{bmatrix} 1 & 0 & 0 \\ 0 & 1 & 0 \\ x_A & y_A & 1 \end{bmatrix}$$

$$T_T = \begin{bmatrix} 0 & 1 & 0 \\ -1 & 0 & 0 \\ (x_A + y_A) & (y_A - x_A) & 1 \end{bmatrix}$$

Problem 2

Find the 3 × 3 transformation matrix for the figures in Fig. 3.12.

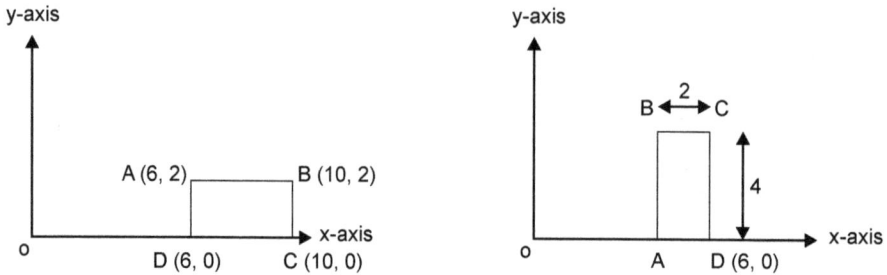

Fig. 3.12

Solution

The total transformation is carried out in the following steps:

Step 1: Translate figure to the origin about point D.

$$t_x = -6 \text{ and } t_y = 0$$

$$T_1 = \begin{bmatrix} 1 & 0 & 0 \\ 0 & 1 & 0 \\ -6 & 0 & 1 \end{bmatrix}$$

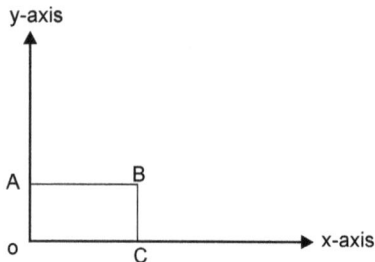

Fig. 3.13 Position of a rectangle after translation

Step 2: Rotate figure in the CCW direction by 90° about the origin.

$$R = \begin{bmatrix} \cos 90 & \sin 90 & 0 \\ -\sin 90 & \cos 90 & 0 \\ 0 & 0 & 1 \end{bmatrix} = \begin{bmatrix} 0 & 1 & 0 \\ -1 & 0 & 0 \\ 0 & 0 & 1 \end{bmatrix}$$

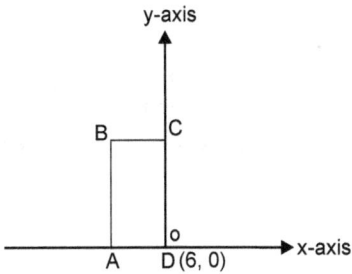

Fig. 3.14 Position of a rectangle after rotation

Step 3: Translate point D back to its original position.

$$t_x = 6 \text{ and } t_y = 0$$

$$T_1 = \begin{bmatrix} 1 & 0 & 0 \\ 0 & 1 & 0 \\ 6 & 0 & 1 \end{bmatrix}$$

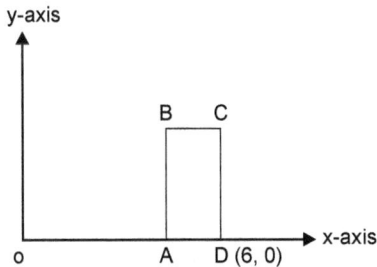

Fig. 3.15 Position of a rectangle after back translation

The final transformation matrix equation is given by

$$[p'] = [p] \cdot [T_T]$$

where T_T = total transformation matrix

$$T_T = \begin{bmatrix} 1 & 0 & 0 \\ 0 & 1 & 0 \\ -6 & 0 & 1 \end{bmatrix} \begin{bmatrix} 0 & 1 & 0 \\ -1 & 0 & 0 \\ 0 & 0 & 1 \end{bmatrix} \begin{bmatrix} 1 & 0 & 0 \\ 0 & 1 & 0 \\ 6 & 0 & 1 \end{bmatrix}$$

$$T_T = \begin{bmatrix} 0 & 1 & 0 \\ -1 & 0 & 0 \\ 0 & -6 & 1 \end{bmatrix} \begin{bmatrix} 1 & 0 & 0 \\ 0 & 1 & 0 \\ 6 & 0 & 1 \end{bmatrix}$$

$$T_T = \begin{bmatrix} 0 & 1 & 0 \\ -1 & 0 & 0 \\ 0 & -6 & 1 \end{bmatrix}$$

Problem 3

Find the 3×3 homogeneous transformation matrix to transform square *ABCD* into another square *A'B'C'D'* as shown in the figure. Side of the original square = 2, coordinates of point *A* (20, 10). Draw the final transformation on a graph paper.

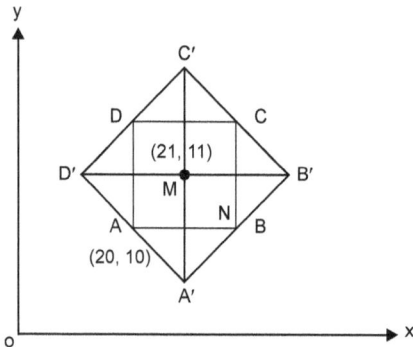

Fig. 3.16

Solution Consider triangle ANA'.

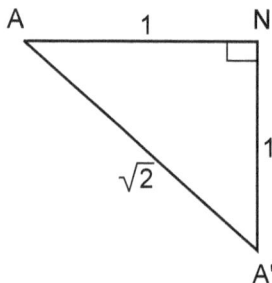

Fig. 3.16(a)

From Fig. 3.16

$$AB = 2$$

$$A'D' = A'A + D'A \quad \text{or} \quad A'B' = A'B + BB'$$

From Fig. 3.16(a)

$$A'A = \sqrt{1+1} = \sqrt{2}$$

$$A'D' = A'B' = \sqrt{2} + \sqrt{2}$$

$$A'D' = A'B' = 2\sqrt{2}$$

$$\text{scaling factor} = \frac{\text{final length}}{\text{original length}} = \frac{A'B'}{AB} = \frac{2\sqrt{2}}{2} = \sqrt{2}$$

The total transformation is carried out in the following steps:

Step 1: Translate center of the original square to the origin.

$$t_x = -21, t_y = -11$$

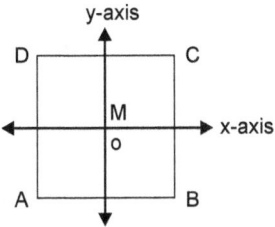

Fig. 3.17 Translate square to the origin about center

Step 2: Scale the figure having $S_x = \sqrt{2}, S_y = \sqrt{2}$

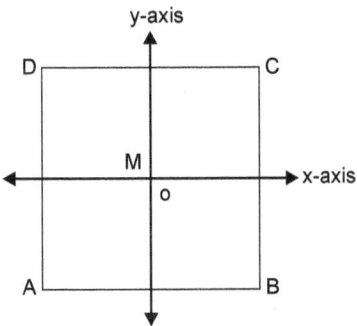

Fig. 3.18 Scale square about the origin

Step 3: Rotate the figure in the CCW direction by 45°.

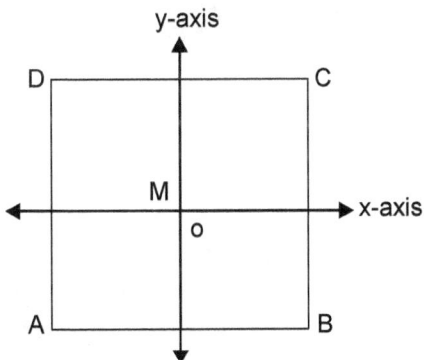

Fig. 3.19 Position of a square after rotation

Step 4: Translate the center back to its original position.

$$t_x = 21 \ t_y = 11$$

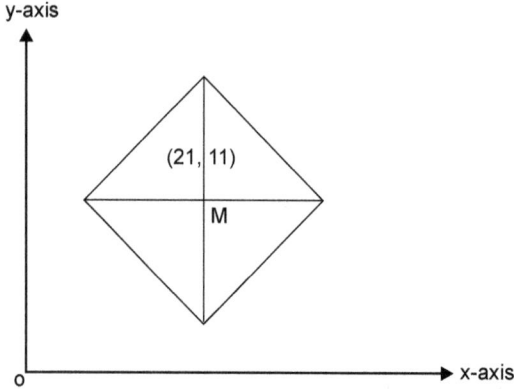

Fig. 3.20 Position of a square after back translation

The final transformation equation is

$$[T_T] = [T_1] \cdot [S][R][T_2]$$

$$T_T = \begin{bmatrix} 1 & 0 & 0 \\ 0 & 1 & 0 \\ -21 & -11 & 1 \end{bmatrix} \cdot \begin{bmatrix} \sqrt{2} & 0 & 0 \\ 0 & \sqrt{2} & 0 \\ 0 & 0 & 1 \end{bmatrix} \cdot \begin{bmatrix} \cos 45 & \sin 45 & 0 \\ -\sin 45 & \cos 45 & 0 \\ 0 & 0 & 1 \end{bmatrix} \cdot \begin{bmatrix} 1 & 0 & 0 \\ 0 & 1 & 0 \\ 21 & 11 & 1 \end{bmatrix}$$

$$T_T = \begin{bmatrix} 1 & 0 & 0 \\ 0 & 1 & 0 \\ -21 & -11 & 1 \end{bmatrix} \begin{bmatrix} \sqrt{2} & 0 & 0 \\ 0 & \sqrt{2} & 0 \\ 0 & 0 & 1 \end{bmatrix} \cdot \begin{bmatrix} \dfrac{1}{\sqrt{2}} & \dfrac{1}{\sqrt{2}} & 0 \\ -\dfrac{1}{\sqrt{2}} & \dfrac{1}{\sqrt{2}} & 0 \\ 21 & 11 & 1 \end{bmatrix}$$

$$T_T = \begin{bmatrix} 1 & 0 & 0 \\ 0 & 1 & 0 \\ -21 & -11 & 1 \end{bmatrix} \begin{bmatrix} 1 & 1 & 0 \\ -1 & 1 & 0 \\ 21 & 11 & 1 \end{bmatrix}$$

$$T_T = \begin{bmatrix} 1 & 1 & 0 \\ -1 & 1 & 0 \\ 11 & -21 & 1 \end{bmatrix}$$

Coordinates of the final figure are given by

$$[p'] = [p][T_T]$$

$$p' = \begin{bmatrix} 20 & 10 & 1 \\ 22 & 10 & 1 \\ 22 & 12 & 1 \\ 20 & 12 & 1 \end{bmatrix} \cdot \begin{bmatrix} 1 & 1 & 0 \\ -1 & 1 & 0 \\ 11 & -21 & 1 \end{bmatrix}$$

$$p' = \begin{bmatrix} 21 & 9 & 1 \\ 23 & 11 & 1 \\ 21 & 11 & 1 \end{bmatrix}$$

3.5 SPECIAL TRANSFORMATION

We have studied the three basic transformations, i.e., translation, scaling, and rotation. Special transformation includes reflection transformation and shear transformation. These are not unique but they are just special cases of basic transformations. First let us see reflection transformation.

3.5.1 Reflection Transformation

Reflection transformation is also called mirror transformation, because it yields a mirror image of the original figure. It is a special case of scaling transformation or a combination of scaling and translation transformation. For any figure to be reflected, it requires an axis of reflection. So, depending upon the position of the axis of reflection, different reflection transformations can be obtained. We discuss some of the positions of the axis of reflection in the following cases.

Case 1: Reflection about the *x*-axis

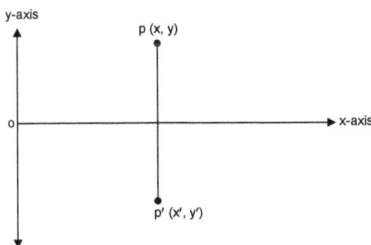

Fig. 3.21 Reflection of a point about the *x*-axis

$$x' = x \qquad \text{...(3.7)}$$

$$y' = -y \qquad \text{...(3.8)}$$

Representing Eqs. (3.7) and (3.8) in matrix form

$$[x'y'] = [x\,y]\begin{bmatrix} 1 & 0 \\ 0 & -1 \end{bmatrix} \qquad \text{...(3.9)}$$

An homogenous coordinate system of Eq. (3.9) is given by

$$[x'y'h] = [x\,y\,h]\begin{bmatrix} 1 & 0 & 0 \\ 0 & -1 & 0 \\ 0 & 0 & 1 \end{bmatrix}$$

Case 2: Reflection about y-axis

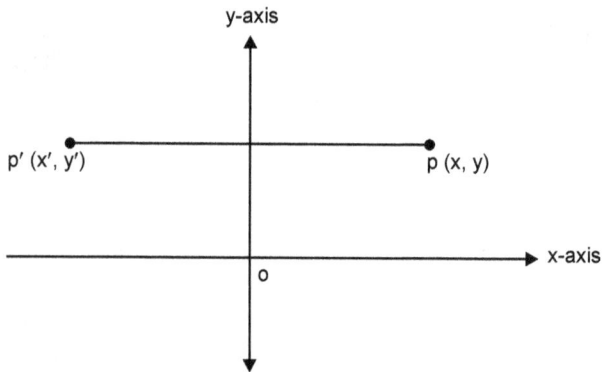

Fig. 3.22 Reflection of a point about the y-axis

$$x' = -x \qquad \text{...(3.10)}$$

$$y' = y \qquad \text{...(3.11)}$$

Representing Eqs. (3.10) and (3.11) in matrix form

$$[x'y'] = [x\,y]\begin{bmatrix} -1 & 0 \\ 0 & 1 \end{bmatrix} \qquad \text{...(3.12)}$$

An homogeneous coordinate system of Eq. (3.12) is given by

$$[x'y'h]=[x\,y\,h]\begin{bmatrix} -1 & 0 & 0 \\ 0 & 1 & 0 \\ 0 & 0 & 1 \end{bmatrix}$$

Case 3: Reflection about the origin

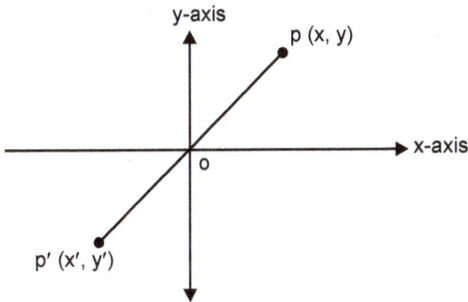

Fig. 3.23 Reflection of a point about the origin

$$x' = -x \qquad\qquad\qquad\qquad ...(3.13)$$

$$y' = -y \qquad\qquad\qquad\qquad ...(3.14)$$

Representing Eqs. (3.13) and (3.14) in matrix form

$$[x'y']=[x\,y]\begin{bmatrix} -1 & 0 \\ 0 & -1 \end{bmatrix} \qquad\qquad ...(3.15)$$

An homogeneous coordinate system of Eq. (3.15) is given by

$$[x'y'h]=[x\,y\,h]\begin{bmatrix} -1 & 0 & 0 \\ 0 & -1 & 0 \\ 0 & 0 & 1 \end{bmatrix}$$

Note:
1. Reflection about the x-axis is the same as scaling transformation with $S_x=+1$ and $S_y=-1$.
2. Reflection about the y-axis is the same as scaling transformation with $S_x=-1$ and $S_y=+1$.
3. Reflection about the origin is the same as scaling transformation with $S_x=-1$ and $S_y=-1$.

Case 4: Reflection of a point about a line $y = b$ (parallel to x-axis)

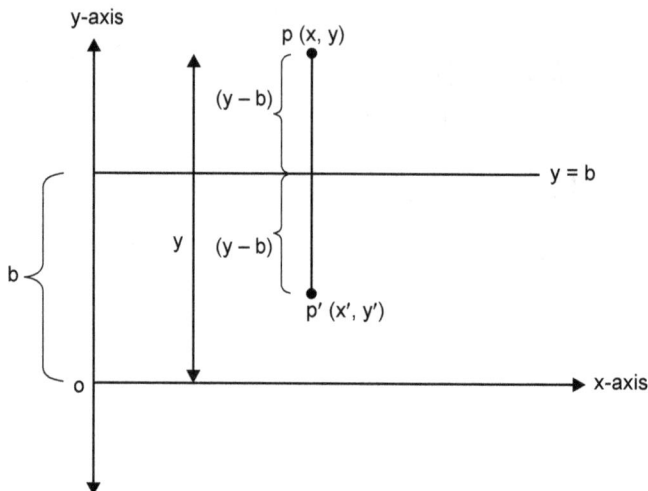

Fig. 3.24 Reflection of a point about a line parallel to the x-axis

$$x' = -x \qquad \text{...(3.16)}$$
$$y' = y - 2\,(y - b)$$
$$y' = y - 2y + 2b$$
$$y' = -y + 2b \qquad \text{...(3.17)}$$

Representing Eqs. (3.16) and (3.17) in matrix form (homogeneous coordinate system)

$$[x'y'\,1] = [x\,y1]\begin{bmatrix} 1 & 0 & 0 \\ 0 & -1 & 0 \\ 0 & 2b & 1 \end{bmatrix}$$

The above matrix confirms that reflection of a point about line $y = b$ is the same as translation followed by scaling. The total transformation is carried out in the following steps:

1. Translate line $y = b$ so as to coincide with x-axis with $t_x = 0$, $t_y = -b$.

2. Now take a reflection of the point about x-axis, which is the same as scaling transformation with $S_x = 1$ and $S_y = -1$.

3. Translate the line from x-axis back to its original position, with $t_x = 0$ and $t_y = b$.

The final transformation matrix is given by

$$[p'] = [p] \cdot [T_T]$$

where $[T_T]$ = total transformation matrix

$$\left[T_T\right]=\left[T_1\right]\left[M\right]\left[T_2\right]$$

$$\left[T_T\right]=\begin{bmatrix} 1 & 0 & 0 \\ 0 & 1 & 0 \\ 0 & -b & 1 \end{bmatrix}\begin{bmatrix} 1 & 0 & 0 \\ 0 & -1 & 0 \\ 0 & 0 & 1 \end{bmatrix}\begin{bmatrix} 1 & 0 & 0 \\ 0 & 1 & 0 \\ 0 & b' & 1 \end{bmatrix}$$

$$\left[T_T\right]=\begin{bmatrix} 1 & 0 & 0 \\ 0 & -1 & 0 \\ 0 & 2b & 1 \end{bmatrix}$$

Case 5: Reflection of a point about a line $x = a$

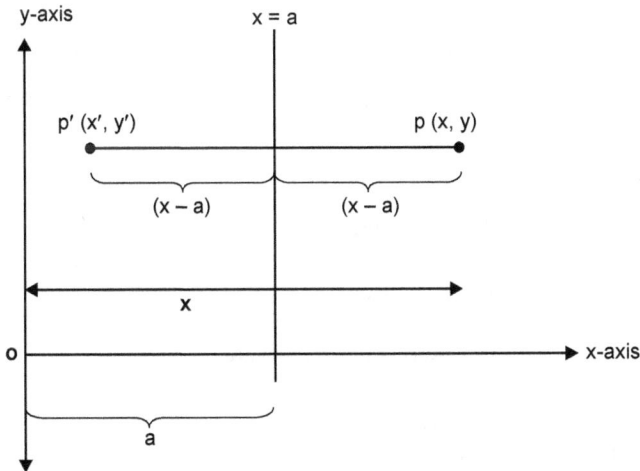

Fig. 3.25 Reflection of a point about a line parallel to the y-axis

$$x' = x - 2\,(x - a)$$
$$x' = x - 2x + 2a$$
$$x' = -x + 2a \qquad\qquad ...(3.18)$$
$$y' = y \qquad\qquad ...(3.19)$$

Representing Eqs. (3.18) and (3.19) in matrix form (homogeneous coordinate system)

$$[x'y'h] = [x\,y\,1] \begin{bmatrix} -1 & 0 & 0 \\ 0 & 1 & 0 \\ 2a & 0 & 1 \end{bmatrix}$$

where

$$[M] = \begin{bmatrix} -1 & 0 & 0 \\ 0 & 1 & 0 \\ 2a & 0 & 1 \end{bmatrix}$$

The above matrix confirms that reflection of a point about line $x = a$ is the same as translation followed by scaling. The total transformation is carried out in the following steps:

1. Translate line $x = a$ so as to coincide with y-axis with $t_x = -a$ and $t_y = 0$.
2. Now take a reflection of the point about y-axis, which is the same as scaling transformation with $S_x = -1$ and $S_y = 1$.
3. Translate the line from x-axis back to its original position, with $t_x = a$ and $t_y = 0$.

The final transformation matrix equation is given by

$$[p'] = [p]\,[T_T]$$

where $[T_T]$ = total transformation matrix

$$[T_T] = [T_1][M][T_2]$$

$$T_T = \begin{bmatrix} 1 & 0 & 0 \\ 0 & 1 & 0 \\ -a & 0 & 1 \end{bmatrix} \begin{bmatrix} -1 & 0 & 0 \\ 0 & 1 & 0 \\ 0 & 0 & 1 \end{bmatrix} \begin{bmatrix} -1 & 0 & 0 \\ 0 & 1 & 0 \\ a & 0 & 1 \end{bmatrix}$$

$$T_T = \begin{bmatrix} -1 & 0 & 0 \\ 0 & 1 & 0 \\ 2a & 0 & 1 \end{bmatrix}$$

Case 6: Reflection of a point about a line $y = x$

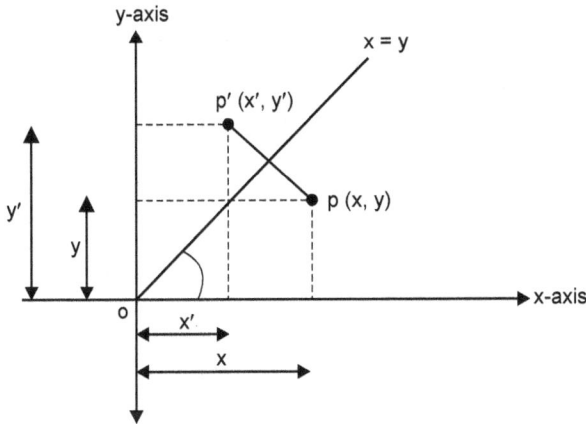

Fig. 3.26 Reflection of a point about a line $45°$ to the x-axis

$$x' = y \qquad\qquad ...(3.20)$$
$$y' = x \qquad\qquad ...(3.21)$$

Representing Eqs. (3.20) and (3.21) in matrix form (homogeneous coordinate system)

$$[x'y'h]=[x\,y1]\begin{bmatrix} 0 & 1 & 0 \\ 1 & 0 & 0 \\ 0 & 0 & 1 \end{bmatrix}$$

where

$$[M]=\begin{bmatrix} 0 & 1 & 0 \\ 1 & 0 & 0 \\ 0 & 0 & 1 \end{bmatrix}$$

Problem 4

Find the reflection matrix of an image about line $y = 2x$.
Solution
Putting $x = 0$ in the equation of line $y = 2x$ we get $y = 0$.
If $y = 0$, we get $x = 0$.
Thus, we infer that the line is passing through the origin.

Comparing the equation of line $y = 2x$ with $y = mx + c$,

m = slope = 2 and $c = y$ = intercept = 0

We know that slope = $\tan \theta$, where θ is the inclination of line with x-axis

Therefore, inclination of the line is given by

$$m = \tan \theta = 2$$

$$\theta = \tan^{-1}(2)$$

$$\theta = 63.43°$$

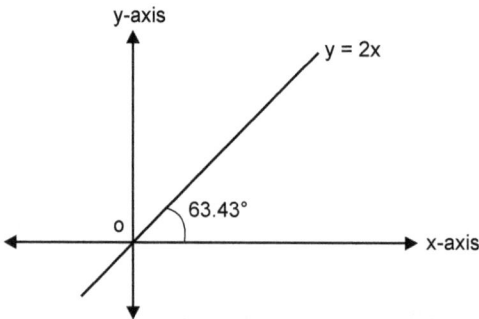

Fig. 3.27 Inclination of a given line

The transformation can be obtained by the following steps:

Step 1: Rotate the line by 63.43° in CW direction so as to coincide with the x-axis.

$$[R_1] = \begin{bmatrix} \cos(-63.43) & \sin(-63.43) & 0 \\ -\sin(-63.43) & \cos(-63.43) & 0 \\ 0 & 0 & 1 \end{bmatrix}$$

$$[R_1] = \begin{bmatrix} 0.447 & -0.8943 & 0 \\ 0.8943 & 0.447 & 0 \\ 0 & 0 & 1 \end{bmatrix}$$

Step 2: Reflection transformation about the x-axis.

$$[M_x] = \begin{bmatrix} 1 & 0 & 0 \\ 0 & -1 & 0 \\ 0 & 0 & 1 \end{bmatrix}$$

Step 3: Back rotation by 63.43° in the CCW direction.

$$[R_2] = \begin{bmatrix} \cos(63.43) & \sin(63.43) & 0 \\ -\sin(63.43) & \cos(63.43) & 0 \\ 0 & 0 & 1 \end{bmatrix}$$

$$[R_2] = \begin{bmatrix} 0.447 & 0.8943 & 0 \\ -0.8943 & 0.447 & 0 \\ 0 & 0 & 1 \end{bmatrix}$$

Thus, total transformation $[T_T] = [R_1] \cdot [M_x] \cdot [R_2]$

$$[T_T] = \begin{bmatrix} 0.447 & -0.8943 & 0 \\ 0.8943 & 0.447 & 0 \\ 0 & 0 & 1 \end{bmatrix} \cdot \begin{bmatrix} 1 & 0 & 0 \\ 0 & -1 & 0 \\ 0 & 0 & 1 \end{bmatrix} \cdot \begin{bmatrix} 0.447 & 0.8943 & 0 \\ -0.8943 & 0.447 & 0 \\ 0 & 0 & 1 \end{bmatrix}$$

$$[T_T] = \begin{bmatrix} -0.6 & 0.8 & 0 \\ 0.8 & 0.6 & 0 \\ 0 & 0 & 1 \end{bmatrix}$$

Problem 5

Determine the transformation matrix for reflection of a point about the line $y = 2x - 6$.

Solution

Put $x = 0$ in equation of line ($y = 2x - 6$); then we get $y = -6$; coordinate $(0, -6)$.
If $y = 0$, then we get $x = 3$; coordinate $(0, -6)$.

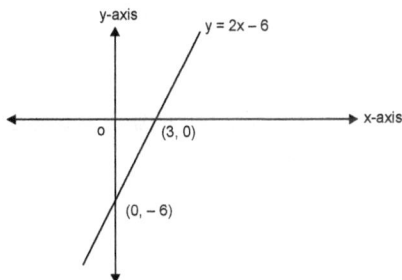

Fig. 3.28 Position of a given line

The transformation can be obtained by the following steps:

Step 1: Rotate the line by 63.43° in the CW direction so as to coincide with the x-axis.

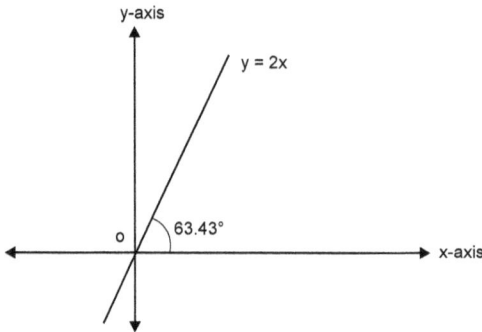

Fig. 3.29 Position of the line after translation

If we compare the equation of line $y = 2x - 6$ with $y = m\,x + c$, we have
$m =$ slope $= 2$ and $c = y =$ intercept $= -6$
We know that slope $= \tan\theta$, where θ is inclination of the line.
Therefore

$$m = tan\,\theta = 2$$

$$\theta = tan^{-1}(2)$$

$$\theta = 63.43°$$

Step 2: Translate the line to the origin by $t_x = -3$, $t_y = 0$.

$$\left[T_1\right] = \begin{bmatrix} 1 & 0 & 0 \\ 0 & 1 & 0 \\ -3 & 0 & 1 \end{bmatrix}$$

Step 3: Rotate the line by 63.43° in CW direction so as to coincide with the x-axis.

$$\left[R_1\right] = \begin{bmatrix} \cos(-63.43) & \sin(-63.43) & 0 \\ -\sin(-63.43) & \cos(-63.43) & 0 \\ 0 & 0 & 1 \end{bmatrix}$$

$$\left[R_1\right] = \begin{bmatrix} 0.447 & -0.8943 & 0 \\ 0.8943 & 0.447 & 0 \\ 0 & 0 & 1 \end{bmatrix}$$

Step 4: Reflection transformation about the x-axis:

$$[M_x] = \begin{bmatrix} 1 & 0 & 0 \\ 0 & -1 & 0 \\ 0 & 0 & 1 \end{bmatrix}$$

Step 5: Back rotation by 63.43° in the CCW direction:

$$[R_2] = \begin{bmatrix} \cos(63.43) & \sin(63.43) & 0 \\ -\sin(63.43) & \cos(63.43) & 0 \\ 0 & 0 & 1 \end{bmatrix}$$

$$[R_2] = \begin{bmatrix} 0.447 & 0.8943 & 0 \\ -0.8943 & 0.447 & 0 \\ 0 & 0 & 1 \end{bmatrix}$$

Step 6: Back-translate the line to the original position by $t_x = 3$, $t_y = 0$.

$$[T_2] = \begin{bmatrix} 1 & 0 & 0 \\ 0 & 1 & 0 \\ 3 & 0 & 1 \end{bmatrix}$$

Total transformation $[T_T] = [T_1] \cdot [R_1] \cdot [M_x] \cdot [R_2] \cdot [T_1]$

$$[T_T] = \begin{bmatrix} 1 & 0 & 0 \\ 0 & 1 & 0 \\ -3 & 0 & 1 \end{bmatrix} \cdot \begin{bmatrix} 0.447 & -0.8943 & 0 \\ 0.8943 & 0.447 & 0 \\ 0 & 0 & 1 \end{bmatrix} \cdot$$

$$\begin{bmatrix} 1 & 0 & 0 \\ 0 & -1 & 0 \\ 0 & 0 & 1 \end{bmatrix} \cdot \begin{bmatrix} 0.447 & 0.8943 & 0 \\ -0.8943 & 0.447 & 0 \\ 0 & 0 & 1 \end{bmatrix} \cdot \begin{bmatrix} 1 & 0 & 0 \\ 0 & 1 & 0 \\ 3 & 0 & 1 \end{bmatrix}$$

$$[T_T] = \begin{bmatrix} 1 & 0 & 0 \\ 0 & 1 & 0 \\ -3 & 0 & 1 \end{bmatrix} \cdot \begin{bmatrix} 0.447 & -0.8943 & 0 \\ 0.8943 & 0.447 & 0 \\ 0 & 0 & 1 \end{bmatrix} \cdot$$

$$\begin{bmatrix} 1 & 0 & 0 \\ 0 & -1 & 0 \\ 0 & 0 & 1 \end{bmatrix} \cdot \begin{bmatrix} 0.447 & 0.8943 & 0 \\ -0.8943 & 0.447 & 0 \\ 3 & 0 & 1 \end{bmatrix}$$

$$[T_T] = \begin{bmatrix} 1 & 0 & 0 \\ 0 & 1 & 0 \\ -3 & 0 & 1 \end{bmatrix} \cdot \begin{bmatrix} 0.447 & -0.8943 & 0 \\ 0.8943 & 0.447 & 0 \\ 0 & 0 & 1 \end{bmatrix} \cdot \begin{bmatrix} 0.447 & 0.8943 & 0 \\ 0.8943 & -0.447 & 0 \\ 3 & 0 & 1 \end{bmatrix}$$

$$[T_T] = \begin{bmatrix} 1 & 0 & 0 \\ 0 & 1 & 0 \\ -3 & 0 & 1 \end{bmatrix} \cdot \begin{bmatrix} -0.6 & 0.8 & 0 \\ 0.8 & 0.6 & 0 \\ 3 & 0 & 1 \end{bmatrix}$$

$$[T_T] = \begin{bmatrix} -0.6 & 0.8 & 0 \\ 0.8 & 0.6 & 0 \\ 4.8 & -2.4 & 1 \end{bmatrix}$$

3.5.2 Shear Transformation

A shear is a transformation that, similar to scale and translate, distorts the shape of an object along either or both the axes. A shear along one axis (say, x-axis) is performed in terms of the point's coordinate in the other axis (y-axis). Thus a shear of 1 in the x-axis will cause the x-coordinate of the point to distort by 1 (y-coordinate).

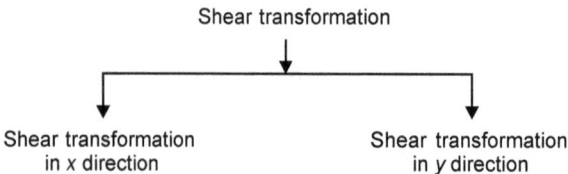

Shear transformation

Shear transformation
in x direction

Shear transformation
in y direction

Fig. 3.30 Classification of a shear transformation

1. The transformation matrix for shear in the x direction is

$$[SH_x] = \begin{bmatrix} 1 & 0 & 0 \\ SH_x & 1 & 0 \\ 0 & 0 & 1 \end{bmatrix}$$

where SH_x = shear factor along the x-axis

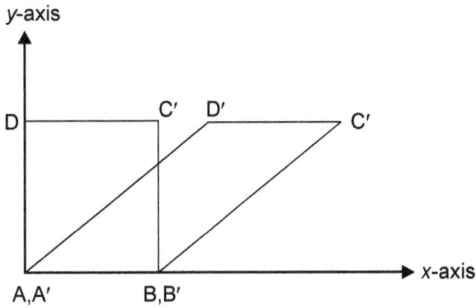

Fig. 3.31 Shear transformation in the x direction

2. The transformation matrix for shear in the y direction is

$$\left[SH_y \right] = \begin{bmatrix} 1 & SH_y & 0 \\ 0 & 1 & 0 \\ 0 & 0 & 1 \end{bmatrix}$$

where SH_y = shear factor along the y-axis

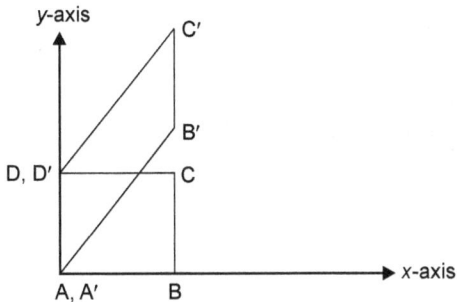

Fig. 3.32 Shear transformation in the y direction

Problem 6

Write the shear transformation of a rectangle *ABCD* with shear parameter *a* = *b* = 2. Also draw the final view of the rectangle *ABCD* in *x* and *y* directions. The vertices of the rectangle are *A* (1, 1), *B* (4, 1), *C* (4, 2), and *D* (1, 2).

Solution

1. Shear transformation in the x direction is

$$[p'] = [p] \cdot [SH_x]$$

$$[p'] = \begin{bmatrix} 1 & 1 & 1 \\ 4 & 1 & 1 \\ 4 & 2 & 1 \\ 1 & 2 & 1 \end{bmatrix} \begin{bmatrix} 1 & 0 & 0 \\ 2 & 1 & 0 \\ 0 & 0 & 1 \end{bmatrix}$$

$$[p'] = \begin{bmatrix} 3 & 1 & 1 \\ 6 & 1 & 1 \\ 6 & 2 & 1 \\ 5 & 2 & 1 \end{bmatrix}$$

2. Shear transformation in the y direction is

$$[p'] = [p] \cdot [SH_y]$$

$$[p'] = \begin{bmatrix} 1 & 1 & 1 \\ 4 & 1 & 1 \\ 4 & 2 & 1 \\ 1 & 2 & 1 \end{bmatrix} \begin{bmatrix} 1 & 2 & 0 \\ 0 & 1 & 0 \\ 0 & 0 & 1 \end{bmatrix}$$

$$[p'] = \begin{bmatrix} 1 & 3 & 1 \\ 4 & 9 & 1 \\ 4 & 10 & 1 \\ 1 & 4 & 1 \end{bmatrix}$$

Problem 7

Fig. 3.33 shows a circle of radius $r = 50$ mm; center A [10, 10] is to be converted into an ellipse with major axis $a = 90$ mm and minor axis $b = 60$ mm by keeping the center at same position. Find the total transformation matrix.

Solution

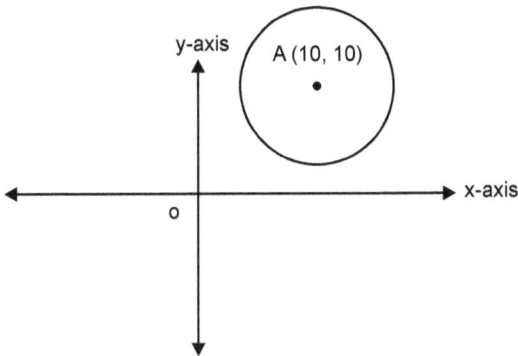

Fig. 3.33 Position of a given circle

Transformation involves the following steps.

1. Translate the circle about the center to the origin.

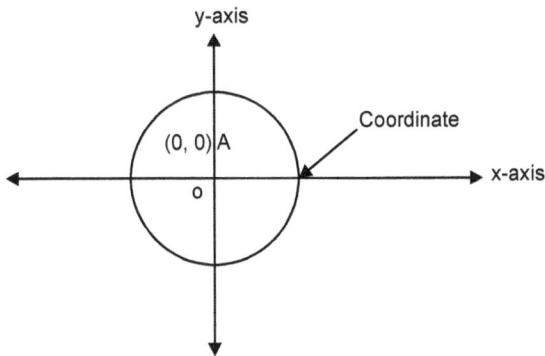

Fig. 3.34 Translating circle about the center to the origin

$$[T_1] = \begin{bmatrix} 1 & 0 & 0 \\ 0 & 1 & 0 \\ -10 & -10 & 1 \end{bmatrix}$$

2. Scaling transformation
The scaling factors are calculated as follows:

$$s_x = \frac{\text{new semi major axis}}{\text{radius}} = \frac{45}{50} = 0.9$$

$$s_y = \frac{\text{new semi major axis}}{\text{radius}} = \frac{30}{50} = 0.6$$

$$[s] = \begin{bmatrix} 0.9 & 0 & 0 \\ 0 & 0.6 & 0 \\ 0 & 0 & 1 \end{bmatrix}$$

3. Translate the center back to the original position.

$$T_2 = \begin{bmatrix} 1 & 0 & 0 \\ 0 & 1 & 0 \\ 10 & 10 & 1 \end{bmatrix}$$

$$[T_T] = [T_1].[S].[T_2]$$

$$[T_T] = \begin{bmatrix} 1 & 0 & 0 \\ 0 & 1 & 0 \\ -10 & -10 & 1 \end{bmatrix}.\begin{bmatrix} 0.9 & 0 & 0 \\ 0 & 0.6 & 0 \\ 0 & 0 & 1 \end{bmatrix}.\begin{bmatrix} 1 & 0 & 0 \\ 0 & 1 & 0 \\ 10 & 10 & 1 \end{bmatrix}$$

$$[T_T] = \begin{bmatrix} 1 & 0 & 0 \\ 0 & 1 & 0 \\ -10 & -10 & 1 \end{bmatrix}.\begin{bmatrix} 0.9 & 0 & 0 \\ 0 & 0.6 & 0 \\ 10 & 10 & 1 \end{bmatrix}$$

$$[T_T] = \begin{bmatrix} 0.9 & 0 & 0 \\ 0 & 0.6 & 0 \\ 1 & 4 & 1 \end{bmatrix}$$

Problem 8

A triangle having vertices (2, 3), (6, 3), and (4, 8) is reflected about the line having equation $y = 3x + 4$. Find the final position of the triangle using 2D transformation.

Solution

$$[p] = \begin{bmatrix} 2 & 3 & 1 \\ 6 & 3 & 1 \\ 4 & 8 & 1 \end{bmatrix}$$

Rotate the line about $y = 3x + 4$.

Put $x = 0$ in equation of a line ($y = 3x + 4$). Then we get $y = 4$; coordinate (0, 4).

And if $y = 0$, we get $x = -\dfrac{4}{3}$; coordinate $(0, -\dfrac{4}{3})$.

Comparing the equation of a line ($y = 3x + 4$) with $y = mx + c$,

m = slope = 3 and $c = y$ = intercept = 4

We know that, slope = $\tan \theta$, where θ is inclination of a line.

Therefore

$$m = \tan \theta = 4$$

$$\theta = \tan^{-1} 4$$

$$\theta = 71.56°$$

The transformation can be obtained by the following steps:

Step 1: Translate the line to the origin by $t_x = 0$, $t_y = -4$.

$$[T_1] = \begin{bmatrix} 1 & 0 & 0 \\ 0 & 1 & 0 \\ 0 & -4 & 1 \end{bmatrix}$$

Step 2: Rotate the line by 71.56° in the CW direction so as to coincide with the x-axis.

$$[R_1] = \begin{bmatrix} \cos(-71.56) & \sin(-71.56) & 0 \\ -\sin(-71.56) & \cos(-71.56) & 0 \\ 0 & 0 & 1 \end{bmatrix}$$

$$[R_1] = \begin{bmatrix} 0.316 & -0.949 & 0 \\ 0.949 & 0.316 & 0 \\ 0 & 0 & 1 \end{bmatrix}$$

Step 3: Reflection transformation about the x-axis:

$$[M_x] = \begin{bmatrix} 1 & 0 & 0 \\ 0 & -1 & 0 \\ 0 & 0 & 1 \end{bmatrix}$$

Step 4: Back rotation by 71.56° in the CCW direction.

$$[R_2] = \begin{bmatrix} \cos(71.56) & \sin(71.56) & 0 \\ -\sin(71.56) & \cos(71.56) & 0 \\ 0 & 0 & 1 \end{bmatrix}$$

$$[R_2] = \begin{bmatrix} 0.316 & 0.949 & 0 \\ 0.949 & 0.316 & 0 \\ 0 & 0 & 1 \end{bmatrix}$$

Step 5: Back-translate the line to the original position by $t_x = 0$, $t_y = 4$.

$$[T_2] = \begin{bmatrix} 1 & 0 & 0 \\ 0 & 1 & 0 \\ 0 & 4 & 1 \end{bmatrix}$$

Total transfromation $[T_T] = [T_1][R_1][M_x][R_2][T_2]$

$$[T_T] = \begin{bmatrix} 1 & 0 & 0 \\ 0 & 1 & 0 \\ 0 & -4 & 1 \end{bmatrix} \cdot \begin{bmatrix} 0.316 & -0.949 & 0 \\ 0.949 & 0.316 & 0 \\ 0 & 0 & 1 \end{bmatrix} \cdot$$

$$\begin{bmatrix} 1 & 0 & 0 \\ 0 & -1 & 0 \\ 0 & 0 & 1 \end{bmatrix} \cdot \begin{bmatrix} 0.316 & 0.949 & 0 \\ 0.949 & 0.316 & 0 \\ 0 & 0 & 1 \end{bmatrix} \cdot \begin{bmatrix} 1 & 0 & 0 \\ 0 & 1 & 0 \\ 0 & 4 & 1 \end{bmatrix}$$

$$[T_T] = \begin{bmatrix} 1 & 0 & 0 \\ 0 & 1 & 0 \\ 0 & -4 & 1 \end{bmatrix} \cdot \begin{bmatrix} 0.316 & -0.949 & 0 \\ 0.949 & 0.316 & 0 \\ 0 & 0 & 1 \end{bmatrix} \cdot \begin{bmatrix} 1 & 0 & 0 \\ 0 & -1 & 0 \\ 0 & 0 & 1 \end{bmatrix} \cdot \begin{bmatrix} 0.316 & 0.949 & 0 \\ 0.949 & 0.316 & 0 \\ 0 & 4 & 1 \end{bmatrix}$$

$$[T_T] = \begin{bmatrix} 1 & 0 & 0 \\ 0 & 1 & 0 \\ 0 & -4 & 1 \end{bmatrix} \cdot \begin{bmatrix} 0.316 & -0.949 & 0 \\ 0.949 & 0.316 & 0 \\ 0 & 0 & 1 \end{bmatrix} \cdot \begin{bmatrix} 0.316 & 0.949 & 0 \\ -0.949 & -0.316 & 0 \\ 0 & 4 & 1 \end{bmatrix}$$

$$[T_T] = \begin{bmatrix} 1 & 0 & 0 \\ 0 & 1 & 0 \\ 0 & -4 & 1 \end{bmatrix} \cdot \begin{bmatrix} 1 & 0.6 & 0 \\ 0 & 0.8 & 0 \\ 0 & 4 & 1 \end{bmatrix}$$

$$[T_T] = \begin{bmatrix} 1 & 0.6 & 0 \\ 0 & 0.8 & 0 \\ 0 & 0.8 & 1 \end{bmatrix}$$

$$[p'] = [p] \cdot [T_T]$$

$$[p'] = \begin{bmatrix} 2 & 3 & 1 \\ 6 & 3 & 1 \\ 4 & 8 & 1 \end{bmatrix} \cdot \begin{bmatrix} 1 & 0.6 & 0 \\ 0 & 0.8 & 0 \\ 0 & 0.8 & 1 \end{bmatrix}$$

$$[p'] = \begin{bmatrix} 2 & 4.4 & 1 \\ 6 & 5.6 & 1 \\ 4 & 9.6 & 1 \end{bmatrix}$$

Problem 9

A triangle *ABC* is to be reflected about its side *BC*. Explain the steps required and determine the resultant transformation matrix. *A* (2, 3), *B* (10, 8), and *C* (−1, 10).

Solution

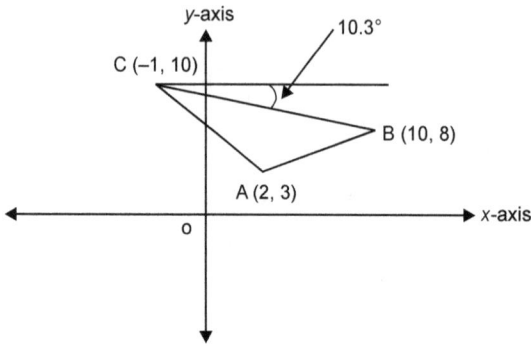

Fig. 3.35 Position of a given triangle

The triangle is to be reflected about side *BC*. Therefore calculate the slope of the line and its angle of inclination with the horizontal.

$$\text{slope of } BC = m = \frac{(y_B - y_C)}{(x_B - x_C)} = \frac{(8-10)}{(10+1)} = \frac{-2}{11}$$

$$\tan\theta = m = \frac{(-2)}{(11)}$$

$$\theta = \tan^{-1} = \frac{(-2)}{(11)} = -10.3°$$

The transformation is carried out by the following steps:

Step 1: Translate the triangle to the origin about point *C*.

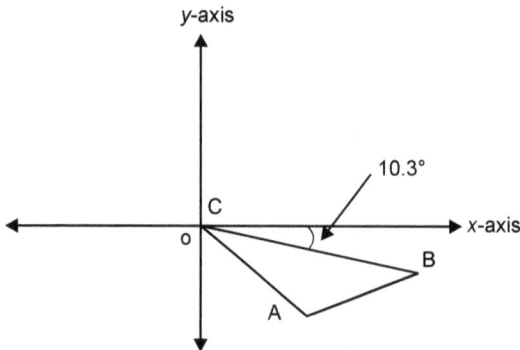

Fig. 3.36 Position of the triangle after translation

$$[T_1] = \begin{bmatrix} 1 & 0 & 0 \\ 0 & 1 & 0 \\ 1 & -10 & 1 \end{bmatrix}$$

Step 2: Rotate the triangle by 10.3° in the CCW direction so as to coincide BC with the x-axis.

$$[R_1] = \begin{bmatrix} \cos(10.3) & \sin(10.3) & 0 \\ -\sin(10.3) & \cos(10.3) & 0 \\ 0 & 0 & 1 \end{bmatrix}$$

$$[R_1] = 1 \begin{bmatrix} 0.98 & 0.18 & 0 \\ -0.98 & 0.98 & 0 \\ 0 & 0 & 1 \end{bmatrix}$$

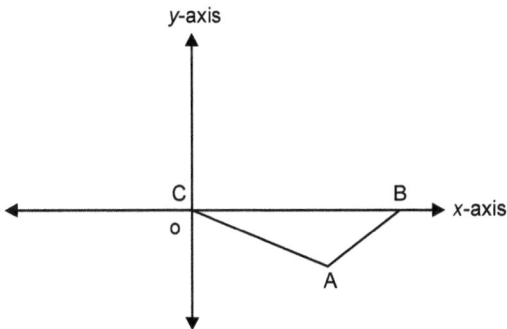

Fig. 3.37 Position of the triangle after rotation

Step 3: Reflection transformation about the x-axis:

$$[M_x] = \begin{bmatrix} 1 & 0 & 0 \\ 0 & -1 & 0 \\ 0 & 0 & 1 \end{bmatrix}$$

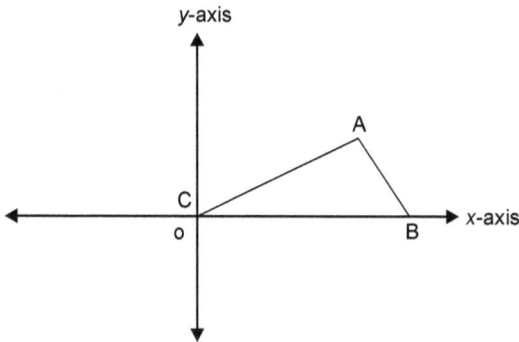

Fig. 3.38 Position of the triangle after reflection about the *x*-axis

Step 4: Back rotation by 10.3° in the CW direction:

$$[R_2] = \begin{bmatrix} \cos(-10.3) & \sin(-10.3) & 0 \\ -\sin(-10.3) & \cos(-10.3) & 0 \\ 0 & 0 & 1 \end{bmatrix}$$

$$[R_2] = \begin{bmatrix} 0.98 & -0.18 & 0 \\ 0.18 & 0.98 & 0 \\ 0 & 0 & 1 \end{bmatrix}$$

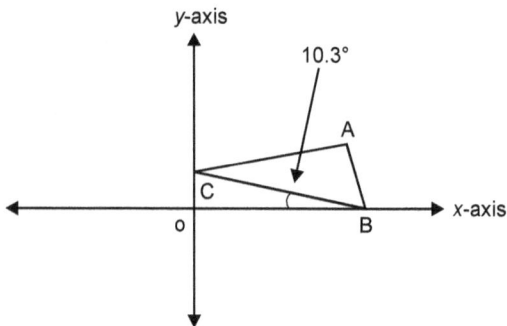

Fig. 3.39 Position of the triangle after back rotation

Step 5: Back-translate the triangle to the original position about *C*.

$$[T_2] = \begin{bmatrix} 1 & 0 & 0 \\ 0 & 1 & 0 \\ -1 & 10 & 1 \end{bmatrix}$$

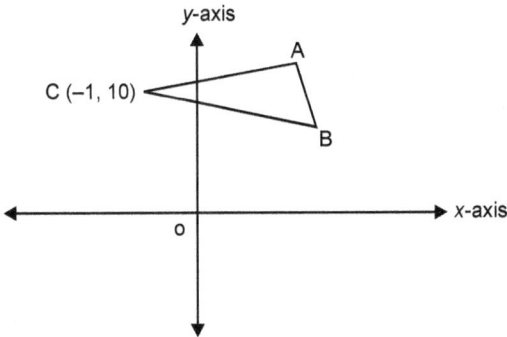

Fig. 3.40 Position of the triangle after back translation

Total transformation $[T_T] = [T_1][R_1][M_x][R_2][T_2]$

$$[T_T] = \begin{bmatrix} 1 & 0 & 0 \\ 0 & 1 & 0 \\ 1 & -10 & 1 \end{bmatrix} \cdot \begin{bmatrix} 0.98 & 0.18 & 0 \\ -0.18 & 0.98 & 0 \\ 0 & 0 & 1 \end{bmatrix} \begin{bmatrix} 1 & 0 & 0 \\ 0 & -1 & 0 \\ 1 & 0 & 1 \end{bmatrix} \cdot$$

$$\begin{bmatrix} 0.98 & -0.18 & 0 \\ 0.18 & 0.98 & 0 \\ 0 & 0 & 1 \end{bmatrix} \cdot \begin{bmatrix} 1 & 0 & 0 \\ 0 & 1 & 0 \\ -1 & 10 & 1 \end{bmatrix}$$

$$[T_T] = \begin{bmatrix} 1 & 0 & 0 \\ 0 & 1 & 0 \\ 1 & -10 & 1 \end{bmatrix} \cdot \begin{bmatrix} 0.98 & 0.18 & 0 \\ -0.18 & 0.98 & 0 \\ 0 & 0 & 1 \end{bmatrix} \cdot \begin{bmatrix} 1 & 0 & 0 \\ 0 & -1 & 0 \\ 0 & 0 & 1 \end{bmatrix} \cdot \begin{bmatrix} 0.98 & -0.18 & 0 \\ 0.18 & 0.98 & 0 \\ -1 & 10 & 1 \end{bmatrix}$$

$$[T_T] = \begin{bmatrix} 1 & 0 & 0 \\ 0 & 1 & 0 \\ 1 & -10 & 1 \end{bmatrix} \cdot \begin{bmatrix} 0.98 & 0.18 & 0 \\ -0.18 & 0.98 & 0 \\ 0 & 0 & 1 \end{bmatrix} \cdot \begin{bmatrix} 0.98 & -0.18 & 0 \\ -0.18 & -0.98 & 0 \\ -1 & 10 & 1 \end{bmatrix}$$

$$[T_T] = \begin{bmatrix} 1 & 0 & 0 \\ 0 & 1 & 0 \\ 1 & -10 & 1 \end{bmatrix} \cdot \begin{bmatrix} 0.93 & -0.37 & 0 \\ 0 & 1 & 0 \\ -1 & 10 & 1 \end{bmatrix}$$

$$[T_T] = \begin{bmatrix} 0.93 & -0.37 & 0 \\ -0.37 & -0.93 & 0 \\ 3.43 & 19 & 1 \end{bmatrix}$$

$$\left[p' \right] = \left[p \right] \cdot \left[T_T \right]$$

$$\left[p' \right] = \begin{bmatrix} 2 & 3 & 1 \\ 10 & 8 & 1 \\ -1 & 10 & 1 \end{bmatrix} \cdot \begin{bmatrix} 0.93 & -0.37 & 0 \\ -0.37 & -0.93 & 0 \\ 3.43 & 19 & 1 \end{bmatrix}$$

$$\left[p' \right] = \begin{bmatrix} 4.26 & 15 & 1 \\ 10 & 8 & 1 \\ -1 & 10 & 1 \end{bmatrix}$$

Problem 10

Segment PQ is marked by (2,2) and (3,7). Point R divides this segment in the ratio of 1:3. If $\begin{bmatrix} A & B \\ C & D \end{bmatrix}$ is any general transformation matrix, then prove that R' will also divide $P'Q'$ in the same ratio.

Solution

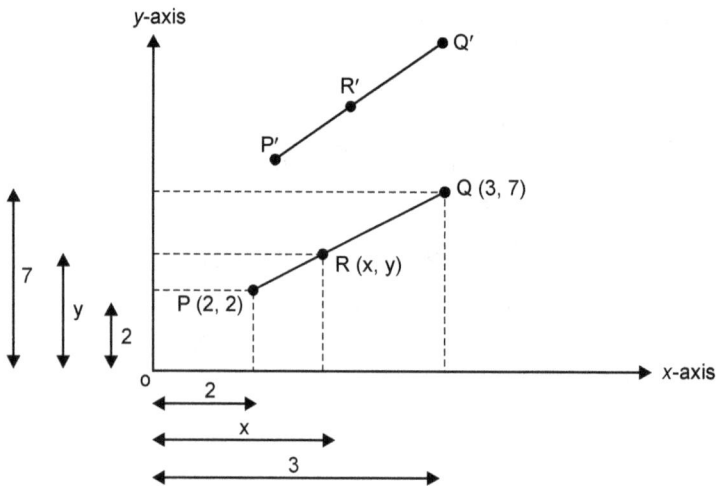

Fig. 3.41 Position of the original and final lines

From the figure

$$x = 2 + \frac{(3-2)}{3} = 2 + \frac{1}{3} = \frac{7}{3}$$

$$y = 2 + \frac{(7-2)}{3} = 2 + \frac{5}{3} = \frac{11}{3}$$

Therefore, $R\left(\dfrac{7}{3}, \dfrac{11}{3}\right)$

$$[P'] = \begin{bmatrix} 2 & 2 \\ \dfrac{7}{3} & \dfrac{11}{3} \\ 3 & 7 \end{bmatrix}$$

$$[T_T] = \begin{bmatrix} A & B \\ C & D \end{bmatrix}$$

$$[P'] = [P] \cdot [T_T]$$

$$[P'] = \begin{bmatrix} 2 & 2 \\ \dfrac{7}{3} & \dfrac{11}{3} \\ 3 & 7 \end{bmatrix} \cdot \begin{bmatrix} A & B \\ C & D \end{bmatrix}$$

$$[P'] = \begin{bmatrix} (2A+2C) & (2B+2D) \\ \left(\dfrac{7}{3}A + \dfrac{11}{3}C\right) & \left(\dfrac{7}{3}B + \dfrac{11}{3}D\right) \\ (2A+7C) & (3B+7D) \end{bmatrix}$$

$$\left(\dfrac{7}{3}A + \dfrac{11}{3}C\right) = (2A+2C) + \dfrac{\left([2A+7C]-[2A+2C]\right)}{a}$$

$$\left(\dfrac{7}{3}A + \dfrac{11}{3}C\right) = (2A+2C) + \dfrac{\left([A+5C]\right)}{a}$$

$$7A + 11C = 6A + 6C + \dfrac{3}{a}(A+5C)$$

$$(A+5C) = \dfrac{3}{a}(A+5C)$$

$$1 = \dfrac{3}{a}$$

$$a = 3$$

Similarly,

$$\left(\dfrac{7}{3}B + \dfrac{11}{3}D\right) = (2B+2D) + \dfrac{\left([3B+7D]-[2B+2D]\right)}{a}$$

$$\left(\dfrac{7}{3}B + \dfrac{11}{3}D\right) = (2B+2D) + \dfrac{\left([B+5D]\right)}{a}$$

$$7B + 11D = 6B + 6D + \frac{3}{a}(A + 5C)$$

$$(B + 5D) = \frac{3}{a}(B + 5D)$$

$$1 = \frac{3}{a}$$

$$a = 3$$

Hence it is proved that R' will also divide $P'Q'$ in 1:3 ratio.

Problem 11

$x + 2y = 9$ and $x + 2y = 3$ are two parallel lines. After transforming by $\begin{bmatrix} A & B \\ C & D \end{bmatrix}$, prove that the lines continue to be parallel.

Solution

The two given lines are $x + 2y = 9$ and $x + 2y = 3$. Convert it into a standard equation of line, that is, $y = mx + c$.

Then

$$y = -0.5x + 4.5 \qquad\qquad …(3.22)$$
$$y = -0.5x + 1.5 \qquad\qquad …(3.23)$$

These two lines are parallel to each other because the slope of these lines are same, that is, -0.5.

If we put $x = 0$ in Eq. (3.22), then $y = 4.5$

Then $y = 4.5$

And if $y = 0$, then $x = 9$.

The line is said to be passing through (0,4.5) and (9,0).

Similarly if we put $x = 0$ in Eq. (3.23), then $y = 1.5$

And $y = 0$ then $x = 3$

The line is said to be passing through (0,1.5) and (3,0).

To transform the first line:

$$\left[P_1' \right] = \begin{bmatrix} 0 & 4.5 \\ 9 & 0 \end{bmatrix} \cdot \begin{bmatrix} A & B \\ C & D \end{bmatrix}$$

$$\left[P' \right] = \begin{bmatrix} 4.5C & 4.5D \\ 9A & 9B \end{bmatrix}$$

Slope of this line is given by

$$m_1 = \frac{y_2 - y_1}{x_2 - x_1} = \frac{\left[9B - 4.5D\right]}{\left[9A - 4.5C\right]}$$

To transform the second line:

$$\left[P_2{'}\right] = \begin{bmatrix} 0 & 1.5 \\ 3 & 0 \end{bmatrix} \cdot \begin{bmatrix} A & B \\ C & D \end{bmatrix}$$

$$\left[P'\right] = \begin{bmatrix} 1.5C & 1.5D \\ 3A & 3B \end{bmatrix}$$

Slope of this line is given by

$$m_2 = \frac{y_2 - y_1}{x_2 - x_1} = \frac{\left[3B - 1.5B\right]}{\left[3A - 1.5C\right]}$$

Multiplying and dividing by 3

$$m_2 = \frac{\left[9B - 4.5D\right]}{\left[9A - 4.5C\right]}$$

As the slope of both transformed lines is same, these lines are parallel to each other.

3.6 INVERSE TRANSFORMATION

The effect of some transformations can be undone by carrying out transformation in the reverse direction. Carrying out reverse or back transformation itself is called inverse transformation. If we know the coordinates of the original point and the sequence of transformation we can find the coordinates of the final point using the following equation:

$$\left[p'\right]_{1 \times 3} = \left[p\right]_{1 \times 3} \cdot \left[T_T\right]_{3 \times 3}$$

$$\left[x'y'h\right]_{1 \times 3} = \left[x\,y1\right]_{1 \times 3} \cdot \left[T_T\right]_{3 \times 3}$$

where

p' = coordinates of the final point

p = coordinates of the original point

$[T_T]$ = total transformation matrix

But if we know the coordinates of the final point and we have to find the coordinates of the original point, then

$$\left[p'\right]_{1\times3} = \left[p\right]_{1\times3} \cdot \left[T_T\right]_{3\times3} \text{ (post multiplier) } ...(3.24)$$

In Eq. (3.24) $[T_T]_{3\times3}$ is post multiplier. Hence after shifting to the left of "=" sign it remains post multiplier.

Since

$$\left[A\right]\cdot\left[B\right] \neq \left[B\right]\cdot\left[A\right]$$

$$\left[p\right]_{1\times3} = \left[p'\right]_{1\times3} \cdot \left[T^{-1}{}_T\right]_{3\times3} \qquad \text{(post multiplier)}$$

Similarly, if we know the coordinates of the original point and the final point, we can find the transformation matrix as follows:

$$\left[p'\right]_{1\times3} = \left[p\right]_{1\times3} \cdot \left[T_T\right]_{3\times3} \qquad \text{(pre multiplier)}$$

$$\left[T_T\right]_{3\times3} = \left[p^{-1}\right]_{3\times1} \cdot \left[p'\right]_{1\times3} \qquad \text{(pre multiplier)}$$

To find the inverse of the matrix:

Let the matrix be
$$p = \begin{bmatrix} a & b & c \\ d & e & f \\ g & h & i \end{bmatrix}$$

Then inverse of [p] is

$$p^{-1} = \frac{a\,\text{Adjoint of } p}{|p|}$$

determinant of $p = |p| = a(ei - hf) - b(di - gf) + c(dh - ge)$

$a\,\text{Adjoint of } p = \left[\text{cofactor of } p\right]^T$

$$\left[\text{cofactor of } p\right] = \begin{bmatrix} (ei-hf) & -(di-gf) & (dh-ge) \\ -(bi-hc) & (ai-gc) & -(ah-gb) \\ (bf-ec) & -(af-dc) & (ae-db) \end{bmatrix}$$

$$\left[\text{cofactor of } p\right]^T = \begin{bmatrix} (ei-hf) & -(bi-hc) & (bf-ec) \\ -(di-gf) & (ai-gc) & -(af-dc) \\ (dh-ge) & -(ah-gb) & (ae-db) \end{bmatrix}$$

$$\left[p^{-1}\right] = \frac{1}{|p|} \begin{bmatrix} (ei-hf) & -(bi-hc) & (bf-ec) \\ -(di-gf) & (ai-gc) & -(af-dc) \\ (dh-ge) & -(ah-gb) & (ae-db) \end{bmatrix}$$

Problem 12

Find the transformation that converts a figure defined by the vertices $A(3, 2)$, $B(2, 1)$, $C(4, 1)$ into another figure defined by the vertices $A'(-3, -1)$, $B'(-4, -2)$, $C'(-2, -2)$.

Solution

Final transformation equation is

$$[p']_{3 \times 3} = [p]_{3 \times 3} \cdot [T_T]_{3 \times 3} \text{ (pre multiplier)}$$

$$[T_T]_{3 \times 3} = [p^{-1}]_{3 \times 3} \cdot [p']_{3 \times 3} \text{ (pre multiplier)} \qquad \dots(3.25)$$

To find the inverse of the matrix:

$$[p] = \begin{bmatrix} 3 & 2 & 1 \\ 2 & 1 & 1 \\ 4 & 1 & 1 \end{bmatrix}$$

Then inverse of $[p]$ is

$$[p^{-1}] = \frac{a \, \text{Adjoint of } p}{|p|}$$

$$\text{determinant of } p = |p| = 3(1 \times 1 - 1 \times 1) - 2(2 \times 1 - 4 \times 1) + 1(2 \times 1 - 4 \times 1)$$

$$|p| = 0 + 4 - 2 = 2$$

$$\text{Adjoint of } p = [\text{cofactor of } p]^T$$

$$[\text{cofactor of } p] = \begin{bmatrix} 0 & 2 & -2 \\ -1 & -1 & 5 \\ 1 & -1 & -1 \end{bmatrix}$$

$$[\text{cofactor of } p]^T = a \, \text{Adjoint of } p = \begin{bmatrix} 0 & -1 & 1 \\ 2 & -1 & -1 \\ -2 & 5 & -1 \end{bmatrix}$$

$$[p^{-1}] = \frac{1}{2} \begin{bmatrix} 0 & -1 & 1 \\ 2 & -1 & -1 \\ -2 & 5 & -1 \end{bmatrix}$$

The matrix of the transformed figure is

$$[p'] = \begin{bmatrix} -3 & -1 & 1 \\ -4 & -2 & 1 \\ -2 & -2 & 1 \end{bmatrix}$$

Putting the values in Eq. (3.25)

$$[T_T] = \frac{1}{2} \begin{bmatrix} 0 & -1 & 1 \\ 2 & -1 & -1 \\ -2 & 5 & -1 \end{bmatrix} \cdot \begin{bmatrix} -3 & -1 & 1 \\ -4 & -2 & 1 \\ -2 & -2 & 1 \end{bmatrix}$$

$$[T_T] = \frac{1}{2} \begin{bmatrix} 2 & 0 & 0 \\ 0 & 2 & 0 \\ -12 & -6 & 2 \end{bmatrix}$$

$$[T_T] = \begin{bmatrix} 1 & 0 & 0 \\ 0 & 1 & 0 \\ -6 & -3 & 1 \end{bmatrix}$$

Looking at the total transformation matrix, we can say that only one transformation is involved and that is a translation transformation with values of $t_x = -6$ and $t_y = -3$. You can cross-check your answer by doing $[p'] = [p] \cdot [T_T]$.

Problem 13

The coordinates of a final figure are

$$P' = (10, 10); \, Q' = (20, 20).$$

The total transformation matrix is carried out by

1. scaling the figure two times horizontally and two times vertically with respect to the origin

2. rotating the figure about the origin through 45° CCW.

Determine the coordinates of the original figure P and Q.

Solution

Final transformation equation is

$$[p']_{2\times3} = [p]_{2\times3} \cdot [T_T]_{3\times3} \text{ (pre multiplier)}$$

$$[p]_{2\times3} = [p']_{2\times3} \cdot [T_T^{-1}]_{3\times3} \text{ (post multiplier)} \qquad ...(3.26)$$

Coordinates of the transformed figure are

$$[p'] = \begin{bmatrix} 10 & 10 & 1 \\ 20 & 20 & 1 \end{bmatrix}$$

Total transformation is given by

$$[T_T] = [S] \cdot [R]$$

Scaling transformation with $s_x = 2$ and $s_y = 2$,

$$[S] = \begin{bmatrix} 2 & 0 & 0 \\ 0 & 2 & 0 \\ 0 & 0 & 1 \end{bmatrix}$$

Rotation transformation by 45° in the CCW direction:

$$[R] = \begin{bmatrix} \cos 45 & \sin 45 & 0 \\ -\sin 45 & \cos 45 & 0 \\ 0 & 0 & 1 \end{bmatrix}$$

$$[R] = \begin{bmatrix} 0.707 & .707 & 0 \\ -0.707 & 0.707 & 0 \\ 0 & 0 & 1 \end{bmatrix}$$

$$[T_T] = \begin{bmatrix} 2 & 0 & 0 \\ 0 & 2 & 0 \\ 0 & 0 & 1 \end{bmatrix} \cdot \begin{bmatrix} 0.707 & 0.707 & 0 \\ -0.707 & 0.707 & 0 \\ 0 & 0 & 1 \end{bmatrix}$$

$$[T_T] = \begin{bmatrix} 1.41 & 1.41 & 0 \\ -1.41 & 1.41 & 0 \\ 0 & 0 & 1 \end{bmatrix}$$

Then inverse of $[T_T]$ is

$$[T_T]^{-1} = \frac{a\,\text{Adjoint of } T_T}{|T_T|}$$

determinant of $[T_T] = |T_T| = 1.41(1.41 \times 1 - 0) - 1.41(-1.41 \times 1 - 0) + 0$

$$|T_T| = 2 + 2 + 0 = 4$$

$$a\,\text{Adjoint of } T_T = \left[\text{cofactor of } T_T\right]^T$$

$$\left[\text{cofactor of } T_T\right]^T = a\,\text{Adjoint of } T_T = \begin{bmatrix} 1.41 & -1.41 & 0 \\ 1.41 & 1.41 & 0 \\ 0 & 0 & 4 \end{bmatrix}$$

$$T_T^{-1} = \frac{1}{4} \begin{bmatrix} 1.41 & -1.41 & 0 \\ 1.41 & 1.41 & 0 \\ 0 & 0 & 4 \end{bmatrix}$$

Putting values in Eq. (3.26)

$$p = \begin{bmatrix} 10 & 10 & 1 \\ 20 & 20 & 1 \end{bmatrix} \cdot \frac{1}{4} \begin{bmatrix} 1.41 & -1.41 & 0 \\ 1.41 & 1.41 & 0 \\ 0 & 0 & 4 \end{bmatrix}$$

$$p = \begin{bmatrix} 7 & 0 & 1 \\ 14 & 0 & 1 \end{bmatrix}$$

The coordinates of the original are $P\,(7, 0)$ and $Q\,(14, 0)$.

EXERCISES

1. Determine a 3×3 homogeneous matrix to transform an equilateral triangle ABC with each side 10 units in length into an isosceles triangle $A'B'C'$ shown in the figure, with an altitude 2.5 times the altitude of the equilateral triangle; the coordinate of point A is $(10, 5)$. Depict the final transformation on a graph paper.

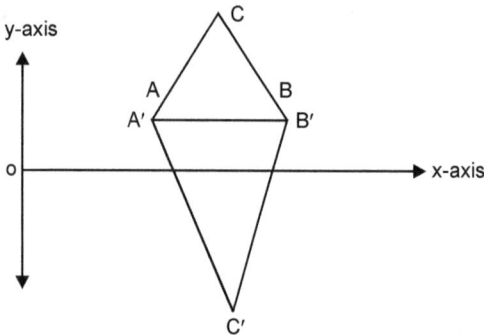

Fig. 3.42

2. Find the reflection of a triangle $A\,(1, 1)$, $B\,(5, 1)$ and $C\,(1, 5)$ about a line $y = 2x + 10$.

3. A rectangle marked by $(4, 4)$, $(4, 5)$, $(5, 4)$ and $(5, 5)$ is to be reflected about the mirror line $2x + 3y = 5$ through necessary transformation. Find concatenated transformation matrix and hence the reflected image.

4. A triangle has vertices as $A\,(1, 1)$, $B\,(1, 2)$, $C\,(2, 2)$. Find the reflection of ABC about a line $y = 3x + 2$. Plot prior and poster images of ABC along with line of reflection on a graph paper.

5. Determine the transformation matrix to transfer square $ABCD$ to rectangle $A'B'C'D'$, $A'B' = 2AB$ and $C'B' = CB$ as shown in figure.

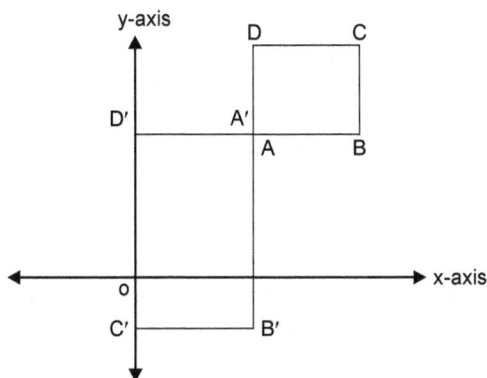

Fig. 3.43

6. Obtain an instant transformation matrix for deriving figure B from figure A. Figure A is described by the vertices A (2, 1), B (4, 1), C (3, 2) and figure B is described by vertices A' (− 4, −2), B' (−2, −2), C' (−3, −1) using inverse transformation.

7. Find the reflection of a diamond-shaped polygon whose vertices are A (−1, 0), B (0, 2), C (−1, 0) and D (0, 2) about line $y = x + 2$.

8. Prove that a 3×3 homogeneous transformation matrix for reflection about the line $y = x$ is equivalent to a reflection about x-axis and rotation by 90° CCW direction.

9. Prove that a rotation about an origin is equivalent to two successive reflections about two coordinate axes.

OBJECTIVE QUESTIONS

2.1 Reflection matrix resembles which basic transformation matrix?
   (*a*) translation   (*b*) scaling
   (*c*) rotation   (*d*) none of the above

2.2 Reflection of a point about the x-axis, followed by a CCW rotation of 90°, is equivalent to reflection about which line?
   (*a*) $x = -y$ (*b*) $y = -x$
   (*c*) $x = y$ (*d*) $x + y = 1$

2.3 A circle, if scaled only in one direction, becomes
   (*a*) parabola   (*b*) hyperbola
   (*c*) ellipse   (*d*) remains a circle

2.4 Which of these are basic transformations?
(a) scaling
(b) rotation
(c) translation
(d) all of the above

2.5 Which transformation in non-homogeneous form is captured by matrix addition?
(a) scaling
(b) rotation
(c) translation
(d) reflection

2.6 In a homogeneous coordinate system, all transformation is captured by matrix
(a) addition
(b) subtraction
(c) multiplication
(d) division

2.7 Transformation effect can be undone by
(a) reverse transformation
(b) forward transformation
(c) inverse transformation
(d) none of the above

2.8 Inverse of any matrix [P] can be found by which formula?

(a) $\dfrac{\text{Adjoint of } p}{P}$

(c) $\dfrac{\text{cofactor of } P}{P}$

(b) $\dfrac{[\text{cofactor of } P]^T}{P}$

(d) $\dfrac{[\text{cofactor of } P]^T}{|P|}$

2.9 The process of combining or multiplying transformation matrices is called
(a) rasterization
(b) transformation
(c) concatenation
(d) reflection

2.10 Shear transformation is classified as a
(a) basic transformation
(b) special transformation
(c) inverse transformation
(d) none of the above

ANSWERS

2.1 (a)	**2.2** (c)	**2.3** (c)	**2.4** (d)
2.5 (c)	**2.6** (c)	**2.7** (d)	**2.8** (d)
2.9 (c)	**2.10** (b)		

4 THREE-DIMENSIONAL TRANSFORMATION

4.1 INTRODUCTION

The real world is composed of three-dimensional images. 3D objects have not only height and width but also depth. Displaying a 3D object on a 2D screen seems to be an impossible task. If height and width are represented by x and y coordinates, then how can the third dimension, depth, be displayed? This problem is solved with techniques used by artists and photographers in producing realistic pictures on paper or film. The difference is that the computer uses a mathematical model instead of a paint brush or lens to create the picture. The complexity of the mathematical model increases with an increase in the realism of a computer-generated picture.

Most engineering problems deal with 3D objects. A variety of patterns, shapes, and techniques are used to represent 3D objects. Whatever method one would use, the 3D object is usually represented in a 3D coordinate system and then mapped onto the 2D system of display. Manipulation, viewing, and creation of object images require the use of 3D object and coordinate transformations. A 3D transformation method is an extension of 2D transformation methods, including the consideration of the z-axis coordinates. In the 3D transformation method, the coordinate of a point is represented by (x, y, z) and the homogeneous coordinate will be $[x\ y\ z\ w]$. The value of w for 3D transformation will be 1. The other coordinates in 3D transformations are:

Coordinates of an original point

$$[P] = [x\ y\ z\ 1]_{1 \times 4}$$

Coordinates of a transformed point

$$[p'] = [x'\ y'\ z'\ 1]$$

4.2 SCALING TRANSFORMATION

Scaling transformation matrix: A scaling transformation is obtained by placing values along the main diagonal of a general 4×4 transformation matrix.

$$[S] = \begin{bmatrix} s_x & 0 & 0 & 0 \\ 0 & s_y & 0 & 0 \\ 0 & 0 & s_z & 0 \\ 0 & 0 & 0 & 1 \end{bmatrix}$$

The above matrix represents scaling with respect to origin, where S_x, S_y, and S_z are scaling factors along the x, y, and z directions, respectively. If the scaling factors S_x, S_y, and S_z are different from each other, the image of an object is distorted. Otherwise, a change in size occurs.

4.3 TRANSLATION TRANSFORMATION

A translation transformation displaces (or translates) a point $p\ (x, y, z)$ along the direction given by the position vector.

Vector $\qquad\qquad \vec{V} = t_x \hat{i} + t_y \hat{j} + t_y \hat{k}$

where $\qquad\qquad\qquad t_x = $ displacement along the x-axis

$\qquad\qquad\qquad\qquad t_y = $ displacement along the y-axis

$\qquad\qquad\qquad\qquad t_z = $ displacement along the z-axis

Translation transformation matrix

$$[T] = \begin{bmatrix} 1 & 0 & 0 & 0 \\ 0 & 1 & 0 & 0 \\ 0 & 0 & 1 & 0 \\ t_x & t_y & t_z & 1 \end{bmatrix}$$

4.4 ROTATION TRANSFORMATION

Rotations in 3D are important in understanding the shape of an object or in verifying different angles of a design. 3D rotation is a more complex phenomenon compared to 2D rotation. 2D rotation is captured about a point and it always happens in the xy plane (or about the z-axis). But 3D rotation can be in an xy plane (or about z-axis), yz plane (or about the x-axis) or zx plane (or about the y-axis). Fig. 4.1 shows three basic rotations in 3D transformation. The coordinate system is right-handed and counterclockwise rotations are assumed to be positive when looking along the axis toward the origin.

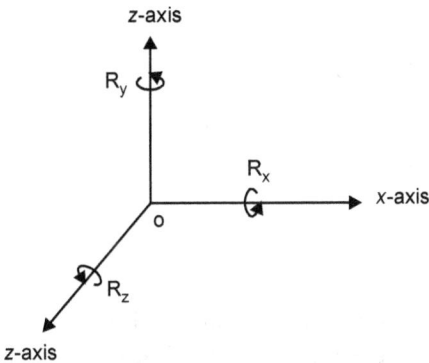

Fig. 4.1 3D rotation

1. Rotation transformation matrix about the x-axis (rotation in y-z plane):

$$[R_x] = \begin{matrix} x & y & z & 1 \\ \begin{bmatrix} 1 & 0 & 0 & 0 \\ 0 & \cos\theta & \sin\theta & 0 \\ 0 & -\sin\theta & \cos\theta & 0 \\ 0 & 0 & 0 & 1 \end{bmatrix} & \begin{matrix} x \\ y \\ z \\ 1 \end{matrix} \end{matrix}$$

2. Rotation transformation matrix about the y-axis (rotation in x-z plane):

$$[R_y] = \begin{matrix} x & y & z & 1 \\ \begin{bmatrix} \cos\theta & 0 & \sin\theta & 0 \\ 0 & 1 & 0 & 0 \\ -\sin\theta & 0 & \cos\theta & 0 \\ 0 & 0 & 0 & 1 \end{bmatrix} & \begin{matrix} x \\ y \\ z \\ 1 \end{matrix} \end{matrix}$$

3. Rotation transformation matrix about the z-axis (rotation in x-y plane):

$$[R_z] = \begin{array}{c} \\ \\ \\ \\ \\ \end{array} \begin{matrix} x & y & z & 1 \\ \begin{bmatrix} \cos\theta & \sin\theta & 0 & 0 \\ -\sin\theta & \cos\theta & 0 & 0 \\ 0 & 0 & 1 & 0 \\ 0 & 0 & 0 & 1 \end{bmatrix} & \begin{matrix} x \\ y \\ z \\ 1 \end{matrix} \end{matrix}$$

Problem 1

Consider a region defined by the position vector

$$[X] = \begin{matrix} x & y & z & 1 \\ \begin{bmatrix} 1 & 1 & 2 & 1 \\ 2 & 1 & 2 & 1 \\ 2 & 2 & 2 & 1 \\ 1 & 2 & 2 & 1 \end{bmatrix} & \begin{matrix} A \\ B \\ C \\ D \end{matrix} \end{matrix}$$

relative to the global *xyz* axis system. It is rotated by 30° about a line parallel to the *x*-axis and passing through point (1.5, 1.5, 1.5, 1). Find the final transformation matrix and final position of the region.

Solution

$$[p] = \begin{bmatrix} 1 & 1 & 2 & 1 \\ 2 & 1 & 2 & 1 \\ 2 & 2 & 2 & 1 \\ 1 & 2 & 2 & 1 \end{bmatrix}$$

Step 1: Translate the line to origin so that it coincides with the *x*-axis:

$$[T_1] = \begin{bmatrix} 1 & 0 & 0 & 0 \\ 0 & 1 & 0 & 0 \\ 0 & 0 & 1 & 0 \\ -1.5 & -1.5 & -1.5 & 1 \end{bmatrix}$$

Step 2: Rotation about the *x*-axis by 30°:

$$[R_x] = \begin{bmatrix} 1 & 0 & 0 & 0 \\ 0 & \cos 30 & \sin 30 & 0 \\ 0 & -\sin 30 & \cos 30 & 0 \\ 0 & 0 & 0 & 1 \end{bmatrix}$$

$$[R_x] = \begin{bmatrix} 1 & 0 & 0 & 0 \\ 0 & 0.866 & 0.5 & 0 \\ 0 & -0.5 & 0.866 & 0 \\ 0 & 0 & 0 & 1 \end{bmatrix}$$

Step 3: Back translation to the original position:

$$[T_2] = \begin{bmatrix} 1 & 0 & 0 & 0 \\ 0 & 1 & 0 & 0 \\ 0 & 0 & 1 & 0 \\ 1.5 & 1.5 & 1.5 & 1 \end{bmatrix}$$

$$[T_T] = T_1 \cdot R_x \cdot T_2$$

$$[T_T] = \begin{bmatrix} 1 & 0 & 0 & 0 \\ 0 & 1 & 0 & 0 \\ 0 & 0 & 1 & 0 \\ -1.5 & -1.5 & -1.5 & 1 \end{bmatrix} \cdot \begin{bmatrix} 1 & 0 & 0 & 0 \\ 0 & 0.866 & 0.5 & 0 \\ 0 & -0.5 & 0.866 & 0 \\ 0 & 0 & 0 & 1 \end{bmatrix} \cdot \begin{bmatrix} 1 & 0 & 0 & 0 \\ 0 & 1 & 0 & 0 \\ 0 & 0 & 1 & 0 \\ 1.5 & 1.5 & 1.5 & 1 \end{bmatrix}$$

$$[T_T] = \begin{bmatrix} 1 & 0 & 0 & 0 \\ 0 & 0.866 & 0.5 & 0 \\ 0 & -0.5 & 0.866 & 0 \\ 0 & 0.95 & -0.549 & 1 \end{bmatrix}$$

$$[p'] = p \cdot T_T$$

$$[p'] = \begin{bmatrix} 1 & 1 & 2 & 1 \\ 2 & 1 & 2 & 1 \\ 2 & 2 & 2 & 1 \\ 1 & 2 & 2 & 1 \end{bmatrix} \cdot \begin{bmatrix} 1 & 0 & 0 & 0 \\ 0 & 0.866 & 0.5 & 0 \\ 0 & -0.5 & 0.866 & 0 \\ 0 & 0.95 & -0.549 & 1 \end{bmatrix}$$

$$[p'] = \begin{bmatrix} 1 & 0.817 & 1.68 & 1 \\ 2 & 0.817 & 1.68 & 1 \\ 2 & 1.683 & 2.183 & 1 \\ 1 & 1.68 & 2.183 & 1 \end{bmatrix}$$

Problem 2

A homogeneous coordinate $[3, 2, 1, 1]$ is translated in the $x, y,$ and z directions by $-2, -2, -2$ respectively followed by successive $45°$ rotation about the y-axis and $60°$ rotation about the x-axis. Find the final position of the homogeneous coordinates.

Solution

$$[p_v] = [3 \ 2 \ 1 \ 1]$$

$$[T_T] = [T] \cdot [R_y] \cdot [R_x]$$

Step 1: Translation:

$$[T] = \begin{bmatrix} 1 & 0 & 0 & 0 \\ 0 & 1 & 0 & 0 \\ 0 & 0 & 1 & 0 \\ -2 & -2 & -2 & 1 \end{bmatrix}$$

Step 2: Rotation about the y-axis by $45°$:

$$[R_y] = \begin{bmatrix} \cos 45 & 0 & \sin 45 & 0 \\ 0 & 1 & 0 & 0 \\ -\sin 45 & 0 & \cos 45 & 0 \\ 0 & 0 & 0 & 1 \end{bmatrix}$$

$$[R_y] = \begin{bmatrix} 0.707 & 0 & 0.707 & 0 \\ 0 & 1 & 0 & 0 \\ -0.707 & 0 & 0.707 & 0 \\ 0 & 0 & 0 & 1 \end{bmatrix}$$

Step 3: Rotation about the x-axis by $60°$:

$$[R_x] = \begin{bmatrix} 1 & 0 & 0 & 0 \\ 0 & \cos 60 & \sin 60 & 0 \\ 0 & -\sin 60 & \cos 60 & 0 \\ 0 & 0 & 0 & 1 \end{bmatrix}$$

$$[R_x] = \begin{bmatrix} 1 & 0 & 0 & 0 \\ 0 & 0.5 & 0.866 & 0 \\ 0 & -0.866 & 0.5 & 0 \\ 0 & 0 & 0 & 1 \end{bmatrix}$$

$$[T_T] = \begin{bmatrix} 1 & 0 & 0 & 0 \\ 0 & 1 & 0 & 0 \\ 0 & 0 & 1 & 0 \\ -2 & -2 & -2 & 1 \end{bmatrix} \cdot \begin{bmatrix} 0.707 & 0 & 0.707 & 0 \\ 0 & 1 & 0 & 0 \\ -0.707 & 0 & 0.707 & 0 \\ 0 & 0 & 0 & 1 \end{bmatrix} \cdot \begin{bmatrix} 1 & 0 & 0 & 0 \\ 0 & 0.5 & 0.866 & 0 \\ 0 & -0.866 & 0.5 & 0 \\ 0 & 0 & 0 & 1 \end{bmatrix}$$

$$[T_T] = \begin{bmatrix} 1 & 0 & 0 & 0 \\ 0 & 1 & 0 & 0 \\ 0 & 0 & 1 & 0 \\ -2 & -2 & -2 & 1 \end{bmatrix} \cdot \begin{bmatrix} 0.707 & -0.61 & 0.35 & 0 \\ 0 & 0.5 & 0.866 & 0 \\ 0.707 & -0.61 & 0.35 & 0 \\ 0 & 0 & 0 & 1 \end{bmatrix}$$

$$[T_T] = \begin{bmatrix} 0.707 & 0 & 0.707 & 0 \\ 0 & 1 & 0 & 0 \\ -0.707 & 0 & 0.707 & 0 \\ 0 & 1.44 & -3.13 & 1 \end{bmatrix}$$

$$[p'] = [p] \cdot [T_T]$$

$$[p'] = [3 \ 2 \ 1 \ 1] \cdot \begin{bmatrix} 0.707 & 0 & 0.707 & 0 \\ 0 & 1 & 0 & 0 \\ 0.707 & 0 & 0.707 & 0 \\ 0 & 1.44 & -3.13 & 1 \end{bmatrix}$$

$$[p'] = [1.41 \ 3.44 \ -1.01 \ 1]$$

Problem 3

A cube of 10 units length has one of its corners at the origin $(0, 0, 0)$ and three edges along three principal axes. If the cube is to be rotated about the z-axis by an angle of 45° in CCW direction, calculate the new position of the cube.

Solution

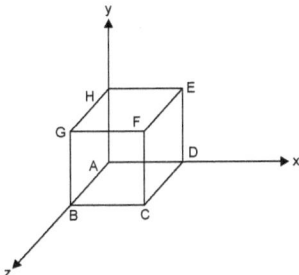

Fig. 4.2

Coordinates of the cube corners are:

A (0   0   0)
B (0   0   10)
C (10 0   10)
D (10 0   0)
E (10 10 0)
F (10 10 10)
G (0   10 10)
H (0   10 0)

$$
[P_v] = \begin{bmatrix}
0 & 0 & 0 & 1 \\
0 & 0 & 10 & 1 \\
10 & 0 & 10 & 1 \\
10 & 0 & 0 & 1 \\
10 & 10 & 0 & 1 \\
10 & 10 & 10 & 1 \\
0 & 10 & 10 & 1 \\
0 & 10 & 0 & 1
\end{bmatrix}
$$

Rotation about the z-axis by 45° in the CCW direction:

$$
[R_z] = \begin{bmatrix}
\cos 45 & \sin 45 & 0 & 0 \\
-\sin 45 & \cos 45 & 0 & 0 \\
0 & 0 & 1 & 0 \\
0 & 0 & 0 & 1
\end{bmatrix}
$$

$$
[R_z] = \begin{bmatrix}
0.707 & 0.707 & 0 & 0 \\
-0.707 & 0.707 & 0 & 0 \\
0 & 0 & 1 & 0 \\
0 & 0 & 0 & 1
\end{bmatrix}
$$

$$
[P'_v] = [P_v] \cdot [R_z]
$$

$$
\left[P'_V\right] =
\begin{bmatrix}
0 & 0 & 0 & 1 \\
0 & 0 & 10 & 1 \\
10 & 0 & 10 & 1 \\
10 & 0 & 0 & 1 \\
10 & 10 & 0 & 1 \\
10 & 10 & 10 & 1 \\
0 & 10 & 10 & 1 \\
0 & 10 & 0 & 1
\end{bmatrix}
\cdot
\begin{bmatrix}
0.707 & 0.707 & 0 & 0 \\
-0.707 & 0.707 & 0 & 0 \\
0 & 0 & 1 & 0 \\
0 & 0 & 0 & 1
\end{bmatrix}
$$

$$
\left[P'_V\right] =
\begin{bmatrix}
0 & 0 & 0 & 1 \\
0 & 0 & 10 & 1 \\
7.07 & 7.07 & 10 & 1 \\
7.07 & 7.07 & 0 & 1 \\
0 & 14.14 & 10 & 1 \\
0 & 14.14 & 10 & 1 \\
-7.07 & 7.07 & 10 & 1 \\
-7.07 & 7.07 & 0 & 1
\end{bmatrix}
$$

4.5 DERIVATION FOR ROTATION ABOUT ANY ARBITRARY LINE IN 3D SPACE

Rotation about an arbitrary axis/line can be captured by transforming the axis/line so as to make it coincide with any of the principal axes and applying one of the three basic 3D rotation matrices. Fig. 4.3 shows an arbitrary line in 3D space about which rotation is to be captured.

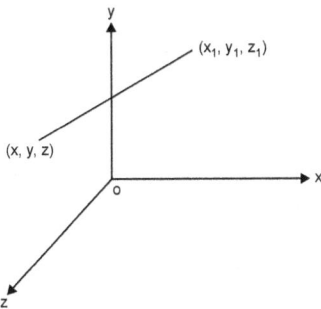

Fig. 4.3 An arbitrary line in 3D space

For deriving the transformation matrix for rotation by an angle θ about any arbitrary line in space, the following transformation must be carried out:

1. Translating the line to the origin:

$$T_1 = \begin{bmatrix} 1 & 0 & 0 & 0 \\ 0 & 1 & 0 & 0 \\ 0 & 0 & 1 & 0 \\ -x & -y & -z & 1 \end{bmatrix}$$

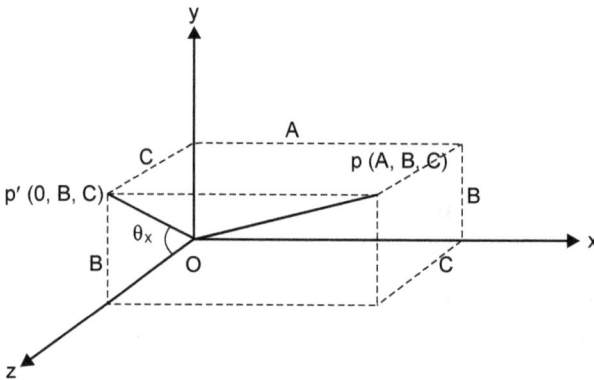

Fig. 4.4 Projection of a line on the y-z plane

2. Rotation of the line about the x-axis to bring the line in the xz plane. For this, the angle by which the line is to be rotated must be computed. To obtain the angle of rotation, project point $p(A,B,C)$ in the yz plane.

Let p' be the projection in the yz plane. The coordinates of p' are $(0,B,C)$.

The length of the segment is given by

$$op' = \sqrt{B^2 + C^2}$$

The angle of rotation about the x-axis so that the line comes in the xz plane will be

$$\cos\theta_x = \frac{C}{\sqrt{B^2 + C^2}}$$

$$\sin\theta_x = \frac{B}{\sqrt{B^2 + C^2}}$$

Putting $$\sqrt{B^2 + C^2} = V$$

$$\text{then } \cos\theta_x = \frac{C}{V}$$

$$\sin\theta_x = \frac{B}{V}$$

Now the rotation transformation matrix about the x-axis is given by

$$[R_x] = \begin{bmatrix} 1 & 0 & 0 & 0 \\ 0 & \cos\theta_x & \sin\theta_x & 0 \\ 0 & -\sin\theta_x & \cos\theta_x & 0 \\ 0 & 0 & 0 & 1 \end{bmatrix} = \begin{bmatrix} 1 & 0 & 0 & 0 \\ 0 & \dfrac{C}{V} & \dfrac{B}{V} & 0 \\ 0 & -\dfrac{B}{V} & \dfrac{C}{V} & 0 \\ 0 & 0 & 0 & 1 \end{bmatrix}$$

The coordinates of point p are $p(A,B,C)$. The line segment $op = \sqrt{A^2 + B^2 + C^2}$

Suppose $$op = \sqrt{A^2 + B^2 + C^2} = L$$

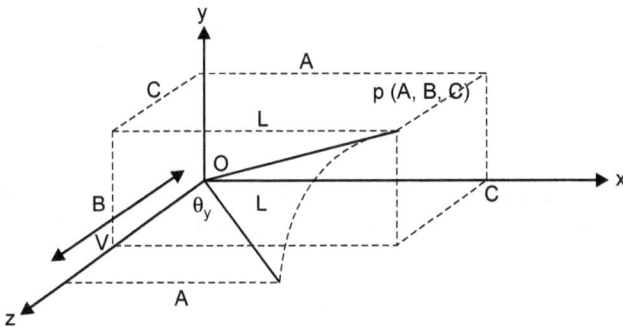

Fig. 4.5 Rotation of a line about the x-axis

After rotating about the x-axis by angle θ_x, the x coordinate will remain unchanged and equal to A. The y coordinate becomes zero and the z coordinate is $\sqrt{B^2 + C^2} = V$.

Now perform rotation of the line about the y-axis by an angle of θ_y to make it coincide with the z-axis.

$$\cos\theta_y = \frac{V}{L} \text{ and } \sin\theta_y = \frac{A}{L}$$

The rotation transformation matrix representing the rotation of a line about y-axis is given by

$$[R_y] = \begin{bmatrix} \cos\theta_y & 0 & \sin\theta_y & 0 \\ 0 & 1 & 0 & 0 \\ -\sin\theta_y & 0 & \cos\theta_y & 0 \\ 0 & 0 & 0 & 1 \end{bmatrix} = \begin{bmatrix} \dfrac{V}{L} & 0 & \dfrac{A}{L} & 0 \\ 0 & 1 & 0 & 0 \\ -\dfrac{A}{L} & 0 & \dfrac{V}{L} & 0 \\ 0 & 0 & 0 & 1 \end{bmatrix}$$

Now after performing rotation about the y-axis, the line will coincide with the z-axis. Now perform rotation about the z-axis by given angle θ.

$$[R_z] = \begin{bmatrix} \cos\theta & \sin\theta & 0 & 0 \\ -\sin\theta & \cos\theta & 0 & 0 \\ 0 & 0 & 1 & 0 \\ 0 & 0 & 0 & 1 \end{bmatrix}$$

Now, the resultant 3D rotation transformation matrix is given by

$$T_T = [T] \cdot [R_x] \cdot [R_y] \cdot [R_z] \cdot [R_y^{-1}] \cdot [R_x^{-1}] \cdot [T^{-1}]$$

Problem 4

Derive the transformation matrix for rotation at 55° CCW about an arbitrary axis in 3D space. The arbitrary axis passes through point A (2, 1, 1, 1) and B (3, 2, 2, 1).

Solution

Consider an arbitrary axis passing through points A (2, 1, 1, 1) and B (3, 2, 2, 1).

Step 1: Translate point A to the origin:

$$[T] = \begin{bmatrix} 1 & 0 & 0 & 0 \\ 0 & 1 & 0 & 0 \\ 0 & 0 & 1 & 0 \\ -2 & -1 & -1 & 1 \end{bmatrix}$$

After translation, the coordinates of point B are given by

$$[3\ 2\ 2\ 1] = \begin{bmatrix} 1 & 0 & 0 & 0 \\ 0 & 1 & 0 & 0 \\ 0 & 0 & 1 & 0 \\ -2 & -1 & -1 & 1 \end{bmatrix} = [1\ 1\ 1\ 1]$$

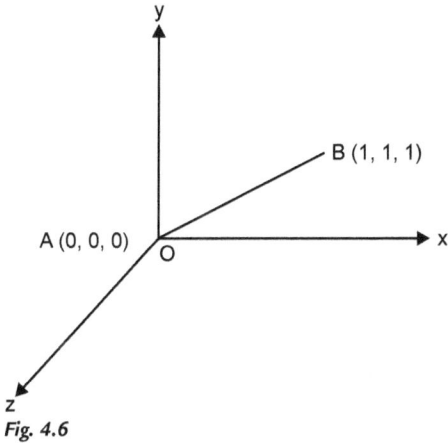

Fig. 4.6

Step 2: Rotate the line about the x-axis to bring it in the yz plane. The coordinates of B' are (A, B, C), that is, $(1, 1, 1)$.

$$\cos\theta_x = \frac{C}{\sqrt{B^2 + C^2}} = \frac{1}{\sqrt{1^2 + 1^2}} = \frac{1}{\sqrt{2}}$$

$$\theta_x = \cos^{-1}\left(\frac{1}{\sqrt{2}}\right) = 45°$$

$$\sin\theta_x = \frac{B}{\sqrt{B^2 + C^2}} = \frac{1}{\sqrt{1^2 + 1^2}} = \frac{1}{\sqrt{2}}$$

Now, the rotation transformation matrix about the x-axis (in the CCW direction) is given by

$$[R_x] = \begin{bmatrix} 1 & 0 & 0 & 0 \\ 0 & \cos\theta_x & \sin\theta_x & 0 \\ 0 & -\sin\theta_x & \cos\theta_x & 0 \\ 0 & 0 & 0 & 1 \end{bmatrix} \begin{bmatrix} 1 & 0 & 0 & 0 \\ 0 & \dfrac{1}{\sqrt{2}} & \dfrac{1}{\sqrt{2}} & 0 \\ 0 & -\dfrac{1}{\sqrt{2}} & \dfrac{1}{\sqrt{2}} & 0 \\ 0 & 0 & 0 & 1 \end{bmatrix}$$

The coordinates of point p are p (A, B, C). The line segment
$$op = \sqrt{A^2 + B^2 + C^2}$$

Suppose $$op = \sqrt{A^2 + B^2 + C^2} = L$$

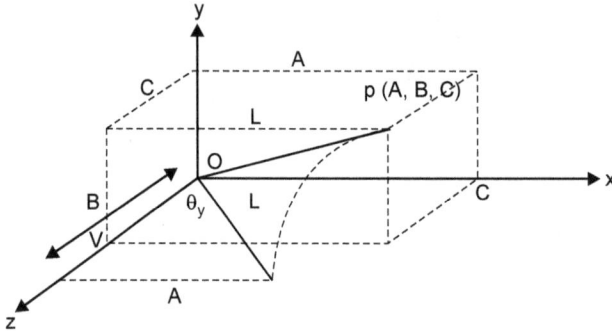

Fig. 4.7 A line in x-z plane

Now, perform rotation of the line about the y-axis by an angle of θ_y to make it coincide with the z-axis.

$$\cos\theta_y = \frac{V}{L} = \frac{\sqrt{B^2 + C^2}}{\sqrt{A^2 + B^2 + C^2}} = \frac{\sqrt{2}}{\sqrt{3}} \text{ and } \sin\theta_y = \frac{A}{L} = \frac{1}{\sqrt{3}}$$

The rotation transformation matrix representing the rotation of a line about the y-axis (in the CW direction) is given by

$$\left[R_y \right] = \begin{bmatrix} \cos\theta_y & 0 & -\sin\theta_y & 0 \\ 0 & 1 & 0 & 0 \\ +\sin\theta_y & 0 & \cos\theta_y & 0 \\ 0 & 0 & 0 & 1 \end{bmatrix} = \begin{bmatrix} \frac{\sqrt{2}}{\sqrt{3}} & 0 & \frac{-1}{\sqrt{3}} & 0 \\ 0 & 1 & 0 & 0 \\ +\frac{1}{\sqrt{3}} & 0 & \frac{\sqrt{2}}{\sqrt{3}} & 0 \\ 0 & 0 & 0 & 1 \end{bmatrix}$$

Now, after performing rotation about the y-axis, the line will coincide with the z-axis. Now perform rotation about the z-axis by given angle 55°.

$$\left[R_z \right] = \begin{bmatrix} \cos 55 & \sin 55 & 0 & 0 \\ -\sin 55 & \cos 55 & 0 & 0 \\ 0 & 0 & 1 & 0 \\ 0 & 0 & 0 & 1 \end{bmatrix} = \begin{bmatrix} 0.573 & 0.819 & 0 & 0 \\ -0.819 & 0.573 & 0 & 0 \\ 0 & 0 & 1 & 0 \\ 0 & 0 & 0 & 1 \end{bmatrix}$$

Now, the resultant transformation is

$$\left[T_T\right]=\left[T\right]\cdot\left[R_x\right]\cdot\left[R_y\right]\cdot\left[R_z\right]\cdot\left[R_y^{-1}\right]\cdot\left[R_x^{-1}\right]\cdot\left[T^{-1}\right]$$

$$\left[T_T\right]=\begin{bmatrix} 1 & 0 & 0 & 0 \\ 0 & 1 & 0 & 0 \\ 0 & 0 & 1 & 0 \\ -2 & -1 & -1 & 1 \end{bmatrix}\cdot\begin{bmatrix} 1 & 0 & 0 & 0 \\ 0 & \dfrac{1}{\sqrt{2}} & \dfrac{1}{\sqrt{2}} & 0 \\ 0 & -\dfrac{1}{\sqrt{2}} & \dfrac{1}{\sqrt{2}} & 0 \\ 0 & 0 & 0 & 1 \end{bmatrix}\cdot\begin{bmatrix} \dfrac{\sqrt{2}}{\sqrt{3}} & 0 & \dfrac{-1}{\sqrt{3}} & 0 \\ 0 & 1 & 0 & 0 \\ \dfrac{1}{\sqrt{3}} & 0 & \dfrac{\sqrt{2}}{\sqrt{3}} & 0 \\ 0 & 0 & 0 & 1 \end{bmatrix}\cdot$$

$$\begin{bmatrix} 0.573 & 0.819 & 0 & 0 \\ -0.819 & 0.573 & 0 & 0 \\ 0 & 0 & 1 & 0 \\ 0 & 0 & 0 & 1 \end{bmatrix}\cdot\begin{bmatrix} \dfrac{\sqrt{2}}{\sqrt{3}} & 0 & +\dfrac{1}{\sqrt{3}} & 0 \\ 0 & 1 & 0 & 0 \\ \dfrac{-1}{\sqrt{3}} & 0 & \dfrac{\sqrt{2}}{\sqrt{3}} & 0 \\ 0 & 0 & 0 & 1 \end{bmatrix}\cdot\begin{bmatrix} 1 & 0 & 0 & 0 \\ 0 & \dfrac{1}{\sqrt{2}} & -\dfrac{1}{\sqrt{2}} & 0 \\ 0 & \dfrac{1}{\sqrt{2}} & \dfrac{1}{\sqrt{2}} & 0 \\ 0 & 0 & 0 & 1 \end{bmatrix}\cdot\begin{bmatrix} 1 & 0 & 0 & 0 \\ 0 & 1 & 0 & 0 \\ 0 & 0 & 1 & 0 \\ 2 & 1 & 1 & 1 \end{bmatrix}$$

Describing a line in 3D space

The 3D equation of a line is given by:

$$x = x_0 + at$$
$$y = y_0 + bt$$
$$z = z_0 + ct$$

Now we could rearrange these three equations as follows:

$$\frac{x-x_0}{a}=t,\frac{y-y_0}{b}=t \text{ and } \frac{z-z_0}{c}=t$$

All the three right-hand sides are the same, so the symmetric form of the straight line is

$$\frac{x-x_0}{a}=\frac{y-y_0}{b}=\frac{z-z_0}{c}$$

As before, the line passes through point (x_0, y_0, z_0) and the constants a, b, and c give the relative gradient in three directions.

Here again the line is passing through the point $(1, 2, 1)$ and here is its equation in symmetry form:

$$\frac{x-1}{1} = \frac{y-2}{1} = \frac{z-1}{1}$$

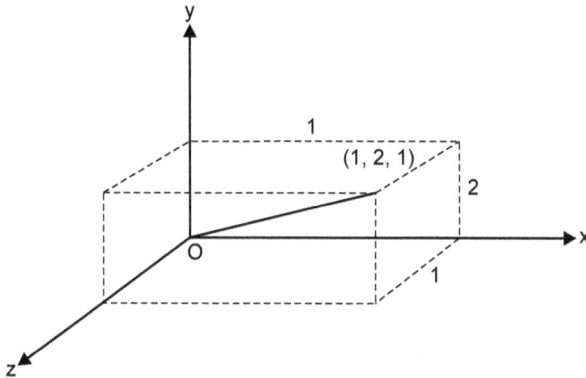

Fig. 4.8 A 3D line

Because this line passes through the origin, the constants a, b, and c are the same as x_0, y_0, z_0 although this is not generally the case.

Problem 5

A triangle PQR is defined by $P\ (3, 3, 7)$, $Q\ (3, 5, 7)$, and $R\ (5, 3, 7)$. Rotate this triangle about axis $\dfrac{x-1}{6} = \dfrac{y-4}{3} = \dfrac{z}{2}$. Upgrade it to homogeneous coordinates for symmetric handling.

Solution

Equation of the line is given by:

$$\frac{x-x_1}{x_2-x_1} = \frac{y-y_1}{y_2-y_1} = \frac{z-z_1}{z_2-z_1}$$

Rewrite the equation of the line in the form of a standard equation.

$$\frac{x-1}{7-1} = \frac{y-4}{7-4} = \frac{z-0}{2-0}$$

$$P_1 \equiv (x_1, y_1, z_1) \equiv (1, 4, 0)$$

$$P_2 \equiv (x_2, y_2, z_2) \equiv (7, 7, 2)$$

Step 1: Translate p_1 to origin.

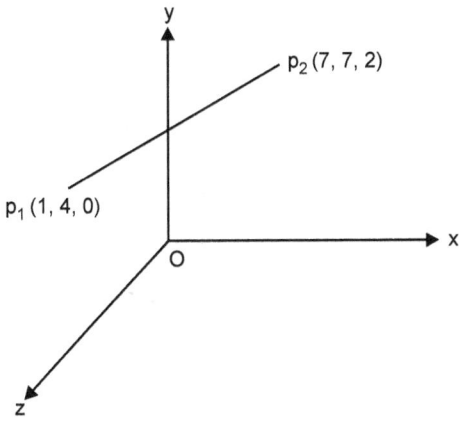

Fig. 4.9 A 3D line

$$[T] = \begin{bmatrix} 0 & 1 & 0 & 0 \\ 0 & 1 & 0 & 0 \\ 0 & 0 & 1 & 0 \\ -1 & -4 & 0 & 1 \end{bmatrix}$$

$P'_2 = x_2 - x_1, y_2 - y_1, z_2 - z_1 = (7-1, 7-3, 2-0)$

$P'_2 = (6, 3, 2)$

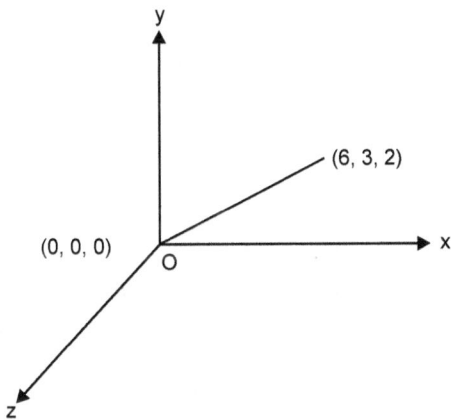

Fig. 4.10

Step 2: Rotate the line about the x-axis in the CCW direction to bring it in the yz plane.

$$[R_x] = \begin{bmatrix} 1 & 0 & 0 & 0 \\ 0 & \dfrac{C}{V} & \dfrac{B}{V} & 0 \\ 0 & -\dfrac{B}{V} & \dfrac{C}{V} & 0 \\ 0 & 0 & 0 & 1 \end{bmatrix} \qquad V = \sqrt{B^2 + C^2} = \sqrt{9+4} = \sqrt{13}$$

$$[R_x] = \begin{bmatrix} 1 & 0 & 0 & 0 \\ 0 & \dfrac{2}{\sqrt{13}} & \dfrac{3}{\sqrt{13}} & 0 \\ 0 & -\dfrac{3}{\sqrt{13}} & \dfrac{2}{\sqrt{13}} & 0 \\ 0 & 0 & 0 & 1 \end{bmatrix}$$

Step 3: Rotation about the y-axis in the CW direction:

Suppose
$$\sqrt{A^2 + B^2 + C^2} = L = \sqrt{36 + 9 + 4} = \sqrt{49} = 7$$

$$[R_y] = \begin{bmatrix} \dfrac{V}{L} & 0 & \dfrac{-A}{L} & 0 \\ 0 & 1 & 0 & 0 \\ \dfrac{A}{L} & 0 & \dfrac{V}{L} & 0 \\ 0 & 0 & 0 & 1 \end{bmatrix} = \begin{bmatrix} \dfrac{\sqrt{13}}{7} & 0 & \dfrac{-6}{7} & 0 \\ 0 & 1 & 0 & 0 \\ \dfrac{6}{7} & 0 & \dfrac{\sqrt{13}}{7} & 0 \\ 0 & 0 & 0 & 1 \end{bmatrix}$$

Step 4: Rotation about the z-axis by a given angle:

$$[R_z] = \begin{bmatrix} \cos\theta_z & \sin\theta_z & 0 & 0 \\ -\sin\theta_z & \cos\theta_z & 0 & 0 \\ 0 & 0 & 1 & 0 \\ 0 & 0 & 0 & 1 \end{bmatrix}$$

Now the resultant transformation:

$$[T_T] = [T] \cdot [R_x] \cdot [R_y] \cdot [R_z] \cdot [R_y^{-1}] \cdot [R_x^{-1}] \cdot [T^{-1}]$$

$$[T_T] = \begin{bmatrix} 1 & 0 & 0 & 0 \\ 0 & 1 & 0 & 0 \\ 0 & 0 & 1 & 0 \\ -1 & -4 & 0 & 1 \end{bmatrix} \cdot \begin{bmatrix} 1 & 0 & 0 & 0 \\ 0 & \dfrac{2}{\sqrt{13}} & \dfrac{3}{\sqrt{13}} & 0 \\ 0 & -\dfrac{3}{\sqrt{13}} & \dfrac{2}{\sqrt{13}} & 0 \\ 0 & 0 & 0 & 1 \end{bmatrix} \cdot \begin{bmatrix} \dfrac{\sqrt{13}}{7} & 0 & \dfrac{-6}{7} & 0 \\ 0 & 1 & 0 & 0 \\ \dfrac{6}{7} & 0 & \dfrac{\sqrt{13}}{7} & 0 \\ 0 & 0 & 0 & 1 \end{bmatrix} \cdot$$

$$\begin{bmatrix} \cos\theta_z & \sin\theta_z & 0 & 0 \\ -\sin\theta_z & \cos\theta_z & 0 & 0 \\ 0 & 0 & 1 & 0 \\ 0 & 0 & 0 & 1 \end{bmatrix} \begin{bmatrix} \dfrac{\sqrt{13}}{7} & 0 & \dfrac{6}{7} & 0 \\ 0 & 1 & 0 & 0 \\ -\dfrac{6}{7} & 0 & \dfrac{\sqrt{13}}{7} & 0 \\ 0 & 0 & 0 & 1 \end{bmatrix} \cdot$$

$$\begin{bmatrix} 1 & 0 & 0 & 0 \\ 0 & \dfrac{2}{\sqrt{13}} & -\dfrac{3}{\sqrt{13}} & 0 \\ 0 & \dfrac{3}{\sqrt{13}} & \dfrac{2}{\sqrt{13}} & 0 \\ 0 & 0 & 0 & 1 \end{bmatrix} \begin{bmatrix} 1 & 0 & 0 & 0 \\ 0 & 1 & 0 & 0 \\ 0 & 0 & 1 & 0 \\ 1 & 4 & 0 & 1 \end{bmatrix}$$

Problem 6

A triangular prism has six vertices as (5, 10, 0), (10, 5, 0), (5, 5, 0), (5, 10, 7), (10, 5, 7), and (5, 5, 7). Rotate the solid about $\dfrac{x-1}{2} = \dfrac{y-2}{3} = \dfrac{z-5}{6}$ through 90°. List the final position of the six vertices after rotation.

Solution

Equation of the line is given by

$$\frac{x-x_1}{x_2-x_1} = \frac{y-y_1}{y_2-y_1} = \frac{z-z_1}{z_2-z_1}$$

Rewrite the equation of the line in the form of a standard equation.

$$\frac{x-1}{3-1} = \frac{y-2}{5-2} = \frac{z-5}{11-5}$$

$$p_1 \equiv (x_1, y_1, z_1) \equiv (1, 2, 5)$$

$$p_2 \equiv (x_2, y_2, z_2) \equiv (3, 5, 11)$$

Step 1: Translate p_1 to origin.

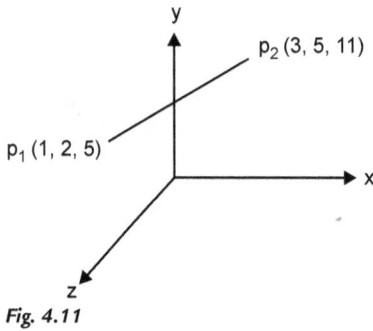

Fig. 4.11

$$[T] = \begin{bmatrix} 1 & 0 & 0 & 0 \\ 0 & 1 & 0 & 0 \\ 0 & 0 & 1 & 0 \\ -1 & -2 & -5 & 1 \end{bmatrix}$$

$$p'_2 = x_2 - x_1, y_2 - y_1, z_2 - z_1$$
$$P'_2 = (2, 3, 6)$$

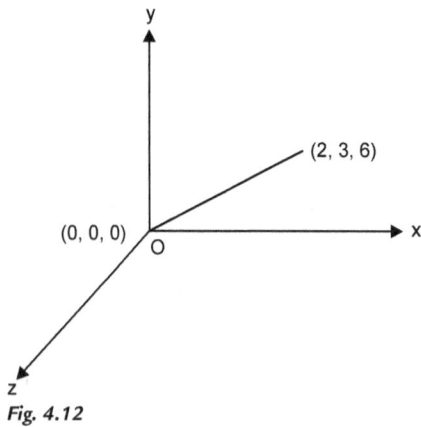

Fig. 4.12

Step 2: Rotating the line about the x-axis in the CCW direction to bring it in the yz plane:

$$[R_x] = \begin{bmatrix} 1 & 0 & 0 & 0 \\ 0 & \dfrac{C}{V} & \dfrac{B}{V} & 0 \\ 0 & -\dfrac{B}{V} & \dfrac{C}{V} & 0 \\ 0 & 0 & 0 & 1 \end{bmatrix} \quad V = \sqrt{B^2 + C^2} = \sqrt{9 + 36} = \sqrt{45}$$

$$[R_x] = \begin{bmatrix} 1 & 0 & 0 & 0 \\ 0 & \dfrac{6}{\sqrt{45}} & \dfrac{3}{\sqrt{45}} & 0 \\ 0 & -\dfrac{3}{\sqrt{45}} & \dfrac{6}{\sqrt{45}} & 0 \\ 0 & 0 & 0 & 1 \end{bmatrix}$$

Step 3: Rotation about the *y*-axis in the CW direction:

Suppose $\sqrt{A^2 + B^2 + C^2} = L = \sqrt{4+9+36} = \sqrt{49} = 7$

$$[R_y] = \begin{bmatrix} \dfrac{V}{L} & 0 & \dfrac{-A}{L} & 0 \\ 0 & 1 & 0 & 0 \\ \dfrac{A}{L} & 0 & \dfrac{V}{L} & 0 \\ 0 & 0 & 0 & 1 \end{bmatrix} = \begin{bmatrix} \dfrac{\sqrt{45}}{7} & 0 & \dfrac{-2}{7} & 0 \\ 0 & 1 & 0 & 0 \\ \dfrac{2}{7} & 0 & \dfrac{\sqrt{45}}{7} & 0 \\ 0 & 0 & 0 & 1 \end{bmatrix}$$

Step 4: Rotation about the *z*-axis by 90°:

$$[R_z] = \begin{bmatrix} \cos 90 & \sin 90 & 0 & 0 \\ -\sin 90 & \cos 90 & 0 & 0 \\ 0 & 0 & 1 & 0 \\ 0 & 0 & 0 & 1 \end{bmatrix} = \begin{bmatrix} 0 & 1 & 0 & 0 \\ -1 & 0 & 0 & 0 \\ 0 & 0 & 1 & 0 \\ 0 & 0 & 0 & 1 \end{bmatrix}$$

Now, the resultant transformation is:

$$[T_T] = [T] \cdot [R_x] \cdot [R_y] \cdot [R_z] \cdot [R_y^{-1}] \cdot [R_x^{-1}] \cdot [T^{-1}]$$

$$[T_T] = \begin{bmatrix} 1 & 0 & 0 & 0 \\ 0 & 1 & 0 & 0 \\ 0 & 0 & 1 & 0 \\ -1 & -2 & -5 & 1 \end{bmatrix} \cdot \begin{bmatrix} 1 & 0 & 0 & 0 \\ 0 & \dfrac{6}{\sqrt{45}} & \dfrac{3}{\sqrt{45}} & 0 \\ 0 & -\dfrac{3}{\sqrt{45}} & \dfrac{6}{\sqrt{45}} & 0 \\ 0 & 0 & 0 & 1 \end{bmatrix} \begin{bmatrix} \dfrac{\sqrt{45}}{7} & 0 & \dfrac{-2}{7} & 0 \\ 0 & 1 & 0 & 0 \\ \dfrac{2}{7} & 0 & \dfrac{\sqrt{45}}{7} & 0 \\ 0 & 0 & 0 & 1 \end{bmatrix}$$

$$\begin{bmatrix} 0 & 1 & 0 & 0 \\ -1 & 0 & 0 & 0 \\ 0 & 0 & 1 & 0 \\ 0 & 0 & 0 & 1 \end{bmatrix} \begin{bmatrix} \dfrac{\sqrt{45}}{7} & 0 & \dfrac{2}{7} & 0 \\ 0 & 1 & 0 & 0 \\ -\dfrac{2}{7} & 0 & \dfrac{\sqrt{45}}{7} & 0 \\ 0 & 0 & 0 & 1 \end{bmatrix} \begin{bmatrix} 1 & 0 & 0 & 0 \\ 0 & \dfrac{6}{\sqrt{45}} & \dfrac{-3}{\sqrt{45}} & 0 \\ 0 & \dfrac{3}{\sqrt{45}} & \dfrac{6}{\sqrt{45}} & 0 \\ 0 & 0 & 0 & 1 \end{bmatrix} \begin{bmatrix} 1 & 0 & 0 & 0 \\ 0 & 1 & 0 & 0 \\ 0 & 0 & 1 & 0 \\ 1 & 2 & 5 & 1 \end{bmatrix}$$

$$[T_T] = \begin{bmatrix} 0.084 & 0.72 & -0.68 & 0 \\ -0.977 & 0.185 & 0.0784 & 0 \\ 0.1836 & 0.6552 & 0.725 & 0 \\ 1.95 & -2.374 & 1.893 & 1 \end{bmatrix}$$

To find the new position of the prism:

$$[P'] = [P][T_T]$$

$$= \begin{bmatrix} 5 & 10 & 0 & 1 \\ 10 & 5 & 0 & 1 \\ 5 & 5 & 0 & 1 \\ 5 & 10 & 7 & 1 \\ 10 & 5 & 7 & 1 \\ 5 & 5 & 7 & 1 \end{bmatrix} \begin{bmatrix} 0.084 & 0.75 & -0.68 & 0 \\ -0.977 & 0.185 & 0.0784 & 0 \\ 0.1836 & 0.6552 & 0.725 & 0 \\ 1.95 & -2.374 & 1.893 & 1 \end{bmatrix}$$

$$[P'] = \begin{bmatrix} -7.394 & 3.1149 & -0.7109 & 1 \\ -2.69 & 5.821 & -4.4910 & 1 \\ -2.51 & 2.18 & -1.1027 & 1 \\ -6.1 & 7.7 & 4.367 & 1 \\ -0.8057 & 10.4084 & 0.5871 & 1 \\ -1.2262 & 6.7742 & 3.97 & 1 \end{bmatrix}$$

4.6 REFLECTION TRANSFORMATION

Reflection transformation is another important modifying transformation of a 3D object. Again, 3D reflection is a more complex phenomenon compared to 2D reflection. 2D reflection is captured about a line in the xy plane. But 3D reflections are captured about three principle planes, that is, the xy plane, yz plane, and zx plane.

Suppose a 3D point having coordinate $p(x, y, z)$ is reflected about the xy plane. The reflected point obtained is $p'(x', y', z')$. Then the coordinates of x and y remain unchanged, whereas the z coordinate changes to negative z. Fig. 4.13 shows the reflection of a point about the xy plane.

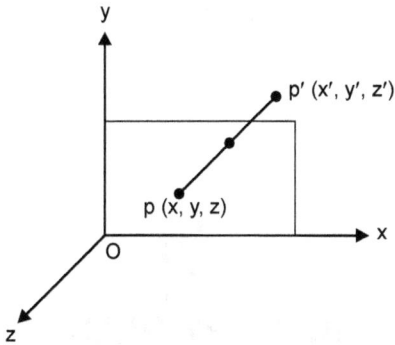

Fig. 4.13 Reflection about the *xy* plane

The parametric equation of reflection is

$$x' = x \qquad \qquad \text{...(4.1)}$$

$$y' = y \qquad \qquad \text{...(4.2)}$$

$$z' = -z \qquad \qquad \text{...(4.3)}$$

Writing these parametric equations in matrix form,

$$[x'\,y'\,z'\,h] = [x\,y\,z\,1] \begin{bmatrix} 1 & 0 & 0 & 0 \\ 0 & 1 & 0 & 0 \\ 0 & 0 & -1 & 0 \\ 0 & 0 & 0 & 1 \end{bmatrix}$$

Reflection transformation matrix is given by

$$[M_{xy}] = \begin{bmatrix} 1 & 0 & 0 & 0 \\ 0 & 1 & 0 & 0 \\ 0 & 0 & -1 & 0 \\ 0 & 0 & 0 & 1 \end{bmatrix}$$

This is similar to the scaling transformation matrix where $s_x = 1$, $s_y = 1$, $s_z = -1$. Similarly, reflection transformation about the *xz* plane is given by

$$[M_{xz}] = \begin{bmatrix} 1 & 0 & 0 & 0 \\ 0 & -1 & 0 & 0 \\ 0 & 0 & 1 & 0 \\ 0 & 0 & 0 & 1 \end{bmatrix}$$

Similarly, reflection transformation about the yz plane is given by

$$\left[M_{yz} \right] = \begin{bmatrix} -1 & 0 & 0 & 0 \\ 0 & 1 & 0 & 0 \\ 0 & 0 & 1 & 0 \\ 0 & 0 & 0 & 1 \end{bmatrix}$$

4.7 REFLECTION ABOUT ANY ARBITRARY PLANE IN 3D SPACE

Reflection about any arbitrary plane can be captured by transforming the plane so as to make it coplanar with any of the principle planes and then applying one of the three basic 3D reflection matrices. To make an arbitrary plane coplanar with a principle plane, a normal to the arbitrary plane is considered. Then a series of transformations is carried out to make the normal to coincide with any of the principle axes. When the normal coincides with any of the principle axes (say the x-axis), the arbitrary plane gets coplanar with the principle plane (the yz plane). Fig. 4.14 shows an arbitrary plane in 3D space and its normal.

Reflection about any arbitrary plane in 3D space is accomplished by the following steps:

1. Translate a known point P, which lies in the reflection plane, to the origin of the coordinate system.
2. Rotate the normal vector to the reflection plane at the origin until it coincides with the positive z-axis; this makes the reflection plane coincide with the principal xy plane.
3. Perform reflection transformation about the xy plane.
4. Perform inverse transformation to place the plane in its original position.

The general transformation is given by

$$\left[T_T \right] = \left[T \right] \cdot \left[R_x \right] \cdot \left[R_y \right] \cdot \left[M_{xy} \right] \cdot \left[R_y^{-1} \right] \cdot \left[R_x^{-1} \right] \cdot \left[T^{-1} \right]$$

$(x_0, y_0, z_0) = (p_x, p_y, p_z)$ are the components of point p in the reflection plane and (C_x, C_y, C_z) are the direction cosines of the normal to the reflection plane.

If the equation of the reflection plane $ax + by + cz + d = 0$ is known, the unit normal to the plane is:

$$[n] = \begin{bmatrix} C_x & C_y & C_z \end{bmatrix} = \frac{[a\ b\ c]}{\sqrt{a^2 + b^2 + c^2}}$$

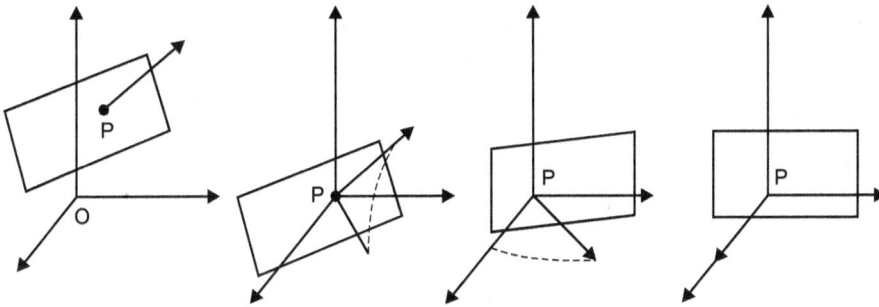

Translation of P to the origin   Rotation of normal about the x-axis   Rotation of normal about the y-axis

Fig. 4.14 3D reflection

Problem 7

A pyramid has coordinates A (10, 10, 10), B (10, 10, 15), C (10, 15, 10), and D (15, 10, 10). Find the reflection of the pyramid about the plane $6x + 2y + 3z = 12$.

Solution

To find the equation of normal to the plane:

Equation of the reflection plane is $6x + 2y + 3z = 12$

By substitution, we have $C_x = 6, C_y = 2, C_z = 3$

$$D = \sqrt{C_x^2 + C_y^2 + C_z^2} = \sqrt{36 + 4 + 9} = \sqrt{49} = 7$$

$$l = \frac{C_x}{D} = \frac{6}{7}$$

$$m = \frac{C_y}{D} = \frac{2}{7}$$

$$n = \frac{C_z}{D} = \frac{3}{7}$$

l, m, n are direction cosines.

Equation of the line in 3D space is given by:

$$\frac{x - x_1}{l} = \frac{y - y_1}{m} = \frac{z - z_1}{n}$$

Equation of the normal line is:

$$\frac{x-x_1}{\dfrac{6}{7}} = \frac{y-y_1}{\dfrac{2}{7}} = \frac{z-z_1}{\dfrac{3}{7}}$$

The points of intersection of the plane and the line will satisfy both the equation of line and the equation of plane. Assuming the point of intersection at $x = 0$ and $y = 0$ in the equation of plane $6x + 2y + 3z = 12$, we have

$3z = 12$ and $z = 4$

Point $(0, 0, 4)$ lies on the plane. The equation of the normal line is

$$\frac{x-0}{\dfrac{6}{7}} = \frac{y-0}{\dfrac{2}{7}} = \frac{z-4}{\dfrac{3}{7}}$$

If we compare it with the standard equation of line in 3D

then

$$\frac{x-x_1}{x_2-x_1} = \frac{y-y_1}{y_2-y_1} = \frac{z-z_1}{z_2-z_1}$$

$$x_1 \equiv (0,0,4)$$

$$(A, B, C) \equiv \left(\frac{6}{7}, \frac{2}{7}, \frac{3}{7}\right)$$

Apply the following transformations:

Step 1: Translate x_1 to the origin.

$$[T] = \begin{bmatrix} 1 & 0 & 0 & 0 \\ 0 & 1 & 0 & 0 \\ 0 & 0 & 1 & 0 \\ 0 & 0 & -4 & 1 \end{bmatrix}$$

Step 2: Rotating the line about the x-axis in the CCW direction to bring it in the yz plane:

$$[R_x] = \begin{bmatrix} 1 & 0 & 0 & 0 \\ 0 & \dfrac{C}{V} & \dfrac{B}{V} & 0 \\ 0 & -\dfrac{B}{V} & \dfrac{C}{V} & 0 \\ 0 & 0 & 0 & 1 \end{bmatrix} \qquad V = \sqrt{B^2 + C^2} = \sqrt{\frac{4}{49} + \frac{9}{49}} = \frac{\sqrt{13}}{7}$$

$$= \begin{bmatrix} 1 & 0 & 0 & 0 \\ 0 & \dfrac{3}{\sqrt{13}} & \dfrac{2}{\sqrt{13}} & 0 \\ 0 & -\dfrac{2}{\sqrt{13}} & \dfrac{3}{\sqrt{13}} & 0 \\ 0 & 0 & 0 & 1 \end{bmatrix}$$

Step 3: Rotation about the y-axis in the CW direction:

Suppose $\qquad \sqrt{A^2 + B^2 + C^2} = L = \sqrt{\dfrac{36}{49} + \dfrac{4}{49} + \dfrac{9}{49}} = \sqrt{1} = 1$

$$[R_y] = \begin{bmatrix} \dfrac{V}{L} & 0 & \dfrac{-A}{L} & 0 \\ 0 & 1 & 0 & 0 \\ \dfrac{A}{L} & 0 & \dfrac{V}{L} & 0 \\ 0 & 0 & 0 & 1 \end{bmatrix} = \begin{bmatrix} \dfrac{\sqrt{13}}{7} & 0 & \dfrac{-6}{7} & 0 \\ 0 & 1 & 0 & 0 \\ \dfrac{6}{7} & 0 & \dfrac{\sqrt{13}}{7} & 0 \\ 0 & 0 & 0 & 1 \end{bmatrix}$$

Step 4: Reflection transformation about the xy plane:

$$[M_{xy}] = \begin{bmatrix} 1 & 0 & 0 & 0 \\ 0 & 1 & 0 & 0 \\ 0 & 0 & -1 & 0 \\ 0 & 0 & 0 & 1 \end{bmatrix}$$

Now the resultant transformation is

$$[T_T] = [T] \cdot [R_x] \cdot [R_y] \cdot [M_{xy}] \cdot [R_y^{-1}] \cdot [R_x^{-1}] \cdot [T^{-1}]$$

$$[T_T] = \begin{bmatrix} 1 & 0 & 0 & 0 \\ 0 & 1 & 0 & 0 \\ 0 & 0 & 1 & 0 \\ 0 & 0 & -4 & 1 \end{bmatrix} \cdot \begin{bmatrix} 1 & 0 & 0 & 0 \\ 0 & \dfrac{3}{\sqrt{13}} & \dfrac{2}{\sqrt{13}} & 0 \\ 0 & -\dfrac{2}{\sqrt{13}} & \dfrac{3}{\sqrt{13}} & 0 \\ 0 & 0 & 0 & 1 \end{bmatrix} \cdot \begin{bmatrix} \dfrac{\sqrt{13}}{7} & 0 & \dfrac{-6}{7} & 0 \\ 0 & 1 & 0 & 0 \\ \dfrac{6}{7} & 0 & \dfrac{\sqrt{13}}{7} & 0 \\ 0 & 0 & 0 & 1 \end{bmatrix} \cdot \begin{bmatrix} 1 & 0 & 0 & 0 \\ 0 & 1 & 0 & 0 \\ 0 & 0 & -1 & 0 \\ 0 & 0 & 0 & 1 \end{bmatrix} \cdot$$

$$\begin{bmatrix} \dfrac{\sqrt{13}}{7} & 0 & \dfrac{6}{7} & 0 \\ 0 & 1 & 0 & 0 \\ \dfrac{-6}{7} & 0 & \dfrac{\sqrt{13}}{7} & 0 \\ 0 & 0 & 0 & 1 \end{bmatrix} \cdot \begin{bmatrix} 1 & 0 & 0 & 0 \\ 0 & \dfrac{3}{\sqrt{13}} & \dfrac{-2}{\sqrt{13}} & 0 \\ 0 & \dfrac{2}{\sqrt{13}} & \dfrac{3}{\sqrt{13}} & 0 \\ 0 & 0 & 0 & 1 \end{bmatrix} \cdot \begin{bmatrix} 1 & 0 & 0 & 0 \\ 0 & 1 & 0 & 0 \\ 0 & 0 & 1 & 0 \\ 0 & 0 & 4 & 1 \end{bmatrix}$$

To find the new position of the prism:

$$[P'] = [P][T_T]$$

$$[P'] = \begin{bmatrix} 10 & 10 & 10 & 1 \\ 10 & 10 & 15 & 1 \\ 10 & 15 & 10 & 1 \\ 15 & 10 & 10 & 1 \end{bmatrix} [T_T]$$

Problem 8

The corners of a wedge-shaped block are:
A [0, 0, 2]; B [0, 0, 3]; C [0, 2, 3]; D [0, 2, 2]; E [−1, 2, 2] and F [−1, 2, 3]. The reflection plane passes through the y-axis at 45° between (−x)-axis and z-axis. Determine the reflection of the wedge.

Solution

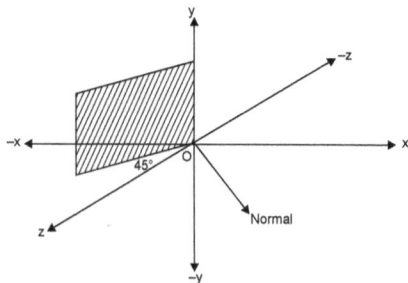

Fig. 4.15 3D reflection

Step 1: Rotation about the y-axis in the CCW direction by $45°$:

$$\left[R_y\right] = \begin{bmatrix} \cos 45 & 0 & \sin 45 & 0 \\ 0 & 1 & 0 & 0 \\ -\sin 45 & 0 & \cos 45 & 0 \\ 0 & 0 & 0 & 1 \end{bmatrix}$$

$$\left[R_y\right] = \begin{bmatrix} 0.7 & 0 & 0.7 & 0 \\ 0 & 1 & 0 & 0 \\ -0.7 & 0 & 0.7 & 0 \\ 0 & 0 & 0 & 1 \end{bmatrix}$$

After rotating about the y-axis the plane coincides with the yz plane. Reflection transformation about the yz plane is given by

$$\left[M_{yz}\right] = \begin{bmatrix} -1 & 0 & 0 & 0 \\ 0 & 1 & 0 & 0 \\ 0 & 0 & 1 & 0 \\ 0 & 0 & 0 & 1 \end{bmatrix}$$

Back rotation about the y-axis:

$$\left[R_y^{-1}\right] = \begin{bmatrix} 0.07 & 0 & 0.7 & 0 \\ 0 & 1 & 0 & 0 \\ -0.07 & 0 & 0.07 & 0 \\ 0 & 0 & 0 & 1 \end{bmatrix}$$

Total transformation is given by

$$\left[T_T\right] = \begin{bmatrix} 0.7 & 0 & 0.7 & 0 \\ 0 & 1 & 0 & 0 \\ -0.7 & 0 & 0.7 & 0 \\ 0 & 0 & 0 & 1 \end{bmatrix} \cdot \begin{bmatrix} -1 & 0 & 0 & 0 \\ 0 & 1 & 0 & 0 \\ 0 & 0 & 1 & 0 \\ 0 & 0 & 0 & 1 \end{bmatrix} \cdot \begin{bmatrix} 0.7 & 0 & 0.07 & 0 \\ 0 & 1 & 0 & 0 \\ -0.7 & 0 & 0.7 & 0 \\ 0 & 0 & 0 & 1 \end{bmatrix}$$

$$= \begin{bmatrix} 0 & 0 & 1 & 0 \\ 0 & 1 & 0 & 0 \\ 0 & 0 & 0 & 0 \\ 0 & 0 & 0 & 1 \end{bmatrix}$$

To find the final position of a wedge-shaped block:

$$[P'] = \begin{bmatrix} 0 & 0 & 2 & 1 \\ 0 & 0 & 3 & 1 \\ 0 & 2 & 3 & 1 \\ 0 & 2 & 2 & 1 \\ -1 & 2 & 2 & 1 \\ -1 & 2 & 3 & 1 \end{bmatrix} \begin{bmatrix} 0 & 0 & 1 & 0 \\ 0 & 1 & 0 & 0 \\ 0 & 0 & 0 & 0 \\ 0 & 0 & 0 & 1 \end{bmatrix}$$

$$[P'] = \begin{bmatrix} 0 & 0 & 0 & 1 \\ 0 & 0 & 0 & 1 \\ 0 & 2 & 0 & 1 \\ 0 & 2 & 0 & 1 \\ 0 & 2 & 0 & 1 \\ 0 & 2 & 0 & 1 \end{bmatrix}$$

4.8 SHEAR TRANSFORMATION

Shearing transformation causes distortions in objects by altering the values of one or more coordinates by an amount proportional to the third, that is, the shear, along any pair of axes that is controlled by a third axis. Off-diagonal terms in the upper 3×3 submatrix of a general transformation matrix produce the effect of sharing. Shearing transformation is captured by the following matrix:

$$[T_{SH}] = \begin{bmatrix} 1 & S_{xy} & S_{xz} & 0 \\ S_{yx} & 1 & S_{yz} & 0 \\ S_{zx} & S_{zy} & 1 & 0 \\ 0 & 0 & 0 & 1 \end{bmatrix}$$

(i) Shear along the x-axis: The following matrix gives shear along the x-axis:

$$\begin{bmatrix} 1 & S_{xy} & S_{xz} & 0 \\ 0 & 1 & 0 & 0 \\ 0 & 0 & 1 & 0 \\ 0 & 0 & 0 & 1 \end{bmatrix}$$

(*ii*) **Shear along the y-axis:** The following matrix gives shear along the y-axis.

$$\begin{bmatrix} 1 & 0 & 0 & 0 \\ S_{yx} & 1 & S_{yz} & 0 \\ 0 & 0 & 1 & 0 \\ 0 & 0 & 0 & 1 \end{bmatrix}$$

(*iii*) **Shear along the z-axis:** The following matrix gives shear along the z-axis.

$$\begin{bmatrix} 1 & 0 & 0 & 0 \\ 0 & 1 & 0 & 0 \\ S_{zx} & S_{zy} & 1 & 0 \\ 0 & 0 & 0 & 1 \end{bmatrix}$$

EXERCISES

1. A cube of 6 mm side having one corner point at $(0, 0, 0)$ is translated by 3 mm in x direction and scaled twice in all directions. Find the final position of the cube.

2. Calculate the 3D homogeneous transformation matrix to carry out a transformation comprising a translation of 20 mm in z direction together with a rotation of 35° about a line parallel to the z-axis through $[20, 20, 0]$.

3. A cube's corner coordinates are $(9, 9, 9)$, $(9, 9, 10)$, $(9, 10, 9)$, $(9, 10, 10)$, $(10, 9, 9)$, $(10, 9, 10)$, $(10, 10, 9)$, and $(10, 10, 10)$. Rotate the cube through 120° about $\dfrac{x-3}{2} = \dfrac{y-1}{2} = z$.

4. A triangle marked by $(5, 5)$, $(10, 5)$, and $(10, 10)$ is to be rotated through 60° CCW about $\dfrac{x-3}{2} = \dfrac{y-1}{2} = z$. Assume the triangle to be in $z = 0$ plane before rotation. Find the coordinates after rotation.

5. A line segment PQ is defined as P $(1, 2, 1, 1)$ and Q $(2, 1, 2, 1)$ in a 3D homogeneous system. Rotate this line segment about an axis $\dfrac{x-2}{1} = \dfrac{y-2}{2} = \dfrac{z}{2}$.

6. A triangle ABC is defined as A $(0, 0, 0)$, B $(1, 2, 3)$, and C $(3, 2, 1)$. Find the reflection of ABC about mirror surface $4x + 7y + 4z + 1 = 0$.

7. Perform the following transformations on a point $P(2, 6, 7)$ using a homogeneous coordinate system.

(a) Translate by 4, 2, 1

(b) Translate by vector $2\hat{i} + 3\hat{j} - \hat{k}$

8. Find out the transformed coordinates of a position vector $3i + 2j - 4k$ subjected to the following multiple transformations successively:

(i) Translation by $-2, -3, 1$

(ii) $45°$ CW rotation about the y-axis

9. A prism is marked by six vertices (8, 6, 0), (6, 6, 0), (6, 8,0), (8, 6, 4), (6, 6, 4), and (6, 8, 4). Find the reflection of this triangular prism about a mirror surface given by $2x + 6y + 3z = 6$.

OBJECTIVE QUESTIONS

4.1 The size of a 3D homogeneous transformation matrix is

(a) 2×2 (b) 3×3

(c) 4×4 (d) 5×5

4.2 A 3D rotation matrix about the x-axis is given by

(a)
$$\begin{bmatrix} \cos\theta & 0 & \sin\theta & 0 \\ 0 & 1 & 0 & 0 \\ -\sin\theta & 0 & \cos\theta & 0 \\ 0 & 0 & 0 & 1 \end{bmatrix}$$

(b)
$$\begin{bmatrix} 1 & 0 & 0 & 0 \\ 0 & \cos\theta & \sin\theta & 0 \\ 0 & -\sin\theta & \cos\theta & 0 \\ 0 & 0 & 0 & 1 \end{bmatrix}$$

(c)
$$\begin{bmatrix} \cos\theta & \sin\theta & 0 & 0 \\ -\sin\theta & \cos\theta & 0 & 0 \\ 0 & 0 & 1 & 0 \\ 0 & 0 & 0 & 1 \end{bmatrix}$$

(d) none of the above

4.3 In a scaling transformation matrix, scaling factors are placed along

(a) horizontal places

(b) vertical places

(c) random places

(d) diagonal places

4.4 Rotation about any arbitrary line in 3D space can be captured by performing a series of transformations to
(*a*)   align the line with any of the principle axes
(*b*)   bring one end of the line on origin
(*c*)   all of the above
(*d*)   none of the above

4.5 Reflection about any arbitrary plane in 3D space can be captured by performing a series of transformations to
(*a*)   align the plane with any of the principle planes
(*b*)   align normal to the plane with any of the principle axes
(*c*)   all of the above
(*d*)   none of the above

4.6 3D rotation matrices are given about
(*a*)   one principle axes   (*b*) two principle axes
(*c*)   three principle axes   (*d*) none of the above

4.7 Distortion in an object by altering the value of one or more coordinates by an amount proportional to the third is called
(*a*)   scaling   (*b*) translation
(*c*)   rotation   (*d*) shear

4.8 A series of transformations required for rotation about any arbitrary line in 3D space is given by
(*a*) $\left[R_x\right]\left[R_y\right]\left[R_z\right]\left[T\right]\left[R_x^{-1}\right]\left[R_y^{-1}\right]\left[T^{-1}\right]$
(*b*) $\left[T\right]\left[R_y\right]\left[R_z\right]\left[R_x\right]\left[R_x^{-1}\right]\left[R_y^{-1}\right]\left[T^{-1}\right]$
(*c*) $\left[T\right]\left[R_y\right]\left[R_z\right]\left[R_x\right]\left[R_x^{-1}\right]\left[R_y^{-1}\right]\left[T^{-1}\right]$
(*d*) $\left[T\right]\left[R_x\right]\left[R_y\right]\left[R_z\right]\left[R_y^{-1}\right]\left[R_x^{-1}\right]\left[T^{-1}\right]$

4.9 Rotation is considered to be positive when it is in a CCW direction when viewed
(*a*)   along the axis towards origin
(*b*)   along the axis away from origin
(*c*)   perpendicular to the axis towards origin
(*d*)   perpendicular to the axis away from origin

4.10 3D reflection matrices are given about
(*a*)   one principle plane   (*b*) two principle planes
(*c*)   three principle planes   (*d*) none of the above

ANSWERS

4.1 (c)	**4.2** (b)	**4.3** (d)	**4.4** (a)
4.5 (c)	**4.6** (c)	**4.7** (d)	**4.8** (d)
4.9 (b)	**4.10** (c)		

5 PARAMETRIC REPRESENTATION OF PLANAR CURVES

Chapter

5.1 INTRODUCTION

A curve can be represented mathematically by a parametric equation. Parametric equations express the coordinates of the points on a curve as functions of a variable called a parameter. For example, the parametric representation of an origin-centered circle of radius r is given by

$$x = r \cos \theta$$

$$y = r \sin \theta$$

$$0 \leq \theta \leq 2\pi$$

where θ is the varying parameter. Together, these equations are parametric representations of a curve. Another common example occurs in kinematics, where the trajectory of a point is usually represented by a parametric equation with time as the parameter. The notion of a parametric equation has been generalized to surfaces, manifolds, and algebraic varieties of higher dimensions, with the number of parameters being equal to the dimension of the manifold or variety, and the number of equations being equal to the dimension of the space in which the manifold or variety is considered (for curves the dimension is one and one parameter is used; for surfaces the dimension is two and two parameters, etc.). The parameter typically is designated as t because parametric equations often represent a physical process in time. However, the parameter may represent some other physical quantity such as a geometric variable, or may merely be selected arbitrarily for convenience. Moreover, more than one set of parametric equations may specify the same curve.

5.2 PARAMETRIC REPRESENTATION OF A CIRCLE

A non-parametric representation of a circle is given by

$$(x - h)^2 + (y - k)^2 = r^2$$

For an origin-centered circle, it is

$$(x)^2 + (y)^2 = r^2$$

For an origin-centered unit circle with $r = 1$,

$$(x)^2 + (y)^2 = 1$$

$$y = \sqrt{1 - x^2}$$

But if we plot the points using non-parametric equation and increase the value of x by 1 and then calculate the corresponding value of y, then the curve would appear to be a poor representation of the circle. Fig. 5.1 shows a curve obtained by a non-parametric equation.

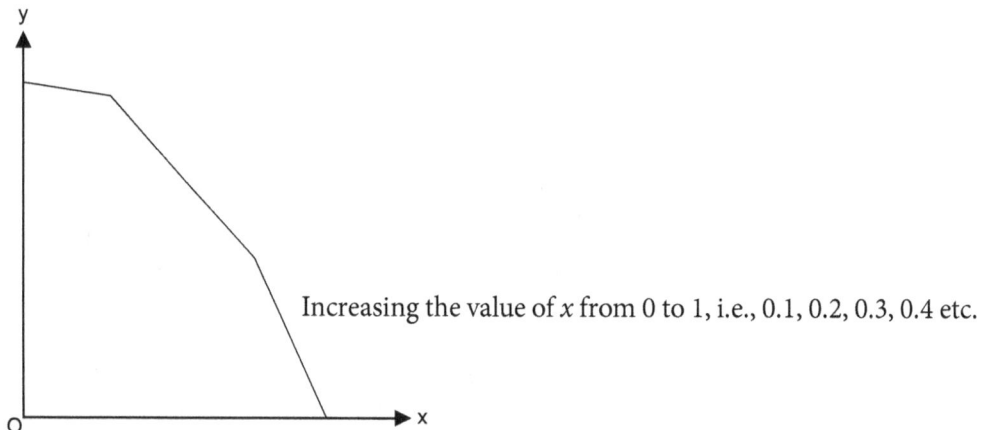

Increasing the value of x from 0 to 1, i.e., 0.1, 0.2, 0.3, 0.4 etc.

Fig. 5.1 Coordinates obtained by a non-parametric equation

Parametric representation of an origin-centered circle of radius r is given by

$$x = r \cos \theta$$

$$y = r \sin \theta$$

$$0 \leq \theta \leq 2\pi$$

where θ is the varying parameter. Noting that the circle is swept out for a range of the parameter θ from 0 to 2π, and assuming that a fixed number of uniformly spaced points on circumference are calculated, that is, $\delta\theta$, the parameter increment between points would be constant. The Cartesian coordinates of any point on an origin-centered circle are

$$x_{(i+1)} = r \cos (\theta_i \cos \delta\theta) \qquad \qquad \text{...(5.1)}$$

$$x_{(i+1)} = r \sin (\theta_i \cos \delta\theta) \qquad \qquad \text{...(5.2)}$$

where θ_i is the value of the parameter that yields the point at $x_i + y_i$
Hence

$$x_i = r \cos \theta_i$$

$$y_i = r \sin \theta_i$$

Applying the sum of angles formula to Eq. (5.1) and Eq. (5.2),

$$x_{(i+1)} = r \left[\cos \theta_i \cos \delta\theta - \sin \theta_i \sin \delta\theta \right]$$

$$y_{(i+1)} = r \left[\cos \theta_i \sin \delta\theta + \sin \theta_i \cos \delta\theta \right]$$

$$x_{(i+1)} = r \cos \theta_i \cos \delta\theta - r \sin \theta_i \sin \delta\theta$$

$$y_{(i+1)} = r \cos \theta_i \sin \delta\theta + r \sin \theta_i \cos \delta\theta$$

Putting $\qquad\qquad x_i = r \cos \theta_i,\ y_i = r \sin \theta_i$

$$x_{(i+1)} = x_i \cos \delta\theta - y_i \sin \delta\theta$$

$$x_{(i+1)} = x_i \sin \delta\theta + y_i \cos \delta\theta$$

represent the rotation of the point $x_i\, y_i$ by $\partial\theta$.

Since $\partial\theta$ is constant and equal to $\dfrac{2\pi}{(n-1)}$, where n is the number of uniformly spaced points on the circle, the values of sin $\partial\theta$ and cos $\partial\theta$ need to be calculated only once.

Problem 1

Generate a circle of radius 2 with center located at (2,2) with eight unique points on the circle.

Solution

Two approaches are considered:

(*i*) Generate an origin-centered circle of radius 2 and then translate the circle by 2 in the *x* and *y* planes.

(*ii*) Generate an origin-centered unit circle, then scale by 2 units and finally translate by 2 units in the *x* and *y* directions.

We will adopt the second approach.

Since the circle is a closed curve, the first point ($\theta = 0$) and the last point ($\theta = 2\pi$) coincide. Thus to obtain *n* equi spaced points on the circle it is necessary to calculate $n + 1$ points. $n = (n + 1) = 8$

Thus

$$\delta\theta = \frac{2\pi}{(n+1-1)} = \frac{2\pi}{n} = \frac{2\pi}{8} = \frac{\pi}{4}$$

Using the parametric equation of the circle and starting with $\theta = 0$ yields initial values of *x* and *y*.

$$x_1 = r\cos\theta_1 - r\cos(0) = 1$$
$$y_1 = r\sin\theta_1 + r\sin(0) = 0$$

Now using the parametric equation of the circle, the other seven points are obtained.

$$\sin\delta\theta = \sin\frac{\pi}{4} = \frac{\sqrt{2}}{2}$$

$$\cos\delta\theta = \cos\frac{\pi}{4} = \frac{\sqrt{2}}{2}$$

and

$$x_2 = x_1\cos\delta\theta - y_1\sin\delta\theta$$
$$= 1 \times \frac{\sqrt{2}}{2} - 0$$
$$= \frac{\sqrt{2}}{2}$$

$$y_2 = x_1\sin\delta\theta - y_1\cos\delta\theta$$
$$= 1 \times \frac{\sqrt{2}}{2} + 0 = \frac{\sqrt{2}}{2}$$

Results of the other points are shown in Table 5.1.

Table 5.1 Coordinates of a circle

i	x_i	y_i
1	1	0
2	$\dfrac{\sqrt{2}}{2}$	$\dfrac{\sqrt{2}}{2}$
3	0	1
4	$-\dfrac{\sqrt{2}}{2}$	$\dfrac{\sqrt{2}}{2}$
5	-1	0
6	$-\dfrac{\sqrt{2}}{2}$	$-\dfrac{\sqrt{2}}{2}$
7	0	-1
8	$\dfrac{\sqrt{2}}{2}$	$-\dfrac{\sqrt{2}}{2}$

Recalling the results of 2D transformation,

$$[T_T]=[S][T]=\begin{bmatrix} 2 & 0 & 0 \\ 0 & 2 & 0 \\ 0 & 0 & 1 \end{bmatrix}\begin{bmatrix} 1 & 0 & 0 \\ 0 & 1 & 0 \\ 2 & 2 & 1 \end{bmatrix}=\begin{bmatrix} 2 & 0 & 0 \\ 0 & 2 & 0 \\ 2 & 2 & 1 \end{bmatrix}$$

$$[x_1,y_1,z_1][T]=\begin{bmatrix} 1 & 0 & 1 \end{bmatrix}\begin{bmatrix} 2 & 0 & 0 \\ 0 & 2 & 0 \\ 2 & 2 & 1 \end{bmatrix}=\begin{bmatrix} 4 & 2 & 1 \end{bmatrix}$$

The final results are shown in Table 5.2.

Table 5.2 Coordinates after transformation

i	x_i	y_i
1	4	2
2	3.41	3.41
3	2	4
4	0.586	3.414
5	0	2
6	0.586	0.586
7	2	0
8	3.414	0.586

5.3 PARAMETRIC REPRESENTATION OF AN ELLIPSE

The desired point distribution can be obtained by considering the parametric representation of an origin-centered ellipse of semi-major axis a and semi-minor axis b given by:

$$x = a \cos \theta$$

$$y = b \sin \theta$$

$$0 \leq \theta \leq 2\pi$$

where θ varies from 0 to 2π and sweeps out the entire ellipse. Again, assuming a fixed number of points on the ellipse's perimeter allows an efficient algorithm to be developed using the sum of angles. The Cartesian coordinates of any point on an origin-centered ellipse are

$$x_{i+1} = a \cos (\theta_i + \delta\theta)$$

$$y_{i+1} = b \cos (\theta_i + \delta\theta)$$

where $\delta\theta = \dfrac{2\pi}{(n-1)}$ is the fixed increment in θ, n is the number of points on the perimeter, and θ_i is the value of the parameter for the point at x_i, y_i.

Using the sum of angles yields

$$x_{(i+1)} = a \left[\cos \theta_i \cos \delta\theta - \sin \theta_i \sin \delta\theta\right] \qquad ...(5.3)$$

$$y_{(i+1)} = b \left[\cos \theta_i \sin \delta\theta + \sin \theta_i \cos \delta\theta\right] \qquad ...(5.4)$$

But

$$x_i = a \cos \theta_i$$

$$y_i = b \sin \theta_i$$

Putting these values in Eqs (5.3) and (5.4)

$$x_{(i+1)} = x_i \cos \delta\theta - \frac{a}{b} y_i \sin \delta\theta$$

$$y_{(i+1)} = \frac{b}{a} x_i \sin \delta\theta + y_i \cos \delta\theta$$

Since $\delta\theta$ and a and b are constants, an efficient algorithm, again utilizing only four multiples—both addition and subtraction within the inner loop—is obtained.

Problem 2

Generate an ellipse with semi-major axis $a = 4$ and semi-minor axis $b = 1$ inclined 30° to the horizontal with center at 2,2. Illustrate using 32 points.

Solution

First, an origin-centered ellipse is generated. To illustrate the results, 32 unique points on the ellipse are generated requiring $n = 33$ because the first and last points coincide. However, to conserve space, only points in the first quadrant are illustrated. Thus the parameter range is:

$$0 \le \theta \le \frac{\pi}{2}$$

$$\delta\theta = \frac{2\pi}{(n-1)} = \frac{2\pi}{32} = \frac{\pi}{16}$$

Starting with $\theta = 0$, the initial values of x and y are:

$$x_1 = a \cos \theta_1 = 4 \cos (0) = 4$$

$$y_1 = b \sin \theta_1 = 1 \sin (0) = 0$$

Then
$$\frac{a}{b} = 4, \frac{b}{a} = \frac{1}{4}$$

and

$$\sin \delta\theta = \sin \frac{\pi}{16} = 0.195$$

$$\cos \delta\theta = \cos \frac{\pi}{16} = 0.981$$

Now using the parametric equation of ellipse,

$$x_2 = x_1 \cos \delta\theta - \frac{a}{b} y_1 \sin \delta\theta$$

$$= 4(0.981) - 4 \times 0 = 3.92$$

$$y_2 = \frac{a}{b} x_1 \sin \delta\theta + y_1 \cos \delta\theta$$

$$= \frac{1}{4} \times 4 \times (0.195) + 0$$

$$= 0.195$$

Results of the other points are shown in Table 5.3.

Table 5.3 Coordinates of the ellipse

i	x_i	y_i
1	4	0
2	3.92	0.195
3	3.696	0.383
4	3.326	.556
5	2.828	0.707
6	2.222	0.831
7	1.531	0.924
8	0.780	0.981

To perform 2D transformation, first rotate about the origin by $\alpha = 30°$ CCW and then translate the center to the point (2,2).

$$[T_T] = [R][T] = \begin{bmatrix} \cos\alpha & \sin\alpha & 0 \\ -\sin\alpha & \cos\alpha & 0 \\ 0 & 0 & 1 \end{bmatrix} \begin{bmatrix} 1 & 0 & 0 \\ 0 & 1 & 0 \\ 2 & 2 & 1 \end{bmatrix}$$

$$= \begin{bmatrix} 0.866 & 0.5 & 0 \\ -0.5 & 0.866 & 0 \\ 0 & 0 & 1 \end{bmatrix} \begin{bmatrix} 2 & 0 & 0 \\ 0 & 2 & 0 \\ 2 & 2 & 1 \end{bmatrix}$$

$$= \begin{bmatrix} 0.866 & 0.5 & 0 \\ -0.5 & 0.866 & 0 \\ 2 & 2 & 1 \end{bmatrix}$$

Applying this transformation to (x, y).

$$\begin{bmatrix} x_1 & y_1 & z_1 \end{bmatrix} [T_T] = \begin{bmatrix} 4 & 0 & 1 \end{bmatrix} \begin{bmatrix} 0.866 & 0 & 0 \\ -0.5 & 0.866 & 0 \\ 2 & 2 & 1 \end{bmatrix} = \begin{bmatrix} 5.464 & 4 & 1 \end{bmatrix}$$

Table 5.4 Coordinates after transformation

i	x_i	y_i
1	5.464	4.0
2	5.3	4.131
3	5.009	4.179
4	4.603	4.144
5	4.096	4.027
6	3.509	3.831
7	2.864	3.565
8	2.185	3.240

5.4 PARAMETRIC REPRESENTATION OF A PARABOLA

Consider an origin-centered parabola opening to the right, that is, with the axis of symmetry being the positive x-axis. The upper limb of such a parabola is shown in Fig. 5.2. In rectangular coordinates, the parabola is represented in non-parametric form by:

$$y^2 = 4\,ax$$

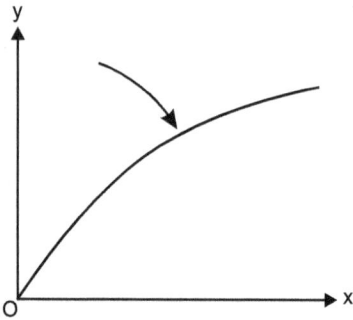

Fig. 5.2 A parabola

A parametric representation is given by:

$$x = \tan^2 \phi$$
$$y = \pm 2\sqrt{a \cdot \tan \phi}$$

where $0 \le \theta \le \dfrac{\pi}{2}$. Although this provides an adequate representation of a parabola, Smith points out that it does not yield a figure with the maximum inscribed area, and this is not the most efficient visual representation.

An alternate parametric representation that does not yield the maximum inscribed area is:

$$x = a,\ \theta^2$$
$$y = 2\ a\theta$$

where $0 \le \theta \le \infty$ sweeps out an entire upper limb of parabola. The parabola, unlike the ellipse, is not a closed curve. Thus the amount of parabola to be displayed must be limited by choosing a minimum and maximum value of θ.

This can be done in a variety of ways. If the range of the x coordinate is limited, then

$$\theta_{min} = \sqrt{\frac{x_{min}}{a}}, \theta_{max} = \frac{y_{max}}{2a} \qquad \qquad ...(5.5a)$$

If the range of the y coordinate is limited, then

$$\theta_{min} = \sqrt{\frac{y_{min}}{2a}}, \theta_{max} = \frac{y_{max}}{2a} \qquad \qquad ...(5.5b)$$

After establishing θ_{min} and/or θ_{max}, the parabola in the first quadrant is generated. Parabolas in other quadrants with displaced centers or at other orientations are obtained using reflection, rotation, and translation.

This parabola can also be generated incrementally. Assuming a fixed number of points on the parabola yields a fixed increment in θ.

Consider $\qquad\qquad \theta_i + 1 = \theta_i + \delta\theta$

The parametric equation of parabola becomes:

$$x_i = a \cdot \theta_i^2$$
$$y_i = 2a\theta_i$$

and

$$\begin{aligned} x_{(i+1)} &= a \cdot (\theta_i + \delta\theta)^2 \\ &= a \cdot \left[\theta_i^2 + 2a\theta_i\delta\theta + \delta\theta^2 \right] \\ &= a \cdot \theta_i^2 + 2a\theta_i\delta\theta + a\delta\theta^2 \\ x_{(i+1)} &= x_i + y_i\delta\theta + a\delta\theta^2 \qquad\qquad ...(5.6) \end{aligned}$$

Similarly

$$\begin{aligned} y_{(i+1)} &= 2a \cdot (\theta_i + \delta\theta) \\ &= 2a \cdot \theta_i + 2a\theta\delta \\ y_{(i+1)} &= y_i + 2a\delta\theta \qquad\qquad ...(5.7) \end{aligned}$$

Problem 3

Generate the parabolic segment in the first quadrant for $1 \leq x \leq 4$ for a parabola given by

$$x = a \cdot \theta^2 = \theta^2 \quad \text{and} \quad y = 2a\theta = 2\theta, \quad \text{i.e., } a = 1$$

Solution

First, it is necessary to determine the limits of θ.

The range of x coordinates is given by $1 \leq x \leq 4$

$$x_{min} = 1 \quad \text{and} \quad x_{max} = 4$$

$$\theta_{min} = \sqrt{\frac{x_{min}}{a}} = \sqrt{\frac{1}{1}} = 1$$

$$\theta_{max} = \sqrt{\frac{x_{max}}{a}} = \sqrt{\frac{4}{1}} = 2$$

For 10 points on the parabolic segment

$$\delta\theta = \frac{(\theta_{max} - \theta_{min})}{n-1} = \frac{2-1}{10-1} = \frac{1}{9}$$

Starting with $\theta_1 = \theta_{min} = 1$, $x_1 = 1$ yelds

$$y_1 = 2a\theta_1 = 2x1x1 = 2$$

From Eqs (5.6) and (5.7)

$$x_2 = x_1 + y_1\delta\theta + a(\delta\theta)^2 = 1 + 2\cdot\frac{1}{9} + 1\cdot\left(\frac{1}{9}\right)^2$$

$$x_2 = 1.235$$

$$y_2 = y_1 + 2a\delta\theta = 2 + 2.1\times\frac{1}{9}$$

$$y_2 = 2.222$$

The final results are shown in Table 5.5.

Table 5.5 Coordinates of the parabola

i	x_i	y_i
1	1.0	2.0
2	1.235	2.222
3	1.494	2.444
4	1.778	2.667
5	2.086	2.889
6	2.420	3.111
7	2.778	3.333
8	3.160	3.556
9	3.568	3.778

Problem 4

Map 15 points of a parabola $y^2 = 4ax$ for x varying from -1.4 to $+1.4$ and $a = 100$. Rotate it through $14.5°$ and shift origin $(-3, -2)$. Generate the numerical solution.

Also write a computer program to generate an image of this parabola.

Solution

Generate the parabolic segment in the first quadrant for x varying from -1.4 to $+1.4$ and $a = 100$.

First it is necessary to determine the limits of θ.

$$x_{min} = 1.4 \text{ and } x_{max} = +1.4$$

$$\theta_{min} = \sqrt{\frac{x_{min}}{a}} = \sqrt{\frac{-1.4}{100}}$$

$$\theta_{max} = \sqrt{\frac{x_{max}}{a}} = \sqrt{\frac{1.4}{100}}$$

$\theta_{min} = \infty$. To solve this problem consider the parabolic segment of the first quadrant only.

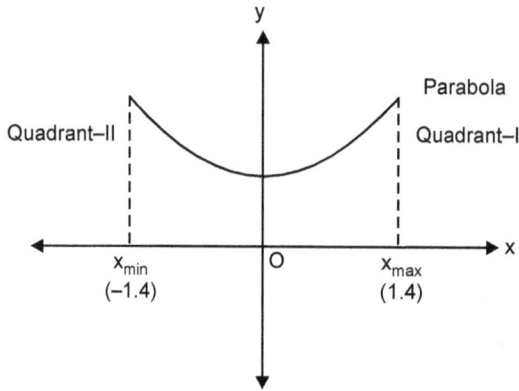

If we consider the parabolic segment only in the first quadrant, then $x_{max} = 1.4$ and $x_{min} = 0$

Therefore

$$\theta_{min} = \sqrt{\frac{x_{min}}{a}} = \sqrt{\frac{0}{100}} = 0$$

$$\theta_{max} = \sqrt{\frac{x_{max}}{a}} = \sqrt{\frac{1.4}{100}}$$

Now calculate the coordinates of the parametric segment in the first quadrant as shown in the previous example.

5.5 PARAMETRIC REPRESENTATION OF A HYPERBOLA

An origin-centered rectangular hyperbola with the x-axis as the axis of symmetry can be generated by the following non-parametric equation:

$$\frac{x^2}{a^2} - \frac{y^2}{b^2} = 1$$

A parametric representation of the hyperbola that yields the polygon with maximum inscribed area is:

$$x = a \cos h\theta$$

$$y = a \sin h\theta$$

The hyperbolic functions are defined as $\cosh\theta = \dfrac{\left(e^{\theta}+e^{-\theta}\right)}{2}$ and $\sinh\theta = \dfrac{\left(e^{\theta}-e^{-\theta}\right)}{2}$.

As θ varies from 0 to ∞ the hyperbola is traced out. The sum of angles formula for $\cos h$ and $\sin h$ are:

$$\cosh(\theta + \delta\theta) = \cosh\delta\theta\ \cosh\delta\theta + \sin\delta\theta\ \sinh\delta\theta$$

$$\sinh(\theta + \delta\theta) = \sinh\delta\theta\ \cosh\delta\theta + \cosh\theta\ \sinh\delta\theta$$

Rewriting the above equations,

$$x_{(i+1)} = a\left[\cosh\delta\theta\ \cosh\delta\theta + \sinh\theta\ \sinh\delta\theta\right]$$

$$y_{(i+1)} = a\left[\sinh\delta\theta\ \cosh\delta\theta + \cosh\theta\sinh\delta\theta\right]$$

$$x_{(i+1)} = x_i\cosh\delta\theta + \frac{a}{b}y_i\sinh\theta\delta$$

$$y_{(i+1)} = \frac{b}{a}x_i\sinh\delta\theta + y_i\cosh\delta\theta$$

Again the maximum and minimum values of θ must be set in order to limit the extent of the hyperbola. Considering the branch of the hyperbola in the first and fourth quadrants and plotting the portion of the hyperbola for $x_{min} \leq x \leq x_{max}$ then:

$$\theta_{min} = \cos h^{-1}\left(\frac{x_{min}}{a}\right)$$

$$\theta_{max} = \cos h^{-1}\left(\frac{x_{max}}{a}\right)$$

where the inverse hyperbolic cosine is obtained from:

$$\cos h^{-1}x = \ln\left(x+\sqrt{x^2-1}\right)$$

Other lines are similarly determined. An example of the first quadrant portion of a hyperbola generated using this technique is shown.

Problem 5

Use the parametric representation to generate eight points on the hyperbolic segment in the first quadrant with $a = 2$, $b = 1$ for $4 \leq x \leq 8$.

Solution

First, the parametric limits are determined.

$$\theta_{\min} = \cos h^{-1}\left(\frac{x_{\max}}{a}\right) = \ln\left(\frac{x_{\max}}{a} + \sqrt{\left(\frac{x_{\max}}{a}\right)^2 - 1}\right)$$

$$= \ln\left(4 + \sqrt{16 - 1}\right)$$

$$= 2.063$$

Similarly

$$\theta_{\min} = 1.317$$

Thus

$$\delta\theta = \frac{\left(\theta_{\max} - \theta_{\min}\right)}{n-1} = \frac{2.063 - 1.317}{7} = 0.107$$

$$\cos h(\delta\theta) = \cos h(0.107) = \frac{\left(e^{0.107} + e^{-0.107}\right)}{2} = 1.006$$

and

$$\sin h(\delta\theta) = \sin h(0.107) = \frac{\left(e^{0.107} - e^{-0.107}\right)}{2} = 0.107$$

With

$$\theta_1 = \theta_{\min}$$
$$x_1 = a\cos h(\theta_{\min}) = 2\cos h(1.317) = 4.00$$
$$y_1 = b\sin h(\theta_{\min}) = 1 \cdot \sin h(1.317) = 1.732$$

Then

$$x_2 = x_1 \cos h\delta\theta + \frac{a}{b} y_1 \sin h\delta\theta$$

$$= 4(1.006) + 2(1.732)(0.107)$$

$$x_2 = 4.393$$

$$y_2 = \frac{b}{a} x_1 \sin h\delta\theta + y_1 \cos h\delta\theta$$

$$= \frac{1}{2}(4)(0.107) + (1.732)(1.006)$$

$$y_2 = 1.956$$

The final results are shown in Table 5.6.

Table 5.6 Coordinates of the hyperbola

i	x_i	y_i
1	4	1.732
2	4.393	1.956
3	4.836	2.201
4	5.334	2.472
5	5.892	2.771
6	6.512	3.102
7	7.218	3.468
8	8	3.873

Problem 6

A hyperbola is defined as

$$\frac{x^2}{9} - \frac{y^2}{16} = 1$$

Compute at least 10 points to map the hyperbola using parametric relationship to support y between -2.5 and $+2.5$. Rotate this hyperbola through $45°$ and shift the origin to $(5, 3)$.

Solution

$$a = 3, \quad b = 4$$

First, the parametric limits are determined.

$$y = b \sin h\theta$$

$$\theta_{max} = \sin h^{-1}\left(\frac{y_{max}}{b}\right) = \sin h^{-1}\left(\frac{+2.5}{4}\right) = 0.590$$

$$\theta_{min} = \sin h^{-1}\left(\frac{y_{min}}{b}\right) = \sin h^{-1}\left(\frac{-2.5}{4}\right) = 0.590$$

Thus

$$\delta\theta = \frac{\left(\theta_{max} - \theta_{min}\right)}{n-1} = \frac{0.590 - \left(-0.590\right)}{10 - 1} = 0.131$$

$$\cos h(\delta\theta) = \cos h \, (0.131) = 0.131$$

and

$$\sin h \, (\delta\theta) = \sin h \, (0.131) = 1.008$$

With

$$\theta_1 = \theta_{min}$$

$$x_1 = a \cos h \, (\theta_{min}) = 3 \cos h \, (-0.590) = 3.537$$

$$y_1 = b \sin h \, (\theta_{min}) = 4 \cos h \, (-0.590) = -2.5$$

Then

$$x_2 = x_1 \cos h\delta\theta + \frac{a}{b} y_1 \sin h\delta\theta$$

$$= 3.567 - 0.246$$

$$x_2 = 3.32$$

$$y_2 = \frac{b}{a} x_1 \sin h\delta\theta + y_1 \cos h\delta\theta$$

$$= 0.619 + \left(-2.52\right)$$

$$y_2 = -1.9$$

The final results are shown in Table 5.7.

Table 5.7 Coordinates of the hyperbola

i	x_i	y_i
1	3.537	– 2.5
2	3.32	– 1.9
3	3.15	– 1.29
4	3.04	– 0.749
5	3.00	– 0.26
6	2.99	0.26
7	3.04	0.749
8	3.15	1.9
9	3.32	1.9
10	3.537	2.5

Total transformation is given by

$$[T_T] = [R][T]$$

$$[R] = \begin{bmatrix} \cos 45 & \sin 45 & 0 \\ -\sin 45 & \cos 45 & 0 \\ 0 & 0 & 1 \end{bmatrix} = \begin{bmatrix} 0.707 & 0.707 & 0 \\ -0.707 & 0.707 & 0 \\ 0 & 0 & 1 \end{bmatrix}$$

$$[T] = \begin{bmatrix} 1 & 0 & 0 \\ 0 & 1 & 0 \\ 5 & 3 & 1 \end{bmatrix}$$

$$[T_T] = \begin{bmatrix} 0.707 & 0.707 & 0 \\ -0.707 & 0.707 & 0 \\ 0 & 0 & 1 \end{bmatrix} \begin{bmatrix} 1 & 0 & 0 \\ 0 & 1 & 0 \\ 5 & 3 & 1 \end{bmatrix} = \begin{bmatrix} 0.707 & 0.707 & 0 \\ -0.707 & 0.707 & 0 \\ 5 & 3 & 1 \end{bmatrix}$$

$$[P'] = \begin{bmatrix} 3.537 & -2.5 & 1 \end{bmatrix} \begin{bmatrix} 0.707 & 0.707 & 0 \\ -0.707 & 0.707 & 0 \\ 5 & 3 & 1 \end{bmatrix} = \begin{bmatrix} 9.268 & 3.733 & 1 \end{bmatrix}$$

Table 5.8 shows the transformed coordinates.

Table 5.8 Coordinates after transformation

i	x_i	y_i
1	9.268	3.733
2	8.691	4.003
3	8.13	4.31
4	7.678	4.61
5	7.30	4.93
6	6.93	5.3
7	6.61	5.788
8	6.31	6.13
9	6.00	6.69
10	5.733	7.268

EXERCISES

1. Generate an origin-centered circle with radius 2 with eight unique points on the circle.

2. Write an algorithm to find the incremental values of x and y using the parametric representation of an ellipse.

3. Generate an ellipse with semi-major axis $a = 6$ and semi-minor axis $b = 2$ with center at $(6, 4)$. Illustrate using eight points.

4. Derive the parametric equations of a parabola.

5. Generate the parabolic segment in the first quadrant for $1.5 \leq x \leq 5.5$ for a parabola given by $x = 4\theta^2$ and $y = 8\theta$.

6. Generate the parabolic segment in first quadrant for x varying as -1.8 to $+2.6$ and $a = 60$.

7. Derive the parametric representation of a hyperbola.

8. A hyperbola is defined as

$$\frac{x^2}{4} - \frac{y^2}{9} = 1$$

   Compute at least eight points to map the hyperbola using a parametric relationship to support y between -1.6 to $+1.6$.

OBJECTIVE QUESTIONS

5.1 Using a non-parametric equation would result in
   (a) poor representation
   (b) high computational time
   (c) non-uniformly spaced points
   (d) all of the above

5.2 Parametric representation of an origin-centered circle of radius "r" is given by $x = r \cos \theta$, $y = \sin \theta$ where varying parameter θ is given by
   (a) $0 \leq \theta \leq \dfrac{\pi}{2}$
   (b) $0 \leq \theta \leq \pi$
   (c) $0 \leq \theta \leq 2\pi$
   (d) $0 \leq \theta \leq 4\pi$

5.3 In kinematics, the trajectory of a point is usually represented by a parametric equation with
   (a) angle as a parameter
   (b) distance as a parameter
   (c) time as a parameter
   (d) none of above

5.4 A parameter in the parametric representation of some physical quantity may be

(*a*) a geometric variable   (*b*) distance

(*c*) time   (*d*) selected arbitrarily for convenience

5.5 "More than one set of parametric equations may specify the same curve"— this statement is

(*a*) true   (*b*) false

(*c*) can't say   (*d*) all of the above

5.6 Parametric representation of an origin-centered ellipse of semi-major axis "*a*" and semi-minor axis "*b*" given by $x = a \cos \theta$, $y = b \sin \theta$, where θ is the varying parameter, is given by

(*a*) $0 \leq \theta \leq \dfrac{\pi}{2}$ (*b*) $0 \leq \theta \leq \pi$

(*c*) $0 \leq \theta \leq 2\pi$ (*d*) $0 \leq \theta \leq 4\pi$

5.7 Parametric representation of a parabola is given by $x = a \cdot \theta^2$, $y = 2a\theta$, where varying parameter θ is given by

(*a*) $0 \leq \theta \leq \dfrac{\pi}{2}$ (*b*) $0 \leq \theta \leq \infty$

(*c*) $0 \leq \theta \leq 2\pi$ (*d*) $0 \leq \theta \leq 4\pi$

5.8 Parametric representation of a parabola is given by $x = a \cdot \theta^2$, $y = 2a\theta$, where $0 \leq \theta \leq \infty$ sweeps out an

(*a*) entire upper limb of parabola   (*b*) entire lower limb of parabola

(*c*) entire parabola   (*d*) minimum inscribed area

5.9 A parabola, unlike a circle and an ellipse, is a

(*a*) open curve   (*b*) closed curve

(*c*) can't say   (*d*) none of these

5.10 A non-origin-centered circle can be generated by

(*a*) generating an origin-centered circle of a given radius and translating it to its center position

(*b*) generating an origin-centered circle of unit radius and then performing transformations (scaling and translation)

(*c*) True

(*d*) False

5.11 A parametric representation of a hyperbola yields a polygon with maximum inscribed area $x = a\cos h\theta$, $y = a\sin h\theta$, where varying parameter θ is given by

(a) $0 \le \theta \le \dfrac{\pi}{2}$

(b) $0 \le \theta \le 4\pi$

(c) $0 \le \theta \le 2\pi$

(d) $0 \le \theta \le \infty$

ANSWERS

5.1 (*d*)	**5.2** (*c*)	**5.3** (*c*)	**5.4** (*d*)
5.5 (*a*)	**5.6** (*c*)	**5.7** (*c*)	**5.8** (*a*)
5.9 (*a*)	**5.10** (*c*)	**5.11** (*d*)	

Chapter 6
PARAMETRIC REPRESENTATION OF SPACE CURVES

6.1 INTRODUCTION TO SPACE CURVES

In the previous chapter we discussed the parametric representation of planar curves. Suppose you wish to make a 2D view of a ship, then you draw it in the xy plane. But if you need to make a 3D model of a ship, then you have to control the path of the space curve meticulously to get the desired profile. Now, to control the profile of the space curve, we have to convert the space curve into its parametric representation. Some examples of space curves are cubic curves, Bézier curves, B-spline curves, non-uniform rational B-splines (NURBS), etc.

6.2 CUBIC SPLINE

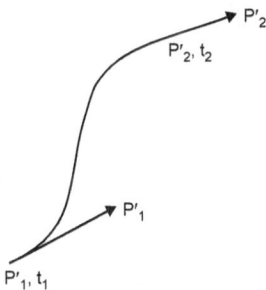

Fig. 6.1 A single-segment cubic curve

The equation of a single-segment parametric cubic spline is given by:

$$P(t) = \sum_{i=1}^{4} B_i t^{i-1} \quad t_1 \leq t \leq t_2$$

where t_1, t_2 are the parameter values at the beginning and end of the segment. Each Cartesian component has a formulation similar to $P(t)$.

$$x(t) = \sum_{i=1}^{4} B_{ix} t^{i-1} \quad t_1 \leq t \leq t_2$$

$$y(t) = \sum_{i=1}^{4} B_{iy} t^{i-1} \quad t_1 \leq t \leq t_2$$

$$z(t) = \sum_{i=1}^{4} B_{iz} t^{i-1} \quad t_1 \leq t \leq t_2$$

Parametric representation of a single cubic curve is given by:

$$P(t) = B_1 + B_2 t + B_3 t^2 + B_4 t^3 \qquad \ldots (6.1)$$

Where t varies from $t_1 \leq t \leq t_2$

Cubic spline is a series of single segment cubic curves

Segment spanning two points where B_1, B_2, B_3, B_4 are the four boundary conditions, and

t is a varying parameter in which $t_1 \leq t \leq t_2$.

$P(t)$ is the position vector of any point on the cubic spline segment

$$P(t) = \begin{bmatrix} x(t) & y(t) & z(t) \end{bmatrix}$$

P_1 and P_2 are position vectors at the ends of the segment.

P'_1 and P'_2 are tangent vectors at the ends of the segment, which are derivatives w.r.t. t.

To find P'_1 and P'_2 let us differentiate Eq. (6.1)

$$P'(t) = B_2 + 2B_3 t + 3B_4 t^2$$

Assuming $t_1 = 0$ and applying four boundary conditions, namely

$$P(0) = P_1 \quad (\text{point at } t = t_1 = 0)$$
$$P(t_2) = P_2 \quad (\text{point at } t = t_2 = 1)$$
$$P'(0) = P'_1 \quad (P' \text{at } t = t_1 = 0)$$
$$P'(t_2) = P'_2 \quad (P' \text{at } t = t_2 = 1)$$

four equations for the unknown $B_i's$ can be obtained as follows:

$$P(t) = B_1 + B_2 t + B_3 t^2 + B_4 t^3 \qquad\qquad\qquad ...(6.2)$$
$$P(0) = B_1$$
$$P'(t) = B_2 + 2B_3 t + 3B_4 t^2$$
$$P'(0) = B_2$$
$$P(t_2) = B_1 + B_2 t^2 + B_3 t_2^2 + B_4 t_2^3$$
$$P'(t_2) = B_2 + 2B_3 t^2 + 3B_4 t_2^2$$

$P(t_2)$ is nothing but P_2, and $P'(t_2)$ is nothing but P'_2.

$$P(t_2) = P_2 = P_1 + P'_1 t_2 + B_3 t_2^2 + B_4 t_2^3 \qquad\qquad ...(6.3)$$
$$P'(t_2) = P'_2 = P'_1 + 2B_3 t_2 + 3B_4 t_2^2 \qquad\qquad\quad ...(6.4)$$

Solving Eqs. (6.3) and (6.4) simultaneously, we get

$$B_3 = \frac{3(P_2 - P_1)}{t_2^2} - \frac{2P'_1}{t_2} - \frac{P'_2}{t_2}$$

Similarly,

$$B_4 = \frac{2(P_1 - P_2)}{t_2^3} - \frac{P'_1}{t_2^2} - \frac{P'_2}{t_2^2}$$

These values of B_1, B_2, B_3, B_4 determine the cubic spline segment.

Substituting the values of B_1, B_2, B_3, B_4 in Eq. (6.2), we have

$$P(t) = P_1 + P'_1 t + \left\{ \frac{3(P_2 - P_1)}{t_2^2} - \frac{2P'_1}{t_2} - \frac{P'_2}{t_2} \right\} t^2$$
$$+ \left\{ \frac{2(P_1 - P_2)}{t_2^3} - \frac{P'_1}{t_2^2} - \frac{P'_2}{t_2^2} \right\} t^3 \qquad\qquad ...(6.5)$$

Eq. (6.5) is for a single cubic spline segment. However, to represent a complete curve, multiple segments are joined together. Two adjacent segments are shown in Fig. 6.2.

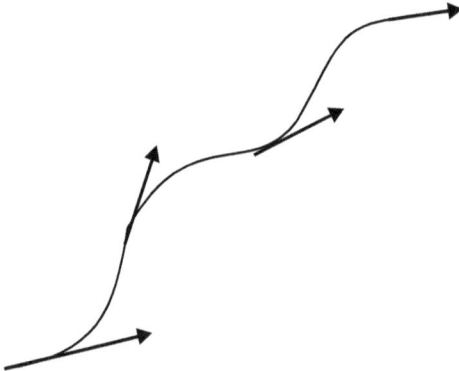

Fig. 6.2 Multi-segment cubic spline

Supposing the position vectors P_1, P_2, P_3, P_4. The tangent vectors P'_1, P'_2, P'_3, P'_4 and parameter values t_2, t_3 and t_4 are known, then applying Eq. (6.5) to each of the two segments yields their shapes.

Finding Tangent Vectors at Internal Points

It is unlikely that the tangent vectors P'_2 and P'_3 at the internal joints between two segments are known. Assuming that the end tangent vectors P'_1 and P'_4 are known, the tangent vector at the internal joints (four-point cubic spline) can be determined.

$$
\begin{bmatrix}
1 & 0 & 0 & 0 \\
t_3 & 2(t_2+t_3) & t_2 & 0 \\
0 & t_4 & 2(t_4+t_3) & t_3 \\
0 & 0 & 0 & 1
\end{bmatrix}
\begin{bmatrix}
P'_1 \\
P'_2 \\
P'_3 \\
P'_4
\end{bmatrix}
=
\begin{bmatrix}
P'_1 \\
\dfrac{3}{t_2 \cdot t_3}\left\{t_2^2\left(P_3-P_2\right)+t_3^2\left(P_2-P_1\right)\right\} \\
\dfrac{3}{t_3 \cdot t_4}\left\{t_3^2\left(P_4-P_3\right)+t_4^2\left(P_3-P_2\right)\right\} \\
P'_4
\end{bmatrix}
$$

Determining a point on the spline segment at τ

Now the position vector at a series of three single-segment joints is given by:

$$P(\tau) = \begin{bmatrix} F_1(\tau) F_2(\tau) F_3(\tau) F_4(\tau) \end{bmatrix} \begin{bmatrix} P_1 \\ P_2 \\ P'_1 \\ P'_2 \end{bmatrix}$$

$$P(\tau) = \begin{bmatrix} F \end{bmatrix} \begin{bmatrix} G \end{bmatrix}$$

where

$$F_1(\tau) = 2\tau^3 - 3\tau^2 + 1$$
$$F_2(\tau) = -2\tau^3 + 3\tau^2$$
$$F_3(\tau) = \tau(\tau^2 - 2\tau + 1) \cdot t^4$$
$$F_4(\tau) = \tau(\tau^2 - \tau) t^4$$
$$t_2 = \sqrt{(x_2 - x_1)^2 + (y_2 - y_1)^2}$$
$$t_3 = \sqrt{(x_3 - x_2)^2 + (y_3 - y_2)^2}$$
$$t_4 = \sqrt{(x_4 - x_3)^2 + (y_4 - y_3)^2}$$

Problem 1

A curve is passing through points A (1, 1, 1) and B (2, 5, −3). It is expected to be a cubic spline; the parameter t ranges from 0 to 1 and the values of the differentials are as follows:

At A:

$$\frac{dx}{dt} = 0.2, \frac{dy}{dt} = 1, \text{ and } \frac{dz}{dt} = 0.3$$

At B:

$$\frac{dx}{dt} = -0.2, \frac{dy}{dt} = -1.2, \text{ and } \frac{dz}{dt} = 0.4$$

Find the cubic spline equation by computing the coordinates of the point and tangent direction at $t = 0.7$.

Solution

Let us solve the problem using a parametric equation.

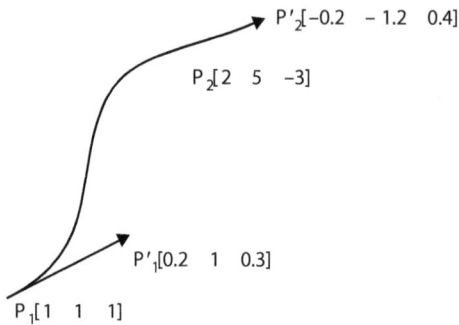

$P'_2[-0.2 \quad -1.2 \quad 0.4]$

$P_2[2 \quad 5 \quad -3]$

$P'_1[0.2 \quad 1 \quad 0.3]$

$P_1[1 \quad 1 \quad 1]$

Fig. 6.3 A cubic curve

The parameter t ranges from 0 to 1, which means $t_2 = 1$. Parametric equation of the spline is given by:

$$P(t) = B_1 + B_2 t + B_3 t^2 + B_4 t^3$$

$$B_1 = P_1 = \left[\left(1 \; 1 \; 1\right)\right]$$

$$B_2 = P'_1 = \left[\left(0.2 \; 1 \; 0.3\right)\right]$$

$$B_3 = \frac{3(P_2 - P_1)}{t_2^2} - \frac{2P'_1}{t_2^2} - \frac{P'_2}{t_2}$$

$$= \frac{3\begin{bmatrix}1 \; 4 \; 4\end{bmatrix}}{1} - \frac{2\begin{bmatrix}0.2 \; 1 \; 0.3\end{bmatrix}}{1} - \frac{\begin{bmatrix}-0.2 \; -1.2 \; 0.4\end{bmatrix}}{1}$$

$$= \begin{bmatrix}3 \; 12 \; -12\end{bmatrix} - \begin{bmatrix}0.4 \; 2 \; 0.6\end{bmatrix} - \begin{bmatrix}-0.2 \; -1.2 \; 0.4\end{bmatrix}$$

$$= \begin{bmatrix}2.8 \; 11.2 \; -13\end{bmatrix}$$

$$B_4 = \frac{2(P_1 - P_2)}{t_2^3} - \frac{P'_1}{t_2^2} - \frac{P'_2}{t_2^2}$$

$$= \frac{2\begin{bmatrix}1 \; -4 \; 4\end{bmatrix}}{1} + \frac{\begin{bmatrix}0.2 \; 1 \; 0.3\end{bmatrix}}{1} + \frac{\begin{bmatrix}-0.2 \; -1.2 \; 0.4\end{bmatrix}}{1}$$

$$= \begin{bmatrix}-2 \; -8.2 \; 8.7\end{bmatrix}$$

Parametric representation of the cubic spline is given by:

$$P(t) = \begin{bmatrix} 1 & 1 & 1 \end{bmatrix} + \begin{bmatrix} 0.2 & 1 & 0.3 \end{bmatrix} t + \begin{bmatrix} 2.8 & 11.2 & -13 \end{bmatrix} t^2 + \begin{bmatrix} -2 & -8.2 & 8.7 \end{bmatrix} t^3$$

$$P(0.7) = \begin{bmatrix} 1 & 1 & 1 \end{bmatrix} + \begin{bmatrix} 0.2 & 1 & 0.3 \end{bmatrix}(0.7) + \begin{bmatrix} 2.8 & 11.2 & -13 \end{bmatrix}(0.7)^2$$

$$+ \begin{bmatrix} -2 & -8.2 & 8.7 \end{bmatrix}(0.7)^3$$

$$P(0.7) = \begin{bmatrix} 1.824 & 4.37 & -2.18 \end{bmatrix}$$

To find the position vector of the tangent:

$$P'(t) = B_2 + 2B_3 t + 3B_4 t^2$$

$$= \begin{bmatrix} 0.2 & 1 & 0.3 \end{bmatrix} + 2\begin{bmatrix} 2.8 & 11.2 & -13 \end{bmatrix} t + 3\begin{bmatrix} -2 & -8.2 & 8.7 \end{bmatrix} t^2$$

$$P'(0.7) = \begin{bmatrix} 0.2 & 1 & 0.3 \end{bmatrix} + 2\begin{bmatrix} 2.8 & 11.2 & -13 \end{bmatrix}(0.7) + 3\begin{bmatrix} -2 & -8.2 & 8.7 \end{bmatrix}(0.7)^2$$

$$P'(0.7) = \begin{bmatrix} 1.18 & 4.626 & -5.111 \end{bmatrix}$$

Problem 2

The direction of the tangent at A (4, 4, 4) is given by (0.25, 3, 0.25). Similarly the tangent at B (5, 6, 7) is given by (2, 1, −2). Generate an equation of the spline connecting these two points. Use a parametric equation defining the parameter "t" and find the position vector and tangent direction at $t = 0.6$. Solve using a parametric equation.

Solution

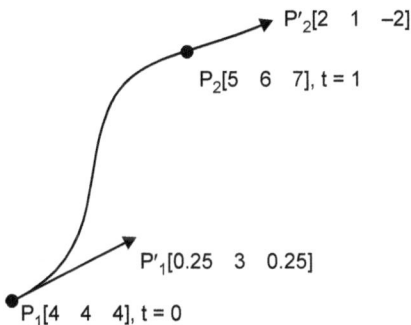

Fig. 6.4 A cubic curve

The parameter t ranges from 0 to 1, which means $t_2 = 1$. Parametric equation of the spline is given by:

$$P(t) = B_1 + B_2 t + B_3 t^2 + B_4 t^3$$

Parametric equation of the cubic spline in Cartesian form is given by:

$$x(t) = B_{1x} + B_{2x}t + B_{3x}t^2 + B_{4x}t^3 \qquad ...(6.6)$$
$$y(t) = B_{1y} + B_{2y}t + B_{3y}t^2 + B_{4y}t^3 \qquad ...(6.7)$$
$$z(t) = B_{1z} + B_{2z}t^2 + B_{3z}t^2 + B_{4z}t^3 \qquad ...(6.8)$$

At P_1, $x = 4$ and $t = 0$. Putting these values in Eq. (6.6), we have

$$B_{1x} = 4$$

At P_2, $x = 5$ and $t = 1$. Putting these values in Eq. (6.6), we have

$$5 = 4 + B_{2x}(1) + B_{3x}(1)^2 + B_{4x}(1)^3$$

$$B_{2x} + B_{3x} + B_{4x} = 1 \qquad ...(6.9)$$

At P_1, $\left(\dfrac{dx}{dt}, \dfrac{dy}{dt}, \dfrac{dz}{dt} \right) = (0.25, 3, 0.25); t = 0$

Differentiating Eq. (6.6) w.r.t. t, we have

$$\frac{dx}{dt} = B_{2x} + 2B_{3x}t + 3B_4t^2 \qquad ...(6.10)$$

At P_1, $\left(\dfrac{dx}{dt} \right) = (0.25); t = 0$

Putting these values in Eq. (6.10),

$$B_{2x} = 0.25$$

So Eq. (6.9) becomes:

$$0.25 + B_{3x} + B_{4x} = 1$$

$$B_{3x} + B_{4x} = 0.75 \qquad ...(6.11)$$

At P_2, $\left(\dfrac{dx}{dt}, \dfrac{dy}{dt}, \dfrac{dz}{dt} \right) = (2, 1, -2); t = 1$

At P_2, $\left(\dfrac{dx}{dt} \right) = (2); t = 1$

Putting these values in Eq. (6.10), we have

$$2 = 0.25 + 2B_{3x} + 3B_{4x}$$

$$2B_{3x} + 3B_{4x} = 1.75 \qquad \qquad ...(6.12)$$

Solving Eqs (6.11) and (6.12) simultaneously, we get

$$\mathbf{B_{3x} = 0.5}$$

$$\mathbf{B_{4x} = 0.25}$$

Parametric equation in terms of $x(t)$ is given by:

$$x(t) = 4 + 0.25t + 0.5t^2 + 0.25t^3 \qquad \qquad ...(A)$$

Parametric equation in terms of $y(t)$ is given by:

$$y(t) = B_{1y} + B_{2y}t + B_{3y}t^2 + B_{4y}t^3$$

At P_1, $y = 4$ and $t = 0$. Putting these values in Eq. (6.7), we have

$$\mathbf{B_{1y} = 4}$$

At P_2, $y = 6$ and $t = 1$. Putting these values in Eq. (6.6), we have

$$6 = 4 + B_{2y}(1) + B_{3y}(1)^2 + B_{4y}(1)^3$$

$$B_{2y} + B_{3y} + B_{4y} = 2 \qquad \qquad ...(6.13)$$

At P_1, $\left(\dfrac{dx}{dt}, \dfrac{dy}{dt}, \dfrac{dz}{dt} \right) = \left(0.25 \ \ 3 \ \ 0.25 \right)$; $t = 0$

Differentiating Eq. (6.7) w.r.t. t,

$$\frac{dy}{dt} = B_{2y} + 2B_{3y}t + 3B_{4y}t^2 \qquad \qquad ...(6.14)$$

At P_1, $\left(\dfrac{dy}{dt} \right) = \left(3 \right)$; $t = 0$

Putting these values in Eq. (6.14),

$$\mathbf{B_{2y} = 3}$$

So Eq. (6.13) becomes:

$$3 + B_{3y} + B_{4y} = 2$$

$$B_{3y} + B_{4y} = -1 \qquad ...(6.15)$$

At P_2, $\left(\dfrac{dx}{dt}, \dfrac{dy}{dt}, \dfrac{dz}{dt} \right) = (2, 1, -2); t = 1$

At P_2, $\left(\dfrac{dy}{dt} \right) = (1); t = 1$

Putting these values in Eq. (6.14)

$$1 = 3 + 2B_{3y} + 3B_{4y}$$

$$2B_{3y} + 3B_{4y} = -2 \qquad ...(6.16)$$

Solving Eqs (6.15) and (6.16) simultaneously, we get

$$\boldsymbol{B_{3y} = -1}$$

$$\boldsymbol{B_{4y} = 0}$$

Parametric equation in terms of $y(t)$ is given by:

$$y(t) = 4 + 3t - t^2 \qquad ...(B)$$

Parametric equation in terms of $z(t)$ is given by:

$$z(t) = B_{1z} + B_{2z}t + B_{3z}t^2 + B_{4z}t^3$$

At P_1, $z = 4$ and $t = 0$. Putting these values in Eq. (6.8), we have

$$\boldsymbol{B_{1z} = 4}$$

At P_2, $z = 7$ and $t = 1$. Putting these values in Eq. (6.8), we have

$$7 = 4 + B_{2z}(1) + B_{3z}(1)^2 + B_{4z}(1)^3$$

$$B_{2z} + B_{3z} + B_{4z} = 3 \qquad ...(6.17)$$

At P_1, $\left(\dfrac{dz}{dt}, \dfrac{dy}{dt}, \dfrac{dz}{dt} \right) = (0.25, 3, 0.25); t = 0$

Differentiating Eq. (6.8) w.r.t. t,

$$\frac{dz}{dt} = B_{2z} + 2B_{3z}t + 3B_{4z}t^2$$

...(6.18)

At P_1, $\left(\dfrac{dz}{dt}\right) = (0.25)$; $t = 0$

Putting these values in Eq. (6.18), we have

$$B_{2z} = 0.25$$

So Eq. (6.17) becomes:

$$0.25 + B_{3z} + B_{4z} = 3$$

$$B_{3z} + B_{4z} = 2.75$$

...(6.19)

At P_2, $\left(\dfrac{dx}{dt}, \dfrac{dy}{dt}, \dfrac{dz}{dt}\right) = (2, 1, -2)$; $t = 1$

At P_2, $\left(\dfrac{dz}{dt}\right) = (-2)$; $t = 1$

Putting these values in Eq. (6.18), we have

$$-2 = 0.25 + 2B_{3z} + 3B_{4z}$$

$$2B_{3z} + 3B_{4z} = -2.25$$

...(6.20)

Solving Eqs (6.19) and (6.20) simultaneously, we get

$$B_{3z} = 10.5$$

$$B_{4z} = -7.75$$

Parametric equation in terms of $z(t)$ is given by:

$$x(t) = 4 + 0.25t + 10.5t^2 - 7.75t^3$$

...(C)

Parametric equation of spline in Cartesian form is given by:

$$x(t) = 4 + 0.25t + 0.5t^2 + 0.25t^3$$

...(A)

$$y(t) = 4 + 3t - t^2$$

...(B)

$$x(t) = 4 + 0.25t + 10.5t^2 - 7.75t^3$$

...(C)

Position vector at $t = 0.6$ is obtained by putting $t = 0.6$ in the above equations.

$$x(0.6) = 4.384$$

$$y(0.6) = 5.44$$

$$z(0.6) = 6.256$$

To find the position of tangent vectors, put the values of the boundary conditions and $t = 0.6$ in the following equations:

$$\frac{dx}{dt} = 0.25 + t + 0.75t^2$$

$$\frac{dy}{dt} = 3 - 2t$$

$$\frac{dz}{dt} = 0.25 + 21t - 23.25t^2$$

At $t = 0.6$,

$$\left(\frac{dx}{dt}, \frac{dy}{dt}, \frac{dz}{dt} \right) = \left(1.12 \quad 1.8 \quad 4.48 \right)$$

6.3 B-SPLINE

B-splines automatically take care of continuity, with exactly one control vertex per curve segment. There are many types of B-splines: their degree may be different (linear, quadratic, cubic, etc.) and they may be uniform or non-uniform. With uniform B-splines, continuity is always one degree lower than the degree of each curve piece. Uniform B-splines do not interpolate control points, unless you repeat a control point three times, but then all derivatives also vanish ($= 0$) at that point. To do interpolation with non-zero derivatives, you must use non-uniform B-splines with repeated knots. To go from a B-spline to a Bézier, both B-spline and Bézier curves represent cubic curves, so either can be used to go from one to the other.

Recall that a point on a curve can be represented by a matrix equation:

- P is the column vector of control points
- M depends on the representation: $M_{\text{B-spline}}$ and $M_{\text{Bézier}}$
- T is the column vector containing t^3, t^2, t, 1

By equating points generated by each representation, we can find a matrix $M_{\text{B-spline->Bézier}}$ that converts B-spline control points into Bézier control points.

B-spline to Bézier matrix

$$M_{\text{B-spline}\rightarrow\text{Bézier}} = \frac{1}{6}\begin{bmatrix} 1 & 4 & 1 & 0 \\ 0 & 4 & 2 & 0 \\ 0 & 2 & 4 & 0 \\ 0 & 1 & 4 & 1 \end{bmatrix}$$

$$\begin{bmatrix} P_{0,\text{Bezier}} \\ P_{1,\text{Bezier}} \\ P_{2,\text{Bezier}} \\ P_{3,\text{Bezier}} \end{bmatrix} = \frac{1}{6}\begin{bmatrix} 1 & 4 & 1 & 0 \\ 0 & 4 & 2 & 0 \\ 0 & 2 & 4 & 0 \\ 0 & 1 & 4 & 1 \end{bmatrix}\begin{bmatrix} P_{0,\text{B-spline}} \\ P_{1,\text{B-spline}} \\ P_{2,\text{B-spline}} \\ P_{3,\text{B-spline}} \end{bmatrix}$$

Advantages

The perspective is invariant, so it can be evaluated in screen space. It can perfectly represent conic sections: circles, ellipses, etc. Piece-wise cubic curves cannot do this.

B-spline Surfaces

• Are defined just like Bézier surfaces:

$$X\left(x,t\right) = \sum_{j=0}^{m}\sum_{k=0}^{n} P_{j,k}\, B_{j,d}(s)B_{k,d}(t)$$

• Continuity is automatically obtained everywhere.

• *But* the control points must be in a rectangular grid.

Blending Functions

$$x\left(t\right) = \sum_{i=0}^{3} P_i\, B_{i,4}\left(t\right)$$

$$= P_0\frac{1}{6}(1-3t+3t^2-t^3)+P_1\frac{1}{6}(4-6t^2+3t^3)+P_2\frac{1}{6}\left(1+3t+3t^2-3t^3\right)+P_3\frac{1}{6}\left(t^3\right)$$

6.4 BÉZIER CURVES

A cubic Bézier curve is used in most graphic applications. This curve is generally used for designing automobile panels. It needs four control points. The curve generally follows the shape of a defining polygon. These four control points completely specify the curve, as shown in Fig. 6.5.

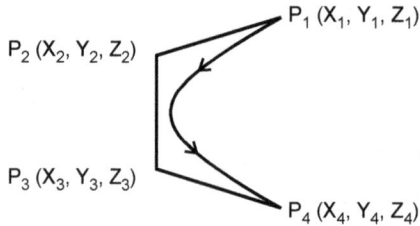

Fig. 6.5 Control points of a Bézier curve

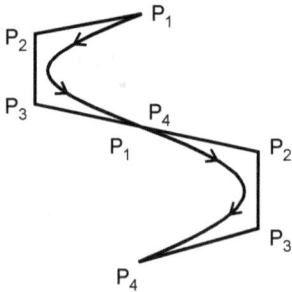

Fig. 6.6 A multi-segment Bézier curve

The curve begins at the first control point and ends at the fourth. Thus, to connect two Bézier curves, join the first control point of the second curve with the fourth control point of the first curve. At the start of the curve, it is tangent to the line connecting the first and second control points. Similarly, at the end of the curve it is tangent to the line connecting the third and fourth control points.

Parametric Equation

- The Bézier curve can be completely described by a parametric equation.

  ➢ $x = x_4 u^3 + 3x_3 u^2(1 - u) + 3x_2 u(1 - u)^2 + x_1(1 - u)^3$

  ➢ $y = y_4 u^3 + 3y_3 u^2(1 - u) + 3y_2 u(1 - u)^2 + y_1(1 - u)^3$

  ➢ $z = z_4 u^3 + 3z_3 u^2(1 - u) + 3z_2 u(1 - u)^2 + z_1(1 - u)^3$

- (x_1, y_1, z_1), (x_2, y_2, z_2), (x_3, y_3, z_3), (x_4, y_4, z_4) are the coordinates of four control points.
- u is the factor that increases from 0 to 1 as the curve moves from the first to the fourth control point.
- (x, y, z) is the coordinate of the pixel representing the Bézier curve.

Properties of a Bézier Curve

- The curve must pass through the first and fourth control points, i.e., P_1 and P_4.
- The curve is tangent to the line (P_1-P_2 and P_3-P_4).
- The Bézier curve has a parametric formulation and equation, which allows it to represent multiple values and shapes.
- If the first and last control points coincide, then the curve is closed (Fig. 6.7).

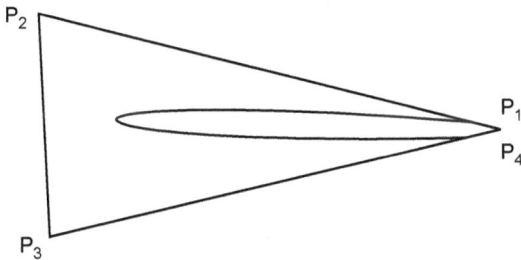

Fig. 6.7 A closed Bézier curve

The curve does not provide localized control, i.e., when moving any one control point, the entire curve changes.

Zero-Order Continuity

- In this case the joint between the two curves must be smooth.
- To achieve zero-order continuity at the joint, it is necessary to control the first control point of the second curve and the fourth control point of the first curve.

Problem 3

The coordinates of four control points related to the curve are

$$P_1 = (2,2,0)$$
$$P_4 = (2,3,0)$$
$$P_3 = (3,3,0)$$
$$P_4 = (3,2,0)$$

Write the equation of the resultant Bézier curve. Also draw the curve by finding the coordinates at $u = 0$, $u = 0.25$, $u = 0.5$, $u = 0.75$ and $u = 1$.

Solution

Parametric equations of the Bézier curve are:

$$x = x_4 u^3 + 3x_3 u^2 (1-u) + 3x_2 u(1-u)^2 + x_1 (1-u)^3$$
$$y = y_4 u^3 + 3y_3 u^2 (1-u) + 3y_2 u(1-u)^2 + y_1 (1-u)^3$$
$$z = z_4 u^3 + 3z_3 u^2 (1-u) + 3z_2 u(1-u)^2 + z_1 (1-u)^3$$

Putting the values of the coordinates, we have:

$$x = 3u^3 + 9u^2 (1-u) + 6u(1-u)^2 + 2(1-u)^3$$
$$y = 2u^3 + 9u^2 (1-u) + 9u(1-u)^2 + 2(1-u)^3$$
$$z = 0$$

For $u = 0$

$$x = 3u^3 + 9u^2 (1-u) + 6u(1-u)^2 + 2(1-u)^3 = 2$$
$$y = 2u^3 + 9u^2 (1-u) + 9u(1-u)^2 + 2(1-u)^3 = 2$$
$$z = 0$$

For $u = 0.25$

$$x = 3u^3 + 9u^2 (1-u) + 6u(1-u)^2 + 2(1-u)^3 = 2.15$$
$$y = 2u^3 + 9u^2 (1-u) + 9u(1-u)^2 + 2(1-u)^3 = 2.56$$
$$z = 0$$

For $u = 0.5$

$$x = 3u^3 + 9u^2(1-u) + 6u(1-u)^2 + 2(1-u)^3 = 2.5$$

$$y = 2u^3 + 9u^2(1-u) + 9u(1-u)^2 + 2(1-u)^3 = 2.75$$

$$z = 0$$

For $u = 0.75$

$$x = 3u^3 + 9u^2(1-u) + 6u(1-u)^2 + 2(1-u)^3 = 2.84$$

$$y = 2u^3 + 9u^2(1-u) + 9u(1-u)^2 + 2(1-u)^3 = 2.56$$

$$z = 0$$

For $u = 1$

$$x = 3u^3 + 9u^2(1-u) + 6u(1-u)^2 + 2(1-u)^3 = 3$$

$$y = 2u^3 + 9u^2(1-u) + 9u(1-u)^2 + 2(1-u)^3 = 2$$

$$z = 0$$

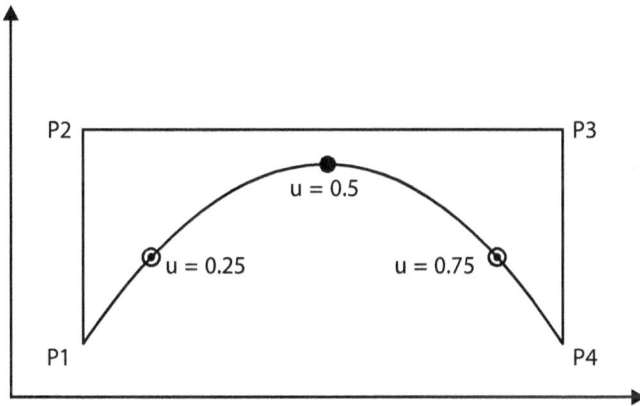

Fig. 6.8 Graphical representation

6.5 NON-UNIFORM RATIONAL B-SPLINES

The non-uniform rational B-spline (NURBS) is a mathematical model commonly used in computer graphics for generating and representing curves and surfaces that offers great flexibility and precision to handle both analytic (surfaces defined by common mathematical formulae) and modeled shapes. The NURBS equation is a general form that can represent both B-spline and NURBS curves. A Bézier curve is a special case of a B-spline curve, so the NURBS equation can also represent Bézier and rational Bézier curves.

- Uniform B-splines are a special case of B-splines.

- Each blending function is the same.

- A blending function starts at $t = -3$, $t = -2$, $t = -1$, ...

- Each blending function is non-zero for 4 units of the parameter.

- Non-uniform B-splines can have blending functions starting and stopping anywhere, and the blending functions are not all the same.

- NURBS are commonly used in computer-aided design (CAD), manufacturing (CAM), and engineering (CAE), and are part of numerous standards used industry-wide, such as IGES, STEP, ACIS, and PHIGS. NURBS tools are also found in various 3D modeling and animation software packages.

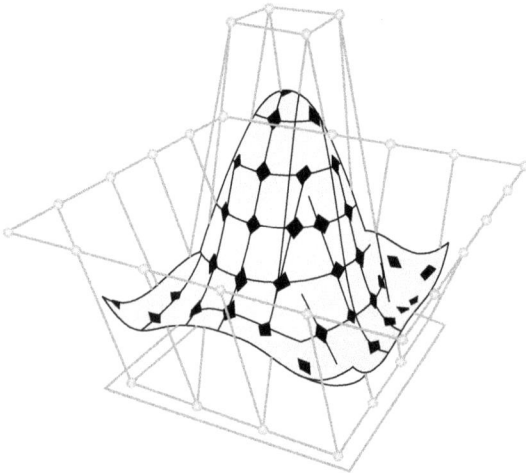

Fig. 6.9 A non-uniform rational B-spline

6.5.1 Control Point

The control points determine the shape of the curve. Typically, each point of the curve is computed by taking a weighted sum of a number of control points. The weight of each point varies according to the governing parameter. Adding more control points allows better approximation to a given curve, although only a certain class of curves can be represented exactly with a finite number of control points.

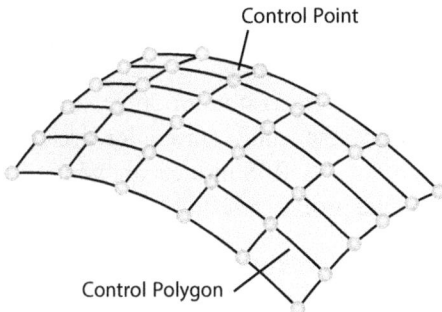

Fig. 6.10 Control polygon and control points on NURBS

The control points can have any dimensionality. 1D points just define a scalar function of the parameter. These are typically used in image processing programs to tune the brightness and color curves. 3D control points are used abundantly in 3D modeling, where they are used in the everyday meaning of the word "point," a location in 3D space. Multidimensional points might be used to control sets of time-driven values, e.g., the different positional and rotational settings of a robot arm. NURBS surfaces are just an application of this.

The knot vector is a sequence of parameter values that determine where and how the control points affect the NURBS curve. Necessary only for internal calculations, knots are usually not helpful to the users of modeling software. Therefore, many modeling applications do not make the knots editable or even visible.

Knot Values

- number of knots =
  num_of_control_points + degree + 1 (or −1 for some APIs)
- The values of knot vectors must be in ascending order.
  - (0, 0, 1, 2, 3) is valid
  - (0, 0, 2, 1, 3) is not valid
- The individual knot values are not meaningful by themselves; only the ratios of the differences between the knot values matter.
  - Hence, the knot vectors (0, 0, 1, 2, 3), and (0, 0, 2, 4, 6) produce the same curve.

Duplicate knot values make a NURBS curve less smooth. At the extreme, a full multiplicity knot in the middle of the knot list means there is a place on the NURBS curve that can be bent into a sharp kink.

NURBS Surfaces

NURBS surfaces are based on curves. The main advantage of using NURBS surfaces over polygons is that NURBS surfaces can create smoother surfaces with fewer control points. NURBS surfaces are especially suited for creating organic smooth surfaces. Besides using primitives, NURBS models are generally constructed by creating curves that will define the profile or shape of an object.

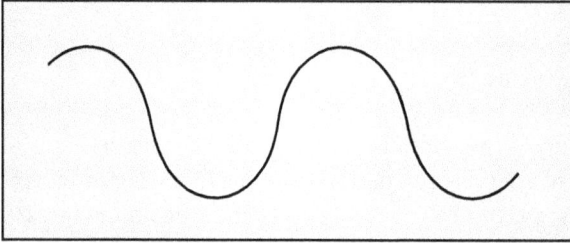

Fig. 6.11 A NURBS curve

NURBS Curves

Control vertices (CVs) control the shape of a curve by pulling the curve out from a straight line. They are the most basic means of controlling NURBS surfaces. In Maya, the first CV or endpoint of a curve is drawn as a box, and the second CV is drawn as a "U". Each additional CV is a dot.

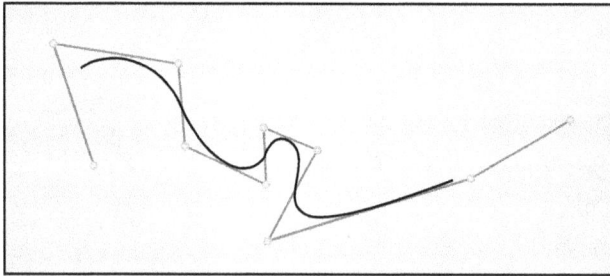

Fig. 6.12 A NURBS curve

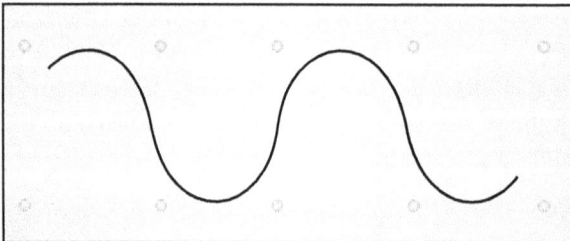

Fig. 6.13 CVs – control points that edit the shape of a curve

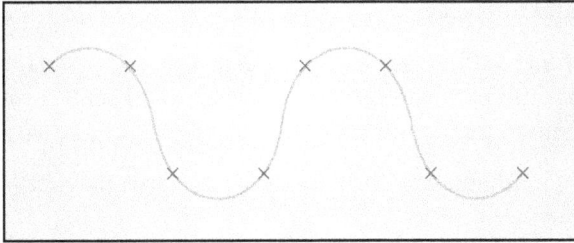

Fig. 6.14 Endpoints reside on a curve and are defined by the shape of the curve

Properties of NURBS

- NURBS have all the properties of a B-spline.

- More versatile modification of a curve becomes possible if the curve is represented by a NURBS equation. It is due to a B-spline curve modified by changing the x, y, and z coordinates, but NURBS curves use homogenous coordinates (x, y, z, h).

- B-splines have degree, control points, and knots, but NURBS have degree, control points, knots, and weights.

  - NURBS equations can exactly represent conic curves (circle, ellipse, parabola, etc.).

  - If projective transformation is applied to a NURBS curve, the result can be constructed from the projective images of its control points.

    Therefore, we do not have to transform the curve to obtain the correct view (without distortion).

- Bézier curves and B-spline curves only satisfy the affine invariance property rather than this projective invariance property. This is because only NURBS curves involve projective transformations.

Rational is generalization of nonrational; thus they carry forward all the analytic and geometric characteristics of their B-spline counterparts.

Also:

– a rational B-spline curve of order k is continuous everywhere.

– curve is invariant to any projective transformation (not only to affine).

– additional control capabilities due to weights.

Uses of NURBS Curves and Surfaces

- They are invariant under affine as well as perspective transformations: operations like rotations and translations can be applied to NURBS curves and surfaces by applying them to their control points.

- They offer one common mathematical form for both standard analytical shapes (e.g., conics) and free-form shapes.

- They provide the flexibility to design a large variety of shapes.

- They reduce memory consumption when storing shapes (compared to simpler methods).

- They can be evaluated reasonably quickly by numerically stable and accurate algorithms.

- Currently, NURBS curves are the standard of curve description in computer graphics.

- They have smooth properties.

- Several ways to control the resulting curve provide great flexibility.

How to Choose a Spline

Bézier curves are good for single segments or patches where a user controls the points. B-splines are good for large continuous curves and surfaces.

NURBS are good when that generality is useful, or when conic sections must be accurately represented (CAD).

EXERCISES

1. The tangent vector at p_1 (1, 3, 1) and p_2 (0, 0, 0) are $i + j + k$ and $- i + 3j - 2k$, respectively. Find the parametric equation of a cubic spline passing through p_1 and p_2. A point p_3 lies on this spline and is defined as distance $(p_1 p_3) =$ distance $(p_2 p_3)$. Find the position vector and tangent direction at point p_3.

2. Generate an equation to cubic spline $P = B_0 + B_1 \cdot t + B_2 \cdot t^2 + B_3 \cdot t^3$ for a point A (3, 4, 5) and B (1, 1, 0). The derivatives along these directions at A are (1, − 1, 0) and at B are (2, − 1, 2). Hence find the coordination at point at $t = 0.25$ on the bridging curve.

3. Explain the Bézier curve. What are its properties?

4. The four vertices of a Bézier polygon are: (1, 1), (2, 3), (4, 3), and (3, 1). Find the equation of the Bézier curve in the parametric form.

5. What do you understand by interpolation and approximation splines? Determine and plot the blending functions of the hermit spline.

6. What is a requirement of synthetic curves? Explain briefly.

OBJECTIVE QUESTIONS

6.1 If the first and last control points of a Bézier curve coincide, then
 (*a*) curve will be closed   (*b*) curve will be open
 (*c*) multiple curves can be joined   (*d*) none of the above

6.2 To join two curves smoothly, it is necessary to control the first control point of the second curve and the last control point of the first curve. This property of the Bézier curve is called
 (*a*) zero-order continuity   (*b*) first-order continuity
 (*c*) third-order continuity   (*d*) higher-order continuity

6.3 In a Bézier curve, trajectory of the curve can be adjusted by controlling
 (*a*) control points   (*b*) segments
 (*c*) curve path   (*d*) none of the above

6.4 A Bézier curve passes through
 (*a*) first and second control points   (*b*) first and third control points
 (*c*) first and fourth control points   (*d*) second and third control points

6.5 A Bézier curve is tangent to segments at
 (*a*) first and second segments   (*b*) first and third segments
 (*c*) first and fourth segments   (*d*) second and third segments

6.6 To join two segments of a cubic spline, the tangent vector at the last point of the first segment and the first point of the second segment must be
 (*a*) same   (*b*) different
 (*c*) unknown   (*d*) none of the above

6.7 A non-uniform rational B-spline used in generating curves and surfaces is a
 (*a*) parametric representation   (*b*) mathematical expression
 (*c*) mathematical model   (*d*) none of the above

6.8 Non-uniform B-splines can have blending functions starting and stopping anywhere and are all

(*a*) same   (*b*) different
(*c*) some same, some different   (*d*) other

6.9 NURBS are part of numerous industry-wide standards such as

(*a*) IGES   (*b*) STEP
(*c*) ACIS   (*d*) PHIGS
(*e*) all of the above

6.10 The control point is computed by taking a weighted sum of a

(*a*) number of control polygons   (*b*) number of knots
(*c*) number of control points   (*d*) none of the above

6.11 The weight of each point varies according to the governing parameter. Adding more control points allows better approximation to a given curve, although only certain curves can be represented exactly with finite control points; these curves are

(*a*) control polygon   (*b*) cubic spline
(*c*) B-spline   (*d*) Bézier curve

6.12 In image processing programs, the brightness and color of the curves can be controlled by

(*a*) control polygon   (*b*) knot
(*c*) control point   (*d*) none of the above

ANSWERS

6.1 (*a*)	**6.2** (*a*)	**6.3** (*a*)	**6.4** (*c*)	**6.5** (*c*)
6.6 (*a*)	**6.7** (*c*)	**6.8** (*b*)	**6.9** (*e*)	**6.10** (*a*)
6.11 (*c*)	**6.12** (*a*)			

7 Chapter PARAMETRIC REPRESENTATION OF SURFACES

7.1 INTRODUCTION TO SURFACES

From the CAD/CAM point of view, surfaces are as important as curves and solids. We need to have an idea of curves for surface creation. In the same way, surfaces form the boundaries of solids. There are two types of surfaces: analytical surfaces and synthetic surfaces. Examples of analytical surfaces are plane surfaces, spheres, and ellipsoids, and examples of synthetic surfaces are bicubic surfaces and Bezier surfaces. The applications of surfaces are in the field of solid modeling of components using CAD software, and representation of data surfaces such as isothermal planes, stress surfaces/contours, etc.

Surface representation is just an extension of representation of curves. We can represent a surface as a series of grid points inside its bounding curves. Surfaces can be in 2D space (planar) or in 3D space (general surfaces). Surface can be described using non-parametric or parametric equations. Surfaces can be represented by equations to pass through all the data points (fitting).

7.2 SURFACE OF REVOLUTION

We know that the simplest method for generating a 3D surface is to revolve a 2D entity, e.g., a line or a plane curve, about an axis in space. Such a surface is called a surface of revolution. The simplest entity that can be rotated about an axis is a point. Provided that it does not lie on the axis, rotating it by 360° (2Π) yields a circle, and rotating it through an angle yields an arc.

Next in complexity is a line segment parallel to and not coincident with the axis of rotation. When rotated through 360° (2Π) it yields a circular cylinder. The radius of a cylinder is the perpendicular distance from the line of the rotation axis. The length of the cylinder is the length of the line segment.

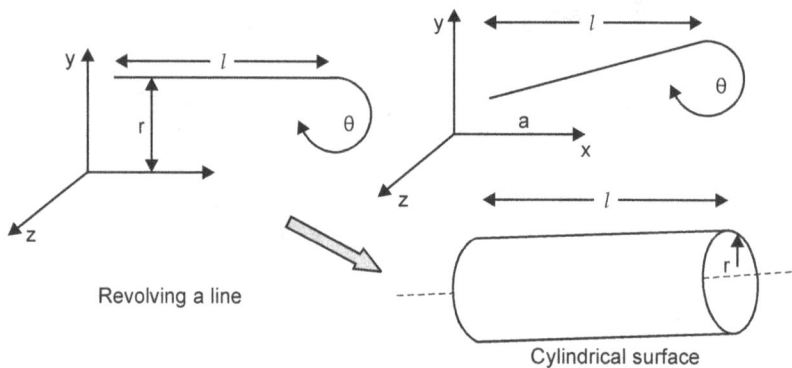

Revolving a line

Cylindrical surface

Fig. 7.1 Revolution of surfaces in parametric form

If the line segment and the axis of rotation are coplanar and the line segment is not parallel to the rotation axis and rotated by 360°, we get a truncated right circular cone. The radius of the cone at each end is the perpendicular distance from the end points of the line segment on the axis of rotation. If the line is perpendicular to the axis of rotation, we get a planar disc. If the line is perpendicular and touches the axis, we get a solid disc.

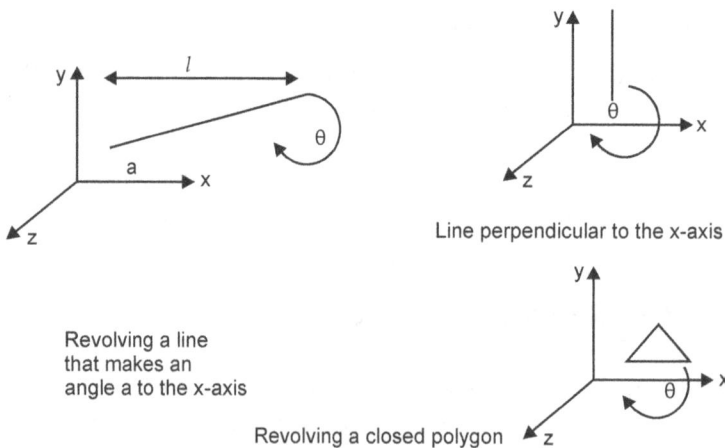

Line perpendicular to the x-axis

Revolving a line
that makes an
angle a to the x-axis

Revolving a closed polygon

Fig. 7.2 Different positions of a line after revolution

- The parametric equation for a point on the surface of revolution is developed by recalling the parametric equation of the entity to be rotated.

- As an example, $P(t) = [x(t)\ y(t)\ z(t)]; 0 \le t \le 1$

- It is the function parameter t.

- Rotation about any axis causes the point to be a function of angle ϕ.

- Thus, a point of surface revolution has two parameters, t and ϕ.

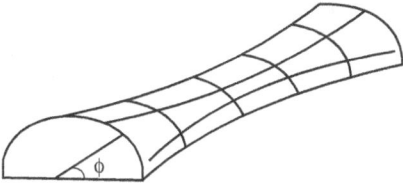

Fig. 7.3 A semi-revolved surface

Fig. 7.3 shows a biparametric function.

For rotation about the x-axis of the entity initially lying in the xy plane, the surface equation would be:

$$Q(t, \phi) = [x(t)\ y(t)\cos \phi\ y(t)\sin \phi] \qquad ...(7.1)$$

Equations of a Line and a Plane in 3D space

Given a point $P = (a, b, c)$, one can draw a vector from the origin to P; such a vector is called the position vector of point P and its coordinates are (a, b, c). Position vectors are usually denoted by $\vec{r}$.

In this section, we derive the equations of lines and planes in 3D space. We do so by finding the conditions for a point that $P = (x, y, z)$ or its corresponding position vector $\vec{r} = (x, y, z)$ must satisfy in order to belong to the object being studied.

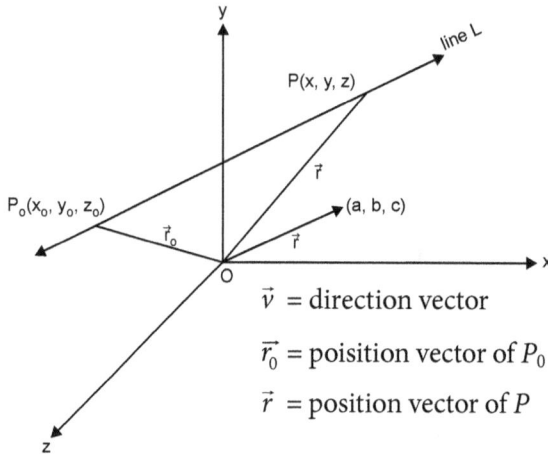

Fig. 7.4

In 3D, like in 2D, a line is uniquely determined when one point and the direction of the line are given. Assume we are given a point $P_0 = (x_0, y_0, z_0)$ on the line and a direction vector $\vec{v} = (a, b, c)$. Our goal is to determine the equation of line L which goes through P_0 and is parallel to $\vec{v}$. Here a, b, c are called the direction numbers of line L.

Let $P(x, y, z)$ be an arbitrary point on line L. We wish to find the coordinates of P that must be satisfied to be on line L.

Vector Equation

In Fig. 7.4, we see that a necessary and sufficient condition for point P to be on line L is that $\overrightarrow{P_0P}$ be parallel to $\vec{v}$. This means there exists a scalar t such that

$$\left(\overrightarrow{P_0P}\right) = t \cdot \vec{v}$$

$$\left(\overrightarrow{P_0P}\right) = \vec{r} - \vec{r_0}$$

$$\vec{r} - \vec{r_0} = t \cdot \vec{v}$$

$$\vec{r} = \vec{r_0} + t \cdot \vec{v}$$

$$t = \text{scalar parameter}$$

$$(x, y, z) = (x_0, y_0, z_0) + t \cdot (a, b, c)$$

$$(x, y, z) = (x_0 + at, y_0 + bt, z_0) + ct$$

$$x = x_0 + at$$

$$y = y_0 + bt$$

$$z = z_0 + ct$$

Problem 1

Consider a line segment with end points $P_1[1\ 1\ 0]$ and $P_2[6\ 2\ 0]$ lying in the xy plane. Rotating the line about the x-axis yields a conical surface. Determine the points on the surface at $t = 0.5$, $\phi = 60°$.

Solution

Parametric equation of the line segment from P_1 to P_2 is:

$$P(t) = [x(t)\ y(t)\ z(t)] = P_1 + (P_2 - P_1)t; \qquad 0 \le t \le 1$$

With Cartesian components,

$$x(t) = x_1 + (x_2 - x_1)t = 1 + 5t$$
$$y(t) = y_1 + (y_2 - y_1)t = 1 + t$$
$$z(t) = z_1 + (z_2 - z_1)t = 0$$

Using Eq. (7.1) point $Q(0.5, 60°)$ on the surface of revolution is:

$$Q(0.5, 60°) = [1 + 5t \quad (1 + t)\cos\phi \quad (1 + t)\sin\phi]$$
$$= [7/3 \quad 3/2\cos 60° \ 3/2\sin 60°]$$
$$= [7/2 \quad 3/4 \quad 1.3]$$
$$= [3.5 \quad 0.75 \quad 1.3]$$
$$x = r\cos\theta, y = \sin\theta; \qquad 0 \le \theta \le \pi$$

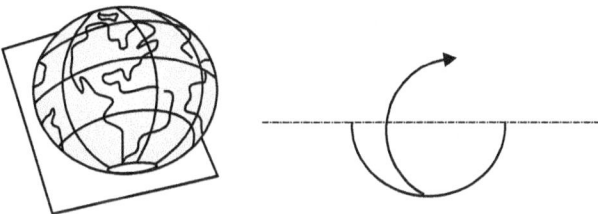

Fig. 7.5 A sphere

Parametric equation of the surface

$$Q(\theta, \phi) = [x(\theta) \quad y(\theta)\cos\phi \quad y(\theta)\sin\phi]; \qquad 0 \le \theta \le \pi; 0 \le \phi \le 2\pi$$
$$= [r\cos\theta \quad r\sin\theta\cos\phi \quad r\sin\theta\sin\phi]$$

Here θ is called latitude angle and ϕ longitude angle

$$x = a\cos\theta; y = b\sin\theta; \qquad 0 \le \theta \le \pi$$

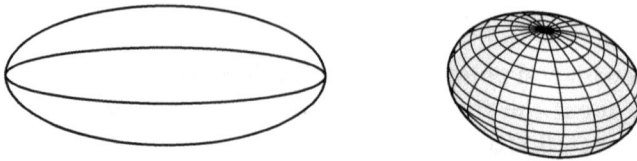

Fig. 7.6 An ellipsoid

Parametric equation of the surface

$$Q(\theta, \phi) = [a \cos \theta \quad b \sin \theta \cos \phi \quad b \sin \theta \sin \phi]; \qquad 0 \leq \theta \leq \pi; 0 \leq \phi \leq 2\pi$$

Or $\quad Q(\theta, \phi) = [b \sin \theta \sin \phi \quad b \sin \theta \cos \phi \quad a \cos \theta]; \qquad 0 \leq \theta \leq \pi; 0 \leq \phi \leq 2\pi$

When the axis of rotation does not pass through the center of the circle or ellipse, we get a torus.

$$x = h + a \cos \theta; y = k + b \sin \theta; \qquad 0 \leq \theta \leq 2\pi$$

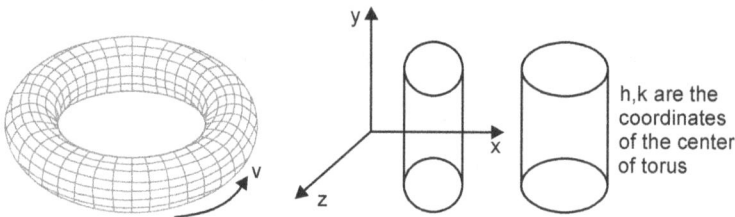

Equation of the surface

Fig. 7.7 A torus

h,k are the coordinates of the center of torus

$$Q(\theta, \phi) = [h + a \cos \theta \, (k + b \sin \theta) \cos \theta \, (\, k + b \sin \theta) \sin \phi];$$
$$0 \leq \theta \leq 2\pi; 0 \leq \phi \leq 2\pi$$

Parametric equation of the surface

$$Q(\theta, \phi) = [a\theta^2 \quad 2a\theta \cos \phi \quad 2a\theta \sin \phi]; \quad 0 \leq \theta \leq \theta_{max}; 0 \leq \phi \leq 2\pi$$
$$x = a\theta^2; y = 2a\theta; \quad 0 \leq \theta \leq \theta_{max}$$

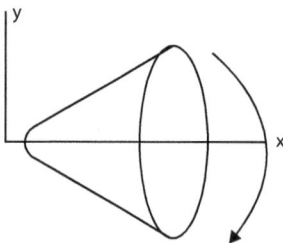

Fig. 7.8 A paraboloid

$$x = a \sec \theta; y = \tan \theta; \qquad 0 \leq \theta \leq \theta_{max}$$

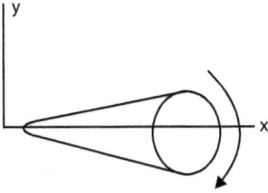

Fig. 7.9 An hyperboloid

Parametric equation of the surface

$$Q(\theta, \phi) = [a \sec \theta \quad b \tan \theta \cos \phi \quad b \tan \theta \sin \phi];$$
$$0 \leq \theta \leq \theta_{max}; 0 \leq \phi \leq 2\pi$$

In general, any space curve can be used to generate a surface of revolution

$$P(t) = [T] [N] [G]$$

$[T]$ = parameter vector

$[N]$ = blending function matrix (normalized)

$[G]$ = geometry information matrix

Now the surface of revolution is defined as:

$$Q(t,\phi) = [T][N][G][S]$$

$$[S_s] = \begin{bmatrix} 1 & 0 & 0 & 0 \\ 0 & \cos\phi & \sin\phi & 0 \\ 0 & 0 & 0 & 0 \\ 0 & 0 & 0 & 1 \end{bmatrix}; t_{min} \leq t \leq t_{max}; 0 \leq \phi \leq 2\pi$$

where

$$[T] = \begin{bmatrix} t_3 & t_2 & t_1 \end{bmatrix}$$

$$[A] = \left(\frac{1}{2}\right) \begin{bmatrix} -1 & 3 & -3 & 1 \\ 2 & -5 & 4 & -1 \\ -1 & 0 & 1 & 0 \\ 0 & 2 & 0 & 0 \end{bmatrix}$$

$$[G] = \begin{bmatrix} P1 \\ P2 \\ P3 \\ P4 \end{bmatrix}$$

7.3 SWEEP SURFACES

Problem 2

A line segment marked by (3.2 4.1 5.5) and (3 4.7 7.8) is rotated about the z-axis through 360°. Generate the parametric equation to the surface of revolution using t and s parameters; both range from 0 to 1. Hence find the equation and position at $Q(t, s)$ at $t = 0.45$ and $s = 0.78$.

Solution

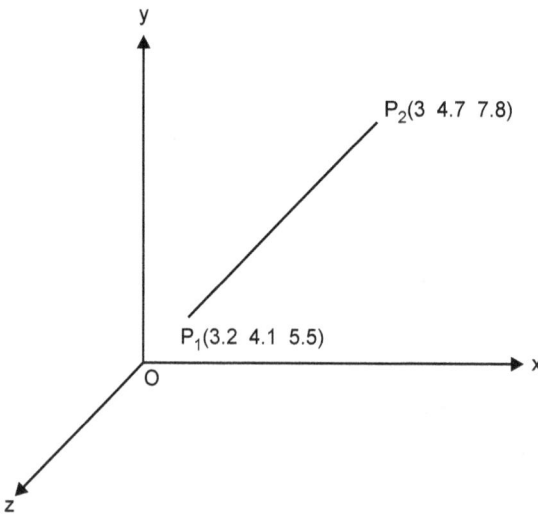

Fig. 7.10 A line in 3D space

Given a line having endpoints P_1 (3.2 4.1 5.5) and P_2 (3 4.7 7.8). This line is rotated about the z-axis to get the surface of revolution.

Parametric representation of the surface of revolution generated is given by:

$$Q(t, s) = [P(t)] \cdot [T_s] \qquad \qquad ...(7.2)$$

where $[P(t)]$ is parametric representation of the geometry to be revolved

$[T_s]$ is sweep transformation

Parametric equation of the line having endpoints P_1, P_2, and t being a varying parameter is given by:

$$P(t) = P_1 + (P_2 - P_1)t \qquad \text{where } 0 \le t \le 1$$

$$[P(t)] = [(x(t) \ y(t) \ z(t) \ 1)] \qquad \qquad ...(7.3)$$

Parametric equation of the line in Cartesian form is given by:

$$x(t) = x_1 + (x_2 - x_1)t$$
$$y(t) = y_1 + (y_2 - y_1)t$$
$$z(t) = z_1 + (z_2 - z_1)t$$
$$x(t) = x_1 + (x_2 - x_1)t$$
$$= 3.2 + [3 - 3.2]t$$
$$= 3.2 - 0.2t$$
$$y(t) = y_1 + (y_2 - y_1)t$$
$$= 4.1 + [4.7 - 4.1]t$$
$$= 4.1 + 0.6t$$
$$z(t) = z_1 + (z_2 - z_1)t$$
$$= 5.5 + [7.8 - 5.5]t$$
$$= 5.5 + 2.3t$$

So parametric equation of the line becomes

$$[P(t)] = [(3.2 - 0.2t) \quad (4.1 + 0.6t) \quad (5.5 + 2.3t) \quad 1]$$

The sweep transformation matrix for rotation by 360° or 2π rad about the z-axis is given by

$$[T_s] = \begin{bmatrix} \cos(2\pi s) & \sin(2\pi s) & 0 & 0 \\ -\sin(2\pi s) & \cos(2\pi s) & 0 & 0 \\ 0 & 0 & 1 & 0 \\ 0 & 0 & 0 & 1 \end{bmatrix}$$

Parametric equation of the surface of revolution is obtained by putting these values in Eq. (7.3).

$$Q(t,s) = \left[(3.2 - 0.2t)(4.1 + 0.6t)(5.5 + 2.3t) \ 1 \right] \begin{bmatrix} \cos(2\pi s) & \sin(2\pi s) & 0 & 0 \\ -\sin(2\pi s) & \cos(2\pi s) & 0 & 0 \\ 0 & 0 & 1 & 0 \\ 0 & 0 & 0 & 1 \end{bmatrix}$$

Now we have obtained the point on this surface at $t = 0.45$ and $s = 0.78$.

So

$$Q(0.45, 0.78) = \left[(3.2 - 0.2(0.45) \ \ (4.1 + 0.6(0.45)) \ \ (5.5 + 2.3(0.45)) \ 1) \right] \times$$

$$\begin{bmatrix} \cos(2\pi(0.78)) & \sin(2\pi(0.78)) & 0 & 0 \\ -\sin(2\pi(0.78)) & \cos(2\pi(0.78)) & 0 & 0 \\ 0 & 0 & 1 & 0 \\ 0 & 0 & 0 & 1 \end{bmatrix}$$

$$Q(0.45, 0.78) = \left[(3.41 \ \ 4.37 \ \ 6.54 \ \ 1) \right]$$

$$\begin{bmatrix} 0.187 & -0.982 & 0 & 0 \\ 0.982 & 0.187 & 0 & 0 \\ 0 & 0 & 1 & 0 \\ 0 & 0 & 0 & 1 \end{bmatrix}$$

$$Q(0.45, 0.78) = \left[4.93 \ \ -2.53 \ \ 6.54 \ \ 1 \right]$$

7.4 HELICAL SPRING

Problem 3

An helical spring is defined by $x = R\cos\theta$, $y = R\sin\theta$ and $z = B\theta$. Assume $R = 5$, $B = 0.8$. Rotate the spring through 60° about the *y*-axis and hence find its orthogonal projection in *xy* plane.

Solution

Parametric equation of the helical spring in a Cartesian form is given by:

$$x = R\cos\theta$$

$$y = R\sin\theta$$

$$z = B\theta$$

where $R = 5$ and $B = 0.8$

Parametric equation of the helical spring is given by:

$$[P(t)] = [(R\cos\theta) \ (R\sin\theta) \ B\theta \ 1]$$

Rotation transformation by 60° about the y-axis is given by

$$R = \begin{bmatrix} \cos 60 & 0 & \sin 60 & 0 \\ 0 & 1 & 0 & 0 \\ -\sin 60 & 0 & \cos 60 & 0 \\ 0 & 0 & 0 & 1 \end{bmatrix}$$

$$[P'] = [P(t)][R]$$

$$= \left[(R\cos\theta)\ (R\sin\theta)\ B\theta\ 1 \right] \begin{bmatrix} \cos 60 & 0 & \sin 60 & 0 \\ 0 & 1 & 0 & 0 \\ -\sin 60 & 0 & \cos 60 & 0 \\ 0 & 0 & 0 & 1 \end{bmatrix}$$

$$= \left[(5\cos\theta)\ (5\sin\theta)\ 0.8\theta\ 1 \right] \begin{bmatrix} 0.5 & 0 & 0.86 & 0 \\ 0 & 1 & 0 & 0 \\ -0.86 & 0 & 0.5 & 0 \\ 0 & 0 & 0 & 1 \end{bmatrix}$$

$$= \left[(2.5\cos\theta - 0.688)\ 5\sin\theta\ (4.3\cos\theta + 0.4\theta)\ 1 \right]$$

$$x' = 2.5\cos\theta$$
$$y' = 5\sin\theta$$
$$z' = 4.3\cos\theta + 0.4\theta$$

Orthogonal projection about the xy plane is given by:

$$\begin{bmatrix} 1 & 0 & 0 & 0 \\ 0 & 1 & 0 & 0 \\ 0 & 0 & 0 & 0 \\ 0 & 0 & 0 & 1 \end{bmatrix}$$

So orthogonal projection of the helical spring about the xy plane is given by:

$$\begin{bmatrix} 1 & 0 & 0 & 0 \\ 0 & 1 & 0 & 0 \\ 0 & 0 & 0 & 0 \\ 0 & 0 & 0 & 1 \end{bmatrix}$$

$$P' = [(2.5\cos\theta - 0.688\theta) \sin\theta \quad (4.3\cos\theta + 0.4\theta) \quad 1)]$$
$$[(2.5\cos\theta - 0.688\theta) \, 5\sin\theta \quad 0 \quad 1)]$$
$$x' = 2.5\cos\theta - 0.688\theta$$
$$y' = 5\sin\theta$$
$$z' = 0$$

EXERCISES

1. Why are surface models required? Name some analytical surfaces and synthetic surfaces.

2. Write the mathematical equations of B-spline and Bezier surfaces.

3. What is the application of synthetic surfaces?

4. Derive the equation of a plane in 3D space.

5. A line has endpoint coordinates as P_1 [2, 3, 0] and P_2 [7, 5, 0]. Rotating the line about the z-axis yields a conical surface. Determine the equation of the surface and find the point at $t = 0.4$, $\phi = 55°$.

6. Derive the surfaces generated by revolving conic sections.

7. Generate the parametric equation of the surface of revolution when a line segment having endpoint coordinates (1.1, 4.3, 6.1) and (3.2, 7.7, 2.1) is rotated about the y-axis through 360°. The t and s parameters range from 0 to 1. Hence find the equation and position at $\theta(t, s)$ at $t = 0.38$, $s = 0.81$.

OBJECTIVE QUESTIONS

7.1 An example of analytical surface is
(a) bicubic surface
(b) Bezier surface
(c) ellipsoid
(d) none of the above

7.2 An example of synthetic curve is
(a) plane surface
(b) bicubic surface
(c) Bezier surface
(d) all of the above

7.3 If a line segment and axis of rotation are coplanar and the line segment is not parallel to the rotation axis, then the solid generated by rotating the line about the axis by 360° is

(a) right circular cone
(b) right circular cylinder
(c) sphere
(d) truncated right circular cone

7.4 When the axis of rotation does not pass through the center of the circle or ellipse, we get a

(a) torus
(b) cylinder
(c) ellipsoid
(d) sphere

7.5 In sweep surfaces, the sweep parameters range from

(a) 0.1 to 1
(b) 1 to 10
(c) 0 to 1
(d) 1 to 100

7.6 In an equation of surface of revolution, θ is called

(a) latitude angle
(b) longitude angle
(c) angle of revolution
(d) none of the above

7.7 In an equation of surface of revolution, ϕ is called

(a) latitude angle
(b) longitude angle
(c) angle of revolution
(d) none of the above

ANSWERS

7.1 (c)	**7.2** (b)	**7.3** (d)	**7.4** (a)	**7.5** (c)
7.6 (a)	**7.7** (b)			

Chapter 8 WINDOWING AND CLIPPING

8.1 INTRODUCTION

An architect may have a graphics program to draw an entire building but be interested in only the ground floor. A businessman may have a map of sales for the entire nation but be interested in only the north-east and south-west. An integrated circuit designer may have a program for displaying an entire chip but be interested in only a few registers. Often, the computer is used in design applications because it can easily and accurately create, store, and modify very complex drawings. When drawings are too complex, they may be difficult to read. In such situations it is useful to display only those portions of the drawing that are of immediate interest. This gives the effect of looking at the image through a window. Furthermore, it is desirable to enlarge these portions to take full advantage of the available display surface. The method of selecting and enlarging portions of a drawing is called *windowing*. The technique of not showing that part of the drawing in which one is not interested is called *clipping*.

8.2 WINDOWING

Windowing is the process of extracting a portion of a database by clipping it to the boundaries of the window. In windowing, we resolve to zoom the larger parts of a picture to lower sizes and still present the whole picture. Fig. 8.1 shows 2D windowing.

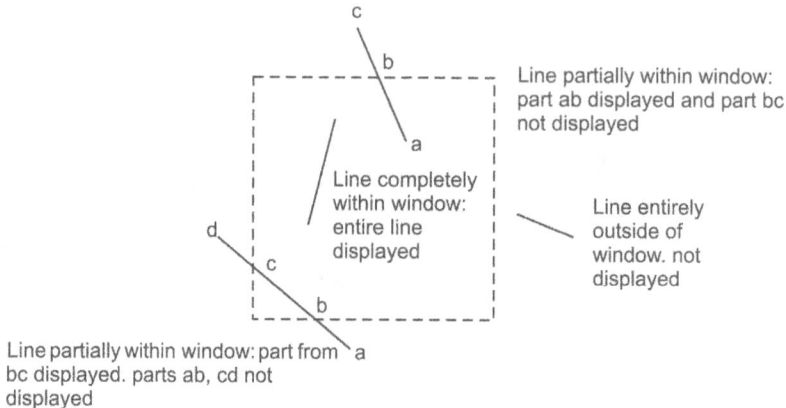

Line partially within window: part ab displayed and part bc not displayed

Line completely within window: entire line displayed

Line entirely outside of window. not displayed

Line partially within window: part from bc displayed. parts ab, cd not displayed

Fig. 8.1 2D windowing (clipping)

In windowing, we are not cutting off the parts beyond the screen size but are trying to prepare them to a size where they become displayable on the screen. In 2D, a window is specified by values for the left, right, bottom, and top edges of a rectangle.

8.3 CLIPPING

Clipping involves determining which lines or portions of lines in the pictures lie outside the window. Those lines or portions of lines are then discarded and not displayed; i.e., they are not passed to the display device. Clipping is useful for copying, moving, or deleting a portion of a scene or picture, e.g., the classical "cut and paste" operation in a windowing system.

In clipping, each line of the display is examined to determine whether or not it is completely inside the window, lies outside the window, or crosses a window boundary. If it is inside, the line is displayed; if it is outside, nothing is drawn. If it crosses the boundary, the point of intersection is determined and only that portion which lies inside the window is displayed.

Clipping is the easiest if the edges of the rectangle are parallel to the coordinate axes. Such a window is called a *regular clipping window*. Irregular windows are also of interest to many applications. Fig. 8.2 shows the clipping process.

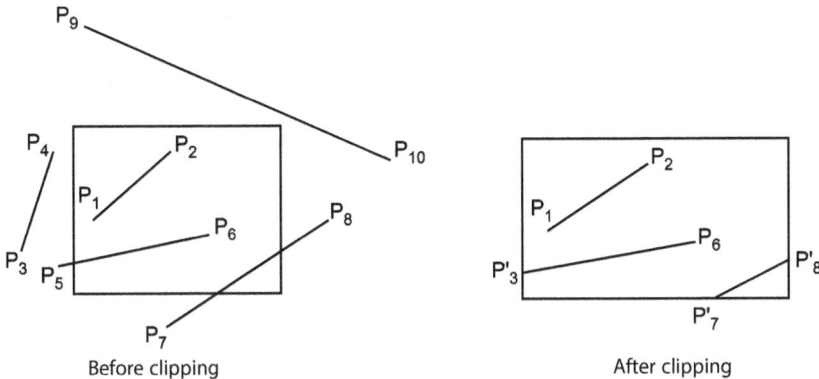

Before clipping   After clipping

Fig. 8.2 The effect of clipping

8.4 NEED FOR WINDOWING AND CLIPPING

The size of a CRT terminal on which pictures are displayed is limited in both its physical dimensions and its resolution. The physical dimensions limit the maximum size of the picture that can be displayed on the screen, and the resolution (number of pixels/inch) limits the quantity of distinct details that can be shown. If the size of a picture to be shown is bigger than the size of the screen, then obviously only a portion of the picture can be displayed. The context is similar to viewing a scene outside the window. While the scene outside is quite large, the portion of the scene that will be visible is limited by the size of the window. Similarly, if we presume that the screen allows us to see pictures as through a window, then any picture whose parts lie outside the limits of the window cannot be shown, and for algorithmic purposes, they have to be "clipped." Note that clipping does not become necessary only when a picture is larger than the window size. If a smaller picture is lying in one corner of the window, parts of it may lie outside of it, or a picture within the limits of the screen may go (partly or fully) outside the window limits, because of transformation done on them. And what is normally not appreciated is that as a result of transformation, parts that were previously outside the window limits may come within limits as well. Hence, in most cases, after each operation on pictures, it becomes necessary to check whether the picture lies within the limits of the screen and, if not, to decide where exactly it reaches the limits of the window and clip it at that point. Further, since it is a regular operation in interactive graphics, the algorithms to do this will have to be pretty fast and efficient. The other related concept is windowing. We don't always cut down the invisible parts of the picture to fit it into the window. The alternate option is to scale down the entire picture to fit it into the window size, i.e., instead of showing only a part of the picture, its dimensions can be zoomed down. In fact, the window can be conceptually divided into more than one window and a different picture can be displayed in each window, each of them "prepared" to fit into the window. In a most general case, one may partly clip a picture and partly transform it by a windowing operation. Also, since the clipped-out parts cannot be discarded by the algorithm, the system should be able to keep track of every window and the status of every picture in each of them and keep making changes as required, all in real time.

8.5 VIEWING TRANSFORMATION

It is often useful to think of two models of the item we are displaying. There is the object model and there is the image of the object which appears on the display. When one speaks of the object, one is actually referring to a model of the object stored in the computer. The object model is said to reside in object space. This model represents the object using physical units of length. In the object space, lengths of an object may be measured in any units from light-years to Angstroms. The lengths of the image on the screen, however, must be measured in screen coordinates.

One must have some way of converting the object space units of measure to those of the image space (screen space). This can be done by scaling transformation. By scaling, we can uniformly reduce the size of the object until its dimensions lie between 0 and 1. Very small objects can be enlarged until their overall dimension is almost 1 unit. The physical dimensions of the object are scaled until they are suitable for display. It may be, however, that the object is too complex to show in its entirety or that we are particularly interested in just a portion of it. We would like to imagine a box about a portion of the object. We would only display what is enclosed in the box. Such a box is called a *window*. It might also happen that we do not wish to use the entire screen for display. We would like to imagine a box on the screen and have the image confined to that box. Such a box in the screen space is called a *viewport*.

When the window is changed, we see a different part of the object shown at the same position on the display. If we change the viewport, we see the same part of the object drawn at a different place on the display. In specifying both window and viewport, we have enough information to determine the translation and scaling transformations necessary to map from the object space to the image space. This can be done with the following three steps. First, the object together with its window is translated until the lower-left corner of the window is at the origin.

Second, the object and window are scaled until the window has the dimensions of the viewport. In effect, this converts object and window into image and viewport. The final transformation step is another translation to move the viewport to its correct position on the screen.

We are really trying to do two things. We are changing the window size to become the size of the viewport (scaling) and we are positioning it at the desired location on the screen (translating). The positioning is just moving the lower-left corner of the window to the viewport's lower-left corner location, but we do this in two steps. We first move the corner to the origin and then move it to the viewport corner location. We take two steps because while it is at the origin, we can perform the necessary scaling without disturbing the corner's position.

The overall transformation which performs these three steps is called *viewing transformation*.

8.6 2D CLIPPING

Fig. 8.3 shows a 2D scene and a regular clipping window. It is defined by left (L), right (R), top (T), and bottom (B) 2D edges.

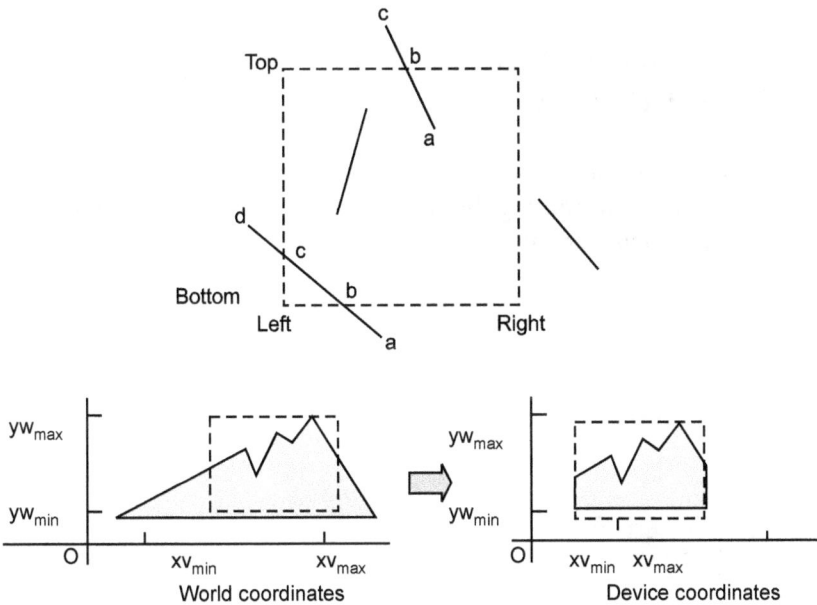

Fig. 8.3 2D clipping window

A regular clipping window is rectangular, with its edges aligned with those of the object space or display device. The purpose of a clipping algorithm is to determine which points, lines, or portions of lines lie within the clipping window. These points, lines, or portions of lines are retained for display; all others are discarded.

Because large numbers of points or lines must be clipped for a typical scene or picture, the efficiency of clipping algorithms is of particular interest. In many cases, the large majority of points or lines are either completely interior to or completely exterior to the clipping window. Therefore, it is important to be able to quickly accept a line like *ab* or a point like *p*, or reject a line like *ij* or a point like *q*. Points are interior to the clipping window provided $x_L <= x <= x_R$ and $y_B <= y <= y_T$ where x_L and x_R are the left and right coordinates of the window and y_B and y_T are the bottom and top coordinates of the window, respectively. The equal sign indicates that points on the window boundary are included within the window.

Lines are interior to the clipping window and hence visible if both endpoints are interior to the window. However, if both endpoints of a line are exterior to the window, the line is not necessarily completely exterior to the window. If both endpoints of a line are completely to the right of, completely to the left of, completely above, or completely below the window, then the line is completely exterior to the window and hence invisible.

8.7 COHEN-SUTHERLAND SUBDIVISION LINE CLIPPING ALGORITHM

The Cohen-Sutherland subdivision line clipping algorithm is a simple and effective procedure for determining the category into which a line segment falls with respect to the rectangular window boundaries.

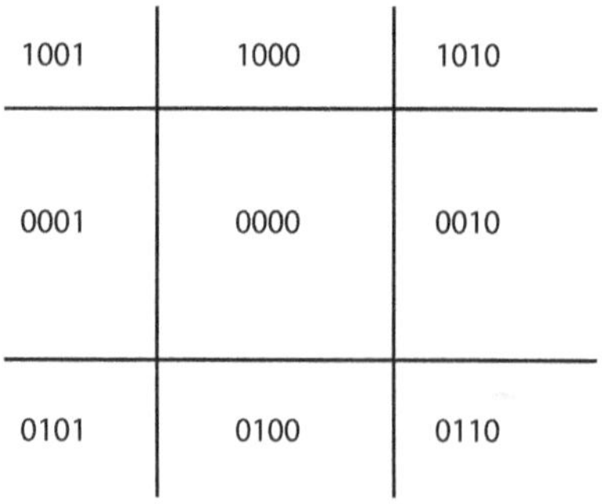

1001	1000	1010
0001	0000	0010
0101	0100	0110

Fig. 8.4 A window boundary

This algorithm has two stages:

1. Assigning a 4-bit code to the endpoints of the line segment being checked, based on the nine regions that include and surround the window as shown in Fig. 8.4.

   Each bit is either set to 1 (true) or 0 (false), starting with the left-most one, according to the following scheme:

   Bit 1 = 1, if endpoint of the line segment is above the window.

   Bit 2 = 1, if endpoint of the line segment is below the window.

   Bit 3 = 1, if endpoint of the line segment is to the right side of the window.

   Bit 4 = 1, if endpoint of the line segment is to the left side of the window.

2. *Categorization of line segment*: The endpoints of the line segment are checked with respect to each other. The following rules are used for categorization:

   Visible: If both endpoints of the line segment have region codes 0000, then the line segment is visible. For example, line segment *AB* is visible in Fig. 8.5.

   Invisible: If the same bit is set to 1 at both endpoints, then the line segment is invisible or the bitwise logical "AND" of the region coded of the endpoints is not (0000), then the line segment is invisible. For example, line segment *EF* with the endpoint codes (1010) and (0010) is invisible.

   Clipping candidate or indeterminate: A line segment is said to be indeterminate it the bit is set to 1 in different locations or if the bitwise logical AND of the region codes of the endpoints is equal to (0000). For example, line segments *CD* and *GH* in Fig. 8.5 have endpoints (1000) and (0010). These line segments may or may not process the window boundaries as line segment *GH* is invisible but line segment *CD* is partially visible and must be clipped.

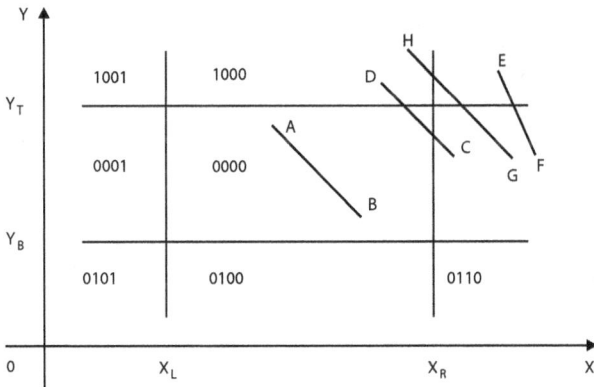

Fig. 8.5 Checking visibility

8.8 INTERSECTION CALCULATION AND CLIPPING

By solving the equations representing both the line and a window boundary, we can easily find the points of intersection between a line segment and a window boundary. For a rectangular window aligned with the coordinate axis, not all four boundaries need to be checked at one time. The window boundary where the intersection will occur can be found as follows (see Fig. 8.6):

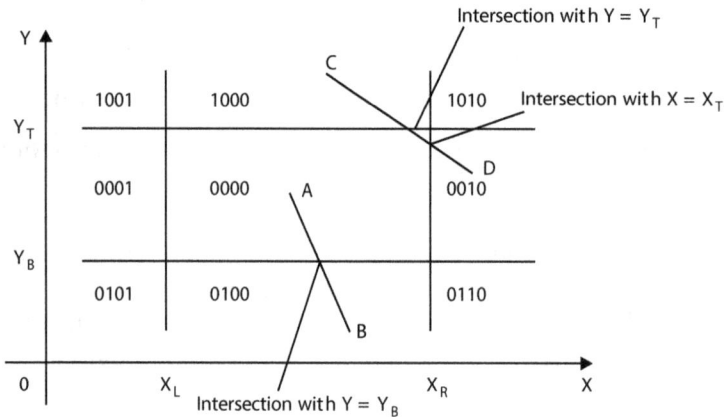

Fig. 8.6 Intersection calculation

If bit $1 = 1$, then the line segment will intersect with $Y = Y_T = Y_{max}$

If bit $2 = 1$, then the line segment will intersect with $Y = Y_B = Y_{min}$

If bit $3 = 1$, then the line segment will intersect with $X = X_R = X_{max}$

If bit $4 = 1$, then the line segment will intersect with $X = X_L = X_{min}$

Once we know the location of points of intersection, we can solve the parametric equation of a line segment and a selected edge of the window as follows:

Consider a line segment joining the endpoints $P(X_1, Y_1, Z_1)$ and $Q(X_2, Y_2, Z_2)$. If the endpoints of intersection lie on the vertical edge (X_L or X_R) then

$$X_i = X_{min} (X_L) \text{ or } X_{max} (X_R)$$

and $$Y_i = Y_1 + m (X_i - X_1)$$

where m = slope of the line

$$= \frac{\left(Y_2 - Y_1\right)}{\left(X_2 - X_1\right)}$$

If the endpoints of intersection lie on the horizontal edge (Y_B or Y_T) then

$$Y_i = Y_{min}\,(Y_B) \text{ or } Y_{max}\,(Y_T)$$

and $X_i = X_1 + m\,(Y_i - Y_1)$

Now we replace the endpoint (X_1, Y_1) with the intersecting point, eliminating the portion of the original line that is outside the window.

The new endpoint is then assigned an update region code and the resulting line is recategorized and handled as above. This iterative process terminates when we finally reach a clipped line that is either visible or invisible.

8.9 MIDPOINT SUBDIVISION ALGORITHM

The Cohen-Sutherland algorithm requires the calculation of the intersection of a line with a window edge. The direct calculation is avoided by performing a binary search for the intersection by always dividing the line at its midpoint. Midpoint subdivision is a useful method of numerical analysis. It is an alternative method to find the point of intersection between the line segment and the window edge. The line segment is separated at its midpoint and the two resulting segments are checked for visibility and clipping. If not totally visible or invisible, the segment is again bisected and the process continues until the intersection with the window boundary is found within the specified tolerance. Fig 8.7 gives an example of this process.

Let $P\,(X_1, Y_1)$ and $Q\,(X_2, Y_2)$ be the endpoints of a line segment PQ. Its midpoint $M\,(X_m, Y_m)$ is found by the following formula:

$$X_m = \frac{\left(X_1, Y_1\right)}{2}$$

$$Y_m = \frac{\left(X_2, Y_2\right)}{2}$$

8.10 ADVANTAGE OF THE MIDPOINT SUBDIVISION ALGORITHM

Midpoint subdivision is efficiently implemented in hardware because division by two is accomplished by a simple bit shift to the right. For example (0100) is the 4-bit binary representation of the number 4. A shift to the right yields (0010) which represents $2 = \dfrac{4}{2}$, when implemented in hardware. The midpoint subdivision process involves only integer values. When implemented in software, it may be slower than the direct calculation method.

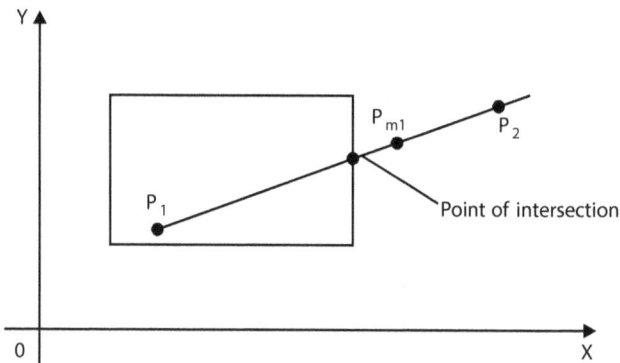

Fig. 8.7 The midpoint subdivision algorithm

8.11 COMPARISON BETWEEN COHEN-SUTHERLAND AND MIDPOINT SUBDIVISION LINE CLIPPING ALGORITHMS

The maximum time-consuming step in the clipping process is the intersection calculation with window boundaries. The Cohen-Sutherland algorithm reduces the calculations by first discarding lines that can be trivially accepted or rejected. The intersection with the window boundaries is then found only for those lines which are clipping candidates. This point is used to break the original line into the new segments which are checked again for trivial acceptance or rejection. The process continues until all segments (original and new) are checked.

The midpoint subdivision algorithm is a special case of the Cohen-Sutherland algorithm, where the intersection is not calculated by equation solving. It is calculated by a midpoint approximation method, which is suitable for hardware complementation, very fast and efficient.

Problem 1

Outcode(A) = 0000

Outcode(D) = 1001

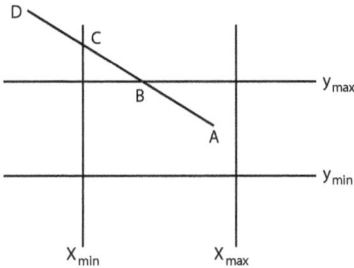

Fig. 8.8 The limits of a window

Solution

- No trivial accept/reject

    Clip (A, D) with $y = y_{max}$, splitting it into (A, B) and (B, D)

- Reject (B, D)

- Proceed with (A, B)

For a line with endpoint coordinates (x_1, y_1) and (x_2, y_2), the y coordinate of the intersection point with a vertical boundary can be obtained as

$$y = y_1 + m(x - x_1) \rightarrow (1)$$

where the x value is set either to x left or x right.

Similarly, if we are looking for the intersection with a horizontal boundary, the x coordinate can be calculated as:

$$x = x_1 + \frac{1}{m}(y - y_1) \rightarrow (2)$$

where y value is set either to y bottom or y top.

Problem 2

Display the corresponding visible portion of a line leaving the outside boundary.

Clip the line with the boundaries $(-1, 1)$ of x and $(-1, 1)$ of y and the points are $\left(\frac{1}{2}, \frac{1}{4}\right)$ and $\left(\frac{1}{2}, \frac{3}{2}\right)$.

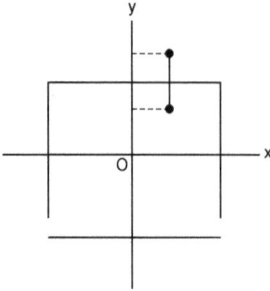

Fig. 8.9 A line

Solution

Given $\qquad\qquad x\,\text{left} = -1 \text{ and } x\,\text{right} = 1$

$$y_{\text{top}} = 1 \text{ and } y_{\text{bottom}} = -1$$

Let $\qquad\qquad A = \left(\dfrac{1}{2}, \dfrac{1}{4}\right) \text{ and } B = \left(\dfrac{1}{2}, \dfrac{3}{2}\right)$

i.e., $A = (0.5, 0.25)$ and $B = (0.5, 1.5)$

So the bitwise position of A is 0000 and of B is 1000. So clearly B is not in the region. So we have to find the horizontal intercept point, i.e., $\left(x = \dfrac{1}{m}\left(y_{\text{top}} - y_1\right) + x_1, y_{\text{top}} \right)$.

$$m = y_2 - y_1 = 1.5 - 0.25 = \infty$$

$$x_2 - x_1 = 0.5 - 0.5$$

$$x = \frac{1}{\infty}(1 - 0.25) + 0.5 = 0.5$$

$$y = 1$$

The point is $(0.5, 1)$.

8.12 POLYGON CLIPPING

The previous discussion concentrated on clipping lines. Now we consider the case of polygon clipping. A polygon can be considered a collection of lines. Polygons are of the following types:

1. **Convex polygon:** A polygon is said to be convex if the line joining any two interior points of the polygon lies completely inside the polygon (Fig. 8.10, left).

2. **Concave or non-convex polygon:** A polygon is said to be non-convex or concave if the line joining any two interior points of the polygon doesn't lie completely inside the polygon (Fig. 8.10, right).

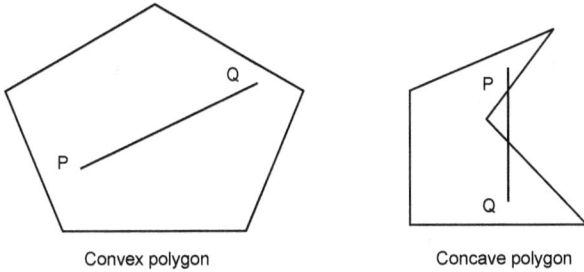

Convex polygon   Concave polygon

Fig. 8.10 Convex and concave polygons

By convention, a polygon with vertices P_1, P_2 .... P_N and edges P_1P_2, P_2P_3, ... P_{i-1} P_i ..... P_N or P_1 is said to be positively oriented if a tour of the vertices in the given order produces a counterclockwise circuit. If a tour of the vertices in the given order produces a clockwise circuit, then it is negatively oriented (Fig. 8.11).

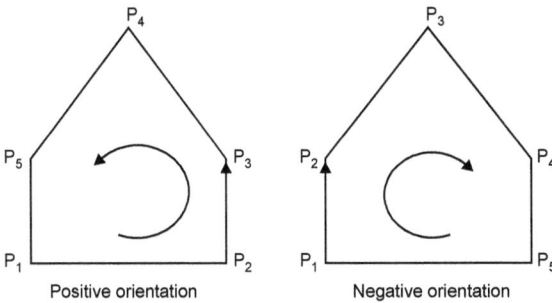

Positive orientation   Negative orientation

Fig. 8.11 Different orientations of a polygon

When a closed polygon is clipped as a collection of lines, the original closed polygon becomes one or more open polygons or discrete lines (Fig. 8.12).

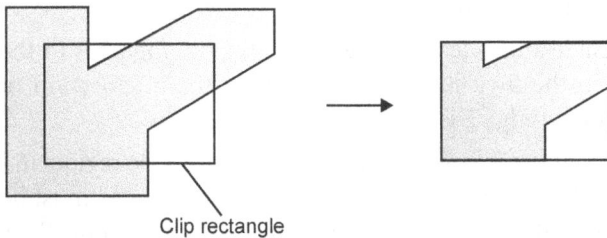

Clip rectangle

Fig. 8.12 Before clipping (closed polygon) and after clipping (open polygon)

8.13 SUTHERLAND-HODGMAN ALGORITHM

The main idea behind the Sutherland-Hodgman algorithm is that it is easy to clip a polygon against a single edge or clipping plane. The procedure is to clip the original polygon and each resulting intermediate polygon against a single edge of the clipping window, each edge in succession. For simplicity we use a rectangular window. The original polygon is defined by a list of vertices $P_1, P_2, P_2, \ldots\ldots, P_N$ which imply a list of edges $P_1 P_2, P_2 P_3 \ldots, P_{N-1} P_{N1} P_N P_1$.

The output of the algorithm is a list of polygon vertices. All these vertices are on the visible side of a clipping window since each edge of the polygon is individually compared with the clipping window so only the relationship between a single edge of a polygon and an edge of the window needs to be considered. Consider an edge SP of the polygon and E being the edge of the window. There are only four possible relationships between SP and E. These relations are shown in Fig. 8.13.

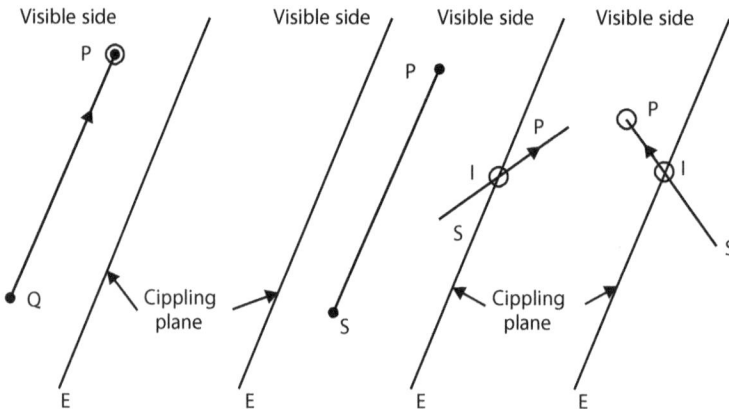

Fig. 8.13 The Sutherland-Hodgman algorithm

1. If edge SP is entirely visible, that is, both S and P are on the visible side, then P is output (Fig. 8.13).

2. If edge SP is entirely invisible, that is, both S and P are on the invisible side, then no output is required (Fig. 8.13).

3. If edge SP is partially visible and is leaving the visible region, then S is in the visible region and P is in the invisible region, and then the intersection of polygon edge SP and window edge E is calculated (Fig. 8.13).

4. If the edge is entering the visible region, that is, S is in the invisible region and P is in the visible region, then the intersection with the window edge must be calculated. Since P is also in the visible region so it must also be output. Thus intersection point I and endpoint P both are output (Fig. 8.13).

The above four steps are used to determine the vertices of our intermediate polygons. Its algorithm proceeds in stages by passing each intermediate polygon to the next stage of the window and clipping is performed. The final edge P_nP_1 must be considered separately. This is done by saving the first point of the polygon as F. Thus the final edge becomes P_nF and is considered exactly as any other edge. Fig. 8.14 gives the flowchart of this algorithm, while Fig. 8.14(a) is applied to every vertex and Fig. 8.14(b) is used for the last vertex only.

8.14 3D CLIPPING

The two common 3D clipping volumes are a rectangular parallelepiped, i.e., a box used for parallel or axonometric projections, and a truncated pyramidal volume, frequently called a frustum of vision, used for perspective projections. These volumes, shown in Fig. 8.15, are six-sided—left, right, top, bottom, near (hither), and far (yon) planes. There is also a requirement to clip to unusual volumes, e.g., the cargo bay of the space shuttle.

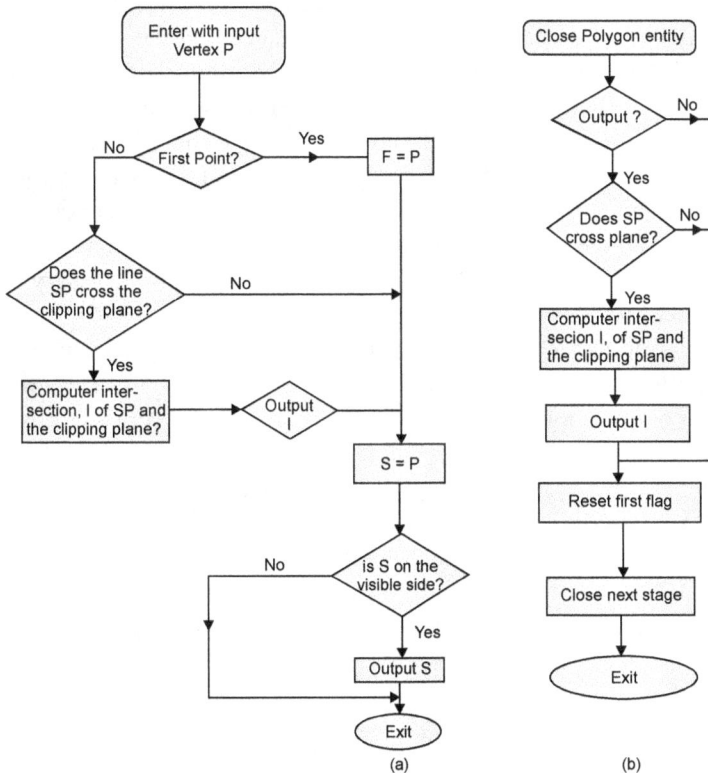

Fig. 8.14 Flowchart for the Sutherland-Hodgman algorithm polygon clipping

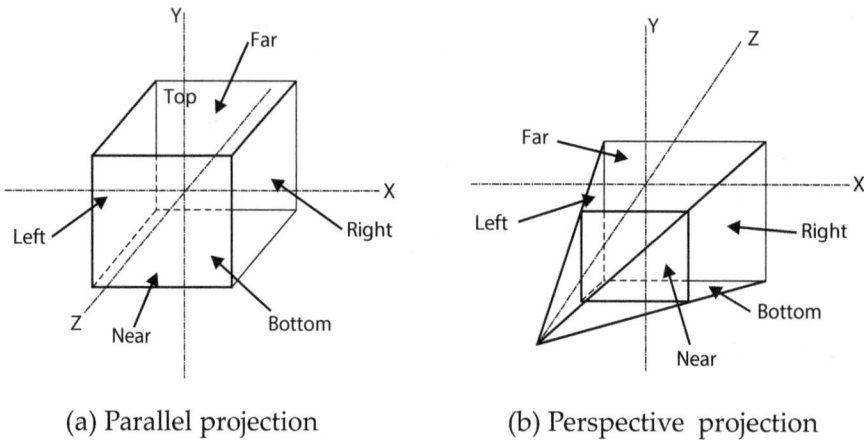

(a) Parallel projection   (b) Perspective projection

Fig. 8.15 3D clipping

As in 2D clipping, lines that are totally visible or trivially invisible can be identified using an extension of the Cohen-Sutherland endpoint codes. For 3D clipping, a 6-bit endpoint code is used. Again, the first bit is the rightmost bit. The bits are set to 1 using an extension of the 2D scheme. First-bit set—if the endpoint is to the left of the window, second-bit set—if the endpoint is to the right of the window, third-bit set—if the endpoint is below the window, fourth-bit set— if the endpoint is above the window, fifth-bit set—if the endpoint is in front of the volume, sixth-bit set—if the endpoint is behind the volume. Otherwise, the bit is set to zero. Again, if both endpoint codes are zero, both ends of the line are visible, and the line is visible. Also, if the bit-by-bit logical intersection of the two endpoint codes is not zero, then the line is totally invisible. If the logical intersection is zero, the line may be partially visible or totally invisible. In this case it is necessary to determine the intersection of the line and clipping volume.

Determining the endpoint codes for a rectangular parallelepiped clipping volume is a straightforward extension of the 2D algorithm. However, the perspective clipping volume shown in Fig. 8.16 requires additional consideration. One technique is to transform the clipping volume into a canonical volume with $x_{right} = 1$, $x_{left} = -1$, $y_{top} = 1$, $y_{bottom} = -1$, at $z_{far} = a$, where $0 < a <= 1$ and the center of projection is at the origin in a left-hand coordinate system, then the endpoint code conditions are considerably simplified. A more straightforward technique, which requires less distortion of the clipping volume, makes the line connecting the center of projection and the center of perspective clipping volume coincident with the z-axis in a right-hand coordinate system, as shown in Fig. 8.16.

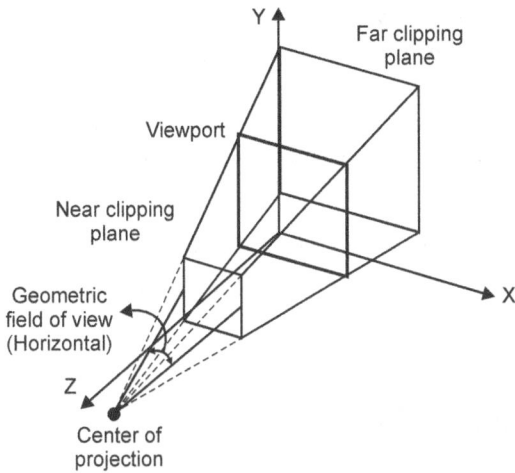

Fig. 8.16 A right-hand coordinate system

8.15 MULTIPLE WINDOWING

Some systems allow the use of multiple windowing; that is, at first the image is created by one or more window transformations on the object. Then, windows are applied to this first image to create a second image. Further windowing transformations may be done until the desired picture is created. Every application of a window transformation allows the user to slice up a portion of the picture and reposition it on the screen. Thus, multiple windowing gives the user freedom to rearrange components of the picture. The same effect may be achieved, however, by applying a number of single-window transformations to the object.

8.16 CHARACTER CLIPPING

Characters or text are generated in software, firmware, or hardware. Characters can be formed from individual lines or strokes or from dot matrix (bitmap) representations. Stroke characters generated in software are treated like any other line; i.e., they can be rotated, translated, scaled, and clipped to arbitrary windows in arbitrary orientations. Dot matrix character representations in software are treated in a similar fashion. The process is, however, somewhat more tedious. In particular, if the character box surrounding the character is clipped to an arbitrary window, then each pixel of the character mask is compared with the clip window to determine if it is inside or outside. If inside, it is activated; if outside, no action is taken. Clipping of hardware-generated characters is more limited. Generally, any character which is not totally visible is eliminated. This is accomplished by clipping the character box against the window. If the entire box is inside the window, the character is displayed; otherwise, it is not. When the rectangular character box is aligned with a rectangular window, only one diagonal of the character box is compared with the window.

When characters are generated in firmware, character clipping facilities may be very limited or very extensive. The extent depends on the clipping algorithm also implemented in firmware.

8.17 APPLICATIONS OF CLIPPING

- Clipping is fundamental to several aspects of computer graphics.

- Typical use of clipping is in selecting only the specific information required to display a particular scene or view from a larger environment.

- Clipping is useful for anti-aliasing.

- Clipping is useful in visible line, visible surface, shadow, and texture algorithms.

- Advanced clipping algorithms are useful for clipping polygonal volumes against polygonal volumes. Such algorithms are used to perform the Boolean operations required for simple solid modelers, e.g., the intersection and union of simple cubical and quadric volumes.

- Clipping is also useful for copying, moving, or deleting a portion of a scene or picture, e.g., the classical "cut and paste" operation in a windowing system.

EXERCISES

1. Explain the difference between a window and a viewport.

2. Explain the need of windowing and clipping.

3. Explain the Cohen–Sutherland line clipping algorithm.

4. Explain the Cohen-Hodgman polygon clipping algorithm.

5. What is aspect ratio? How do you solve the problem of aspect ratio while performing window-to-viewport transformation?

6. For the rectangular window boundaries given as $x_{min} = 2$, $x_{max} = 8$, $y_{min} = 2$ and $y_{max} = 8$, check the visibility of the following segments using the Cohen-Sutherland algorithm and, if necessary, clip them against the appropriate window boundaries.

Line EF: E (3, 10) and F (6, 12)

Line GH: G (4, 1) and H (10, 6)

7. Compare Cohen-Sutherland and midpoint subdivision line clipping algorithms.

8. Write a short note on 3D clipping.

9. Write some of the applications of clipping.

OBJECTIVE QUESTIONS

8.1 The line $2x - y + 4 = 0$, if clipped against this window, will connect the point
(*a*) (0, 1) and (3, 3)   (*b*) (0, 1) and (2, 3)
(*c*) (1, 2) and (4, 2)   (*d*) none of the above

8.2 In the Cohen-Sutherland clipping algorithm using region codes, a line is already clipped if the
(*a*) codes of the endpoint are same
(*b*) logical AND of the endpoint code is not 0000
(*c*) logical OR of the endpoint code is 0000
(*d*) logical AND of the endpoint code is 0000
(*e*) (*a*) and (*b*)

8.3 The method of selecting and enlarging a portion of a drawing is called
(*a*) viewing   (*b*) view port
(*c*) windowing   (*d*) clipping

8.4 The technique of not showing that part of the drawing which one is not interested is called
(*a*) windowing   (*b*) clipping
(*c*) viewing   (*d*) view port

8.5 If the edges of the rectangular window are parallel to the coordinate axes, then such a window is called
(*a*) rectangular window   (*b*) standard window
(*c*) parallel window   (*d*) regular window

8.6 Conversion from object space units of measure to those of the image space is captured by which transformation?
(*a*) scaling   (*b*) reflection
(*c*) translation   (*d*) rotation

8.7 When an entire image is to be confined into a box, then that box in the screen space is called a
(*a*) window   (*b*) view port
(*c*) both of these   (*d*) none of the above

8.8 A line clipping algorithm is presented by a
(*a*) visibility algorithm   (*b*) Cohen-Sutherland algorithm
(*c*) midpoint subdivision algorithm   (*d*) Cyrus-Beck algorithm
(*e*) all of above

8.9 Polygon clipping algorithm is presented by
(*a*) Cohen-Sutherland algorithm   (*b*) Cyrus-Beck algorithm
(*c*) Cohen-Hodgeman algorithm   (*d*) none of the above

8.10 Applications of clipping include
(*a*) selecting a specific information
(*b*) antialiasing
(*c*) copying, moving, deleting a portion of picture
(*d*) all of the above

ANSWERS

8.1 (*d*)	**8.2** (*e*)	**8.3** (*c*)	**8.4** (*b*)
8.5 (*d*)	**8.6** (*a*)	**8.7** (*b*)	**8.8** (*e*)
8.9 (*c*)	**8.10** (*d*)		

9 Chapter GENERATION OF A 3D MODEL

9.1 INTRODUCTION

Geometric modeling has created wonders in the fields of aerospace design, marine engineering, aesthetics, interior decoration, architectural engineering, etc. Design can be better visualized the in the 3D view than a 2D projected view. Existing models can be easily and quickly modified. An important step in product design development, i.e., prototyping, is completely removed by the introduction of geometric modeling. Hence, development cycle time is reduced considerably. This is why newer and improved products are coming on the market at a rapid speed. Geometric models are generated by the creation of basic geometric objects, the transformation of elements, and the creation of geometric entities. The geometric modeling approach involves:

1. Wireframe modeling
2. Surface modeling
3. Solid modeling

9.2 WIREFRAME MODELING

A wireframe model is a wired frame structure where wires represent the edges of the geometry. Two approaches can be adopted to make a wireframe model, i.e., the conventional approach and the procedural approach. In the conventional approach, the entire geometry is placed in the data structure. Wireframe models are created with relative ease, and they require less memory and less computation time. Another advantage of the wireframe model is that it allows one to see the interior of the design and check the behavior of its inner components. Testing can be done quickly. Figure 9.1 shows a geometric figure and its wireframe model. The limitation of wireframe modeling is that all the lines in a wireframe model are visible to the observer. Consequently, the lines that indicate the edges of the rear part are visible right through the front surface. This makes the image somewhat confusing to the observer, and in some cases the model interpretation becomes difficult, as shown in Fig. 9.2.

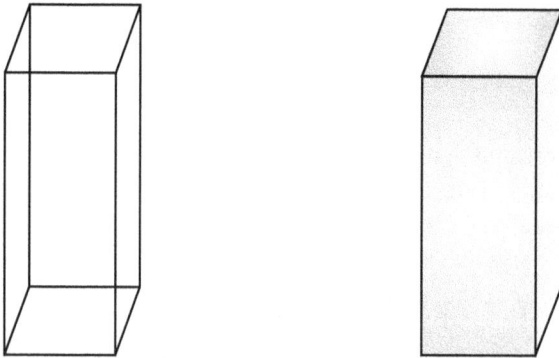

Fig. 9.1 Wireframe modeling

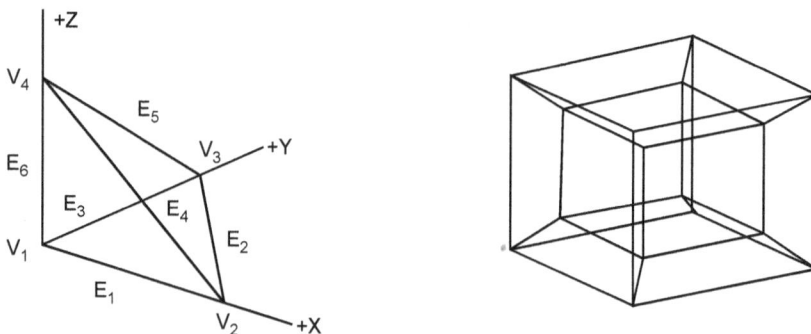

Fig. 9.2 Wireframe models

Advantages of wireframe modeling

➢ Easy to construct

➢ Most economical in use of time and memory

➢ Models solid objects

Disadvantages of wireframe modeling

➢ Unable to determine computationally important information on mass properties (e.g., volume, mass, moment, etc.) and lines of intersection between two faces of intersecting models

➢ Cannot guarantee that the model definition is correct, complete, or manufacturable

➢ Complex models are difficult to interpret

9.3 SURFACE MODELING

Surface models use various surface elements to represent parts of the geometry. These surface elements are connected to form surface models. A wireframe model can be converted into a surface model by defining the surfaces. Similar to wireframe entities, existing CAD/CAM systems provide designers with both analytic and synthetic surface entities. Surface models can be constructed using a large variety of surface features often provided by CAD systems. A plane is the most basic feature used to represent a surface element. More complex shapes can be defined by tabulated cylinders, ruled surfaces, surfaces of revolution, sculptured surfaces, sweep surfaces, and fillet surfaces.

Analytic entities include

• Plane surfaces

• Ruled surfaces

• Surfaces of revolution

• Tabulated cylinders

Synthetic entities include

• Bicubic Hermite spline surfaces

• B-spline surfaces

• Rectangular and triangular Bezier patches

- Rectangular and triangular Coons patches

- Gordon surfaces

Plane surface: This is the simplest surface. It requires three non-coincident points to define an infinite plane, as shown in Fig. 9.3.

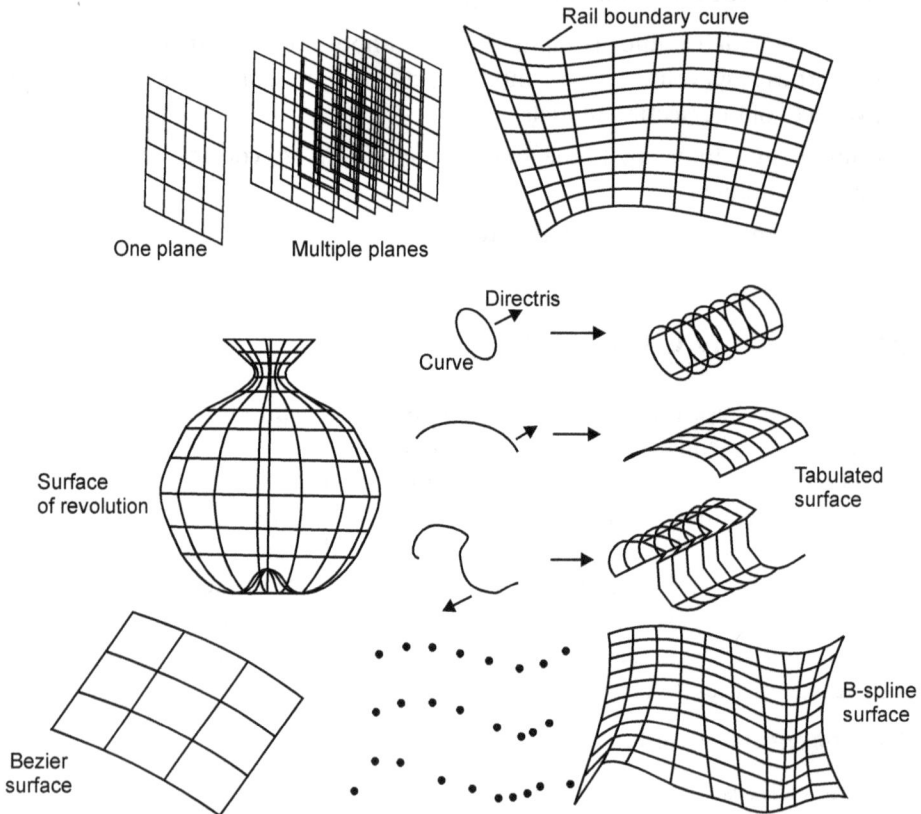

Fig. 9.3 Surface types

Ruled (lofted) surface: This is a linear surface. It interpolates linearly between two boundary curves that define the surface (rails). Rails can be any wireframe entity. This entity is ideal to represent surfaces that do not have any twists or kinks.

Surface of revolution: A surface of revolution is generated by revolving a given curve about an axis.

Tabulated cylinder: This is a surface generated by translating a planar curve a certain distance along a specified direction (axis of the cylinder).

Bezier surface: This is a surface that approximates given input data. It is different from the previous surfaces in that it is a synthetic surface. Similar to the Bezier curve, it does not pass through all given data points. It is a general surface that permits twists and kinks. The Bezier surface allows only global control of the surface.

B-spline surface: This is a surface that can approximate or interpolate given input data (Fig. 9.3). It is a synthetic surface. It is a general surface like the Bezier surface but with the advantage of permitting local control of the surface.

Advantages of surface modeling

➢ Smooth varying surfaces are used

➢ Analysis becomes easy

➢ Strength and weakness can be obtained

➢ Visual inspection can be done

Disadvantages of surface modeling

➢ More computations are required

➢ Hidden and internal surfaces cannot be seen

➢ Complex shapes having side patches cannot be viewed

9.4 SOLID MODELING

Solid modeling is the most advanced method of geometric modeling in three dimensions. It is a representation of the solid parts of an object on a computer. The typical geometric model is made up of wireframes that show the object in the form of wires. Providing surface representation to the wire, 3D views of geometric models make the object appear solid on the computer screen; this is called solid modeling. A wireframe model and its solid model are shown in Fig. 9.4. In CAD systems there are a number of representation schemes for solid modeling, which include:

• Primitive creation functions

• Constructive solid geometry (CSG)

• Boundary representation (BREP)

• Sweeping

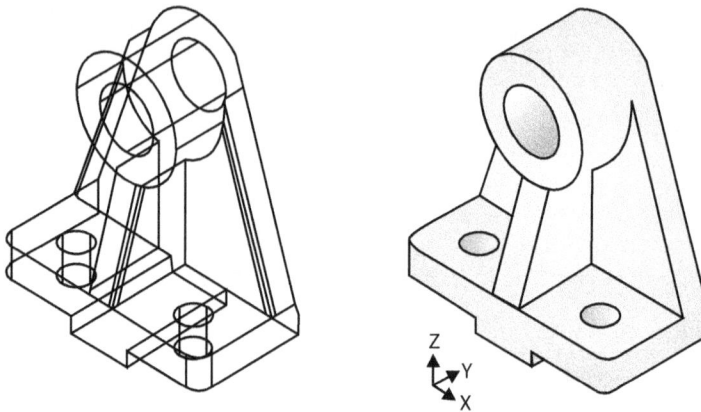

Fig. 9.4 Solid modeling

9.4.1 Primitive Creation Functions

These functions retrieve a solid of a simple shape from primitive solids stored in the program in advance and create a solid of the same shape but of the size specified by the user.

9.4.2 Constructive Solid Geometry

Objects are represented as a combination of simpler solid objects (primitives). The primitives, such as cube, cylinder, cone, torus, sphere, etc., are shown in Fig. 9.5. Copies or "instances" of these primitive shapes are created and positioned. A complete solid model is constructed by combining these "instances" using a set of specific logic operations (Boolean operations). These operations include union, difference, and intersection.

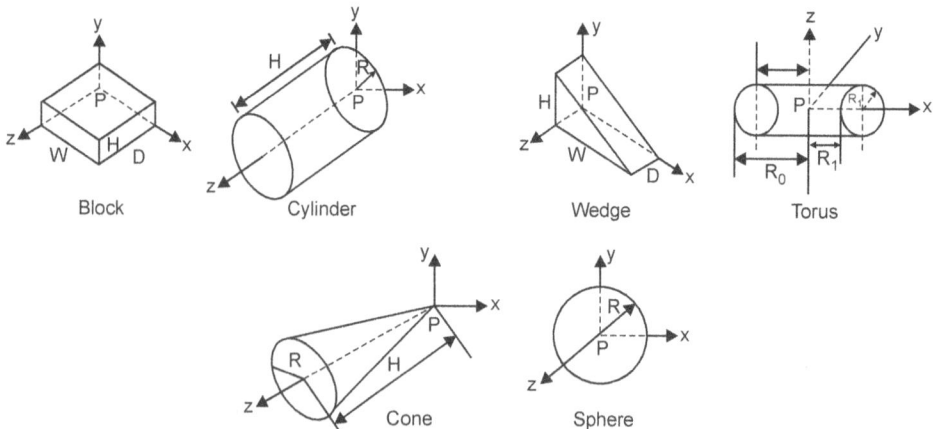

Fig. 9.5 Primitives

Union: The sum of all points in each of the two defined sets (logical "OR"). It is also referred to as add, combine, join, merge, etc. An example of a union operation is shown in Fig. 9.7(*a*).

Difference: The points in a source set minus the points common to a second set (logical "NOT"). Set must share a common volume. It is also referred to as subtraction, remove, cut, etc. An example of a difference operation is shown in Fig. 9.7(*b*).

Intersection: Those points common to each of the two defined sets are represented after an intersection operation (logical "AND"). The set must share a common volume. Intersection is also referred to as common, conjoin, etc. An example of an intersection operation is shown in Fig. 9.7(*c*).

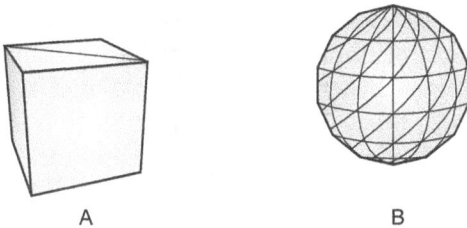

A   B

Fig. 9.6 More primitives

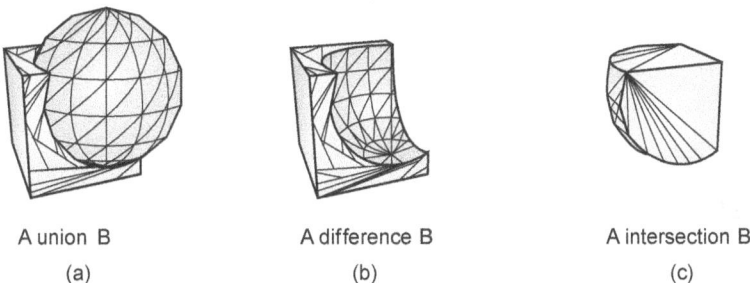

A union B   A difference B   A intersection B

(a)   (b)   (c)

Fig. 9.7 Boolean expressions

Boolean expressions in CSG

Two cylinders of different diameters are used as primitives. The cylinder with larger diameter is Block A, the cylinder with smaller diameter is Block B. Block A union ($\cup$) Block B is represented by Fig. 9.8(*a*). The Boolean expression for this operation is represented as ($A \cup B$). Block A intersection ($\cap$) Block B is represented by Fig. 9.8(*b*). The Boolean expression for this operation is represented as ($A \cap B$). Block A difference (−) Block B is represented by Fig. 9.8(*c*). The Boolean expression for this operation is represented as ($A - B$). Block B difference (−) Block A is represented by Fig. 9.8(*d*). The Boolean expression for this operation is represented as ($B - A$).

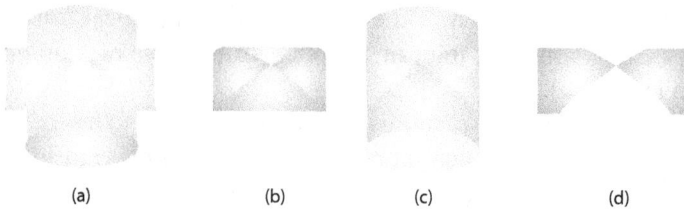

| (a) | (b) | (c) | (d) |

Fig. 9.8 Boolean operations

CSG expression and tree

Every solid constructed using the CSG technique has a corresponding CSG expression, which in turn has an associated CSG tree. The CSG tree is a representation of the final design. Recall that the same solid may have different CSG expressions/trees. For example, three blocks (Block 1, Block 2, Block 3) are shown in Fig. 9.9. Many combinations of Boolean expressions are possible to achieve the final result. One might punch a hole from Block 1 first and then compute the union of this result with Block 2, or Block 1 and Block 2 are connected by union and then compute the difference of this result with Block 3. As a result, CSG representations are not unique.

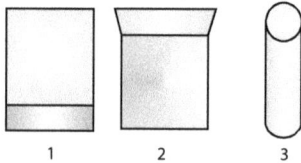

| 1 | 2 | 3 |

Fig. 9.9 CSG trees

The Boolean expression for the solid model shown in Fig. 9.9(*a*) can be written as:

$$Result\ 1 = (\{Block\ 1 \cup Block\ 2\} \cup Block\ 3)$$

This expression can be converted to an expression tree of the design. The CSG expression tree for Result 1 is shown in Fig. 9.10.

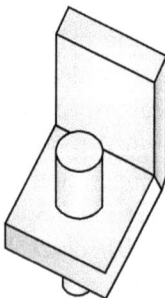

Fig. 9.9 A solid model using union (Result 1)

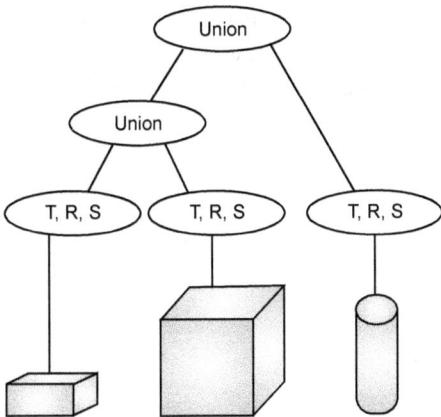

Fig. 9.10 CSG expression tree for Result 1

The Boolean expression for the solid model shown in Fig. 9.11 can be written as:

$$Result\ 2 = (\{Block\ 1 \cup Block\ 2\} - Block\ 3)$$

The CSG expression tree for Result 2 is shown in Fig. 9.12.

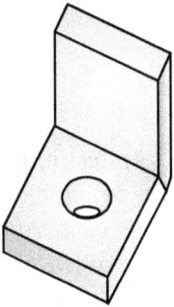

Fig. 9.11 A solid model using union (Result 2)

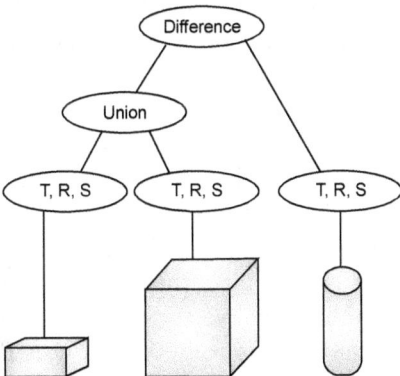

Fig. 9.12 CSG expression tree for Result 2

Another example of solid modeling using CSG is shown in Fig. 9.12. It has three primitives: a cubical block, a cylinder, and a sphere. First, the block and the cylinder are united with each other and sphere is subtracted (difference) from the result.

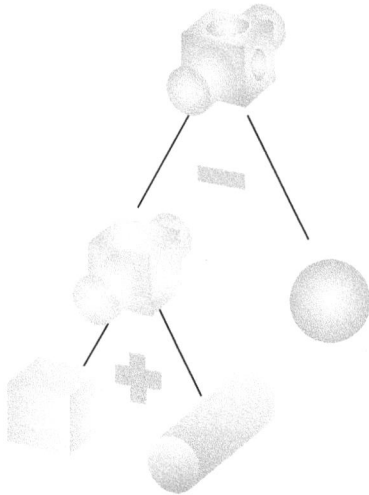

Fig. 9.12 Solid modeling using CSG

9.4.3 Boundary Representation

Solid models are defined by their enclosing surfaces or boundaries. This technique consists of geometric information about the faces, edges, and vertices of an object with the topological data on how these are connected. Boundary representation, or B-rep for short, can be considered an extension of the wireframe model. The merit of a B-rep is that a solid is bounded by its surface and has its interior and exterior. The surface of a solid consists of a set of well-organized faces, each of which is a piece of some surface, e.g., a surface patch. Faces may share vertices and edges that are curve segments. Therefore, this is an extension to the wireframe model by adding face information to the latter. There are two types of information: topological and geometric. Topological information provides the relationships among vertices, edges, and faces, similar to that used in a wireframe model. In addition to connectivity, topological information also includes the orientation of edges and faces. Geometric information is usually equations of the edges and faces. The orientation of each face is important. Normally, a face is surrounded by a set of vertices. Using the right-handed rule, the ordering of these vertices for describing a particular face must guarantee that the normal vector of that face is pointing to the exterior of the solid. Normally, the order is counterclockwise. If that face is given by an equation, the equation must be rewritten so that the normal vector at every point on the part that is being used as a face points to the exterior of the solid. Therefore, by inspecting normal vectors, one can immediately tell the inside and outside of a solid. This orientation must be done for all faces. Fig. 9.13 shows boundary representation in topological and geometric information.

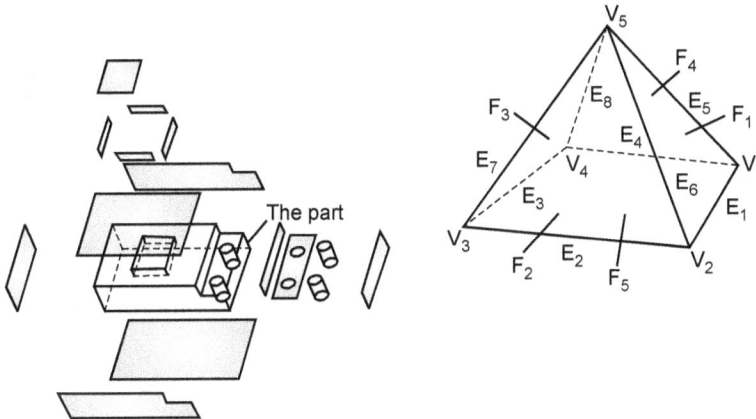

Fig. 9.13 Boundary representation

The B-Rep Scheme

The basis of a B-rep scheme is that a solid model is bounded by a set of faces. A solid model contains faces, vertices, loops, edges, bodies, etc. Only boundary surfaces of the model are stored and the volumetric properties are calculated by the Gauss divergence theorem. This theorem relates surface integrals to volume integrals. Using this scheme, a variety of solids depending on the primitive surfaces (curved, planar, sculptured) can be modeled. There are two types of solid models in the scheme:

1. **Polyhedral solids:** Polyhedral models consist of straight edges, e.g., a non-cylindrical surface, box, wedge, combination of two, or more non-cylindrical bodies. Polyhedral solids can have blind or through holes and 2D or 3D faces, with no dangling edges. A valid polyhedral abides by Euler's equation:

$$F - E + V - L = 2(B - G)$$

where

$$F = \text{face}$$
$$E = \text{edge}$$
$$V = \text{vertices}$$
$$L = \text{inner loop}$$
$$B = \text{bodies}$$
$$G = \text{through holes}$$

A simple polyhedral has no holes; each face is bounded by a single set of connected edges (bounded by one loop of edges).

Euler's equation for a simple polyhedral can be reduced to: $F - E + V = 2$

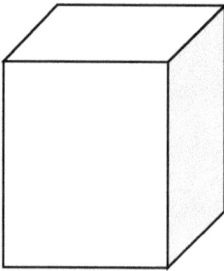

Fig. 9.14 A simple polyhedral

For the box shown in Fig. 9.14, $F = 6$, $E = 12$, and $V = 8$.

Examples of other types of polyhedral are shown in Fig. 9.15.

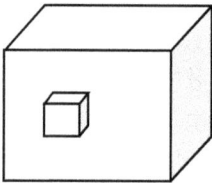   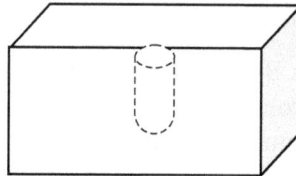

    (a)   (b)

Fig. 9.15 (a) A polyhedral with two loops; (b) a polyhedral with a blind hole

2. **Curved solids:** A curved solid is similar to a polyhedral object but it has curved faces and edges. Spheres and cylinders are examples of curved solids (Fig. 9.16).

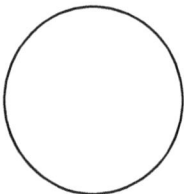   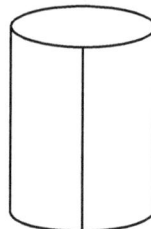

Sphere: F = 1, V = 1, E = 0   Cylinder: F = 3, E = 3, V= 2

Fig. 9.16 Curved solids

Primitives: In B-rep, a model is made up of the following primitives:

- **Vertex:** a point in space

- **Edge:** a finite, non-intersecting curve bounded by two vertices that are not necessarily distinct

- **Face:** a finite connected, non-self-intersecting region of a closed oriented surface, bounded by one or more loops

- **Loop:** an ordered alternating sequence of vertices and edges. It defines a non-self-intersecting closed space curve, which may be a boundary of a face

- **Body:** an entity that has faces, edges, and vertices; a minimum body is a point

A B-rep scheme is closely related to the traditional drafting method.

9.4.4 Sweeping

Sweeping is a modeling function in which a planar closed domain is translated or revolved to form a solid. When the planar domain is translated, the modeling activity is called translational sweeping; when the planar region is revolved, it is called swinging, or rotational sweeping, as shown in Fig. 9.17.

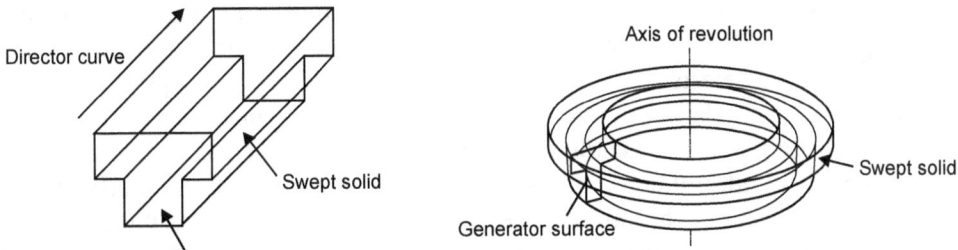

Fig. 9.17 Sweeping

9.5 ADVANTAGES OF SOLID MODELING

- Solid modeling is one of the most important applications of CAD software and it has become increasingly popular of late. Solid modeling helps the designer to see the designed object as if it were the real manufactured product.

- Solid modeling can be seen from various directions and in various views. This helps the designer to be sure that the object looks exactly as they want it to be. It also allows the designer to see what other changes can be made to the object.

9.6 APPLICATIONS OF SOLID MODELING

Solid modeling is used for creating not only solid models of machine parts, but also buildings, electric circuits, and even the human body Solid modeling software is used for a large variety of applications, including:

1. **Engineering:** Engineering design professionals use solid modeling to see what the designed product will actually look like. Architects and civil engineers use it to see the layout of a designed building.

2. **Entertainment industry:** The animation industry has been using solid modeling to create characters and objects.

3. **Medical industry:** Modern imaging scanners create solid models of the internal body parts design medical devices, etc.

9.7 RENDERING

Rendering is a technique of creating realistic images on a computer monitor. The image we see on a computer monitor is made up of a large number of illuminated dots called pixels. Creating a picture involves a number of stages. In the first stage, models of objects are generated, then viewing specifications and lighting conditions are selected. The creation of realistic pictures is an important goal in fields such as simulation, design, entertainment, research, and education. Examples of simulation systems include flight simulators, designs of 3D objects such as automobiles and buildings, and computer-generated cartoons in entertainment. Realistic images have become an essential tool in research and education.

The color of any specific point in a model is a function of the physical material properties of that surface. Two general shading algorithms are used for this purpose:

1. **Local illumination:** Local illumination algorithms describe only how individual surfaces reflect or transmit light. They predict the intensity, spectral character, and distribution of the light being reflected from that surface. Only the light coming directly from the light source itself is considered in shading.

2. **Global illumination:** Global illumination is commonly used to describe all forms of indirect light. It is often assumed to encompass all of global illumination.

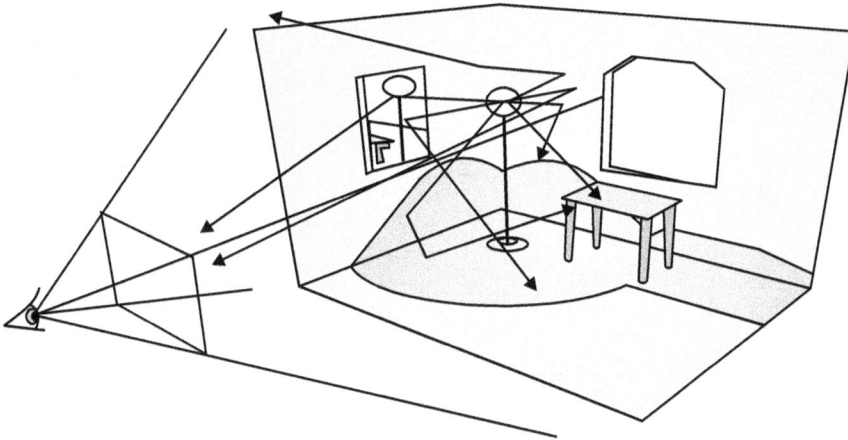

Fig. 9.18 Diffuse reflection

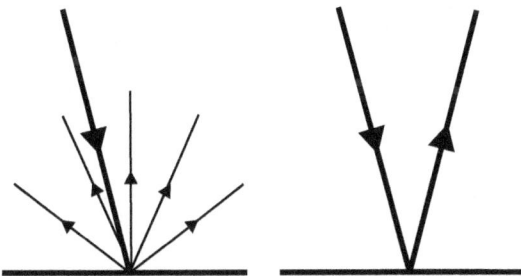

Fig. 9.19 Specular reflection

9.7.1 Scanline Rendering

Scanline rendering is used to demonstrate a visible surface. It is widely used for movie effects, due to its speed and realism. It has the side effect of only being able to "see" one pixel at a time, and therefore cannot create shadows naturally.

9.7.2 Ray Trace Rendering

A ray is traced back from the eye position, through the pixel on the monitor, until it intersects with a surface. When an imaginary line drawn from the eye, through a pixel, into a scene strikes a polygon, three things happen. First, the color and brightness values are calculated based on direct illumination from lights directly striking that polygon. Next, the angles of reflection and refraction are calculated, as shown in Fig. 9.20. The ray tracing process repeats once again, and so on, until a maximum number of iterations is reached or until no more surfaces are intersected. When all the rays have completed their journeys, the intensity and color values are combined and the pixel is painted. Ray tracing is very versatile. It can accurately account for the global illumination characteristics of direct illumination, shadows, specular reflections (e.g. mirrors), and refraction through transparent materials.

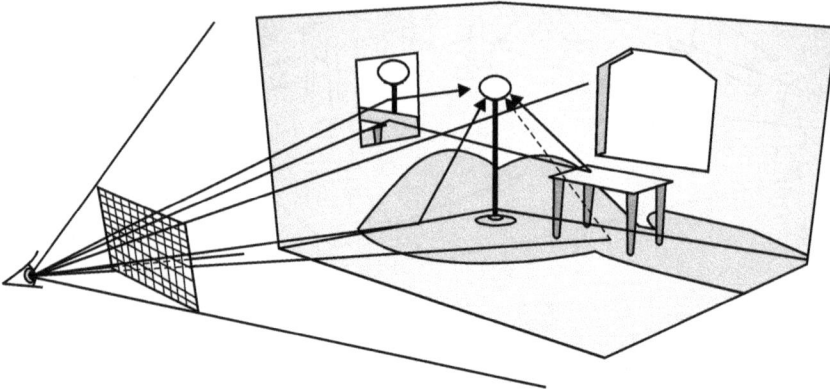

Fig. 9.20 Ray trace rendering

Advantages of ray tracing

- Reflections and refraction are calculated accurately
- Shadows can be calculated as well

Disadvantages of ray tracing:

- The process can be computationally expensive
- Not all behaviors of light are accounted for

9.7.3 Radiocity Rendering

This is the ability of a material's physical properties to reflect light and to impinge upon other materials. Consider the intersections of two walls at a corner (i.e., orthogonal to each other), one painted white and the other red. If a red object is in front of a white object, some of the red will appear on the white background. The rate at which energy leaves a surface is called radiocity. It is the sum of the rates at which the surface emits energy and reflects or transmits it from that surface or other surfaces. Fig. 9.21 shows rendering using radiocity.

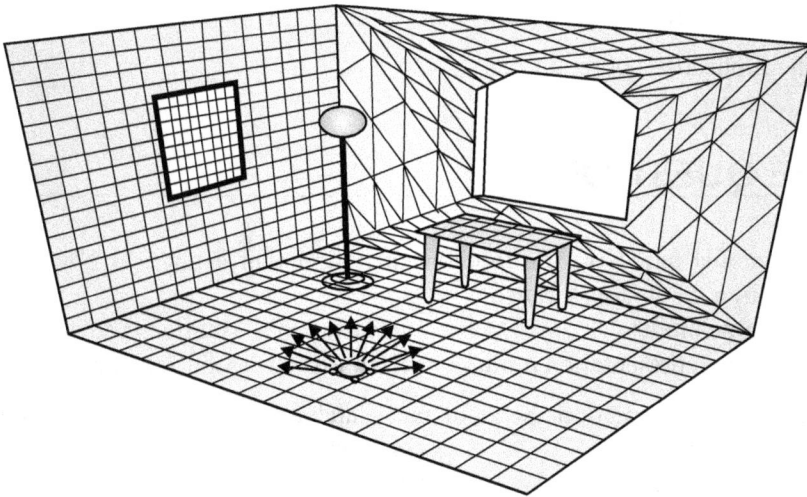

Fig. 9.21 Rendering using radiocity

- All energy emitted or reflected by every surface is accounted for by its reflection from or absorption by other surfaces.

- The amount of light distributed from each mesh element to every other mesh element is calculated; the final radiocity values are stored for each element of the mesh

Applications of radiocity

- Generating images that are much closer to reality

- Remote viewing of buildings

- Animation

- Producing photorealistic models and lifelike video games

EXERCISES

1. What do you mean by solid modeling? What are the techniques of solid modeling used in practice?

2. Explain wireframe modeling. Explain its advantages.

3. Write a short note on the approaches of solid modeling.

4. What do you mean by surface modeling?

5. Write the applications of rendering.

OBJECTIVE QUESTIONS

9.1 A solid model based on the topological notion that a physical object is bounded by a set of faces is called
(*a*) wireframe model   (*b*) surface of revolution model
(*c*) boundary representation model   (*d*) constructive solid geometry model

9.2 In boundary representation, the topological database is created by performing
(*a*) Euler operation   (*b*) Euclidean calculations
(*c*) Boolean operations   (*d*) set theory

9.3 A solid model based on the topological notion that a physical object can be divided into a set of primitives is called
(*a*) wireframe model   (*b*) surface of revolution model
(*c*) boundary representation model   (*d*) constructive solid geometry

9.4 The process of development of a solid model by combining primitives using Boolean operators is called
(*a*) transformation   (*d*) Euler operation
(*c*) set theory   (*d*) Euclidean operation

9.5 Common volumes shared by two primitives are obtained by following which Boolean operation?
(*a*) union   (*b*) intersection
(*c*) difference   (*d*) division

9.6 Difference Boolean operation is also referred as logical
(*a*) OR   (*b*) AND
(*c*) NAND   (*d*) NOT

9.7 Union Boolean operation is also referred as logical
(*a*) OR   (*b*) AND
(*c*) NAND   (*d*) NOT

9.8 Intersection Boolean operation is also referred as logical
(*a*) OR   (*b*) AND
(*c*) NAND   (*d*) NOT

9.9 CSG expression for union operation is given by
(a) $A \cup B$ (b) $A \cap B$
(c) $A - B$ (d) $A + B$

9.10 CSG expression for intersection operation is given by
(a) $A \cup B$ (b) $A - B$
(c) $A + B$ (d) $A \cap B$

9.11 In sweeping, what type of generator surface is translated or revolved to form a solid model?
(a) planar open domain (b) planar closed domain
(c) non-planar open domain (d) non-planar closed domain

9.12 Scan line, ray trace, and radiocity are types of
(a) solid modeling (b) clipping
(c) rendering (d) windowing

9.13 Advantages of wireframe modeling are
(a) it requires less memory (b) less computational time
(c) it allows to see the interior of the design (d) all of the above

9.14 Inability to determine computational information on mass properties is the disadvantage of which 3D modeling technique?
(a) wireframe modeling (b) solid modeling
(c) constructive solid geometry (d) boundary representation

9.15 Plane surfaces, ruled surfaces, and surface of revolution are examples of
(a) synthetic entities (b) analytical entities
(c) both (a) and (b) (d) neither (a) nor (b)

9.16 Hermite spline surfaces, B-spline surfaces, Bezier patches, and Coon patches are examples of
(a) synthetic entities (b) analytical entities
(c) both (a) and (b) (d) neither (a) nor (b)

9.17 In a CAD system, solid modeling schemes include
(a) primitive creation function (b) constructive solid modeling
(c) sweeping (d) boundary representation
(e) all of the above

9.18 In CSG, objects are represented as a combination of simpler solid objects called
(a) derivatives (b) Boolean operators
(c) models (d) primitives

9.19 B-rep is an extension by adding face information to
    (*a*) wireframe modeling   (*b*) solid modeling
    (*c*) constructive solid geometry   (*d*) none of the above

ANSWERS

9.1 (*c*)	**9.2** (*a*)	**9.3** (*d*)	**9.4** (*c*)	**9.5** (*b*)
9.6 (*d*)	**9.7** (*a*)	**9.8** (*b*)	**9.9** (*a*)	**9.10** (*d*)
9.11 (*b*)	**9.12** (*c*)	**9.13** (*d*)	**9.14** (*a*)	**9.15** (*b*)
9.16 (*b*)	**9.17** (*e*)	**9.18** (*d*)	**9.19** (*a*)	

Chapter 10 PROJECTIONS

10.1 INTRODUCTION

3D viewing operations are more complex than 2D viewing, not only because of the additional dimensions, but also because of limited display surface. In 2D, simple mapping produces an image; in 3D, there are many options depending on how the model is to be viewed—front, side, top, back. There is also a mismatch between the 3D model and the 2D image. To overcome all these differences, projection must be used to map the 2D projection plane; various types of projection are used in order to generate multiple views of a model. Therefore, projection is an important concept of the 3D viewing process.

10.2 PROJECTIONS

The problem of projecting a n-dimensional object into a 2D surface has been studied by engineers, architects, and artists for many years. In general, projections transform points in a coordinate system of n-dimensions into points in a coordinate system of a dimension less than n.

Computer graphics has long been used for studying n-dimensional objects by projecting them into 2D for viewing. We shall here limit our discussion to the projection from 3D to 2D.

The projection of a 3D object is defined by straight rays, emanating from the center of projection (CP), passing through each point of the object and intersecting a projection (or view) plane to form the projection. In general, the center of projection is at a finite distance from the projection plane. In some cases, the center of projection tends to be at infinity. Fig. 10.1 shows two different types of projections.

The class of projections with which we deal here is known as planar geometric projection because projection is onto a plane rather than onto a curved surface and uses straight rather than curved projection. Planar geometric projections can be divided into two classes: perspective and parallel. The distinction lies in the relation of the center of projection to the projection plane.

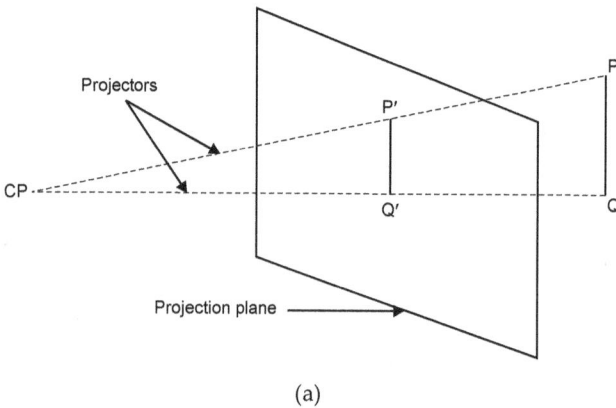

(a)

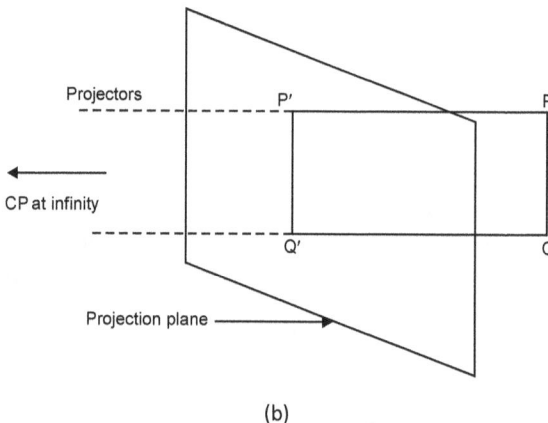

(b)

Fig. 10.1 (a) Perspective projection, (b) parallel projection

If the center of projection is at a finite distance from projection plane, then the projection is perspective, as shown in Fig. 10.1(a). Now, as the center of projection moves towards infinity, the projectors become parallel; hence the projection is called parallel, as shown in Fig. 10.1(b).

10.2.1 Perspective Projection

The center of projection is located at a finite distance from the projection plane. When a perspective projection is defined, its center of projection is explicitly specified: the center of projection is a point and has homogeneous coordinates of the form $(x, y, z, 1)$. The visual effect of a perspective projection is similar to that of a photographic system and of the human visual system, called perspective foreshortening. The size of perspective projection of an object varies inversely with the distance of that object from the center of projection. The perspective projection of objects tends to look realistic, but it is not useful for recording the exact shape and measurements of the objects. Distance cannot be taken from the projection. The perspective projection gives a realistic image but loses the true dimensions. A perspective projection is described mathematically by prescribing the following:

1. **Center of projection (CP):** A point where lines of projection (which are not parallel to the projection plane) appear to meet. The eye of the artist generally acts as a center of projection when they prepare realistic images of 3D objects.

2. **The view plane or projection plane:** The view plane is determined by:

   (a) Reference point $R_0 (X_0, Y_0, Z_0)$

   (b) Unit vector, $\vec{N} = n_1 \hat{i} + n_2 \hat{j} + n_3 \hat{k}$ which is normal to the plane

3. **The location of an object:** A point $P(x, y, z)$ located in the world coordinate system. The objective of perspective projection is to determine the image point $P'(x', y, z')$ on the view plane—see Fig. 10.2.

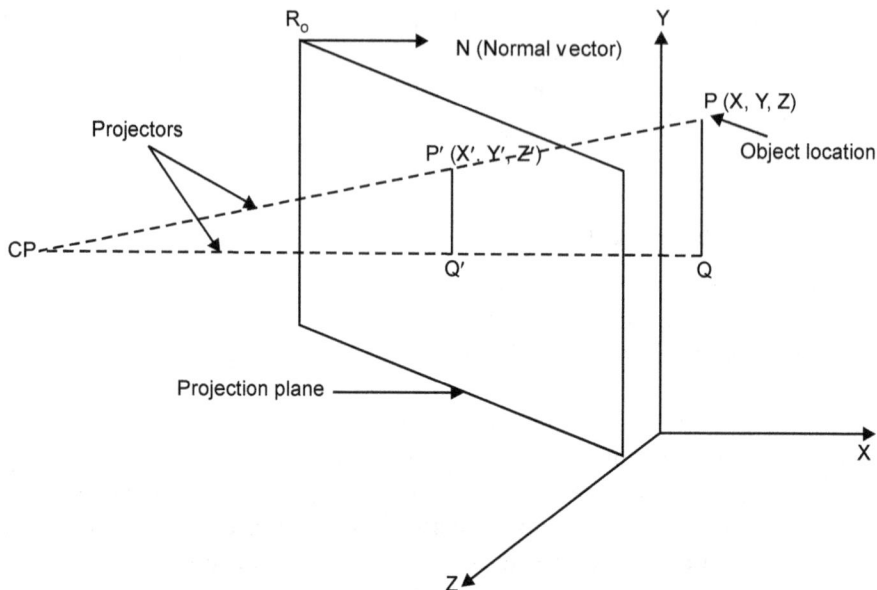

Fig. 10.2 Location of the object and the image in the perspective projection

Perspective projections are characterized by:

(a) Perspective foreshortening: This is the illusion that objects and lengths appear smaller as their distance from the center of projection increases. The size of an object (d) varies inversely with the distance of that object (r) from the center of projection, that is, $d \infty \dfrac{1}{r}$.

(b) Vanishing points: The perspective projection of any set of parallel lines that are not parallel to the projection plane coverage to a point called the vanishing point (VP). In 3D, the parallel lines meet only at infinity, so the VP can be thought of as the projection of a point at infinity. Therefore, there is an infinity of VPs, one for each of the infinity of directions in which a line can be oriented.

If a set of lines (projectors) is parallel to one of the three principal axes, the VP is called an axis vanishing point (or principal vanishing point). There are almost three such points, corresponding to the number of principal axes cut by the projection plane.

For example, if the projection plane cuts only the z-axis (i.e. normal to it) then the z-axis has a VP, because lines parallel to the x- or y-axis are also parallel to the projection planes and then have no VP. Perspective projections are categorized by their number of principal VPs, i.e., by the number of axes the projection plane cuts. Thus, there are three types of perspective projections.

1-point perspective projection: 1-point perspective projection occurs when the projection plane is perpendicular to one of the principal axes (let it be z-axis). In this case the center of projection is located along one of the three coordinate axes. The other two centers are at infinity. So horizontal lines remain horizontal and vertical lines remain vertical. Fig. 10.3 shows two different 1-point perspective projections of a cube. In this case, lines parallel to the x- and y-axis do not converge; only lines parallel to the z-axis do so.

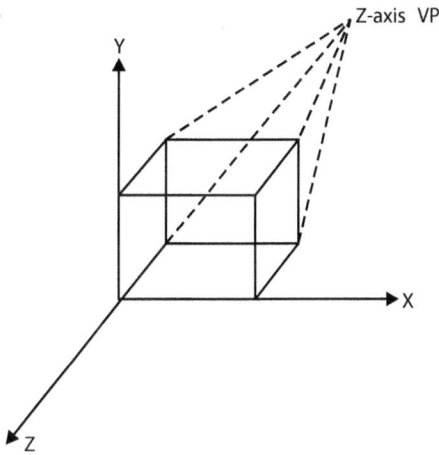

Fig. 10.3 1-point perspective projection

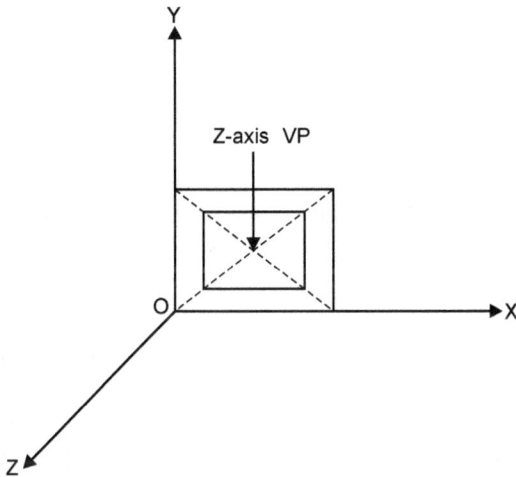

Fig. 10.4 2-point perspective projection

2-point perspective projection: 2-point perspective projection occurs when the projection plane intersects two principal axes. Let these axes be z- and x-axis. Therefore, lines parallel to the y-axis do not converge in the projection. 2-point perspective projection is used in architectural, engineering, industrial design, and advertising drawings. Fig. 10.4 shows the construction of a 2-point perspective projection.

3-point perspective projection: 3-point perspective projection occurs when the projection plane intersects all three principal axes. These are used less frequently, since they add little realism beyond that afforded by the 2-point perspective. See Fig. 10.5.

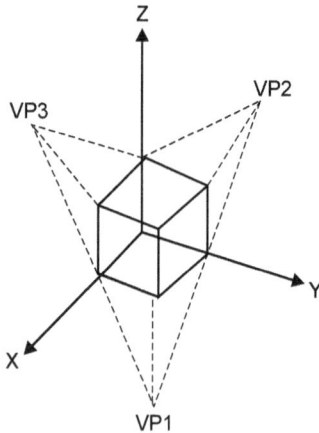

Fig. 10.5 3-point perspective projection

10.2.2 Parallel Projection

The center of projection is located at infinity in parallel projection, because all of the projections (or lines of projections) are parallel to each other. The parallel projection is a less realistic view because perspective foreshortening is lacking, although there can be different constant foreshortening along each axis. Parallel projection can be used to preserve the true dimensions of an object but does not produce a realistic picture. Parallel projections have been used by engineers and draftsmen in order to create working drawings.

In parallel projections, the projection (or image) is obtained at a location on the projection plane where the parallel lines of projection intersect the projection plane. These lines of projections are drawn from the object location along a particular direction. The direction of projection is explicitly given (see Fig. 10.6).

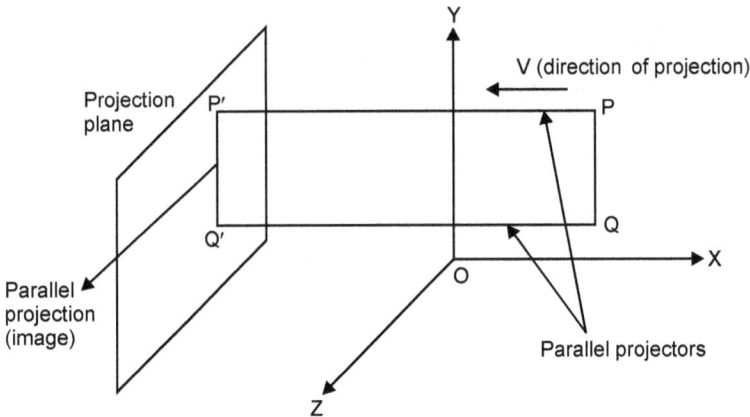

Fig. 10.6 Parallel projection

Depending on the relation between direction of projection and normal to the projection plane, the parallel projections are categorized into two types:

(a) Orthographic parallel projection

(b) Oblique parallel projection

10.2.2.1 Orthographic Parallel Projection

In orthographic parallel projection, directions of projection (lines of projection) are perpendicular to the plane of projection as shown in Fig. 10.7. Orthographic parallel projections are mainly of two types.

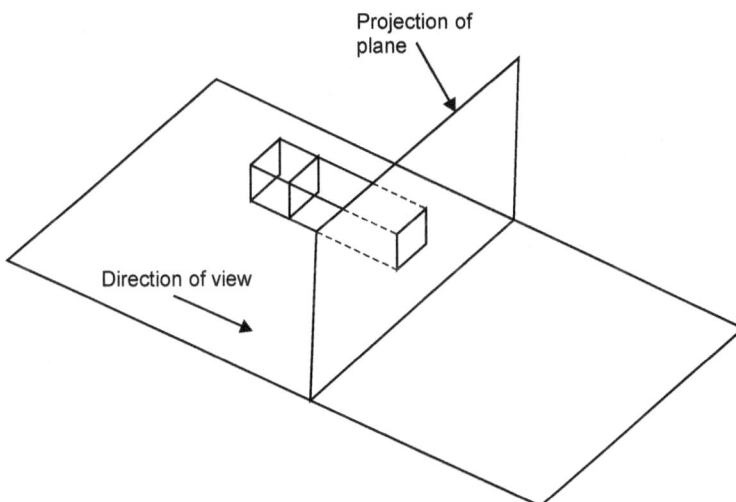

Fig. 10.7 Orthographic projection

(i) *Multi-view orthographic parallel projection:* The projection plane is perpendicular to the principal axis and the direction of projection is parallel to the principal axis. These projections are mainly of the following types:

(a) front elevation

(b) top elevation or plane elevation

(c) side elevation

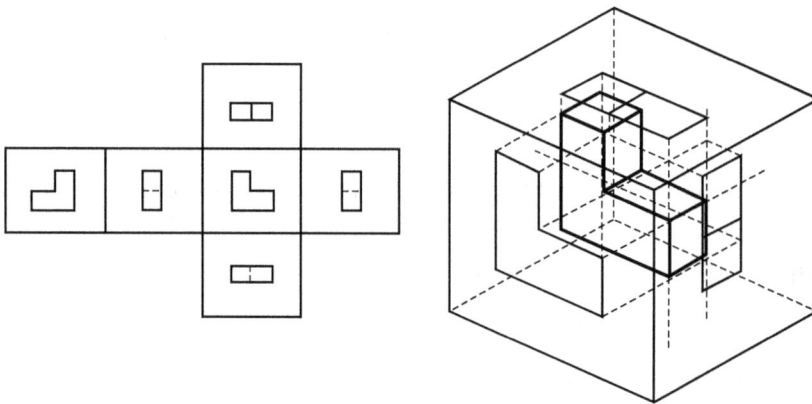

Fig. 10.8 Multi-view orthographic parallel projection

Fig. 10.8 shows the construction of multi-view orthographic parallel projection. These types of projections are generally used in engineering drawing to project multiple views (or faces) of machine parts or buildings. Since each projection depicts only one face of an object, the 3D nature of the projected object can be difficult to deduce.

(ii) *Axonometric orthographic parallel projections:* Projection planes are not perpendicular to a principal axis and therefore show multiple faces of an object at once. Axonometric orthographic parallel projection is shown in Fig. 10.9. It can resemble perspective projection in this way, but differs in that the shortening is uniform, rather than being related to the distance from the center of projection.

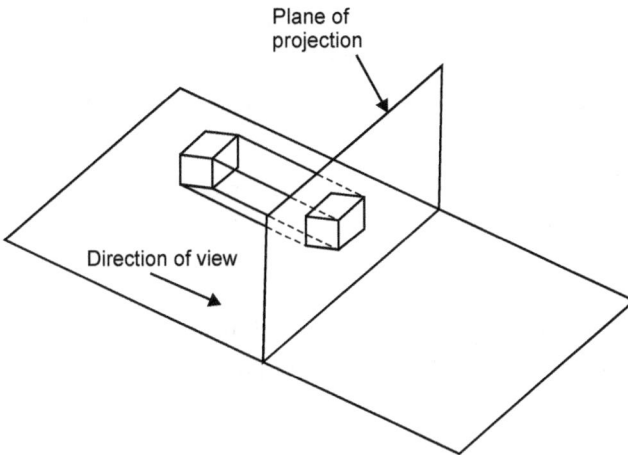

Fig. 10.9 Axonometric orthographic parallel projections

Parallelism of lines is preserved but angles are not; distance can be measured along each principal axis with different scale factors. Axonometric orthographic parallel projections are categorized into three types:

(a) **Isometric:** The isometric projection is commonly used. In this case, the projection plane normal (i.e. the direction of projection) makes equal angles with each principal axis. The projection plane normal is represented in the following vector form:

$$n_x \hat{i} + n_y \hat{j} + n_z \hat{k}$$

$$\left| n_x \right| = \left| n_y \right| = \left| n_z \right|$$

$$\pm n_x = \pm n_y = \pm n_z$$

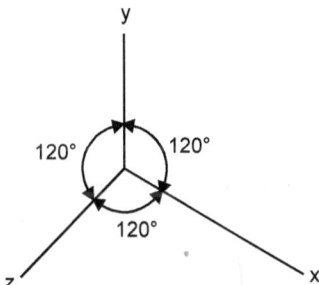

Fig. 10.10 Isometric projectors

There are just eight directions that satisfy the above conditions. Therefore, in this type of projection, the angles between the principal axes are all equal to 120° as shown in Fig. 10.10. In isometric projection all three principal axes are equally foreshortened, due to this measurement along the axes being made to the same scale ("iso" means equal and "metric" means measure).

(b) Diametric: In this case the direction of projection makes equal angles with exactly two of the principal axes.

(c) Trimetric: In this case, the direction of projection makes unequal angles with all the principal axes.

10.2.2.2 Oblique Projection

The projections are inclined with respect to the projection plane; also, one of the faces of the object is kept parallel to the projection plane. Fig. 10.11 shows oblique projection. Oblique projection combines the properties of multi-view orthographic projection with those of axonometric projection. The projection plane is normal to the principal axes, so the projection of the face of the object must be parallel to the projection plane. This allows the measurement of angles and distances. Oblique projection is categorized into two types:

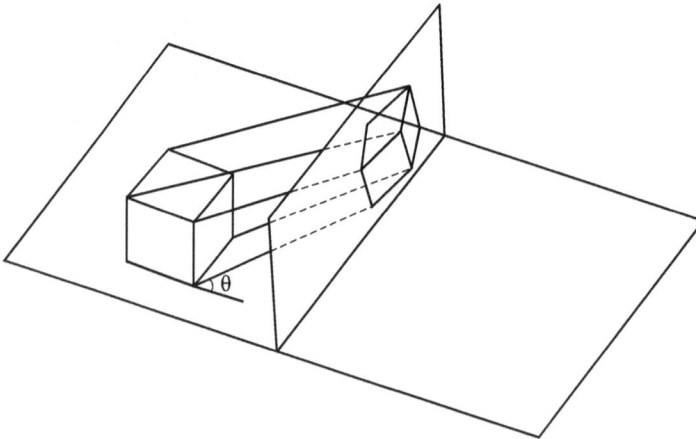

Fig. 10.11 Oblique projection

(a) Cavalier: In this case the direction of projection makes a 45° angle with the projection plane. Due to this, the projection of a line perpendicular to the projection plane has the same length as the line itself. That is, there is no foreshortening along this direction. Fig. 10.12 shows cavalier projection of the unit cube into the *xy* plane and shows all the edges of the cube project at unit length. If the direction of projection makes a 45° angle with the projection plane, then the direction of projection is given by the vector, and if angle is 30° then the direction of projection is given by the vector.

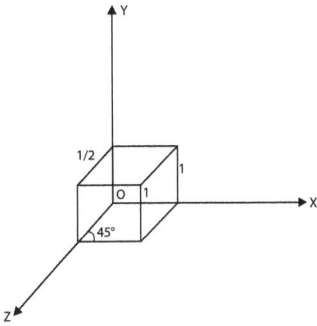

Fig. 10.12 Cavalier projection in the *xy* plane

(*b*) **Cabinet projection:** In this case the lines of projection make $\tan^{-1}(2) = 63.4°$ angle with the projection plane; due to this, the lines perpendicular to the projection plane project at one half their length. Cabinet projection produces more realistic image, due to foreshortening. Fig. 10.13 shows cabinet projection of a unit cube into the *xy* plane.

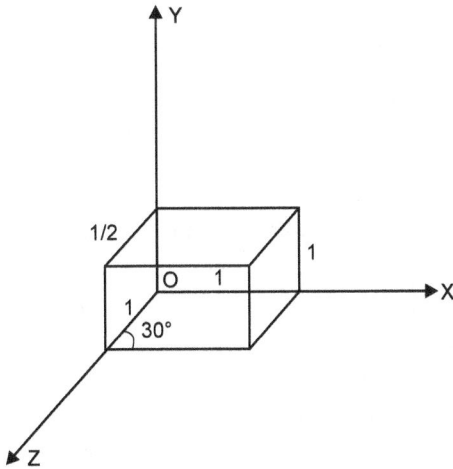

Fig. 10.13 Cabinet projection

Edges parallel to the *x*-axis and the *y*-axis are projected at unit length and the edge is parallel to *z*-axis at half of the original length. If the line of projection makes an angle of 45° with the projection plane, then the direction of projection of given by the vector:

$$\vec{V} = \frac{\sqrt{2}}{4}\, \hat{i} + \frac{\sqrt{2}}{4}\, \hat{j} - \hat{k}$$

If the angle is 30° then the direction of projection is given by the vector:

$$\vec{V} = \frac{\sqrt{3}}{4}\ \hat{i} + \frac{1}{4}\ \hat{j} - \hat{k}$$

10.2.3 Differentials Between Parallel Projection and Perspective Projection

	Perspective Projection	Parallel Projection
1.	The center of projection is at a finite distance from the projection plane.	The center of projection is at an infinite distance from the projection plane.
2.	The lines of projection or projectors converge to a point; that is, lines of projection appear to meet at a point on the view plane called the vanishing point.	Projectors are parallel.
3.	To define perspective projection, we explicitly specify the center of projection.	To define parallel projection we specify the direction of projection.
4.	The visual effect is similar to that of a photographic system and of the human visual system; this feature is known as perspective shortening.	This is used by drafters and organizers to create a working drawing of an object which preserves its scale and shape.
5.	The size of the projection of an object varies inversely with the distance of that object from the center of projection.	The scale and shape of an object is preserved; there can be different constant foreshortening along each axis.
6.	Perspective projection of an object looks realistic, due to perspective foreshortening and vanishing points.	Parallel projection is a less realistic view because perspective foreshortening is lacking.
7.	Perspective projection is not useful for recording the exact shape and measurement of the objects.	Parallel projection is useful for exact measurement and shape of objects.
8.	Perspective projections are categorized by their number of principal vanishing points and by the number of axes the projection plane cuts.	Parallel projections are categorized by the relation between the direction of projection and normal to the projection plane.

Mathematical description of a parallel projection

In order to determine parallel projection we have to prescribe:

1. the direction of projection, which is prescribed by the given vector $\vec{V}$. If $\vec{V}$ is normal to the projection plane then the parallel projection is called orthographic, otherwise it is called oblique.

2. the projection plane or view plane, which is specified by its reference point R_0 (X_0, Y_0, Z_0) and normal vector $\vec{N} = n_1\hat{i} + n_2\hat{j} + n_3\hat{k}$.

3. the location $P(x, y, z)$ of an object in the world coordinate system. Now our objective is to determine the location of image $P'(x', y', z')$ by using the above three parameters (see Fig. 10.14).

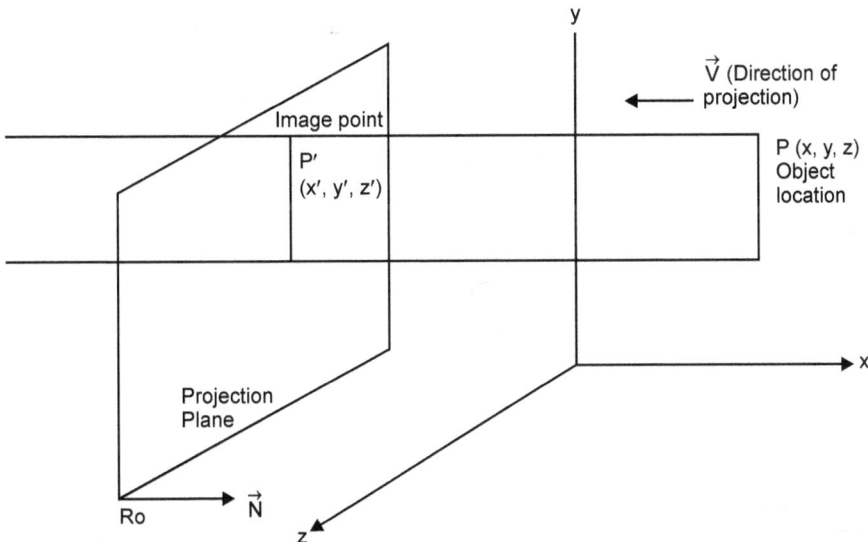

Fig. 10.14 Location of an object and an image in parallel projection

10.3 SOLVED PROBLEMS

Problem 1

Obtain standard perspective projection onto the *xy* plane.

Solution

Consider a point $P(z, y, z)$ in space as shown in Fig. 10.15. Let $P'(x', y', 0)$ be the perspective projection of $P(x, y, z)$ onto the *xy* plane, with the center of projection along the *z*-axis at a distance d from the projection plane.

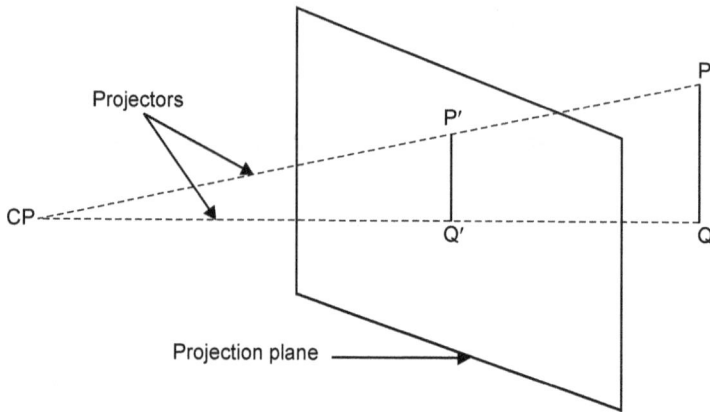

Fig. 10.15 Perspective projection

The perspective projection of point p can be found as follows:

(i) Looking along the y-axis towards the origin as CAP and COP′ are similar. See Fig. 10.16.

Therefore,

$$\frac{x'}{x} = \frac{d}{d-z}$$

or $$x' = \frac{dx}{d-z}$$ ...(10.1)

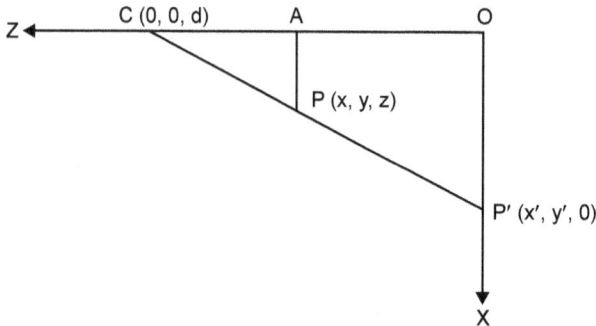

Fig. 10.16 Direction of view along the y-axis

(ii) Looking along the x-axis towards the origin as CBP and COP′ are similar. See Fig. 10.17.

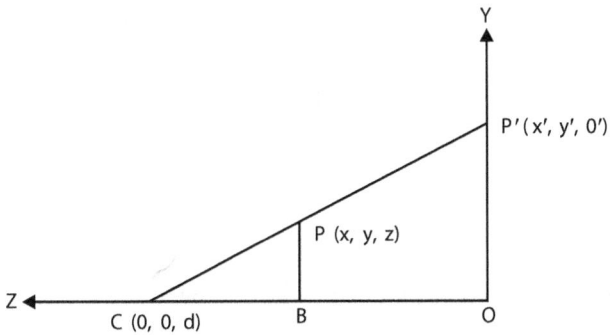

Fig. 10.17 Direction of view along the x-axis

Therefore,

$$\frac{y'}{y} = \frac{d}{d-z}$$

or

$$y' = \frac{dx}{d-z} \qquad \qquad ...(10.2)$$

On the basis of Eqs (10.1) and (10.2), the projected point becomes

$$\begin{bmatrix} x' & y' & z' & 1 \end{bmatrix} = \begin{bmatrix} \dfrac{dx}{d-z} & \dfrac{dy}{d-z} & 0 & 1 \end{bmatrix}$$

$$\begin{bmatrix} x' & y' & z' & 1 \end{bmatrix} = \begin{bmatrix} x & y & z & 1 \end{bmatrix} \begin{bmatrix} d & 0 & 0 & 0 \\ 0 & d & 0 & 0 \\ 0 & 0 & 0 & -1 \\ 0 & 0 & 0 & d \end{bmatrix}$$

$$[P'] = [P][M_{\text{PER}}\hat{k}]$$

where

$$[M_{\text{PER}}\hat{k}] = \begin{bmatrix} d & 0 & 0 & 0 \\ 0 & d & 0 & 0 \\ 0 & 0 & 0 & -1 \\ 0 & 0 & 0 & d \end{bmatrix}$$

If the center of projection is located along the x-axis, then the perspective projection matrix $M_{PER}i$ becomes:

$$[M_{PER}\hat{i}] = \begin{bmatrix} 0 & 0 & 0 & -1 \\ 0 & d & 0 & 0 \\ 0 & 0 & d & 0 \\ 0 & 0 & 0 & d \end{bmatrix}$$

If the center of projection is located along the y-axis, the perspective projection matrix $M_{PER}j$ becomes:

$$[M_{PER}\hat{j}] = \begin{bmatrix} d & 0 & 0 & 0 \\ 0 & 0 & 0 & -1 \\ 0 & 0 & d & 0 \\ 0 & 0 & 0 & d \end{bmatrix}$$

Problem 2

A tetrahedron is defined by the coordinates of its vertices as follows $P_1 (3, 4, 0)$, $P_2(1, 0, 4)$, $P_3(2, 0, 5)$, $P_4(4, 0, 3)$. Find the perspective projection onto the projection plane at $z = 0$. The center of projection should be located at $d = -5$ (as negative side of z-axis).

Solution

Here $\qquad\qquad\qquad\qquad\qquad d = -5$

Therefore, perspective matrix along the z-axis is given by:

$$[M_{PER}\hat{k}] = \begin{bmatrix} -5 & 0 & 0 & 0 \\ 0 & -5 & 0 & 0 \\ 0 & 0 & 0 & 1 \\ 0 & 0 & 0 & -5 \end{bmatrix}$$

The projected points are obtained as follows:

$$\begin{bmatrix} P_1' & P_2' & P_3' & P_4' \end{bmatrix} = \begin{bmatrix} P_1 & P_2 & P_3 & P_4 \end{bmatrix} [M_{PER}\hat{k}]$$

$$= \begin{bmatrix} 3 & 4 & 0 & 1 \\ 1 & 0 & 4 & 1 \\ 2 & 0 & 5 & 1 \\ 4 & 0 & 3 & 1 \end{bmatrix} \begin{bmatrix} -5 & 0 & 0 & 0 \\ 0 & -5 & 0 & 0 \\ 0 & 0 & 0 & 0 \\ 0 & 0 & 0 & -5 \end{bmatrix}$$

$$= \begin{bmatrix} -15 & -20 & 0 & -5 \\ -5 & 0 & 0 & -9 \\ -10 & 0 & 0 & -10 \\ -20 & 0 & 0 & -8 \end{bmatrix}$$

$$= \begin{bmatrix} 3 & 4 & 0 & 1 \\ \dfrac{5}{9} & 0 & 0 & 1 \\ 1 & 0 & 0 & 1 \\ \dfrac{10}{4} & 0 & 0 & 1 \end{bmatrix}$$

$$P_1'(3, 4, 0), \quad P_2'\left(\frac{5}{9}, 0, 0\right), \quad P_3'(1,0,0), \quad P_4'\left(\frac{10}{4}, 0, 0\right)$$

Problem 3

Find the standard perspective projection of a unit cube on the *xy* plane with $d = 5$ units. Refer to Fig. 10.18.

Solution

Here $\qquad\qquad d = 5$

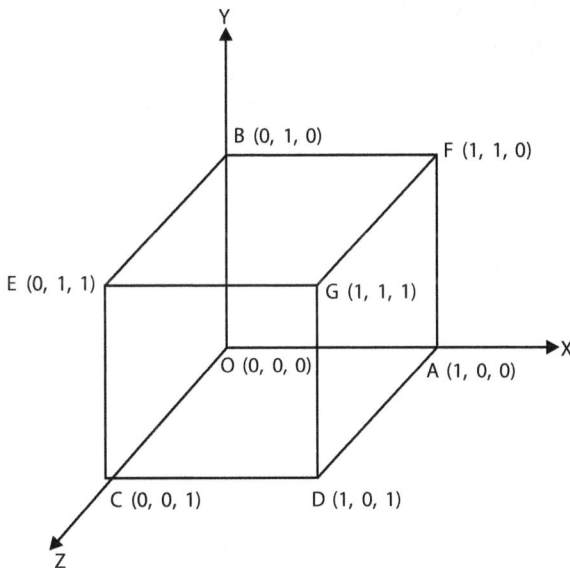

Fig 10.18 A unit cube

The perspective projection along the z-axis is given by:

$$M_{\text{PER}}\hat{k} = \begin{bmatrix} 5 & 0 & 0 & 0 \\ 0 & 5 & 0 & 0 \\ 0 & 0 & 0 & -1 \\ 1 & 0 & 0 & 5 \end{bmatrix}$$

The unit cube is represented by the following matrix:

$$P = \begin{bmatrix} 0 & 0 & 0 & 1 \\ 1 & 0 & 0 & 1 \\ 0 & 1 & 0 & 1 \\ 0 & 0 & 1 & 1 \\ 1 & 0 & 1 & 1 \\ 1 & 1 & 0 & 1 \\ 0 & 1 & 1 & 1 \\ 1 & 1 & 1 & 1 \end{bmatrix} \begin{matrix} O \\ A \\ B \\ C \\ D \\ E \\ F \\ G \end{matrix}$$

The projected points are determined as follows:

$$[P'] = [P][M_{\text{PER}}\hat{k}]$$

$$= \begin{bmatrix} 0 & 0 & 0 & 1 \\ 1 & 0 & 0 & 1 \\ 0 & 1 & 0 & 1 \\ 0 & 0 & 1 & 1 \\ 1 & 0 & 1 & 1 \\ 1 & 1 & 0 & 1 \\ 0 & 1 & 1 & 1 \\ 1 & 1 & 1 & 1 \end{bmatrix} \begin{bmatrix} 5 & 0 & 0 & 0 \\ 0 & 5 & 0 & 0 \\ 0 & 0 & 0 & -1 \\ 1 & 0 & 0 & 5 \end{bmatrix}$$

$$
= \begin{bmatrix}
0 & 0 & 0 & 5 \\
5 & 0 & 0 & 5 \\
0 & 5 & 0 & 5 \\
0 & 0 & 0 & 4 \\
5 & 0 & 0 & 4 \\
5 & 5 & 0 & 5 \\
0 & 5 & 0 & 4 \\
5 & 5 & 0 & 4
\end{bmatrix}
$$

$$
P' = \begin{bmatrix}
0 & 0 & 0 & 1 \\
1 & 0 & 0 & 1 \\
0 & 1 & 0 & 1 \\
0 & 0 & 0 & 1 \\
\dfrac{5}{4} & 0 & 0 & 1 \\
1 & 1 & 0 & 1 \\
0 & \dfrac{5}{4} & 0 & 1 \\
\dfrac{5}{4} & \dfrac{5}{4} & 0 & 1
\end{bmatrix}
\begin{matrix}
O' \\ A' \\ B' \\ C' \\ D' \\ E' \\ F' \\ G'
\end{matrix}
$$

Therefore, projected points are $O'(0, 0, 0)$, $A'(1, 0, 0)$, $B'(0, 1, 0)$, $C'(0, 0, 0)$, $D'\left(\dfrac{5}{4}, 0, 0\right)$, $E'(1, 1, 0)$, $F'\left(0, \dfrac{5}{4}, 0\right)$ $G'\left(\dfrac{5}{4}, \dfrac{5}{4}, 0\right)$

Problem 4

Obtain standard 2-point and 3-point perspective projections.

Solution

In order to obtain 2-point and 3-point perspective projections, it is required to create a 4×4 homogeneous coordinate transformation matrix with two or three of the top three elements on the fourth row having non-zero values. This matrix is then multiplied by an orthographic projection matrix.

For a 2-point perspective projection, the transformation matrix is written as:

$$\begin{bmatrix} 1 & 0 & 0 & p \\ 0 & 1 & 0 & q \\ 0 & 0 & 1 & 0 \\ 0 & 0 & 0 & 1 \end{bmatrix} \text{ or } \begin{bmatrix} 1 & 0 & 0 & 0 \\ 0 & 1 & 0 & q \\ 0 & 0 & 1 & r \\ 0 & 0 & 0 & 1 \end{bmatrix}$$

For a 3-point perspective projection, the transformation matrix is written as:

$$\begin{bmatrix} 1 & 0 & 0 & p \\ 0 & 1 & 0 & q \\ 0 & 0 & 1 & r \\ 0 & 0 & 0 & 1 \end{bmatrix}$$

These matrices can also be obtained by concatenation of the appropriate 1-point perspective transformation matrices:

$$\begin{bmatrix} 1 & 0 & 0 & p \\ 0 & 1 & 0 & 0 \\ 0 & 0 & 1 & 0 \\ 0 & 0 & 0 & 1 \end{bmatrix}\begin{bmatrix} 1 & 0 & 0 & 0 \\ 0 & 1 & 0 & q \\ 0 & 0 & 1 & 0 \\ 0 & 0 & 0 & 1 \end{bmatrix} = \begin{bmatrix} 1 & 0 & 0 & p \\ 0 & 1 & 0 & q \\ 0 & 0 & 1 & 0 \\ 0 & 0 & 0 & 1 \end{bmatrix}$$

EXERCISES

1. Obtain 2-point and 3-point perspective projections of a unit cube.

2. Obtain 2-point perspective projection of a unit cube obtained by rotating the cube 30° about the y-axis and translating it by $(0, 3, -3)$. The center of projection is at $(0, 0, 2)$.

3. Obtain perspective projection of any point in the plane $z = d$ by standard perspective projection.

4. By standard perspective projection, obtain the projection of a line joining the points $a(2, 2, 2d)$ and $b(-1, 1, 0)$, when the projection plane is $z = d$ and center of projection is at $(0, 0, d)$.

OBJECTIVE QUESTIONS

10.1 Subcategories of orthographic projection are
  (*a*) isometric, diametric, trimetric   (*b*) cavalier, cabinet, isometric
  (*c*) cavalier, cabinet   (*d*) isometric, cavalier, trimetric

10.2 When the center of projection is located at a finite distance from the projection plane, this projection method is called
  (*a*) orthographic projection   (*b*) perspective projection
  (*c*) parallel projection   (*d*) planar geometric projection

10.3 Perspective projections are characterized by perspective foreshortening in which
  (*a*) the object appears bigger as its distance from the center of projection increases
  (*b*) the object appears smaller as its distance from the center of projection increases
  (*c*) the object appears unchanged as its distance from the center of projection changes
  (*d*) none of the above

10.4 In 3D perspective projection, the vanishing point can be thought of as
  (*a*) finite distance
  (*b*) infinity
  (*c*) two times the distance of the object from the projection plane
  (*d*) three times the distance of the object from the projection plane

10.5 1-point perspective projection occurs when the projection plane is
  (*a*) parallel to one of the principle axes
  (*b*) inclined to one of the principle axes
  (*c*) perpendicular to one of the principle axes
  (*d*) none of the above

10.6 In parallel projection, the center of projection is located at
  (*a*) finite distance
  (*b*) infinity
  (*c*) two times the distance of the object from the projection plane
  (*d*) four times the distance of the object from the projection plane

10.7 In orthographic parallel projection, the direction of projectors is
(a) parallel to the plane of projection
(b) inclined to the plane of projection
(c) obliqued to the plane of projection
(d) perpendicular to the plane of projection

10.8 A multi-view projection method is
(a) isometric   (b) diametric
(c) triametric   (d) none of the above

10.9 Projection planes are not perpendicular to a principle axis and show multiple faces of an object at once; such a type of projection is called
(a) orthographic projection   (b) oblique projection
(c) parallel projection   (d) axonometric projection

10.10 In oblique projection, projectors are
(a) parallel to the plane of projection
(b) inclined to the plane of projection
(c) perpendicular to the plane of projection
(d) none of the above

10.11 In cavalier projection, the angle between the projector and the plane of projection is
(a) 30°   (b) 45°
(c) 63.4°   (d) 120°

ANSWERS

10.1 (a)	**10.2** (b)	**10.3** (b)	**10.4** (b)	**10.5** (c)
10.6 (b)	**10.7** (d)	**10.8** (d)	**10.9** (d)	**10.10** (b)
10.11 (b)				

11 Chapter GRAPHICS PROGRAMS IN C LANGUAGE

11.1 PROGRAM-1

/* PROGRAM FOR LINE GENERATION USING DDA ALGORITHM */

```c
#include<stdio.h>
#include<conio.h>
#include<graphics.h>
#include<math.h>
void main()
{
  int xA, xB, yA, yB, dx, dy, i;
  float xincr, yincr, x, y, DENO;
  int gd = DETECT,gm;
  initgraph(&gd, &gm,"c:\\tc\\bgi");
  printf("Enter the start pt co-ordinates");
  scanf("%d%d", &xA, &yA);
  printf("Enter end point co-ordinates");
  scanf("%d%d", &xB, &yB);
  dx = xB - xA;
  dy = yB - yA;
  if (abs (dy) < = abs (dx))
      DENO = abs(dx);
  else
      DENO = abs(dy);
  xincr = dx/DENO;
```

291

```
    yincr = dy/DENO;
    x = xA;
    y = yA;
    for(i = 0; i< = abs (DENO); i++)
    {
        putpixel(floor(x), floor(y), 2);
        x = x + xincr;
        y = y + yincr;
    }
    getch();
}
```

11.2 PROGRAM-2

/* PROGRAM FOR LINE GENERATION USING BRESENHAM'S LINE GENERATION ALGORITHM */

```
#include<graphics.h>
#include<stdio.h>
#include<math.h>
#include<conio.h>
void main()
{
  int xa, ya, xb, yb;
  int dx, dy;
  int x, y;
  int p;
  int i;
  int signx, signy;
  int gd = DETECT,gm;
  initgraph(&gd, &gm,"c: \\tc\\bgi");
  printf("enter start point coordinate");
  scanf("%d%d", &xa, &ya);
  printf("enter end point coordinate");
  scanf("%d%d", &xb, &yb);
  dx = xb - xa;
  dy = yb - ya;
  x = xa;
  y = ya;
  if (dx > = 0)
      signx = +1;
  else
      signx = -1;
  if (dy > = 0)
      signy = +1;
  else
      signy = -1;
  if (abs(dy) < abs(dx))
  {
      p = (2 * dy * signy) - (dx * signx);
      for (i = 0; i < = dx * signx; i++)
```

```
    {
        putpixel(floor(x),floor(y),RED);
        if (p < 0)
        {
            x = x + signx;
            y = y;
            p = p + (2 * dy * signy);
        }
        else
        {
            x = x + signx;
            y = y + signy;
            p = p + (2 * dy * signy) - (2 * dx * signx);
        }
    }
}
else
{
    p = (2 * dx * signx - dy * signy);
    for( i =0; i < = dy * signy; i++)
    {
        putpixel(floor(x),floor(y),RED);
        if (p < 0)
        {
            x = x;
            y = y + signy;
            p = p + 2 * dx * signx;
        }

        else
        {
            x=x+signx;
            y=y+signy;
            p=p+(2*dx*signx)-(2*dy* signy);
        }
    }
}
getch();
}
```

11.3 PROGRAM-3

/* PROGRAM FOR CIRCLE GENERATION USING BRESENHAM'S MIDPOINT CIRCLE GENERATION ALGORITHM */

```
#include<conio.h>
#include<stdio.h>
#include<math.h>
#include<graphics.h>
void main()
```

```
{
  int xc, yc, R, p, i;
  int x, y;
  int gd = DETECT, gm;
  initgraph(&gd, &gm,"c:\\tc\\bgi");
  printf("Enter the co-ordinates of Centre of Circle");
  scanf("%d%d",&xc,&yc);
  printf("Enter Radius of Circle");
  scanf("%d", &R);
  x = 0;
  y = R;
  p = 1 - R;
  for (i = 0; x < = y; i++)
  {
      putpixel((x + xc), (y + yc), CYAN);
      if(p < 0)
      {
          x = x + 1;
          y = y;
          p = p + 2 * x + 3;
      }
      else
      {
          x = x + 1;
          y = y - 1;
          p = p + 2 * x - 2 * y + 5;
      }
      putpixel((x + xc), (-y + yc), CYAN);
      putpixel((-x + xc), (y + yc), CYAN);
      putpixel((-x + xc), (-y + yc), CYAN);
      putpixel((y + xc), (x + yc), CYAN);
      putpixel((y + xc), (-x + yc), CYAN);
      putpixel((-y + xc), (x + yc), CYAN);
      putpixel((-y + xc), (-x + yc), CYAN);
  }
  getch();
}
```

11.4 PROGRAM-4

/* PROGRAM FOR ELLIPSE GENERATION USING BRESENHAM'S MIDPOINT ELLIPSE GENERATION ALGORITHM */

```
#include<graphics.h>
#include<math.h>
#include<stdio.h>
#include<conio.h>
void main()
```

```c
{
  int rx, ry, xc, yc, x1, y1, x2, y2, p1, p2, i, j;
  float gd = DETECT,gm;
  initgraph(&gd, &gm,"c:\\tc\\bgi");
  printf("enter the center of the ellipse");
  scanf("%d%d", &xc, &yc);
  printf("enter semi_major and semi_minor axis");
  scanf("%d%d", &rx, &ry);
  x1 = 0;
  y1 = ry;
  p1 = (ry^2 - ry*rx^2);
  for(i = 0; x1 * ry^2 < y1*rx^2; i++)
  {
      if(p1 < 0)
      {
          x1 = x1+1;
          y1 = y1;
          p1 = p1 + (2*x1 + 3) * ry^2;
      }
      else
      {
          x1 = x1 + 1;
          y1 = y1 - 1;
          p1 = p1 + (2 * x1 + 3) * ry^2 + (2 - 2*y1) * rx^2;
      }
      putpixel(x1 + xc, y1 + yc, 1);
      putpixel(-x1 + xc, y1 + yc, 1);
      putpixel(x1 + xc, -y1 + yc, 1);
      putpixel(-x1 + xc, -y1 + yc, 1);
  }
  x2 = rx;
  y2 = 0;
  p2 = rx^2 - rx*ry^2;
  for(j = 0; x2*ry^2 > y2*rx^2; j++)
  {
      if(p2 < 0)
      {
          x2 = x2;
          y2 = y2 + 1;
          p2 = p2 + (2*y2 + 3)*rx^2;
      }
      else
      {
          x2 = x2 - 1;
          y2 = y2 + 1;
          p2 = p2 + (2 * y2 + 3) * rx^2 - (2 * x2 - 2) * ry^2;
      }
      putpixel(x2 + xc, y2 + yc, 1);
      putpixel(-x2 + xc, y2 + yc, 1);
      putpixel(x2 + xc, -y2 + yc, 1);
      putpixel(-x2 + xc, -y2 + yc, 1);
  }
  getch();
}
```

11.5 PROGRAM-5

/* PROGRAM FOR 2D TRANSLATION TRANSFORMATION */

```c
#include<graphics.h>
#include<stdio.h>
#include<conio.h>
#include<math.h>
void main()
{
  int n = 5, i, b[10], tx, ty;
  int a[ ] = {100, 100, 200, 100, 200, 200, 100, 200, 100, 100};
  int gd = DETECT, gm;
  initgraph(&gd, &gm,"c:\\tc\\bgi");
  drawpoly(n, a);
  printf("Enter The Value of tx&ty");
  scanf("%d%d", &tx, &ty);
  for(i = 0; i< =1 0; i = i + 2)
  {
      b[i] = a[i] + tx;
  }
  for(i = 1; i< = 9;i = i + 2)
  {
      b[i] = a[i] + ty;
  }
  setcolor(4);
  drawpoly(n, b);
  getch();
}
```

11.6 PROGRAM-6

/* PROGRAM FOR 2D ROTATION TRANSFORMATION */

```c
#include<graphics.h>
#include<stdio.h>
#include<conio.h>
#include<math.h>
void main()
{
  int n = 5, i, b[10];
  float o;
  int a[] = {100, 100, 200, 100, 200, 200, 100, 200, 100, 100};
  int gd = DETECT, gm;
  initgraph(&gd, &gm,"c:\\tc\\bgi");
  drawpoly(n, a);
  printf("enter the value of angle o");
  scanf("%f", &o);
  o = o*(3.14/180);
  for (i = 0; i < = 10; i = i + 2)
```

```
    {
        b[i] = a[i] * cos(o) - a[i + 1]*sin(o);
        b[i + 1] = a[i] * sin(o) + a[i + 1] * cos(o);
    }
    setcolor(3);
    drawpoly(n, b);
    getch();
}
```

11.7 PROGRAM-7

/* PROGRAM FOR TRANSLATION FOLLOWED BY SCALING TRANSFORMATION */

```
#include<graphics.h>
#include<stdio.h>
#include<conio.h>
#include<math.h>
void main()
{
  int n = 5, i, b[10], tx, ty, sx, sy;
  int a[ ] = {100,100,200,100,200,200,100,200,100,100};
  int gd = DETECT,gm;
  initgraph(&gd, &gm," c:\\tc\\bgi");
  drawpoly(n, a);
  printf("Enter The Value Of tx&ty&sx&sy");
  scanf("%d%d%d%d", &tx, &ty, &sx, &sy);
  for(i = 0; i < = 10; i = i + 2)
  {
      b[i] = a[i] * sx + (1 - sx) * tx;
  }
  for(i = 1; i < = 9; i = i + 2)
  {
      b[i] = a[i] * sy + (1 - sy) * ty;
  }
  setcolor(5);
  drawpoly(n, b);
  getch();
}
```

/* PROGRAM FOR SCALING ABOUT A POINT */

```
#include<stdio.h>
#include<conio.h>
#include<graphics.h>
#include<math.h>
void main ()
{
  int n = 5, b[10], sx, sy, i;
  int a[10] = {100, 100, 200, 100, 200, 200, 100, 200, 100, 100};
```

```
int gd = DETECT,gm;
initgraph(&gd, &gm," c:\\tc\\bgi");
drawpoly(n, a);
printf("Enter the value of sx and sy");
scanf("%d%d", &sx, &sy);
for(i = 0; i < = 9; i + = 2)
{
    b[i] = a[i] * sx + 100 * (1 - sx);
    b[i + 1] = a[i + 1] * sy + 100 * (1 - sy);
}
setcolor(3);
drawpoly(n,b);
getch();
}
```

/* PROGRAM FOR ROTATION ABOUT A POINT */

```
#include<stdio.h>
#include<conio.h>
#include<graphics.h>
#include<math.h>
void main ()
{
  int n = 5, b[10], i;
  int a[10]={100, 100, 200, 100, 200, 200, 100, 200, 100, 100};
  float ang;
  int gd = DETECT, gm;
  initgraph(&gd, &gm," c:\\tc\\bgi");
  drawpoly(n, a);
  printf("Enter the value ang");
  scanf("%f", &ang);
  for(i = 0; i < = 9; i + = 2)
  {
      b[i] = a[i] * cos(ang) - a[i + 1] * sin(ang) + 100 *
  (1 - cos(ang)) + 100 * sin(ang);
      b[i + 1] = a[i] * sin(ang) + a[i + 1] * cos(ang) - 100 *
  sin(ang) - 100 * (cos(ang) - 1);
  }
  setcolor(3);
  drawpoly(n,b);
  getch();
}
```

/* PROGRAM FOR SHEAR TRANSFORMATION */

```
#include<stdio.h>
#include<conio.h>
#include<graphics.h>
#include<math.h>
void main()
{
  int n = 5, b[10], shx, i;
  int a[10] = {100, 100, 200, 100, 200, 200, 100, 200, 100, 100};
```

```
int gd = DETECT,gm;
initgraph(&gd, &gm," c:\\tc\\bgi");
drawpoly(n, a);
printf("enter the value of shx");
scanf("%d", &shx);
for(i = 0; i < = 3; i + = 2)
{
b[i] = a[i];
b[i + 1] = a[i + 1];
}
for(i = 4; i < = 7; i + = 2)
{
b[i] = a[i] + shx;
b[i + 1] = a[i + 1];
}
  for(i = 8; i < = 9; i + = 2)
{
b[i] = a[i];
b[i + 1] = a[i + 1];
}
setcolor(4);
drawpoly(n, b);
getch();
}
```

/* PROGRAM FOR REFLECTION TRANSFORMATION */

```
#include<stdio.h>
#include<conio.h>
#include<math.h>
#include<graphics.h>
void main()
{
int n = 5, b[10], i, c, x;
int a[10] = {100, 100, 200, 100, 200, 200, 100, 200, 100, 100};
float ang;
int gd = DETECT, gm;
initgraph(&gd, &gm," c:\\tc\\bgi");
drawpoly(n, a);
printf("enter the value of x and y intercept");
scanf("%d%d", &x, &c);
printf("enter the angle");
scanf("%f", &ang);
line(0, c, x, 0);
ang = ang * 3.14159/180;
for(i = 0; i < = 9; i + = 2)
{
b[i] = a[i] * cos(2 * ang) - a[i + 1] * sin(2 * ang) + c * sin(2 * ang);
b[i + 1] = - a[i] * sin(2 * ang) - a[i + 1] * cos(2 * ang) + c *
    (1 - cos(2 * ang));
}
drawpoly(n,b);
getch();
}
```

11.8 PROGRAM-8

/* PROGRAM FOR ALL 3D TRANSFORMATIONS */

```c
#include<stdio.h>
#include<conio.h>
#include<graphics.h>
#include<math.h>
int maxx,maxy,midx,midy;
void axis()
{
getch();
cleardevice(); //clear the graphics screen
line(midx, 0, midx, maxy);
line(0, midy, maxx, midy);
}
void main()
{
int gd, gm, x, y, z, o, x1, x2, y1, y2;
detectgraph(&gd, &gm);  //determine graphics driver
initgraph(&gd, &gm," c:\\tc\\bgi"); //initialize the graphics system
setfillstyle(0, getmaxcolor());  //set fill pattern & colour
maxx = getmaxx();
maxy = getmaxy();
midx = maxx/2;
midy = maxy/2;
axis();
bar3d(midx + 100, midy - 150, midx + 60, midy - 100,10,1);
printf("\Enter the translation factor");
scanf("%d%d", &x, &y);
axis();
printf("After translation");
bar3d(midx + 100, midy - 150, midx + 60, midy - 100,10,1); //draw a bar
bar3d(midx + x + 100, midy - (y + 150), midx + x + 60, midy -
    (y + 100), 10, 1); //draw a bar
axis();
bar3d(midx + 100, midy - 150, midx + 60, midy - 100,10,1); //draw a bar
printf("Enter the scaling factor");
scanf("%d%d%d", &x, &y, &z);
axis();
printf("After scaling");
bar3d(midx + 100, midy - 150, midx + 60, midy - 100,10,1); //draw a bar
bar3d(midx + (x * 100), midy - (y * 150),midx + (x * 60), midy -
    (y * 100), 10 * z, 1);
axis();
bar3d(midx + 100, midy - 150, midx + 60, midy - 100,10,1);
printf("Enter the rotation angle");
scanf("%d", &o);
x1 = 50 * cos(o * 3.14/180) - 100*sin(o * 3.14/180);
y1 = 50 * sin(o * 3.14/180) + 100 * cos(o * 3.14/180);
x2 = 60 * cos(o * 3.14/180) - 90 * sin(o * 3.14/180);
y2 = 60 * sin(o * 3.14/180) + 90 * cos(o * 3.14/180);
axis();
```

```
printf("After rotating about Z-axis");
bar3d(midx + 100,midy - 150, midx + 60, midy - 100,10,1);
bar3d(midx + x1, midy - y1, midx + x2, midy - y2, 10,1);
axis();
printf("After rotating about x-axis");
bar3d(midx + 100, midy - 150, midx + 60, midy - 100,10,1); //draw a bar
bar3d(midx + 100, midy - x1, midx + 60, midy - x2, 10,1);
axis();
printf("After rotating about Y-axis");
bar3d(midx + 100, midy - 150, midx + 60, midy - 100,10,1); //draw a bar
bar3d(midx + x1, midy - 150, midx + x2, midy - 100,10,1);  //draw a bar
getch();
closegraph(); //shutdown current graphics  system
}
```

/* PROGRAM FOR ALL 3D TRANSFORMATIONS */

```
#include<graphics.h>
#include<stdio.h>
#include<math.h>
#include<conio.h>
#include<stdlib.h>
int x1, y1, x2, y2;
void draw_cube(double edge[20][3])
{
int i;
cleardevice();
for (i = 0; i < 19; i++)
{
x1 = edge[i][0] + edge[i][2]*(cos(2.3562));
y1 = edge[i][1] - edge[i][2]*(sin(2.3562));
x2 = edge[i + 1][0] + edge[i + 1][2]*(cos(2.3562));
y2 = edge[i + 1][1] - edge[i + 1][2]*(sin(2.3562));
line(x1 + 320, 240 - y1, x2 + 320, 240 - y2);
}
line(320, 240, 320, 25);
line(320, 240, 550, 240);
line(320, 240, 150, 410);
getch();
}
void trans(double edge[20][3])
{
int a, b, c, i;
printf("Enter the Translation Factors:");
scanf("%d%d%d", &a, &b, &c);
for(i = 0; i < 20; i++)
{
edge[i][0] + = a;
edge[i][0] + = b;
edge[i][0] + = c;
}  draw_cube(edge);
}
void scal(double edge[20][3])
```

```c
{
int a, b, c, i;
printf("Enter Scaling factor:");
scanf("%d%d%d", &a, &b, &c);
for(i = 0; i < 20; i++)
{
 edge[i][0] = edge[i][0]*a;
 edge[i][1] = edge[i][1]*b;
 edge[i][2] = edge[i][2]*c;
}
draw_cube(edge);
}
void rotate(double edge[20][3])
{
 int ch, i;
 float temp, theta, temp1;
 printf("\nrotation about \n1.x axis\n2.y axis \n3.z axis\nenter your
     choice");
 scanf("%d", &ch);
 switch (ch)
 {
  case 1:
   printf("\n Enter the angle=\t");
   scanf("%f",&theta);
   theta = (theta*3.14)/180;
   for(i = 0; i < 20; i++)
   {
   edge[i][0] = edge[i][0];
   temp = edge[i][1];
   temp1 = edge[i][2];
   edge[i][1] = temp*cos(theta) - temp1*sin(theta);
   edge[i][2] = temp*sin(theta) + temp1*cos(theta);
   }
  draw_cube(edge);
  break;
  case 2:
   printf("\n Enter The Angle : =");
   scanf("%f", &theta);
   theta = (theta*3.14)/180;
   for(i = 0; i < 20; i++)
   {
    edge[i][1] = edge[i][1];
    temp = edge[i][0];
    temp1 = edge[i][2];
    edge[i][0] = temp*cos(theta) + temp1*sin(theta);
    edge[i][2] = -temp*sin(theta) + temp1*cos(theta);
   } draw_cube(edge);
   break;
  case 3:
   printf(" Enter The Angle: =");
   scanf("%f", &theta);
   theta = (theta*3.14)/180;
   for(i = 0; i < 20; i++)
```

```
  {
   edge[i][2]=edge[i][2];
   temp=edge[i][0];
   temp1=edge[i][1];
   edge[i][0]=temp*cos(theta)-temp1*sin(theta);
   edge[i][1]=temp*sin(theta)+temp1*cos(theta);
  }
  draw_cube(edge);
  break;
 }
}
void reflection(double edge[20][3])
{
int ch,i;
double temp,theta,temp1;
printf("\nreflection about \n1.x axis\n2.y axis \n3.z axis\n enter
   your choice");
scanf("%d",&ch);
switch (ch)
{
 case 1:
 for(i = 0; i < 20; i++)
 {
  edge[i][0] = edge[i][0];
  edge[i][1] = -edge[i][1];
  edge[i][2] = -edge[i][2];
 }
 draw_cube(edge);
 break;
 case 2:
  for(i = 0; i < 20; i++)
  {
   edge[i][1] = edge[i][1];
   edge[i][0] = -edge[i][0];
   edge[i][2] = -edge[i][2];
  }
  draw_cube(edge);
  break;
 case 3:
  for(i = 0; i < 20; i++)
  {
   edge[i][2] = edge[i][2];
   edge[i][0] = -edge[i][0];
   edge[i][1] = -edge[i][1];
  }
  draw_cube(edge);
  break;
}
}
void main()
{
int gd=DETECT,gm,i,ch;
char choice;
do
```

```
{
double edge1[20][3]= {  100,0,0,  100,100,0,  0,100,0,  0,100,100,
   0,0,100,  0,0,0,  100,0,0,  100,0,100, 100,75,100,  75,100,100,
   100,100,75,  100,100,0,  100,0,75,  100,75,100,  75,100,100,
   0,100,100, 0,100,0,  0,0,0,  0,0,100,  100,0,100  };
initgraph(&gd,&gm,"t:\\bgi");
cleardevice();
printf("\n1.Translation"); printf("\n2.Scaling"); printf("\
   n3.Rotation"); printf("\n4.reflection"); printf("\n Enter your
   choice:");
scanf("%d",&ch);
draw_cube(edge1);
switch(ch)
{
case 1:
trans(edge1);
break;
case 2:
scal(edge1);
break;
case 3:
rotate(edge1);
break;
case 4:
reflection(edge1);
break;
}
getch();
cleardevice();
printf("Do you want to continue : [y/n] ");
choice = getch();
}
while(choice = = 'Y'||choice = = 'y');
}
```

11.9 PROGRAM-9

/* COHEN-SUTHERLAND 2D LINE CLIPPING */

```
#include<stdio.h>
#include<graphics.h>
int  i,, xwmin, xwmax, ywmin, ywmax;
int x1, y1, x2, y2, code1[4], code2[4], flag, flag1;
int newx1, newx2, newy1, newy2;
void inter();
int reject();
void main()
{
int gd = DETECT, gm;
initgraph(&gd, &gm,"");
printf("Enter the window coordinates\n");
scanf("%d %d %d %d", &xwmin, &ywmin, &xwmax, &ywmax);
```

```
printf("enter the line coordinates\n");
scanf("%d %d %d %d", &x1, &y1, &x2, &y2);
printf("Before clipping\n");
setcolor(RED);
rectangle(xwmin, ywmin, xwmax, ywmax);
line(x1, y1, x2, y2);
if(x1 < xwmin)code1[0] = 1;
if(x1 > xwmax)code1[1] = 1;
if(y1 < ywmin)code1[2] = 1;
if(y1 > ywmax)code1[3] = 1;
if(x2 < xwmin)code2[0] = 1;
if(x2 > xwmax)code2[1] = 1;
if(y2 < ywmin)code2[2] = 1;
if(y2 > ywmax)code2[3] = 1;
getch();
clrscr();
printf("After clipping\n");
setcolor(BLUE);
rectangle(xwmin, ywmin, xwmax, ywmax);
flag = accept();
if(flag = = 1)
{
setcolor(BLUE);
line(x1, y1, x2, y2);
}
else flag1 = reject();
if(flag1 = = 1)
{
return;
}
else
{
inter();
newx1 = x1;
newy1 = y1;
newx2 = x2;
newy2 = y2;
printf("%d %d %d %d", newx1, newy1, newx2, newy2);
line(newx1, newy1, newx2, newy2);
}
getch();
}
int accept()
{
for(i = 0; i < 4; i++)
{
if(code1[i] = = 0 && code2[i]==0)
flag = 1;
}
flag = 0;
return(flag);
}
int reject()
```

```
{
for(i = 0; i < 4; i++)
{
if(code1[i] ! = 0 && code2[i] ! = 0)
flag 1 = 1;
}
flag 1 = 0;
return(flag 1);
}
void inter()
{
m = (y2 - y1)/(x2 - x1);
if(code1[0] = = 1)
{
y1 = y1 + (xwmin - x1)*m;
x1 = xwmin;
}
if(code1[1] = = 1)
{
y1 = y1 + (xwmax - x1)*m;
x1 = xwmax;
}
if(code1[2] = = 1)
{
x1 = x1 + ((ywmin - y1)/m);
y1 = ywmin;
}
if(code1[3] = = 1)
{
x1 = x1 + ((ywmax - y1)/m);
y1 = ywmax;
}
if(code2[0] = = 1)
{
y2 = y2 + (xwmin - x2)*m;
x2 = xwmin;
}
if(code2[1]==1)
{
y2 = y2 + ((xwmax - x2)*m);
x2 = xwmax;
}
if(code2[2] == 1)
{
x2 = x2 + ((ywmin - y2)/m);
y2 = ywmin;
}
if(code2[3] == 1)
{
x2 = x2 + ((ywmax - y2)/m);
y2 = ywmax;
}
return(x1, y1, x2, y2);
}
```

11.10 PROGRAM-10

/* COHEN-HOGGMAN POLYGON CLIPPING */

```c
#include <stdio.h>
#include <graphics.h>
#include <conio.h>
#include <math.h>
#include <process.h>
#define TRUE 1
#define FALSE 0
typedef unsigned int outcode;
outcode compoutcode(float x,float y);
enum {  TOP = 0x1,
BOTTOM = 0x2,
RIGHT = 0x4,
LEFT = 0x8
};
float xmin,xmax,ymin,ymax;
void clip(float x0, float y0, float x1, float y1)
{
outcode outcode0,outcode1,outcodeout;
int accept = FALSE,done = FALSE;

outcode0 = CompOutCode(x0, y0);
outcode1 = CompOutCode(x1, y1);
do
{
  if(!(outcode0|outcode1))
  {
    accept = TRUE;
    done = TRUE;
  }
  else
  if(outcode0 & outcode1)
    done = TRUE;
  else
  {
    float x, y;
    outcodeOut = outcode0?outcode0:outcode1;
    if(outcodeOut & TOP)
    {
     x = x0 + (x1 - x0) * (ymax - y0)/(y1 - y0);
     y = ymax;
    }
    else if(outcodeOut & BOTTOM)
    {
     x = x0 + (x1 - x0)*(ymin - y0)/(y1 - y0);
     y = ymin;
    }
    else if(outcodeOut & RIGHT)
    {
     y = y0 + (y1 - y0) * (xmax - x0)/(x1 - x0);
```

```
  x = xmax;
 }
 else
 {
  y = y0 + (y1 - y0) * (xmin - x0)/(x1 - x0);
  x = xmin;
 }
 if(outcodeOut = = outcode0)
 {
  x0 = x;
  y0 = y;
  outcode0 = CompOutCode(x0, y0);
 }
 else
 {
  x1 = x;
  y1 = y;
  outcode1 = CompOutCode(x1, y1);
 }
 }
}while(done==FALSE);
if(accept)
 line(x0, y0, x1, y1);
outtextxy(150, 20, "POLYGON AFTER CLIPPING");
rectangle(xmin, ymin, xmax, ymax);
}
outcode CompOutCode(float x, float y)
{
 outcode code = 0;
 if(y > ymax)
 code| = TOP;
else if(y < ymin)
 code| = BOTTOM;
if(x > xmax)
 code| = RIGHT;
else if(x < xmin)
 code| = LEFT;
return code;
}
void main( )
{
float x1, y1, x2, y2;
/* request auto detection */
int gdriver = DETECT, gmode, n, poly[14], i;
clrscr( );
printf("Enter the no of sides of polygon:");
scanf("%d", &n);
printf("\nEnter the coordinates of polygon\n");
 for(i = 0; i < 2 * n; i++)
{
    scanf("%d", &poly[i]);
}
poly[2*n] = poly[0];
poly[2*n + 1] = poly[1];
```

```
printf("Enter the rectangular coordinates of clipping window\n");
scanf("%f%f%f%f", &xmin, &ymin, &xmax, &ymax);
/* initialize graphics and local variables */
initgraph(&gdriver, &gmode, "c:\\tc\\bgi");
outtextxy(150, 20, "POLYGON BEFORE CLIPPING");
drawpoly(n + 1, poly);
rectangle(xmin, ymin, xmax, ymax);
getch( );
cleardevice( );
for(i = 0; i < n; i++)
clip(poly[2*i], poly[(2*i) + 1], poly[(2*i) + 2], poly[(2*i) + 3]);
getch( );
restorecrtmode( );
}
```

Chapter 12 OpenGL with Computer Graphics

12.1 INTRODUCTION

OpenGL (Open Graphics Library) is the computer industry's standard application program interface (API) for defining 2D and 3D graphic images. Prior to OpenGL, any company developing a graphical application typically had to rewrite the graphics part of it for each operating system and had to be cognizant of the graphics hardware as well. With OpenGL, an application can create the same effects in any operating system using any OpenGL-adhering graphics adapter.

OpenGL specifies a set of "commands" or immediately executed functions. Each command directs a drawing action or causes special effects. A list of these commands can be created for repetitive effects. OpenGL is independent of the windowing characteristics of each operating system, but provides special "glue" routines for each operating system that enable OpenGL to work in that system's windowing environment. OpenGL comes with a large number of built-in capabilities requestable through the API. These include hidden surface removal, alpha blending (transparency), antialiasing, texture mapping, pixel operations, viewing and modeling transformations, and atmospheric effects (fog, smoke, and haze).

Silicon Graphics, makers of advanced graphics workstations, initiated the development of OpenGL. Other companies on the industrywide Architecture Review Board include DEC, Intel, IBM, Microsoft, and Sun Microsystems.

There is no cost to developing an application using the OpenGL API. Although OpenGL is not itself a development "toolkit," such toolkits are available, including the Silicon Graphics object-oriented programming 3D graphics toolkit Open Inventor.

12.1.1 Graphical Functions of OpenGL

1. **Alpha blending:** It provides a means to create transparent objects. Using alpha information an object can be defined as anything from totally transparent to totally opaque.

2. **Color–index mode:** Color buffers store color indices rather than red, green, blue, and alpha color components.

3. **Display list:** The contents of a display list may be preprocessed and might therefore execute more efficiently than the same set of OpenGL commands executed in immediate mode.

4. **Double buffering:** It is used to provide smooth animation of objects. Each successive scene of an object in motion can be constructed in the back or "hidden" buffer and then displayed. This allows only complete images to be displayed on the screen.

5. **Feedback:** This is a mode where OpenGL will return the processed geometric information (colors, pixel positions, etc.) to the application as comported to rendering them into the frame buffer.

6. **Immediate mode:** Execution of OpenGL commands when they are called rather than from a display list.

7. **Materials lighting and shading:** It is the ability to accurately compute the color of any point given the material properties of the surface.

8. **Pixel operations:** Storing, transforming, mapping, and zooming.

9. **Polynomial evaluators:** To support non-uniform rational B-splines (NURBS).

10. **Selection and picking:** It is a mode in which OpenGL determines whether certain user-identified graphics primitives are rendered into a region of interest in the frame buffer.

11. **Texture mapping:** It is a process of applying an image to a graphics primitive. The technique is used to generate realism in images.

12. **Z-buffering:** Z-buffering is used to keep track of whether one part of an object is closer to the viewer than another; it is important in hidden surface removal.

Any visual computing application requiring maximum performance—from 3D animation to CAD to visual simulation—can exploit high-quality, high-performance OpenGL capabilities. These capabilities allow developers in diverse markets such as broadcasting, CAD/CAM/CAE, entertainment, medical imaging, and virtual reality to produce and display incredibly compelling 2D and 3D graphics.

Developer-driven Advantages

- **Industry standard:** An independent consortium, the OpenGL Architecture Review Board, guides the OpenGL specification. With broad industry support, OpenGL is the only truly open, vendor-neutral, multiplatform graphics standard.

- **Stable:** OpenGL implementations have been available for more than seven years on a wide variety of platforms. Additions to the specification are well controlled, and proposed updates are announced in time for developers to adopt changes. Backward compatibility requirements ensure that existing applications do not become obsolete.

- **Reliable and portable:** All OpenGL applications produce consistent visual display results on any OpenGL API-compliant hardware, regardless of operating system or windowing system.

- **Evolving:** Because of its thorough and forward-looking design, OpenGL allows new hardware innovations to be accessible through the API via the OpenGL extension mechanism. In this way, innovations appear in the API in a timely fashion, letting application developers and hardware vendors incorporate new features into their normal product release cycles.

- **Scalable:** OpenGL API-based applications can run on systems ranging from consumer electronics to PCs, workstations, and supercomputers. As a result, applications can scale to any class of machine that the developer chooses to target.

- **Easy to use:** OpenGL is well structured, with an intuitive design and logical commands. Efficient OpenGL routines typically result in applications with fewer lines of code than those that make up programs generated using other graphics libraries or packages. In addition, OpenGL drivers encapsulate information about the underlying hardware, freeing the application developer from having to design for specific hardware features.

- **Well-documented:** Numerous books have been published about OpenGL, and a great deal of sample code is readily available, making information about OpenGL inexpensive and easy to obtain.

How Does OpenGL Work?

OpenGL is a procedural rather than a descriptive graphics API. Instead of describing the scene and how it should appear, the programmer actually prescribes the steps required to achieve a certain appearance or effect. These steps involve calls to this highly portable API, which includes about 250 distinct commands and functions (about 200 in the core OpenGL and another 50 in the OpenGL Utility Library).

Software Implementation

A software implementation can run just about anywhere as long as the system has the ability to display the generated graphics image. Fig 12.1 shows the typical place that OpenGL and software implementation occupy when an application is running, Windows applications wanting to create output on screen usually call a Windows API called GDI (Graphics Device Interface). The GDI contains methods that allow a user to write text in a window, draw simple 2D lines, etc.

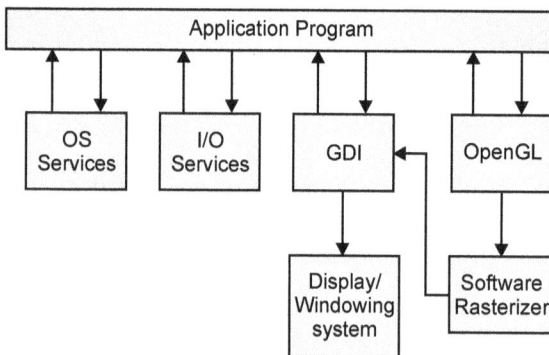

Fig. 12.1 OpenGL's place in a typical application program

A software implementation of OpenGL takes graphics requests from an application and constructs a color image of the 3D graphics. It then supplies this image to the GDI for display on the monitor. On the other operating systems, the process is pretty equivalent, but the GDI is replaced with that operating system's native display services.

Hardware Implementations

A hardware implementation of OpenGL usually takes the form of a graphics card driver. Fig. 12.2 shows its relationship to the applications. The OpenGL API calls are passed to a hardware driver. This driver does not pass its output to the windows' GDI for display; the driver interfaces directly with the graphics display hardware.

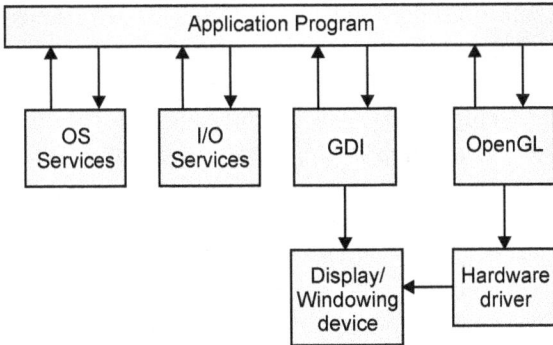

Fig. 12.2 Hardware implementation

A hardware implementation is often referred to as an accelerated implementation because hardware-silted 3D graphics usually outperforms software-only implementation.

OpenGL Rendering Pipeline

Most implementation of OpenGL has a similar order of operations, a series of processing stages called an OpenGL rendering pipeline. Geomantic data follow the path through the row of boxes that include unpacking of vertices and vertex operations, while pixel data (image) are treated differently for part of the process. Both types of data undergo the same final steps (rasterization and fragment operations) before the final pixel data is written into the frame buffer.

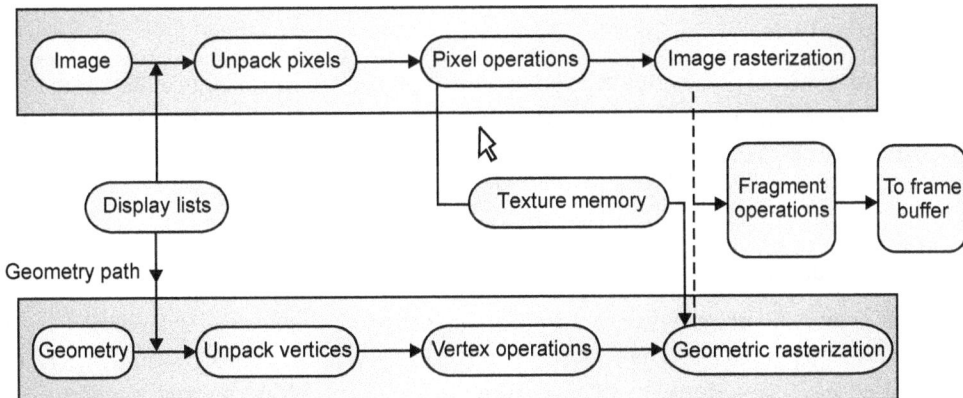

Fig. 12.3 An OpenGL rendering pipeline

One problem is that this program does not display completely drawn frames; instead we watch the drawing as it happens.

Most OpenGL implementation provides double-buffering hardware or software that supplies two complete color butters. One is displayed while the other is being drawn. When the drawing of a frame is complete, the two buffers are swapped, so the one that was being viewed is now used for drawing and vice versa. With double-buffering, every frame is shown only when the drawing is complete; the viewer never sees a partially drawn frame.

For some OpenGL implementation, in addition to simply swapping the viewable and drawable buffers, the routine for buffer swapping waits until the current screen refresh period is over so that the previous buffer is completely displayed, starting from the beginning.

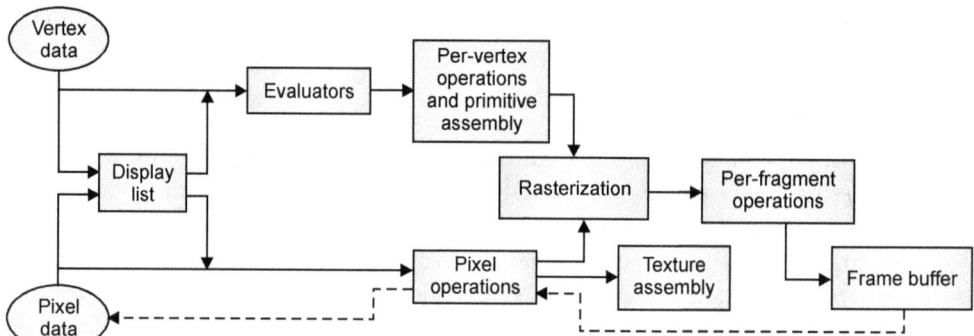

Fig. 12.4 The order of operations

Display Lists

All data, whether they describe geometry or pixels, can be saved in a display list for current or later use. (The alternative to retaining data in a display list is processing the data immediately, also known as immediate mode.) When a display list is executed, the retained data is sent from the display list just as if it were sent by the application in immediate mode.

Evaluators

All geometric primitives are eventually described by vertices. Parametric curves and surfaces may be initially described by control points and polynomial functions called basis functions. Evaluators provide a method to derive the vertices used to represent the surface from the control points. The method is polynomial mapping, which can produce surface normal, texture coordinates, colors, and spatial coordinate values from the control points.

Per-Vertex Operations

For vertex data, next is the "per-vertex operations" stage, which converts the vertices into primitives. Some vertex data (e.g., spatial coordinates) are transformed by 4 × 4 floating-point matrices. Spatial coordinates are projected from a position in the 3D world to a position on your screen.

Primitive Assembly

Clipping, a major part of primitive assembly, is the elimination of portions of geometry that fall outside a half-space, defined by a plane. Point clipping simply passes or rejects vertices; line or polygon clipping can add additional vertices depending upon how the line or polygon is clipped.

In some cases, this is followed by perspective division, which makes distant geometric objects appear smaller than closer objects. Then viewport and depth (z coordinate) operations are applied. If culling is enabled and the primitive is a polygon, it then may be rejected by a culling test. Depending upon the polygon mode, a polygon may be drawn as points or lines.

Pixel Operations

While geometric data takes one path through the OpenGL rendering pipeline, pixel data takes a different route. Pixels from an array in system memory are first unpacked from one of a variety of formats into the proper number of components. Next the data are scaled, biased, and processed by a pixel map. The results are clamped and then either written into texture memory or sent to the rasterization step.

If pixel data is read from the frame buffer, pixel-transfer operations (scale, bias, mapping, and clamping) are performed. Then these results are packed into an appropriate format and returned to an array in system memory.

There are special pixel copy operations to copy data in the frame buffer to other parts of the frame buffer or to the texture memory. A single pass is made through the pixel transfer operations before the data is written to the texture memory or back to the frame buffer.

Texture Assembly

An OpenGL application may wish to apply texture images onto geometric objects to make them look more realistic. If several texture images are used, it's wise to put them into texture objects so that you can easily switch among them.

Some OpenGL implementations may have special resources to accelerate texture performance. There may be specialized, high-performance texture memory. If this memory is available, the texture objects may be prioritized to control the use of this limited and valuable resource.

Rasterization

Rasterization is the conversion of both geometric and pixel data into *fragments*. Each fragment square corresponds to a pixel in the frame buffer. Line and polygon stipples, line width, point size, shading model, and coverage calculations to support antialiasing are taken into consideration as vertices are connected into lines or the interior pixels are calculated for a filled polygon. Color and depth values are assigned for each fragment square.

Fragment Operations

Before values are actually stored into the frame buffer, a series of operations are performed that may alter or even throw out fragments. All these operations can be enabled or disabled.

The first operation which may be encountered is texturing, where a texel (texture element) is generated from texture memory for each fragment and applied to the fragment. Then fog calculations may be applied, followed by the scissor test, the alpha test, the stencil test, and the depth-buffer test (the depth buffer is for hidden surface removal). Failing an enabled test may end the continued processing of a fragment's square. Then, blending, dithering, logical operation, and masking by a bitmask may be performed.

Simple Animation in OpenGL

1. Drawing rectangles in OpenGL

```
#include <GL/gl.h>
#include <GL/glu.h>
#include <GL/glut.h>
void setup ()
{
glClearColor(1.0f, 0.0f, 0.0f, 0.0f); }
void display(){
glClear(GL_COLOR_BUFFER_BIT);
glColor3f(0.0f, 0.0f, 0.0f);
glRectf(-0.75f, 0.75f, 0.75f, -0.75f);
glFlush();
glutSwapBuffers();
}
int main(int argc, char *argv[])
{
glutInit(&argc, argv);
glutInitDisplayMode(GLUT_RGB | GLUT_SINGLE);
glutInitWindowSize(400, 300);
```

```
glutInitWindowPosition(200, 100
glutCreateWindow("Hello World");
glutDisplayFunc(display);
glutMainLoop();
return 0;
}
```

2. Drawing lines in OpenGL

```
#include <GL/gl.h>
#include <GL/glu.h>
#include <GL/glut.h>
void setup()
{
    glClearColor(1.0, 1.0, 1.0, 1.0);
    gluOrtho2D(-10.0, 10.0, -10.0, 10.0);
}
void display()
{
    glClear(GL_COLOR_BUFFER_BIT);
    glColor3f(1.0, 0.0, 1.1);
    glPointSize(5.0);
glBegin(GL_LINES);
        glVertex2f(-10.0, 0.0);  // left - x negative
        glVertex2f(10.0, 0.0);   // right - x positive
        glVertex2f(0.0, 10.0);   // top - y positive
        glVertex2f(0.0, -10.0);  // bottom - y negative
    glEnd();
    glFlush();
}
int main(int argc, char *argv[])
{
    glutInit(&argc, argv);
    glutInitDisplayMode(GLUT_SINGLE | GLUT_RGB);
    glutInitWindowPosition(200, 100);
    glutInitWindowSize(400, 300);
    glutCreateWindow("Hello World");
    glutDisplayFunc(display);

    setup();
    glutMainLoop();
    return 0;
}
```

3. Drawing points in OpenGL

```
#include <GL/gl.h>
#include <GL/glu.h>
#include <GL/glut.h>
void setup()
{

    glClearColor(0.0, 0.0, 0.0, 1.0);
    gluOrtho2D(-10.0, 10.0, -10.0, 10.0);
}
```

```
void display()
{
    glClear(GL_COLOR_BUFFER_BIT);
    glColor3f(0.0, 1.0, 0.1);
    glPointSize(5.0);
    glBegin(GL_POINTS);
        glVertex2f(1.0, 1.0);
        glVertex2f(2.0, 2.0);
        glVertex2f(3.0, 3.0);
        glVertex2f(4.0, 4.0);
        glVertex2f(5.0, 5.0);
    glEnd();

    glFlush();
}
    int main(int argc, char *argv[])
{
    glutInit(&argc, argv);
    glutInitDisplayMode(GLUT_SINGLE | GLUT_RGB);
    glutInitWindowPosition(200, 100);
    glutInitWindowSize(400, 300);
    glutCreateWindow("Hello World");
    glutDisplayFunc(display);
    setup();
    glutMainLoop();
    return 0;
}
```

4. Drawing a polygon in OpenGL

```
#include <GL/gl.h>
#include <GL/glu.h>
#include <GL/glut.h>
void setup()
{
    glClearColor(1.0, 1.0, 1.0, 1.0);
    gluOrtho2D(-01.0, 10.0, -01.01, 10.0);
}
    void display()
{
        glClear(GL_COLOR_BUFFER_BIT);
        glColor3f(1.0, 0.0, 0.0);
        glBegin(GL_POLYGON);
        glVertex2f(0.5, 0.5);
        glVertex2f(0.5, 5.0);
        glVertex2f(5.0, 5.0);
        glEnd();
        glBegin(GL_LINES);
        glVertex2f(-10.0, 0.0);
        glVertex2f(10.0, 0.0);
        glVertex2f(0.0, -10.00);
        glVertex2f(0.0, 10.0);
        glEnd();
    glFlush();
```

```
}
int main(int argc, char *argv[])
{
    glutInit(&argc, argv);
    glutInitDisplayMode(GLUT_SINGLE | GLUT_RGB);
    glutInitWindowPosition(200, 100);
    glutInitWindowSize(400, 300);
    glutCreateWindow("Hello World");
    glutDisplayFunc(display);

    setup();
    glutMainLoop();

    return 0;
}
```

EXERCISES

1. Explain event-driven programming with different OpenGL utilities. Explain how the program makes use of these utilities.
2. Derive the transformation from window to viewport.
3. Explain line clipping with the Cohen-Sutherland line clipping algorithm.
4. How is the deCasteljau algorithm used for Bezier curve? Explain for four points.
5. Consider a knot vector $t = \{0, 0, 0, 0.3, 0.5, 0.5, 0.6, 1, 1, 1\}$ and solve for knot assignment.

OBJECTIVE QUESTIONS

12.1 The value of aspect ratio of a golden rectangle is
(*a*) 1.6085   (*b*) 1.618034
(*c*) 1.628876   (*d*) 1.652157

12.2 Which one is a v-contour generated curve?
(*a*) v varies while u is constant   (*b*) u varies while v is constant
(*c*) u and v both vary same time   (*d*) none of these

12.3 Changing the position of control point Pi only affects the curve $P(u)$ on interval
(*a*) $[u_i, u_{i+p+1})$ (*b*) $[u_{i-1}, u_{i+p+1})$
(*c*) $[u_i, u_{i+1})$ (*d*) $[u_i, u_{i+p})$

12.4 Clamped B-spline curve $P(t)$ passes through
(*a*) two middle control points   (*b*) two end control points
(*c*) both (*a*) and (*b*)   (*d*) neither (*a*) nor (*b*)

12.5 The technique used to produce a transformation of one object into another is known as
(*a*) morphing   (*b*) betweening
(*c*) blindfolding   (*d*) cutaway

ANSWERS

12.1 (*b*)   **12.2** (*b*)   **12.3** (*a*)   **12.4** (*b*)   **12.5** (*a*)

13 PROGRAMMING GRAPHICS USING OPENGL

13.1 APPLICATION OF COMPUTER-GENERATED IMAGES

Computer graphics have the ability to picturize real-life objects with dazzling realism. But it also gives us the ability to draw things that could never be viewed in reality. These imaginary objects are described by an algorithm in a computer program.

13.1.1 Computer-Aided Design

Computer-aided design (CAD) is the use of computer systems to aid in the creation, modification, analysis, or optimization of a design. Prior to the advent of CAD, the development of any type of design or prototype was done manually. As such, development was typically tedious and time-consuming, often hampered by costly trial and error. Since it digitizes and simplifies the entire design process, CAD has all but replaced the traditional drawing board. CAD methods are now routinely used in the design of buildings, automobiles, aircraft, watercraft, spacecraft, computers, textiles, and many other products.

Computer graphics have been widely used in design processes, particularly for engineering and architectural systems. Designers can easily rotate the object or zoom in for a clear and closer look to carry out manipulation. For some design applications, the object is first displayed in a wireframe outline form that shows its overall shape and internal features. Wireframe displays also allow designers to quickly see the effects of interactive adjustments to design shapes by a grid of connected lines.

Figs. 13.1 and 13.2 show the pictorial view of CAD in designing a crank mechanism.

For example, a building plan might contain separate overlays for its structural, electrical, and plumbing components. With CAD, layers are equivalent to transparent overlays. As with overlays, you can display, edit, and print layers separately or in combination. You can name layers to help track content, and lock layers so they can't be altered. Assigning settings such as color, linetype, or lineweight to layers helps you comply with industry standards. You can also use layers to organize drawing objects for plotting. Assigning a plot style to a layer makes all the objects drawn on that layer plot in a similar manner.

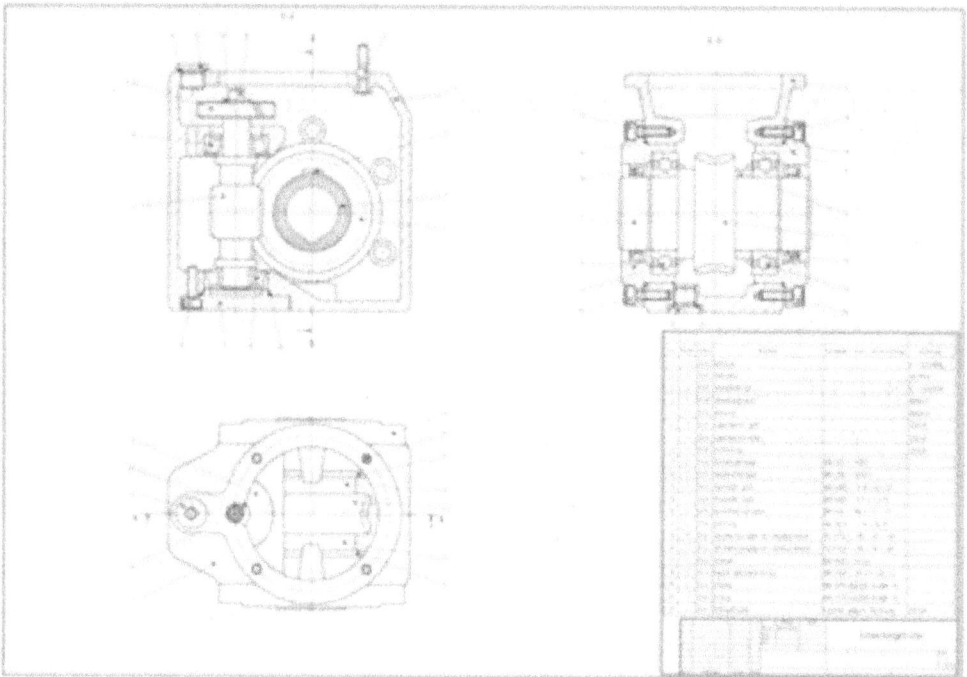

Fig. 13.1 2D drawing

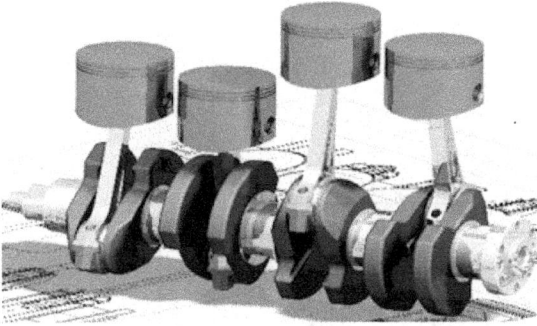

Fig. 13.2 A 3D model

Computer-Aided Architectural Design

Computer graphics are also helpful to architects who design and model buildings. Computer-aided architectural design (CAAD) is used to design 2D floor plans and 3D schematics of houses, office buildings, schools, hospitals, and other structures. When creating buildings, flawless planning is a must. Aside from the actual architecture and layout of a structure, the CAAD program is used to determine proper specifications, including measurements, volumes, and weights, before construction even begins. Render version shows the 3D view of the structure. Computer graphics allow an architect to adjust the position of doors and windows and to display different textures of bricks or wall paint. With the help of interactive controls provided by computer graphics, the architect can walk through the building and the client will be able to experience how the house will look when it is built, as shown in Fig. 13.3.

13.1.2 Image Processing

Every year we see improvement in the field of image processing as a result of blending with computer graphics. In computer graphics, a computer is used to create a picture. Image processing is a type of computation using mathematical operations in any form of signal processing for which the input is an image, such as a photograph or video frame. The output of image processing may be either an image or a set of characteristics or parameters related to the image.

The primary goal of computer graphics is to create pictures and images, realizing them based on a model or description. However, the primary goal of image processing is to improve the quality of the image. It includes sharpening edges, fixing color combinations, removing the noise from the image, and enhancing contrast. Two principal applications of image processing are improving picture quality and machine perception of visual information.

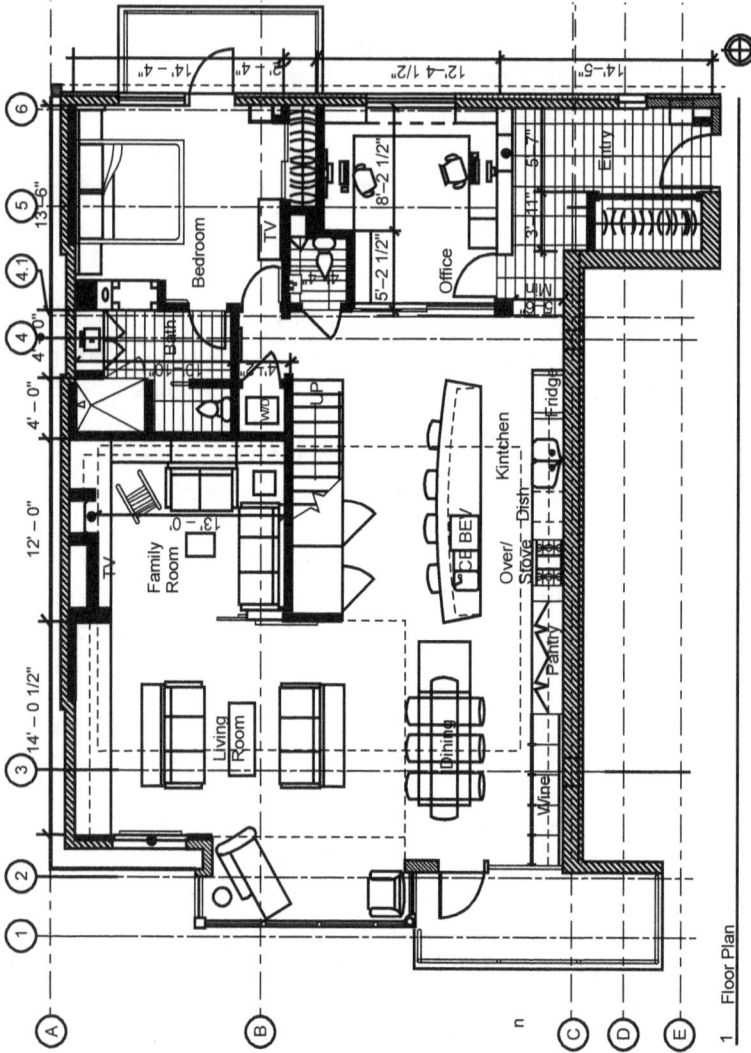

Fig. 13.3 Floor plan of a house

To apply image-processing methods, we must first digitize an image. Then digital methods can be applied to rearrange picture parts, enhance color separations, or improve the quality of shading. An example of image-processing methods to enhance the quality of a picture is shown in Fig. 13.4. These techniques are extensively used to analyze satellite photos. OpenGL routines can be used to identify certain features in an image and make them more noticeable and comprehensible. In computer graphics, images are manually made from physical models of objects, environments, and lighting instead of being acquired from natural scenes, as in most animated movies.

Fig. 13.4 Satellite images

13.1.3 Process Monitoring

Computer graphics are used in highly time-critical systems like air traffic control, power plants, and factories that need to be closely monitored. An operator carefully monitors the things; he gets up-to-date information that can be interpreted instantly. Calculations are made in the system after every interval and data are transmitted to a monitoring station to be converted into graphical information.

For example, an air traffic control system displays the locations of nearby airplanes. The operator can see the schematic representation of the whole situation at a glance. Numerous indicators can change color or flash to alert operator, when they require attention.

13.1.4 Entertainment and Publishing

Computer graphics are commonly used in the production of movie, music videos, television shows, books, and games. In recent years, the cost of computer graphics systems has reduced dramatically, due to the development of new hardware tools and powerful software with increased performance.

Music videos use graphics in several ways. Graphic objects can be combined with live action, or graphics and image processing techniques can be used to produce a transformation of one object into another, called morphing. An example of morphing images is shown in Fig. 13.5.

In computer games, when a player moves a joystick or presses a button, the computer-generated image responds instantly. Special hardware is installed to speed up processing to generate successive images.

Fig. 13.5 Morphing

A paintbrush program allows artists to paint pictures on the screen of a video monitor. Actually, the picture is usually painted electronically on a graphics tablet (digitizer) using a stylus, which can simulate different brush strokes, brush widths, and colors. A paintbrush program such as Adobe Photoshop may be used to create characters.

13.1.5 Simulation

Some highly complex systems like air traffic control need to be analyzed in real time, while others might never be built in real world at all, but still exist in the form of an equation or algorithm in a computer. These algorithms can still be tested and considered as if they exist in reality; they run through their paces and simulated results are obtained, which is very valuable information for setting benchmarks for others.

Simulation of a system is represented by running the system's model. It can be used to explore and gain insights into new technology and to estimate the performance of systems too complex for analytical solutions.

In today's world, a variety of such systems can be beneficially simulated, like the effect of global warming due to an increase in hydrocarbons, analysis of air pollutant dispersion using atmospheric dispersion modeling, design of complex systems such as aircraft and logistics, design of noise barriers to effect roadway noise mitigation, or modeling car crashes to test safety mechanisms in new vehicle models.

A simple example is the flight simulator. The system is composed of an airplane, with shape and flying parameters, along with air, landing runway, oceans, mountains, and, of course, other planes. During simulation, the pilot moves the controls, and the computer programs calculate speed and new positions of the simulated plane. The pilot can see the simulated result. It is a very difficult and demanding application to write, as it must respond so rapidly. Fig. 13.6 shows a simulated airplane's cockpit.

Computer graphics have the ability to display objects as if they physically exist, but they are only models inside a computer.

Fig. 13.6 The control panel of a simulated airplane

13.2 DRAWING FIGURES USING OPENGL

Section 13.2.1 covers the basic writing of OpenGL programs and the concept of device-independent programming. Section 13.2.2 discusses the basic primitives of OpenGL available for graphics design and various data types and states used in OpenGL. Section 13.2.3 gives an idea of how to perform line drawing operations in OpenGL and also discusses the concept of polylines, polygons, and aligned polygons. Lastly, section 13.2.4 discusses the features of OpenGL related to keyboard and mouse interactions.

13.2.1 Getting Started with Making Pictures

When talking about the various disciplines of engineering, computer graphics is similar in that it provides a means to write a program and test cases that create a variety of pictures. For a beginner it is better to start with the basics of the graphic task. Once you are familiar with those, you can shift to writing complicated programs that produce complex pictures.

Similar to the other programming constructs, you need a programming environment so that you can write and execute your program on it. When we talk about the graphics operation, we also need hardware devices like CRT display — a screen — and a predefined library of software tools which help us draw graphics primitives.

Every graphics program starts with an initialization phase, in which you define the desired display mode and area by setting appropriate coordinating points. Initialization depends on whether you define the entire screen or some window-based system for drawing.

In Fig. 13.7 the entire screen is used for drawing and we just initialized display mode as "graphics mode." The values of coordinates x and y are defined in right and downward directions respectively. In Fig. 13.8 a window-based system is shown whose coordinate value grows in right and downward directions, correspondingly. The main feature of this mode is that it can support multiple window displays on the screen at the same time. In Fig. 13.9 a slight variation in window mode is performed where the coordinate value of Y increases in upward direction.

Each system has some initialization tool that helps users to get started. We start our discussion with the *setpixel* command, which defines the values of x and y coordinate system value and the color value. The syntax of setpixel is *setPixel* $(x, y, color)$. In some systems we call this command *putpixel()*, *setpixel()*, or *drawpoint()*. Similarly, we have a line command which draws a line between (x_1, y_1) and (x_2, y_2). Sometimes it may be called *drawline()* or simply *Line()*. A sample command can be given as follows. The result of this command is displayed in Fig. 13.7.

> *line*(130, 60, 180, 80);
> *line*(180, 80, 0, 250);

Instead of having a *line ()* command, some systems have a *moveto(x, y)* and *lineto(x, y)*. The arguments of *moveto* command define the starting point of the line and the arguments of the *lineto* command define the ending point of the line. The operation of the command is analogous to the working of a pen plotter. Once the line has been drawn, the new position becomes the starting position.

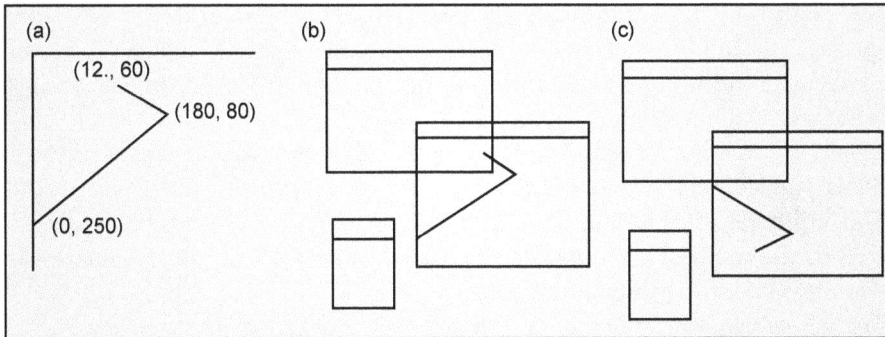

Fig. 13.7 Different types of display layouts

As already said, each environment uses a different set of commands for drawing primitives, so porting from one environment to another is difficult. The programmer has to explicitly define the library tool at the start of the program to make necessary changes in the overall structure of the program.

13.2.2 Device-Independent Programming and OpenGL

The concept of device-independent programming allows the user to write a single program and compile it on many environments which produce nearly the same result on each display. OpenGL supports device-independent programming. When you port your program from one environment to another, it only requires installing library files on the new machine and you can just run the program on that machine with the same parameters and callings. OpenGL is sometimes called an Application Programming Interface because it is a collection of routines that users can call and produce the required graphics result. The programmer is only aware of the interface.

OpenGL is very useful for drawing 3D scenes as compared to 2D scenes. However, it still works better for 2D objects. We will discuss most of the graphics algorithms and their implementation using the concept of OpenGL primitives. In most circumstances it may not be possible to implement the algorithm using OpenGL. In such scenarios you need to develop an application that doesn't use OpenGL at all.

13.2.3 Event-Driven Programming

One of the important properties of window-based graphics systems is that they are event-driven, which means they respond to some event such as clicking the mouse or pressing a key on the keyboard. If multiple events take place on the window, the system automatically manages a queue regarding the applicability of the event on a first-come-first-served basis. When programmers write any program, they simply associate a *callback* function with it, so that when the event gets executed and it is removed from the queue, it simply executes the *callback* function associated with it.

OpenGL provides some utility toolkits to manage various events. One such utility is: *glutMouseFunc (myMouse);*

This utility registers for the function *myMouse,* which is responsible for events related to the mouse. The programmer can manually set the functionalities in *myMouse* to handle various commands.

The following program segment gives an outline of an event-driven program.

```
void main ()
{
        Initialize things
        Create a screen window
        glutDisplayFunc (myDisplay);
        glutReshapeFunc (myReshape);
        glutMouseFunc (myMouse);
        glutKeyboardFunc (myKeyboard);
        perhaps initialize other things
        glutMainLoop();
}
```

Now, we will discuss each of the outline's four functions.

- *glutDisplayFunc (myDisplay):* This command is useful when the screen window redraws its issue on a redraw event. It sometimes occurs when the user opens a new window and rolls it over an existing window. Here the function is regarded as the callback function for a redraw event.

- *glutReshapeFunc(myReshape):* When users want to resize the window, they simply drag the corner of the window to the new required position. Here the *myReshape* is an event-driven utility called a "Reshape" event.

- *glutMouseFunc(myKeyboard):* When we press one of the mouse buttons, an event related to the mouse is issued. Here the *myMouse*() function is called when the event is executed.

- *glutKeyboardFunc(myKeyboard):* Similar to the mouse-related operation, when we press any key on the keyboard, an event-related function *myKeyboard*() is executed. The function automatically takes the argument as the key is pressed.

If the program doesn't make use of the mouse, then the corresponding mouse-related events have no effect. This is also the case with other event utilities.

13.2.4 Opening a Window for Drawing

Opening a new window for drawing is completely system-dependent. As OpenGL functions are device-independent, they provide no support for window control. But the OpenGL utility toolkit provides support for window operation.

The following program segment states the outline of the main program that draws graphics on a screen window. You will see that we have defined the five functions that call for an OpenGL toolkit utility. You need to just copy your program and set the appropriate parameters. A brief description of these commands is given below.

```
void main (intargc, char** argv)
{
        glutInit(&argc, argv);
        glutInitDisplayMode(GLUT_SINGLE | GLUT_RGB);
        glutInitWindowSize (1024, 768);
        glutInitWindowPosition (100, 150);
        glutDisplayFunc (myDisplay);
        glutReshapeFunc (myReshape);
        glutMouseFunc (myMouse);
        glutKeyboardFunc (myKeyboard);
        myInit ();
        glutMainLoop ();
}
```

- *glutInit (&argc, argv):* This function is responsible for the initialization of toolkit. The arguments &argc and &argv are standard command line information.

- *glutInitDisplayMode (GLUT_SINGLE | GLUT_RGB):* This function defines how the display should be initialized. The argument GLUT_SINGLE indicates that a single window should be initialized and the color of that will be defined by the amount of red, green, and blue passed in the second argument.

- *glutInitWindowSize (1024, 768):* This function indicates that the screen resolution should be 1024 pixels wide and 768 pixels high. It is a static allocation, but the user can alter it while running the program.

- *glutInitWindowPosition(100, 150):* This function is similar to the previous one, as it defines the position of the window 100 pixels from the left edge and 150 pixels down from the top.

- *glutCreateWindow("my first attempt"):* This function opens a new window and puts a title on it — my first attempt — in the title bar.

The remaining callback functions of the program are as discussed earlier. Programmers should ensure that they initialize each and every callback function and *myInit()* function.

13.2.5 Drawing Basic Graphics Primitives

If we want to create a graphics window, we should initialize the function with proper parameters and callback functions. Our first approach towards graphics designing is to create a window of appropriate size defined by the coordinate system.

We show in this example a window 1024 pixels wide and 768 pixels high. The value of the first 1024 pixels vary from 0 left edge to 1023 right edge direction. Similarly, the corresponding 768 pixels vary from 0 top edge to 767 down edge direction. Fig. 13.8 shows the output of window initialization.

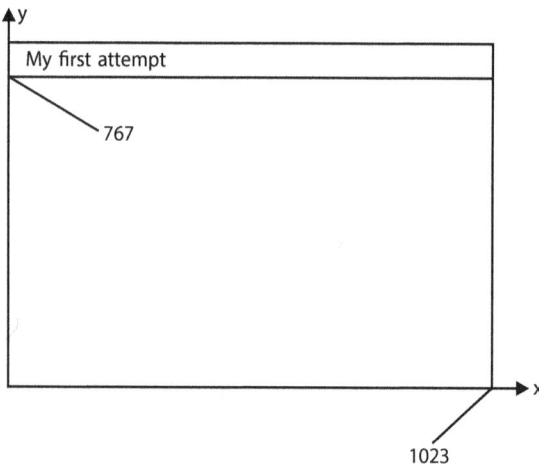

Fig. 13.8 A coordinate system initialization

We will first discuss the basic primitives. Most primitives are defined by one or more vertices such as points, lines, polylines, polygons, etc. To draw such primitives, you have a function body starting with glBegin() and ending with glEnd(). The following functions define the initialization of points at various locations in the 1024 × 768 graphic window.

```
glBegin(GL_POINTS);
        glVertex2i(130, 70);
        glVertex2i(150, 80);
        glVertex2i(200, 100);
    glEnd();
```

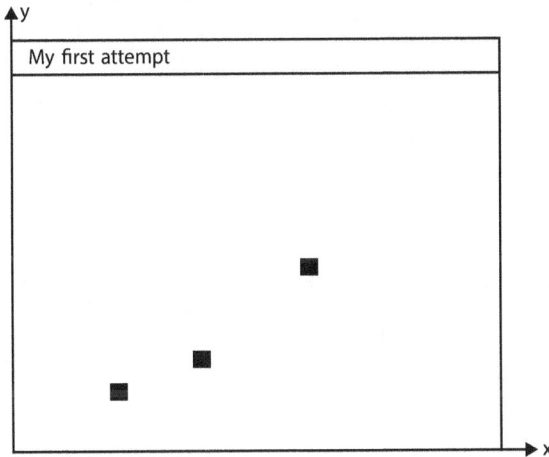

Fig. 13.9 Drawing three dots at a specified position

Similar to GL_POINTS, we can also set it to the GL_LINES and GL_POLYGON, etc. These commands send the vertex information in a pipeline manner, which is then forwarded to several processing steps.

The function *glVertex2i()* is based on the argument size and argument types.

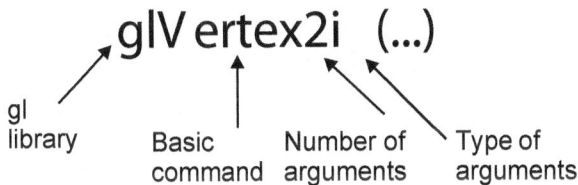

Fig. 13.10 Command format for OpenGL

In Fig. 13.10, the prefix gl stands for a function in OpenGL library (differs from glut as utility tool). It is followed by the command root, on which the command should be applicable. The numeric value indicates the number of arguments passed to the command, and finally i indicates the type of argument as integer.

We can set the number of arguments of the command as per our requirement, similarly the type as integer, float, etc.

13.2.6 Data Types and "States" in OpenGL

When we talk about the data type, OpenGL works on specific data types such as 32-bit integers. Some applications, like C, C++, support different data type sizes, such as 16-bit and 32-bit integer formats. OpenGL doesn't take the wrong input format, or it will produce a wrong result. The same criterion is applicable for float and double data types. To deal with these problems, OpenGL supports predefined built-in data type names such as GLint and GLdouble. The various data types and their corresponding OpenGL type names are given in Fig. 13.11.

Data types	C or C++ type name	OpenGL type name	Suffix used
8-bit integer	Signed char	GLbyte	b
16-bit integer	Short	GLshort	s
32-bit integer	Int	GLint	i
32-floating point	Float	GLfloat	f
64-bit floating point	Double	GLdouble	d

Fig. 13.11 Data types and their equivalent OpenGL type names and suffix

Now, if you are defining your syntax as glVertex2i() then it will demand 32-bit integers while your system supports 16-bit only. So if you want to put a dot on the graphics windows you should carefully pass the arguments as Glint or GLfloat. A sample program for drawing a dot on screen is as follows:

```
Void drawDot(GLint x, GLint y)
{
        glBegin(GL_POINTS);
        glVertex2i(x, y);
        glEng();
}
```

An attractive feature of OpenGL is that it maintains the state information regarding variables such as color, size of dot, background color, etc. The value assigned to a variable remains stable until a new value is assigned to it. Let's take an example of point size. We use the command glPointSize() for it, which takes floating point arguments. If the argument portion contains three parameters, then it draws three points on the side of the window where the value of red, green, and blue lies between 0.0 and 1.0. Some examples of the commands are:

```
glcolor3f(1.0, 0.0, 0.0) //set drawing colour to red
glcolor3f(1.0, 1.0, 0.0) //set drawing colour to yellow.
```

Similarly, if you want to define the background color then you should give command as glClearColor(red, green, blue, alpha). Here alpha is the degree of transparency.

13.2.7 Establishing a Coordinate System

A sample coordinate system initialization is given in the following program segment.

```
Void myInit (void)
{
        glMatrixMode (GL_PROJECTION);
        glLoadIdentity ();
        gluOrtho2D (0, 1024.0, 0, 768.0);
}
```

The command myInit() is used for establishment. The transformation takes place in OpenGL at regular intervals, so we allow MatrixMode to deal with such transformations. Required dimensions are set in Ortho2–D function.

Now at this stage we are ready with one simple, complete program.

```
#include<windows.h>                  // Use as per your system need.
#include<gl/Gl.h>
#include<gl/glut.h>
Void myInit(void)
{
      glClearColor (1.0, 1.0, 1.0, 0); // set the background as white
      glColor3f (0.0f, 0.0f, 0.0f);   // set the drawing color
      glPointSize (5.0);          // a dot of 5 by 5 pixels
      glMatrixMode (GL_PROJECTION);
      glLoadIdentity ();
      gluOrtho2D (0.0, 1024.0, 0.0, 768.0);
}
Void myDisplay (void)
{
      glClear (GL_COLOR_BUFFER_BIT);    //clear the screen
      glBegin (GL_POINTS);             //draw three points specified by
                                       coordinate values
      glVetrex2i (130, 70);
      glVetrex2i (150, 80);
      glVetrex2i (200, 100);
      glEnd ();
      glFlush ();                      //send the output values to
                                       display screen
}
```

```
Void main (intargc, char** argv)
{
    glutInit(&argc,argv);                  // Initialization of toolkit
    glutInitDisplayMode(GLUT_SINGLE|GLUT_RGB); //display mode setting
    glutInitWindowSize(1024,768;            //window size setting
    glutInitWindowPosition(100,150);        //window position setting on the
                                             screen
    glutCreateWindow("my first attempt");    //Open the screen window
    glutDisplayFunc (myDisplay);            // register for redraw function
                                             myInit();
    glutMainLoop ();                        //go into loop
}
```

The program simply draws three dots on the screen. We can extend the dot quantity manually. As previously discussed, myInit() initializes the coordinate system, point size, background color, etc. The particular drawing is encapsulated in the myDrawing() function. At last we use the glFlush() to ensure that the processed data is sent over the screen.

Now we will move toward drawing the dots constellation pattern. We will take a simple example of representing the Big Dipper to state our idea.

Example 1

Fig. 13.12 represents a pattern of 7 dots on the screen as the Big Dipper. This scene is often seen in the night sky.

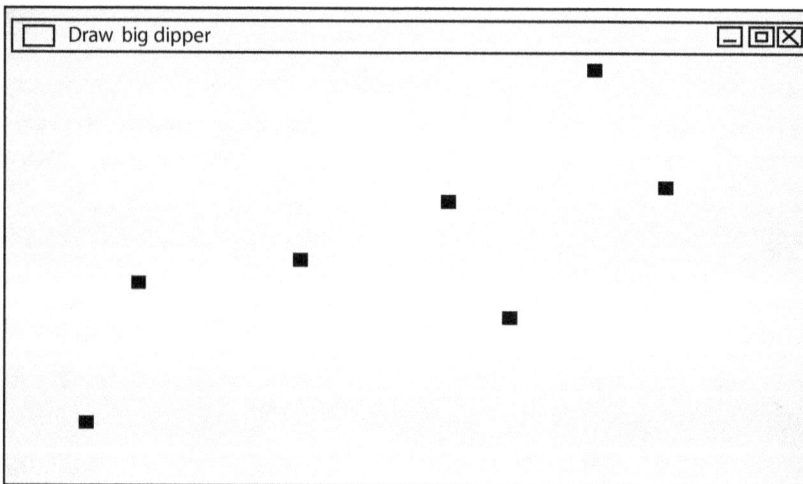

Fig. 13.12 A simple dot constellation

We can assign the names and respective positions of the dots in the screen. For example, dot (289, 190) is assigned the name of Dubhe. This representation is applicable to others also.

13.2.8 Making a Line Drawing

In computer graphics line drawing is a very fundamental concept. Almost every graphic makes use of basic line primitives to make complicated graphics. The simple line drawing command in OpenGL starts with *glBegin()* function, where the arguments are passed as GL_LINES. The body of the function contains the two vertex endpoints between which the line has to be drawn. Each vertex is assigned with the type and coordinate systems. A sample program is:

```
glBegin(GL_LINES);
        glVertex2i(60, 135);
        glVertex2i(180, 56);
    glEnd();
```

If more than two points are defined between glBegin() and glEnd(), then these points are taken as a pair and a separate line is drawn for them. The selection of vertex points is based on the corresponding coordinate values of x and y.

```
glBegin(GL_LINES);
        glVertex2i(10, 20);    //First Horizontal line as both
                               vertex set have same y coordinates
        glVertex2i(40, 20);
        glVertex2i(20, 10);    //First Vertical line as both
                               vertex set have same x coordinates
        glVertex2i(20, 40);
    glEnd();
    glFlush();
```

The color of the line is set in the same way as for points. The command is *glColor3f()*. The width is defined by *glLineWidth(4.0)*.

Drawing Polylines and Polygons

A polyline is simply a collection of connected line segments. Each of the segments is defined by the coordinate values of points. The basic structure of a polyline can be given as:

$$p_0 = (x_0, y_0), p_1 = (x_1, y_1), p_2 = (x_3, y_3) \ldots p_n = (x_m, y_n)$$

The following program segment discusses the drawing of a polyline.

```
glBegin(GL_LINE_STRIP);
            glVertex2i(20, 10);
            glVertex2i(50, 10);
            glVertex2i(20, 80);
            glVertex2i(50, 80);
    glEnd();
    glFlush();
```

The thickness and color of the polyline is assigned in the same way as previously discussed.

Line Drawing Using *Moveto* () and *Lineto* ()

The *moveto* and *lineto* is an alternative approach for polyline drawing. The command *moveto()* takes the argument as points from which the line has to be drawn and the command *lineto()* takes the arguments to which the line has to be drawn. We can call the *moveto()* value current position.

So a line from (x_0, y_0) to (x_1, y_1) can be drawn simply by calling *moveto* (x_0, y_0) and *lineto* (x_1, y_1). A polygon can be drawn similarly by using a loop for the connecting line segments.

```
moveto(x[0], y[0]);
For(int i=1; i<n; i++)
lineto (x[i], y[i]);
```

A sample program defining *moveto()* and *lineto()* is as follows:

```
GLintPoint              // global current position
Void moveto (GLint x, GLint   y)
{
        CP.x = x;
        CP.y = y;
}
Void lineto (GLint x, GLint y)
{
        glBegin (GL_LINES);
                glVertex2i (CP.x, Cp.y);
                glVertex2i (x, y);
        glEnd ();
        glFlush ();
        CP.x = x; CP.y = y;
}
```

Drawing Aligned Rectangles

This is a special case of a polyline in which the rectangles are aligned with the sides.

glRecti(GLint x₁; GLint y₁; GLint x₂; GLint y₂)

$$glRecti(GLint\ x_1;\ GLint\ y_1;\ GLint\ x_2;\ GLint\ y_2)$$

This command draws an aligned rectangle based on given endpoints. We can also fill the rectangle's color, for which we need only to embed the following code:

```
glClearColor(1.0, 1.0, 1.0, 1.0);     //set background as white
glClear(GL_COLOR_BUFFER_BIT);          //clear the window
glColor3f(0.6, 0.6, 0.6);      // Setting colour as bright gray
glRecti(20, 20, 100, 70);
glColor3f(0.2, 0.2, 0.2);      // Setting colour as dark gray
glRecti(70, 50, 150, 130);
glFlush();
```

Aspect Ratio of Aligned Rectangles

We can calculate the aspect ratio of aligned rectangles as the ratio of its weight and height. The shape of aligned rectangles depends on the aspect ratio.

$$\text{Aspect ratio} = \frac{\text{width}}{\text{height}}$$

Examples of rectangles with different aspect ratios are shown in Fig. 13.13.

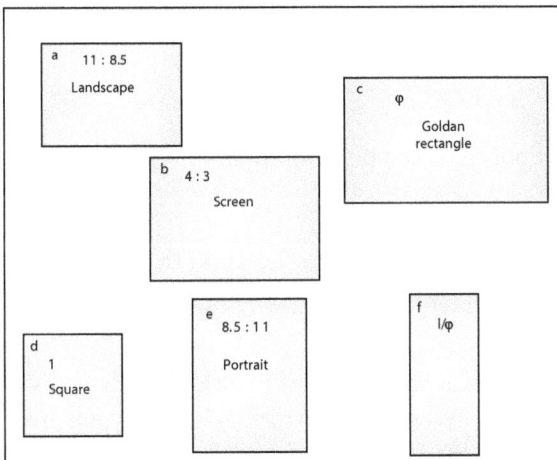

Fig. 13.13 Aspect ratios of aligned rectangles

If the width is larger than the height, it is called a landscape rectangle. A rectangle with an aspect ratio of 1.618034 is called a golden rectangle. Similarly, if the aspect ratio equals 1, then it is called a square rectangle. For a portrait rectangle the width is less than its height. The last rectangle is tall and skinny with an aspect ratio of $\frac{1}{\varphi}$ where $\varphi = 1.618034$.

Filling Polygons

The restriction on a polygon's color filling is that it should be convex. A polygon is said to be convex if the line connecting two points in the polygon lies entirely within it. Some convex and non-convex shapes are given in Fig. 13.14.

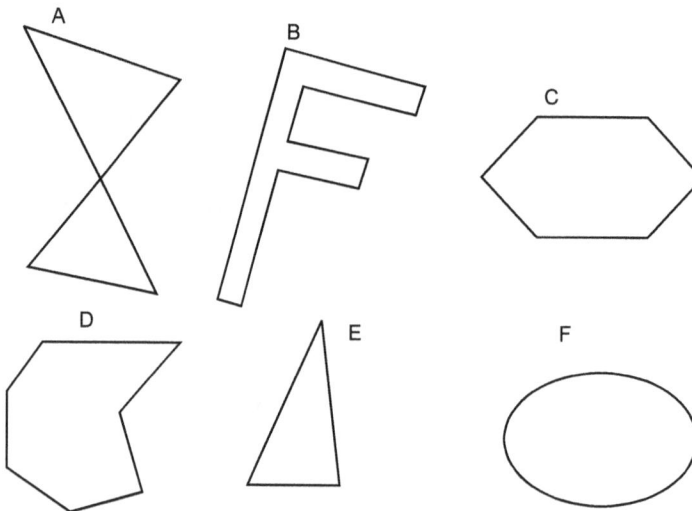

Fig. 13.14 Convex and non-convex polygons

A program syntax to draw convex polygons can be as follows:

```
glBegin(GL_POLYGON)
        glVertex2f(x₀, y₀);
        glVertex2f(x₁, y₁);
        .......
        glVertex2f(xₙ, yₙ);
glEnd();
```

Now it can be filled with a simple color or a strip of colors. Various types of algorithms are available which assign different color textures to the polygon area.

13.2.9 Other Graphics Primitives in OpenGL

Beside the objects discussed so far, OpenGL also supports five other objects of different shapes. Fig. 13.15 gives an idea of the objects' shapes. To draw them we adopt the same procedure as before but make changes in the *glBegin*() body area.

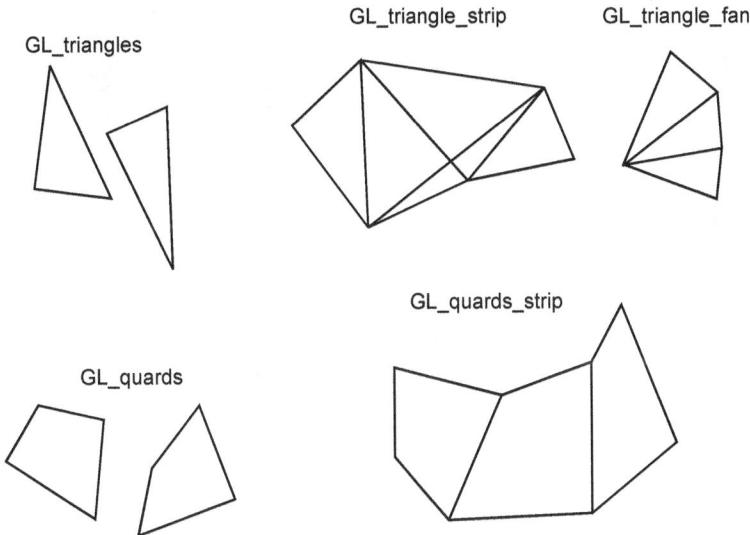

Fig. 13.15 Other geometric primitive types

The functionality of each of them is discussed below:

- GL_TRIANGLES: It takes the three vertices among the given vertices set and prepares a triangle for each.
- GL_QUADS: It is similar to the previous one but it takes four vertices at a time and prepares a quadrilateral for each of them.
- GL_TRIANGLE_STRIP: Among the series of the vertices it takes the three vertices and prepares the triangle series to connect with each other. All the triangles are traversed in the same direction.
- GL_TRIANGLE_FAN: It draws a series of connected triangles but in all of them one vertex is common so that they can prepare a fan-like architecture.
- GL_QUADS_STRIP: Similar to the triangle strip, it creates a series of connected quad literals by taking four vertices at a time. All the quad literals have the same direction either clockwise or anticlockwise.

13.2.10 Simple Interaction with Mouse and Keyboard

A graphics application must be interactive because only an interactive graphics application can allow a user to navigate and control the drawing of objects. Hardware devices such as a mouse and a keyboard play an important role in this. The pointing devices allow the user to go to a specific location and make a clicking at that. Whenever the user presses a button on keyboard or clicks on the screen with a mouse, an event happens. The OpenGL utility toolkit allows users to write the callback function that allows programs to execute when an event happens. We will discuss some of these utility commands here:

- *glutMouseFunc (myMouse)* : This utility registers all the event functionalities related to mouse clicking actions.

- *glutMotionFunc (myMovedMouse)* : This utility registers functionalities when the movements of the mouse take place.

- *glutKeyboardFunc (myKeyboard)*: This utility registers the event functionalities related to keyboard actions.

The next step is to learn how a program makes use of these utilities. We will discuss them one by one.

Mouse Interaction

When we click a mouse button, data is sent to the application. But how this data transfer takes place? We should use the callback function myMouse() which contains four parameters.

$$\text{void myMouse (int button, int state, int } x, \text{ int } y)$$

As soon as the mouse events occur, the system calls the register function and supplies these four parameter values. The parameter button takes one of the three values:

GLUT_LEFT_BUTTON
GLUT_RIGHT_BUTTON
GLUT_MIDDLE_BUTTON

The parameter state takes the value as either GLUT_UP or GLUT_DOWN. The x and y take the values from the pixel representation on which clicking takes place. Normally the variable x takes its pixel value from the left of the window and y takes the value from the bottom end of the window.

Mouse Motion

In a normal application program, when we press one of the keys, an event occurs. In such a scenario the mouse motion utility takes place. *myMovedMouse()* is an OpenGL utility command associated with this event. The syntax is as follows:

glutMotionFunc(myMovedMouse) ;

Here the callback function is *myMovedMouse(int x, int y)*. The parameters *x* and *y* take the values of position of the mouse.

Keyboard Interaction

When we press a button on the keyboard, an event takes place. The callback function mykeyboard() is registered with the functionalities related to these events. The syntax can be given as below:

void myKeyboard (unsigned int key, int *x*, int *y*)

The parameter key takes the ASCII value of the key pressed by the user. The integer variables *x* and *y* take the mouse pixel location values.

13.3 DRAWING TOOLS

Sections 13.3.1 and 13.3.2 discuss world coordinates, world window, and its transformation to viewports. This transformation simplifies the application of the program in the reasonable coordinate systems of display devices. The section also discusses how to achieve a desired drawing using proper window and viewport. The aspect ratio of window and viewport plays an important role in all types of transformation. Section 13.3.3 discusses the classical clipping algorithms and their implementation in real-time scenarios.

Section 13.3.4 includes information about initialization and variable handling concepts required for graphics programming. Implementation using the OpenGL environment is also included for high-performance computing of graphics programs. The tools available can be used to make complex graphics. Encapsulated variables are used to protect the details from intermediate mishandling.

Section 13.3.5 includes routines that add relatively simple subroutines into the programmer's toolkit. Section 13.3.6 includes how to use regular polygons to create interesting drawings, and Section 13.3.7 includes arc and circle drawing algorithms using OpenGL. At the end, case studies discuss details about clipping, window to viewport transformation, and the development of inherent classes as a tool kit.

Section 13.3.8 covers how to develop curves using parametric forms. Curves in both 2D and 3D space are also included.

The basic unit of a screen window's coordinate system is the pixel. The width of the screen is the number of pixels present in the x-axis of the screen, and the height of the screen is the same in the y-axis. The positive values of x and y are considered for the coordinate system. The easiest way to think about coordinate systems is in term of x varying from 1 or −1 and the same for the y-axis.

In this chapter, objects are considered to be present in a world coordinate system. It is usually calculated using the Cartesian xy coordinate system used in mathematics, based on a convenient units system. The method for conversion of the world coordinate system to a world window and then viewport using automatically scaled and shifted objects makes it simple for the programmer to draw a picture in the screen window. The world window specifies which part of the scene should be drawn. Whatever lies inside the window is included and whatever remains is clipped away.

The rectangular viewport is the window on the screen. Mapping between the world window and the viewport is done in such a way that entire objects in the world are considered for the world window and mapped automatically to the viewport after substantial clipping operations. This window/viewport approach makes it much easier to zoom and pan for a detailed view of the scene. We will first look at mapping and then clipping.

13.3.1 World Coordinates, World Windows, and Viewports

Fig. 13.16 illustrates the concept of the world window and viewport. The coordinate system of window and viewport is specified by the programmer. It is represented by the rectangle shown in the figure. The window is mapped in the world coordinate system. The viewport is a portion of the screen window. Proper shifting and scaling operations are required to map the world window with the viewport.

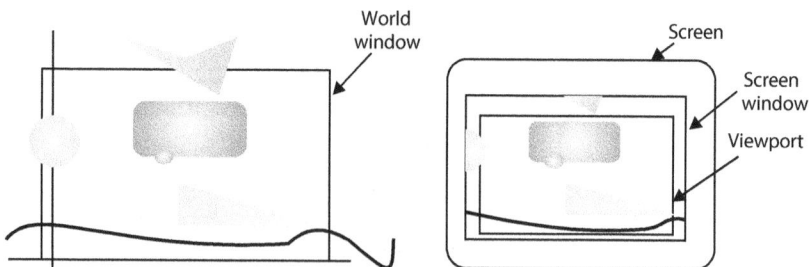

Fig. 13.16 World window, screen window, and viewport

Consider the mathematical representation of cos (x) in pictorial format. As the value of x may vary from $-\infty$ to $+\infty$, the value of y varies from $+1$ to -1. A plot of cos (x) is shown in Fig. 13.17.

```
voidTransformxy(void)
{
        glBegin(GL_LINE_STRIP);
        for(GLfloat x = -4.0; x < 4.0; x += 0.1)
        {
             GLfloat y = cos(3.14159 * x) / (3.14159 * x);
             glVertex2f(x, y);
        }
        glEnd();
        glFlush();
}
```

The key concept is how the transform xy () function creates the values using scaling and shifting operations, so that the picture appears properly on the screen window is.

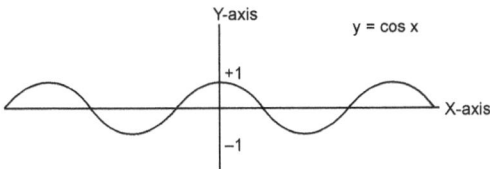

Fig. 13.17 A plot of cos(x) function

13.3.2 Mapping Between Window and Viewport

Figure 13.18 shows a world window and viewport in more detail. The borders of the world window are described as w_1, w_2, w_3, and w_4. The viewport is described by the coordinate system of the screen window by v_1, v_2, v_3 and v_4.

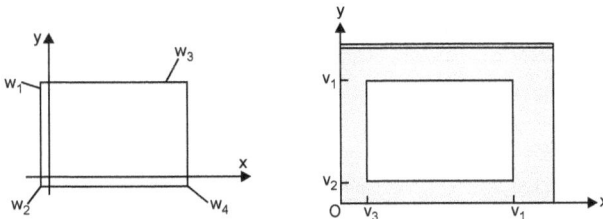

Fig. 13.18 Specifications of window and viewport

The world window is of any size, shape, and present at any position. The viewport lies entirely within the screen window. The aspect ratio of the world window and viewport may differ. We will also discuss how to coordinate the viewport with the aspect ratio so that it always matches with the entire window after resizing by the user.

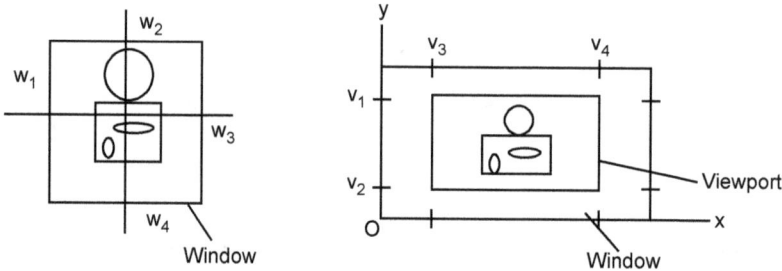

Fig. 13.19 Mapping of a window to viewport with distortion

Mapping is also called transformation. The transformation from window to viewport is called window-to-viewport mapping. The mapping creates the point for viewport (V_x, V_y) from points (x, y) in a world coordinate system. The mapping should always be in proper proportion. Let us consider the following linear formulae for proportionate mapping.

$$V_x = C^* x + D$$
$$V_y = E^* y + F \qquad \qquad ...(13.1)$$

where C, D, E and F are positive constants, in which C, E are scaling factors of x, y and D, F are positive or negative shifts in x and y directions. In order to calculate the values of C, D, E and F we have to do mapping between the coordinate systems of the window and viewport as shown in Fig. 13.20.

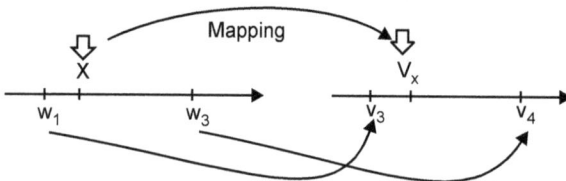

Fig. 13.20 Mapping between x and V_x

$$\frac{(V_x - v_4)}{v_4 - v_3} = \frac{x - w_1}{w_3 - w_1}$$

Or

$$V_x = \frac{v_4 - v_3}{w_3 - w_1} x + \left(v_3 - \frac{v_4 - v_3}{w_3 - w_1} w_1 \right) \quad\quad ...(13.2)$$

Thus $\quad\quad C = \dfrac{v_4 - v_3}{w_3 - w_1}$ and $D = \left(v_3 - \dfrac{v_4 - v_3}{w_3 - w_1} w_1 \right)$

Similarly,

$$\frac{\left(V_y - v_1 \right)}{v_1 - v_2} = \frac{x - w_4}{w_4 - w_2}$$

Thus $\quad\quad C = \dfrac{v_1 - v_2}{w_4 - w_2}$ and $D = \left(v_2 - \dfrac{v_1 - v_2}{w_4 - w_2} w_4 \right)$

Mapping is bidirectional, i.e., mapping can be from window to viewport or viewport to window. In order to apply Eq. 13.2 the following properties are important:

(a) if x is at the window's left edge: $x = w_1$, then V_x is at the viewport's left edge: $s_x = v_1$.

(b) if x is at the window's right edge then s_x is at the viewport's right edge.

(c) if x is fraction f of the way across the window, then V_x is fraction f of the way across the viewport.

(d) if x is outside the window to the left, $(x < w_1)$, then s_x is outside the viewport to the left $(V_x < v_1)$.

Similarly, if x is outside the window then V_x is to the right of viewport.

OpenGL implementation

OpenGL is a command-oriented language. Window-to-viewport transformation is a very simple task in OpenGL. The *glVertex2*()* command automatically passes each vertex through a sequence of transformation according to the desired mapping. The automatic clipping of objects outside the window is done by the same function. We need to just set the transformation property.

gluOrtho2D() is used for setting the world window and *glViewport()* is used for setting the viewport in 2D graphics.

void gluOrtho2D(GLdouble left, GLdouble right, GLdouble bottom, GLdouble top);

where lower left corner (*left, bottom*) and upper right corner (*right, top*) are used to represent window coordinates.

voidglViewport(GLint x, GLint y, GLint width, GLint height);

where lower left corner (*x, y*) and upper right corner (*x* + width, *y* + height) are used to represent viewport coordinates.

The default size of viewport is the entire screen window. By default, the data structure of OpenGL is a marix. Therefore the *gluOrtho2D()* function is presided by *glMatrixMode*(GL_PROJECTION) and *glLoadIdentity()* functions.

```
glMatrixMode(GL_PROJECTION);
glLoadIdentity();
gluOrtho2D(0.0, 4.0, 0.0, 2.0); // sets the window
glViewport(50,70, 380, 260); // sets the viewport
```

glVertex 2*(*x, y*) is used to do mapping of Eq. 2.

Example 2

Plotting the co-function

The OpenGL program requires just defining the window and viewport. We want to plot the function from closely spaced *x*-values between −5.0 and 5.0 into a viewport with width 640 and height 480 using the following OpenGL program:

```
voidTransformxy(void) // plot the cos function, using world coordinates
{
        glMatrixMode(GL_PROJECTION);
        glLoadIdentity();
        gluOrtho2D(-5.0, 5.0, -0.3, 1.0);
        glViewport(0, 640, 0, 640 - 480);
        glBegin(GL_LINE_STRIP);
        for(GLfloat x = -4.0; x < 4.0; x += 0.1) // draw the plot
            glVertex2f(x, cos(3.14159 * x) / (3.14159 * x));
        glEnd();
        glFlush();
}
```

Setting the window and viewport automatically

There are two ways to set the size of window and viewport: one is to set the size of both as per dimensions entered by the user in the program and other way is to set everything automatically as per default settings in OpenGL. For this instance, let us consider automatic sizing of window and viewport.

Setting the window

Generally the programmer doesn't have any idea about the size of the object in world coordinates. The object may be any picture of known size or data generated by some unknown procedure. In such conditions, the most convenient way is to rely on the automatic size determination function of the application.

The general approach is to set the boundary of the object in terms of a rectangle such that it contains the entire object in the scene. This rectangular boundary is also called the extent of the object. Fig. 13.21 contains the representation of extents in a proper way.

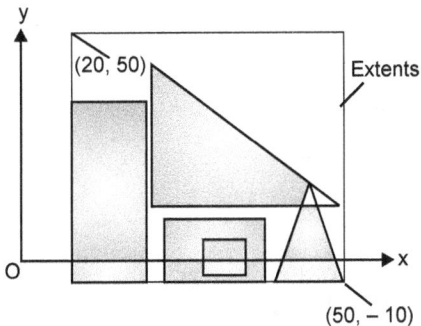

Fig. 13.21 Figures with extents

If $P[]$ contains all the points of lines present in the figure, then the extremes of x and y coordinates in array P are considered the extremes of the object to be displayed in the window.

Automatic setting of the viewport to preserve aspect ratio

An undistorted version of a figure is possible if the aspect ratio of the viewport and the actual window is the same. A simple idea is to find the largest possible viewport that can be visible on the window screen of the display. Suppose the screen window is of width W and height H and aspect ratio of the world window is A, then either $A < \left(\dfrac{W}{H}\right)$ or $A > \left(\dfrac{W}{H}\right)$. In the first case the viewport extends fully along the width of the window but leaves unused space along the y direction of the screen window. In the second case the viewport extends fully along the height of the window but leaves unused space along the x direction of the screen window.

Resizing the screen window

In a Microsoft Windows-based system, a simple drag-and-drop operation of a mouse from one of the corners of an image can change the size of the window in run time. The OpenGL utility tool kit contains *glutReshape()* to reshape the window whenever required.

glutReshape(myReshape); specifies the function called on a resize event.

Making a matched viewport

The common approach to prevent distortion is that the aspect ratio of the viewport matches with the aspect ratio of the world window. The following OpenGL program creates a matching viewport that is visible in the new screen window of a display device with its extreme size.

```
if(A> W/H) // use (global) window aspect ratio
        setViewport(0, W, 0, W/R);
else
        setViewport(0, H * R, 0, H);
```

The routine obtains the new size of the viewport according to the default size of the screen window.

13.3.3 Line Clipping

Clipping is an important task for a graphics application. It is generally used to remove or add portions of the world window to the screen window of display devices. In OpenGL the object is automatically clipped using specified inbuilt algorithms in the world window. Since clipping is automatic in an OpenGL environment, we are concentrating on tools that incorporate clipping for the programmer. Instead of skipping the concept, it is included by considering the absence of an OpenGL environment for graphics programming in a general sense.

We include a general clipping algorithm to understand the clipping process. These algorithms can be used in general routines in the absence of an OpenGL environment.

In this section we concentrate on the Cohen-Sutherland line clipping algorithm. The input to the algorithm is a line segment with endpoint p_1, p_2 and returns the line segment with an endpoint that fits inside the viewport or screen window.

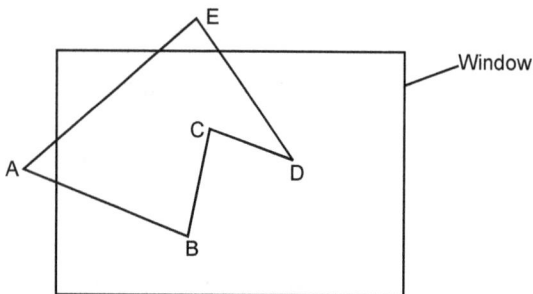

Fig. 13.22 Line clipping at the window's boundary

Fig. 13.22 illustrates the action required to be performed by the clipper.

- If the entire line lies within the window, it returns 1.
- If the entire line lies outside the window, it returns 0.
- If one endpoint is inside the window and one is outside, the function clips the portion of the segment that lies outside the window and returns 1.
- If both endpoints are outside the window, but a portion of the segment passes through it, it clips both ends and returns 1.

The Cohen-Sutherland line clipping algorithm

This algorithm has two common cases that can be quickly detected. They are called "trivially accept" and "trivially reject." If the line lies completely within the boundary of window, then this line is trivially accepted, and if it is completed outside the window then it is trivially rejected.

The Cohen-Southerland algorithm uses an inside-outside codeword for detection of a line inside, outside, or on the boundary of the window. The codeword contains four bits as represented below.

T/F	T/F	T/F	T/F

First bit: True if P is to the left of the window
Second bit: True if P is above the window
Third bit: True if P is to the right of the window
Fourth bit: True if P is below the window
If P is inside the window then codeword values are FFFF; otherwise nine values are possible:

TTFF	FTFF	FTFF
TFFF	FFFF	FFTF
TFFT	FFFT	FFTT

- Trivial accept: If both points have codeword FFFF
- Trivial reject: If the codeword has an *F* in the same position, i.e., both points are either left, above, below, or on the right of the window.

Condition for chopping the line

The Cohen-Sutherland algorithm is based on a divide-and-conquer strategy. It discards the portion of the line which is outside the window and uses the same strategy for the remaining portion. The loop discards after four iterations since it requires at most four iterations for trivial acceptance and rejection to be assured.

```
do{
        form the code words for p1 and p2
        if (trivial accept) return 1;
        if (trivial reject) return 0;
        chop the line at the "next" window border; discard the "outside"
          part;
} while(1);
```

Fig. 13.23 contains the clip segment routine for line clipping algorithm. The inputs p_1 and p_2 are called in with its (x, y) values by reference. Array W is a matrix for storing values of the rectangle representing the screen's window.

```
intclipSegment(Point2& p1, Point2& p2, RealRect W)
{
do{
    if(trivial accept) return 1; // some portion survives
    if(trivial reject) return 0; // no portion survives
    if(p1 is outside)
    {
      if(p1 is to the left) chop against the left edge
        else if(p1 is to the right) chop against the right edge
        else if(p1 is below) chop against the bottom edge
        else if(p1 is above) chop against the top edge

    }
    else // p2 is outside
    {
        if(p2 is to the left)chop against the left edge
          else if(p2 is to the right)chop against the right edge
          else if(p2 is below) chop against the bottom edge
          else if(p2 is above)chop against the top edge
      }
}while(1);
}
```

Fig. 13.23 Pseudo-code for Cohen-Sutherland line clipper

13.3.4 Drawing Polygons, Circles, and Arcs Using OpenGL

OpenGL provides various tools to draw regular shapes like polygons, circles, and arcs. These shapes play vital roles in the development of graphics applications.

Drawing polygons

Polygons are an important family of shapes commonly used in computer graphics. The regular polygon is one category of polygons. Polygons are called regular if all their sides are of the same length and the adjacent sides meet each other forming equal interior angles.

The different shapes of regular polygons with n sides are shown in Fig. 13.24.

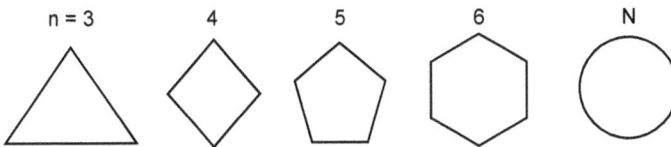

Fig. 13.24 Shapes of regular polygons

If the number of lines are very large then the shapes of polygons appear like circles. The general equation of polygons with n vertices is

$$P_i = \left(R\cos\left(\frac{2\pi i}{n}\right), R\sin\left(\frac{2\pi i}{n}\right) \right), \text{ for } i = 0, \cdots, n-1 \qquad \qquad \text{...(13.3)}$$

where P_i is vertices of polygons with (x, y) coordinates. Fig. 13.25 is a polygon with six vertices and the interior angle between two adjacent lines is 60 degrees.

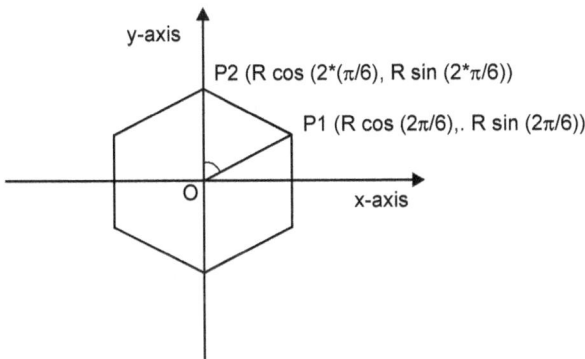

Fig. 13.25 Vertices of an hexagon from Eq. 13.3

The OpenGL implementation of a polygon with n vertices centered at (C_x, C_y), with radius R, and rotated through RA degrees is shown in Fig. 13.26:

```
void polygon(int n, float cx, float cy, float R, float RA)
{ // assumes global Canvas object, cvs
      if(n < 3) return; // bad number of sides
      double angle = RA * 3.14159265 / 180; // initial angle
          double angleInc = 2 * 3.14159265 /n; //angle increment
          cvs. moveTo(R + cx, cy);
      for(int k = 0; k < n; k++) // repeat n times
      {
          angle += angleInc;
          cvs.lineTo(R * cos(angle) + cx, R * sin(angle) + cy);
      }
}
```

Fig. 13.26 OpenGL implementation of a regular polygon with n vertices in memory

13.3.5 Drawing Circles and Arcs

Drawing a circle is same as drawing polygons. The difference is only in the number of vertices we have to select. The function *DCircle()* shown in Fig. 13.27 creates a 70-sided polygon by simply passing parameter to function *polygon(int n, float cx, float cy, float R, float RA)*.

```
void DCircle(Point2 center, float radius)
{
constintnumVerts = 70; // use larger for a better circle
    polygon(numVerts, center.getX(), center.getY(), radius, 0)
}
```

Fig. 13.27 Drawing a circle based on 70-sided polygons

Drawing arcs

An arc is significantly described by the position of center C and its radius R. The circle is a special case of an arc with a sweep of 360 degrees. The diagrammatic representation of an arc is shown in Fig. 13.28:

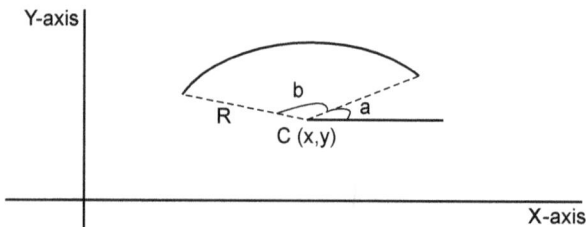

Fig. 13.28 Arc representation in a 2D coordinate system

The angles a and b are sweeps of an arc in an anticlockwise direction along the *x*-axis. The OpenGL implementation of the arc formulated from the concept of the polygon is shown in Fig. 13.29. *R* is the radius of the arc, *SA* is the starting angle, *S* is the sweep, and center is the position of the midpoint of the arc along the (*x*, *y*) coordinate system.

```
void drawArc(Point2 center, float R, float SA, float S)
{ // startAngle and sweep are in degrees
      constint n = 30; // number of intermediate segments in arc
        float angle = SA * 3.14159265 / 180; // initial angle in
          radians
        float angleInc = S * 3.14159265 /(180 * n); // angle
          increment
      float cx = center.getX(), cy = center.getY(); cvs.moveTo
        (cx + R * cos(angle), cy + R * sin(angle)); for(int
        k = 1; k < n; k++, angle += angleInc)
      cvs.lineTo(cx + R * cos(angle), cy + R * sin(angle));
}
```

Fig. 13.29 Function for creating an arc

13.4 TRANSFORMATION OF OBJECTS

13.4.1 Transformation

Transformations are a fundamental feature of computer graphics and are central to OpenGL as well as to most other graphics systems. Transformation is used to translate and scale the objects of the real world to their final size and position in the viewport. The fundamentals of computer graphics are transformation and representation of points and lines in space. With the help of an appropriate drawing algorithm, points and lines can be joined to draw an object. Computer graphics have the ability to transform these points and lines. They are required to scale, translate, rotate, distort, or develop a perspective view of an object in order to visualize it.

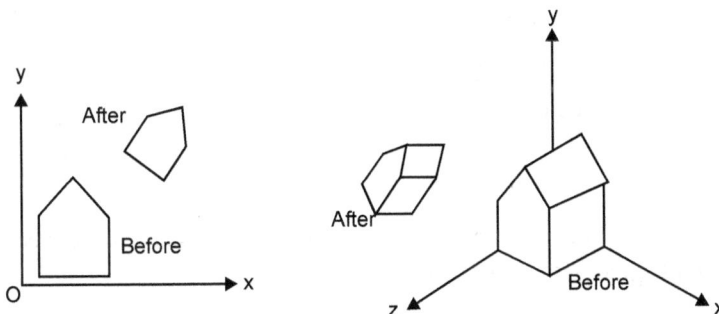

Fig. 13.30 Objects before and after they are transformed

Figure 13.30 shows a view of a simple house; (*a*) is a 2D view while (*b*) is a 3D view, drawn before and after; each of its points has been transformed. Firstly, the house has been scaled down in size, rotated, and then moved up. The overall transformation here is a combination of three more elementary ones: scaling, rotation, and translation.

Transformation with OpenGL

The main goal is to produce graphical drawings of objects that have been transformed to proper size, position, and orientation so that it can present the desired view. Today a lot of platforms are available, such as OpenGL, which provide a sequence of operations or graphics pipeline to all the points under consideration. The object is produced after analyzing each point.

The transformation given in figure is called Current Transformation (CT). CT provides a crucial tool for the manipulation of a graphical object, and an application programmer needs to know what adjustment to make in CT so as to produce a desired transformation.

Transformation can be viewed in two ways: object transformation and coordinate transformation. An object transformation alters the coordinate of each point of the object, keeping the coordinate system fixed. A coordinate transformation defines a new coordinate system in terms of the old one, and then represents all the object points in this new system. These two views are closely connected and each has its own advantage, but implementation is somewhat different.

13.4.2 Affine Transformation

Affine transformation is the most common transformation used in computer graphics. It possesses very useful properties which make it so easy to handle. The properties are to scale, rotate, and reposition figures.

In affine transformations, the coordinates of Q are linear combinations of six constants $m_{11}, m_{13}, m_{13}, m_{21}, m_{22}, m_{23}$.

$$\begin{pmatrix} Q_x \\ Q_y \\ 1 \end{pmatrix} = \begin{pmatrix} m_{11}P_x + m_{12}P_y + m_{13} \\ m_{21}P_x + m_{22}P_y + m_{23} \\ 1 \end{pmatrix}$$

Q_x consists of portions of both P_x and P_y, and similarly Q_y. This cross between the x and y components gives rise to rotations and shears.

Geometric Effects of 2D Affine Transformations

Geometric effects produced due to affine transformations are a combination of four elementary transformations, i.e., translation, scaling, rotation, and shear. These are called elementary because they can only be applied one at a time.

Translation

To translate a picture into a different position on a graphics display, the translation part of affine transformation arises from the third column of the translation matrix; so in ordinary coordinates $Q = P + d$, where offset vector d has components (m_{13}, m_{23}).

$$\begin{pmatrix} Q_x \\ Q_y \\ 1 \end{pmatrix} = \begin{pmatrix} 1 & 0 & m_{13} \\ 0 & 1 & m_{23} \\ 0 & 0 & 1 \end{pmatrix} \begin{pmatrix} P_x \\ P_y \\ 1 \end{pmatrix}$$

Scaling

A scaling changes the size of a picture and involves two scale factors, S_x and S_y, for the x- and y-coordinates, respectively:

$$(Q_x, Q_y) = (S_x P_x, S_y P_y)$$

Thus the matrix for a scaling by itself is simple.

Transforming Points and Objects:

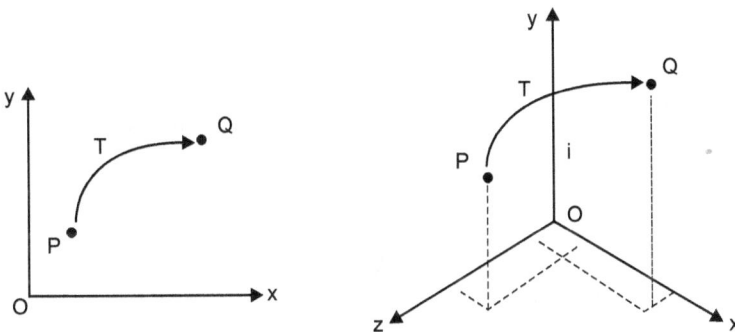

Fig. 13.31 Mapping points into a new position

Fig. 13.31 shows transformation of point P to Q in 2D and 3D views using an algorithm or formula. The point P is mapped to point Q; we can say that Q is the image of P under transformation T.

In the case of 2D, points P and Q are represented by $\tilde{P}$ and $\tilde{Q}$

$$\tilde{P} = \begin{pmatrix} P_x \\ P_y \\ 1 \end{pmatrix}, \tilde{Q} = \begin{pmatrix} Q_x \\ Q_y \\ 1 \end{pmatrix}$$

The transformation operates on the representation $\tilde{P}$ and produces the representation $\tilde{Q}$ according to a function $T()$.

$$\begin{pmatrix} Q_x \\ Q_y \\ 1 \end{pmatrix} = T \begin{pmatrix} P_x \\ P_y \\ 1 \end{pmatrix}$$

Or simply

$$\tilde{Q} = T(\tilde{P})$$

The function $T()$ could be complicated.

$$\begin{pmatrix} Q_x \\ Q_y \\ 1 \end{pmatrix} = \begin{pmatrix} \cos(P_x)e^{-P_y} \\ \dfrac{\ln(P_y)}{1+P_x^2} \\ 1 \end{pmatrix}$$

$$\begin{pmatrix} S_x & 0 & 0 \\ 0 & S_y & 0 \\ 0 & 0 & 1 \end{pmatrix}$$

Scaling also includes refection around an axis. Fig. 13.32 shows scaling and reflection around the x-axis.

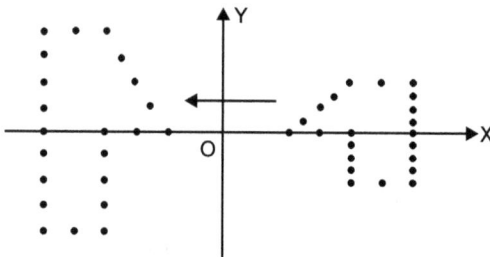

Fig. 13.32 A scaling and a reflection

Rotation

Rotation is a fundamental graphics operation in which a figure about a given point is rotated through an angle.

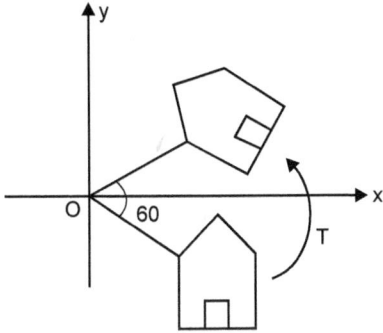

Fig. 13.33 Rotation of points through 60°

Fig. 13.33 shows a set of points rotated about the origin through an angle of $\theta = 60°$. $T(\ )$ is a rotation about the origin; the offset vector $\boldsymbol{d}$ is zero and $Q = T(P)$ has the form

$$Q_x = P_x \cos(\theta) - P_y \sin(\theta)$$
$$Q_y = P_x \sin(\theta) + P_y \cos(\theta)$$

In matrix form,

$$\begin{pmatrix} \cos(\theta) & -\sin(\theta) & 0 \\ \sin(\theta) & \cos(\theta) & 01 \\ 0 & 0 & 1 \end{pmatrix}$$

The Inverse of an Affine Transformation

When you apply transformation T to a point, you may want the original point back to its previous position. To remove the effect of transformation we apply another transformation called inverse transformation and it is denoted by T^{-1}.

If point P is mapped into point Q according to $Q = MP$, simply pre-multiply both sides by the inverse of M, denoted M^{-1}, and write

$$P = M^{-1} Q$$

The inverse of M is given by

$$M^{-1} = \frac{1}{\det M} \begin{pmatrix} m_{22} & -m_{12} \\ -m_{21} & m_{11} \end{pmatrix}$$

The elementary inverse transformations are as follows:

Scaling:

$$M^{-1} = \begin{pmatrix} \dfrac{1}{S_x} & 0 & 0 \\ 0 & \dfrac{1}{S_y} & 0 \\ 0 & 0 & 1 \end{pmatrix}$$

Rotation:

$$M^{-1} = \begin{pmatrix} \cos(\theta) & \sin(\theta) & 0 \\ -\sin(\theta) & \cos(\theta) & 0 \\ 0 & 0 & 1 \end{pmatrix}$$

Shearing:

$$M^{-1} = \begin{pmatrix} 1 & 0 & 0 \\ -h & 1 & 0 \\ 0 & 0 & 1 \end{pmatrix}$$

Translation:

$$M^{-1} = \begin{pmatrix} 1 & 0 & -m_{13} \\ 0 & 1 & -m_{23} \\ 0 & 0 & 1 \end{pmatrix}$$

Affine transformation: 3D approach

3D affine transformation is the same as 2D but has more complex expression and difficulty in visualizing. We use coordinate frames; in OpenGL, a vertex V at (x, y, z) is represented as

$$V = \begin{bmatrix} x \\ y \\ z \end{bmatrix}$$

Scaling:

3D scaling can be represented as

$$S(\alpha_{x'},\alpha_{y'},\alpha_z) = \begin{bmatrix} \alpha_x & 0 & 0 \\ 0 & \alpha_y & 0 \\ 0 & 0 & \alpha_z \end{bmatrix}$$

where α_x, α_y and α_z represent the scaling factors in x, y, and z directions, respectively. We can obtain the transformed V' of vertex V as follows:

$$V' = SV = \begin{bmatrix} \alpha_x & 0 & 0 \\ 0 & \alpha_y & 0 \\ 0 & 0 & \alpha_z \end{bmatrix}\begin{bmatrix} x \\ y \\ z \end{bmatrix} = \begin{bmatrix} \alpha_x\, x \\ \alpha_y\, y \\ \alpha_z\, z \end{bmatrix}$$

Rotation

3D rotation operates about an axis of rotation (2D rotation operates about a center of rotation). 3D rotations about the x, y, and z axes for an angle θ (measured in counterclockwise manner) can be represented as

$$R_z(\theta) = \begin{bmatrix} \cos\theta & -\sin\theta & 0 \\ \sin\theta & \cos\theta & 0 \\ 0 & 0 & 1 \end{bmatrix}, R_x(\theta) = \begin{bmatrix} 1 & 0 & 0 \\ 0 & \cos\theta & -\sin\theta \\ 0 & \sin\theta & \cos\theta \end{bmatrix}, R_y(\theta) = \begin{bmatrix} \cos\theta & 0 & \sin\theta \\ 0 & 1 & 0 \\ -\sin\theta & 0 & \cos\theta \end{bmatrix}$$

The rotational angles about x, y, and z axes, denoted as θ_x, θ_y, and θ_z, are known as Euler angles, which can be used to specify any arbitrary orientation of an object.

Translation

Translation does not belong to linear transformation, but can be modeled via a vector addition as follows:

$$\begin{bmatrix} x \\ y \\ z \end{bmatrix} + \begin{bmatrix} d_x \\ d_y \\ d_z \end{bmatrix} = \begin{bmatrix} x+d_x \\ y+d_y \\ z+d_z \end{bmatrix}, \text{ where } \begin{bmatrix} d_x \\ d_y \\ d_z \end{bmatrix} \text{ is the translational vector}$$

13.4.3 Drawing 3D Scenes Using OpenGL

OpenGL contains functions that establish a window and viewport, and that do line drawing through *moveTo()* and *lineTo()*. The main emphases are on transforming objects in order to orient and position them as desired in a 3D scene.

2D drawing so far has actually used a special case of 3D viewing, based on a simple parallel projection. Viewing the scene looks along the one axis at the window, a rectangle lying in the remaining two planes. OpenGL provides the three functions *glScaled(..)*, *glRotated(..)*, and *glTranslated(..)* for applying modeling transformations to a shape.

The graphics pipeline implemented by OpenGL does its major work through matrix transformations, so we will first look into what each of the matrices in the pipeline does. At this point it is important only to grasp the basic idea of how each matrix operates: Each vertex of an object is passed through this pipeline with a call such as *glVertex3d(x, y, z)*. The vertex is multiplied by the various matrices shown; it is clipped if necessary, and if it survives clipping it is ultimately mapped onto the viewport. Each vertex encounters three matrices:

1. The model view matrix
2. The projection matrix
3. The viewport matrix

The model view matrix basically provides what we have been calling the CT. It combines two effects: the sequence of modeling transformations applied to objects and the transformation that orients and positions the camera in space (hence its peculiar name "model views"). Although it is a single matrix in the actual pipeline, it is easier to think of it as the product of two matrices, a modeling matrix M, and a viewing matrix V.

The projection matrix scales and shifts each vertex in a particular way, so that all those that lie inside the view volume will lie inside a standard cube that extends from -1 to 1 in each dimension. This matrix effectively squashes the view volume into the cube centered at the origin. This cube is a particularly efficient boundary against which to clip objects. Scaling the block in this fashion might badly distort it, of course, but this distortion will be compensated for in viewport transformation. The projection matrix also reverses the sense of the z-axis, so that increasing values of z now represent increasing values of depth of a point from the eye.

Finally, the viewport matrix maps the surviving portion of the block into a "3D viewport." This matrix maps the standard cube into a block shape whose x and y values extend across the viewport (in screen coordinates), and whose z-component extends from 0 to 1 and retains a measure of the depth of point.

Three functions are used to set modeling transformations:

- *glScaled(s_x, s_y, s_z)*; Post-multiply the current matrix by a matrix that performs a scaling by s_x in x, by s_y in y, and by s_z in z. Put the result back in the current matrix.

- *glTranslated*(d_x, d_y, d_z); Post-multiply the current matrix by a matrix that performs a translation by d_x in x, by d_y in y, and by d_z in z. Put the result back in the current matrix.

- *glRotated*(angle, u_x, u_y, u_z); Post-multiply the current matrix by a matrix that performs a rotation about the axis that passes through the origin and the point (u_x, u_y, u_z). Put the result back in the current matrix.

13.5 CURVE AND SURFACE DESIGN

Graphic scenes contain many different kinds of objects such as trees, flowers, clouds, rocks, water, bricks, glass, etc. We want an organized way to describe and represent a much richer set of shapes that occur in computer graphics and in CAD programs.

Polygon and quadric surfaces provide precise descriptions for simple Euclidean objects such as polyhedrons and ellipsoids. Other shapes are designed by some analysis program as the best possibility for a particular job, such as aircraft wings, gears, and other engineering structures with curved shapes and procedural methods.

Some shapes such as logarithmic spirals and the path of a planet as it sweeps about sun have a concise mathematical formulation that makes them easy to analyze, but it is of little help when we want to write a routine to draw them. Thus we need ways to convert it from one kind of representation to another that is more suited to certain tasks. Other shapes are more freeform and are based on data rather than mathematical expression. These we could handle in a program also, perhaps in order to find where one such curve intersects another.

13.5.1 Description of Curves

Polynomials are fundamental mathematical objects and are frequently used in computer graphics because they are well behaved and efficient to compute.

We can represent a polynomial in two ways:

1. **Nonparametric form:** When we write object descriptions directly in terms of the coordinates of the reference frame in use, the representation is nonparametric. For example, we can represent a surface with either of the following Cartesian functions:

$$f(x, y, z) = 0 \quad \text{or} \quad z = f(x, y)$$

The first form is an implicit expression for the surface, and the second form gives an explicit representation, with x and y as the independent variables, and z as the dependent variable.

2. Parametric form: Euclidean curves are one-dimensional objects, and positions along the path of a 3D curve can be described with a single parameter u. That is, we can express each of the three Cartesian coordinates in terms of parameter u, and any point on the curve can then be represented with the following vector point function:

$$P(u) = (x(u), y(u), z(u))$$

Often, the coordinate equations can be set up so that parameter u is defined over the unit interval from 0 to 1. For example, a circle in the xy plane with center at the coordinate origin could be defined in the parametric form as:

$$x(u) = r\cos(2\pi u), \ y(u) = r\sin(2\pi u), \ z(u) = 0, \ 0 \le u \le 1$$

Curved or plane Euclidean surfaces are 2D objects, and a position on a surface can be described with two parameters, u and v. A coordinate position on the surface is then represented with the parametric vector function

$$P(u, v) = (x(u, v), y(u, v), z(u, v))$$

where the Cartesian coordinate values for x, y and z are expressed as functions of parameters u and v. As with curves, it is often possible to arrange the parametric description so that parameters u and v are defined over the range from 0 to 1. A spherical surface with center at the coordinate origin can be described as follows:

$$x(u, v) = r\sin(\pi u)\cos(2\pi v)$$

$$y(u, v) = r\sin(\pi u)\sin(2\pi v)$$

$$z(u, v) = r\cos(\pi u)$$

where r is the radius of the sphere. Parameter u describes lines of constant latitude over the surface, and parameter v describes lines of constant longitude. By keeping one of these parameters fixed while varying the other over a subinterval of the range from 0 to 1, we are able to plot latitude and longitude lines for any spherical section.

NOTE: In general, it is more convenient to represent an object in computer graphics algorithms in terms of parametric equation.

Things to remember: An Lth-degree polynomial in t is a function given by:

$$a_0 + a_1 t + a_2 t^2 + \ldots \ldots \ldots \ldots + a_L t^L$$

where the constants $a_0, a_1, \ldots \ldots a_L$ are its coefficients, each associated with one of the powers of t.

Polynomial Curves of Degree 1

Polynomial curves of degree 1 yield a straight line. The curve whose parametric equation is $P(t) = a_0 + a_1^t$ is a straight line which passes through a_0 at time 0, and through $a_0 + a_1$ at time 1. Here we can see that $P(t)$ is actually two equations, one for $x(t)$ and one for $y(t)$. In the 3D world, there is a third equation for $z(t)$.

Polynomial Curves of Degree 2

$$x(t) = at^2 + 2bt + c$$

$$y(t) = dt^2 + 2et + f$$

where a, b, and so on are constants. This curve is always a parabola.

Implicit Form of Degree 2

$$F(x, y) = Ax^2 y + Cy^2 + Dx + Ey + F$$

where A, C, and so on are constants. It is assumed that A and C are not both 0, which produce a degenerative curve. The above equation represents a conic section by examining the signs of coefficients A and C:

If $AC > 0$, it is an ellipse

If $AC = 0$, it is a parabola

If $AC < 0$ it is an hyperbola

The conic that is described depends on the value of eccentricity ε. Eccentricity measures how far off the curve is from a perfect circle (eccentricity = 0). Fig. 13.34 shows curves with different eccentricity.

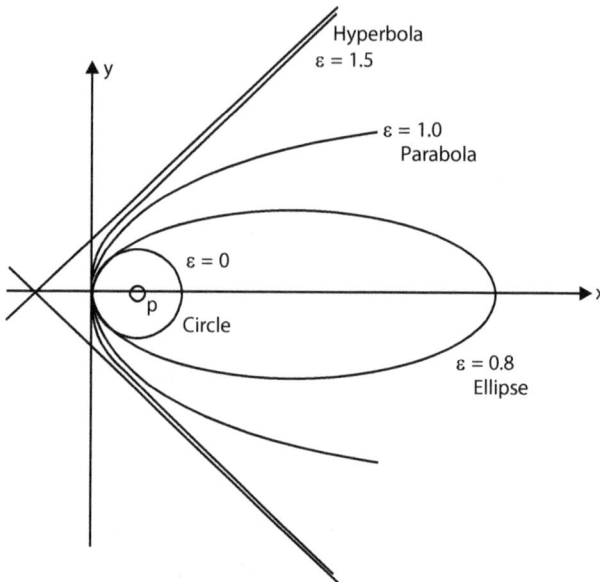

Fig. 13.34 Conic sections with different eccentricities

Polynomial curves of degree 3 or higher

Curves with first and second degree polynomials are easily understood. But things get more complicated when the polynomials are of a higher degree. It is always possible to find an implicit form of a given polynomial functions for $x(t)$ and $y(t)$, but if an implicit form is given we can't easily convert it into parametric form when the degree of the polynomial is greater than or equal to 3.

Cubic polynomials prove very useful in curve and surface design. Bezier and B-Spline curves are cubic polynomials, and they provide a powerful approach to curve design. But this method won't start with an implicit form and try to parameterize it. Rather it will start with a collection of control points carefully set down by the designer and allow a specific algorithm to generate points along the curve, so the designer, if necessary, can edit the position of the control points and view the curve again. This approach is visual, allowing the designer to see the progress of the curve design as the process continues.

Rational Parametric Forms

x and y are each defined as a ratio of two polynomials.

$$P(t) = \frac{P_0(1-t)^2 + 2w(1-t) + P_2 t^2}{(1-t)^2 + wt(1-t) + t^2}$$

where P_0, P_1, and P_2 are three points in the plane. They are called control points as they control the shape of the curve; w is called a weighted parameter.

The equation for $P(t)$ is actually two equations: one each for $x(t)$ and $y(t)$.

$$x(t) = \frac{x_0(1-t)^2 + 2x_1\, wt(1-t) + x_2 t^2}{(1-t)^2 + 2wt(1-t) + t^2}$$

$$y(t) = \frac{y_0(1-t)^2 + 2y_1\, wt(1-t) + t^2}{(1-t)^2 + 2wt(1-t) + t^2}$$

where x_0 and y_0 are the components for P_0.

At $t = 0$, the right-hand side collapses simply to (x_0, y_0); this curve passes through, or interpolates, the point P_0. At $t=1$, it passes through P_2. For t in between 0 and 1, $P(t)$ depends on all three points in a complicated way.

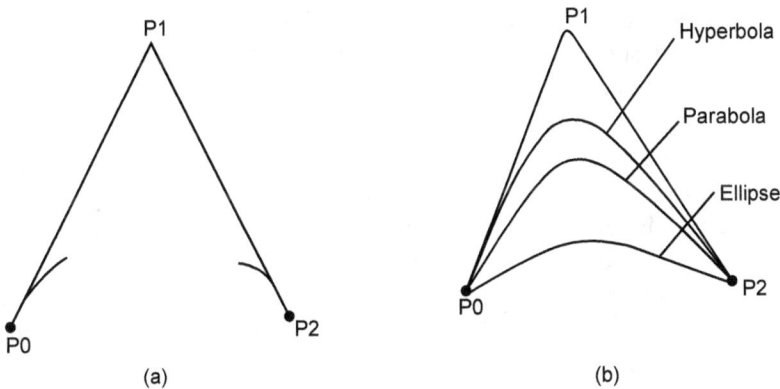

Fig. 13.35 Generating conics with rational quadratics

Fig. 13.35(a) has three control points and shows how the curve emerges from P_0 as t increases from 0 and ends up at P_2 as t approaches 1. The curve in Fig. 13.35(b) is one of the conic sections, and the type of curve depends on the value of w.

If $w < 1$, it is an ellipse

If $w = 1$, it is a parabola

If $w > 1$, it is an hyperbola

Rational parametric forms provide a way to generate conic sections parametrically.

13.5.2 Designing Bezier Curves

There are two main classes of curve generation algorithms.

1. **Interpolation:** This algorithm generates a curve $P(t)$ that passes exactly through the control points and forms a smooth curve.

2. **Approximation:** This algorithm generates a curve $r(t)$ that approximates the control points. $R(t)$ is attracted towards each control point in turn, but doesn't actually pass through all of them.

Bezier curves (approximating curves) were developed to assist in car design. The de Casteljau algorithm is used to draw them.

The de Casteljau algorithm

The de Casteljau algorithm uses a sequence of points P_0, P_1, and P_2,... to construct a well-defined value for point $P(t)$ at each value of t from 0 to 1. Thus it provides a way to generate a curve from a set of points. Changing the points changes the curves. The de Casteljau algorithm is based on a sequence of familiar tweening steps that are easy to implement.

Because tweening is such a well-behaved procedure, it is possible to deduce many valuable properties of the curves that it generates.

Let us first talk about tweening:

Tweening is the process of generating intermediate frames between two images to give the appearance that the first image evolves smoothly into the second image. Tweening is used mainly for art and animation. It's simplest if the two figures are polylines based on the same number of points.

The concept of tweening is simply moving a point (or a series of points) from its initial position to a final position. The equation for tweening along a straight line is a linear interpolation:

$$P = A(1 - t) + Bt \qquad \qquad ...(13.4)$$

where A is the initial position of the object and B is its final position and t is the time varying from 0 to 1.

Tweening Three Points to Obtain a Parabola

Start with three points P_0, P_1, and P_2 as shown in the Fig. 13.36. Choose some value of t between 0 and 1, suppose $t = 0.3$, and locate point A that is fraction t of the way along the line from P_0 to P_1. Similarly, locate B at fraction t along the line between endpoints P_0 and P_1 using the same t.

From Eq. (4) the new points can be expressed as

$$A(t) = (1 - t) P_0 + tP_1$$

$$B(t) = (1 - t) P_1 + tP_2 \qquad \qquad ...(13.5)$$

Now repeat linear interpolation on these points (t is same).

Find the point $P(t)$ that lies fraction t of the way between A and B:

$$P = A(1 - t) + Bt \qquad \qquad ...(13.6)$$

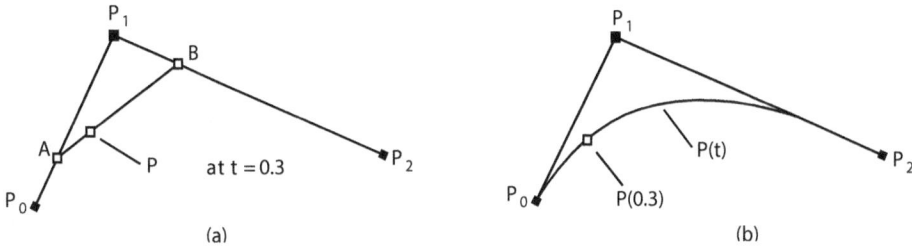

Fig. 13.36 The de Casteljau algorithm for three points

If we take $t = 0.5$, $P(0.5)$ is simply the "midpoint between midpoints" for the three given points. If this process is carried out for every t between 0 and 1, the curve $P(t)$ will be generated. Substitute Eq. (13.5) into Eq. (13.6) to get the parametric equation of curve.

$$P(t) = (1 - t)^2 P_0 + 2t(1 - t)P_1 + t^2 P_2$$

The above parametric form of equation $P(t)$ is quadratic in t, so the equation is a parabola. It will still be a parabola even if t is allowed to vary from $-\infty$ to ∞.

Thus we have a well-defined process that can generate a smooth parabolic curve based on the three given points.

What if more than three control points are used?

The most commonly used family of Bezier curves is based on four control points.

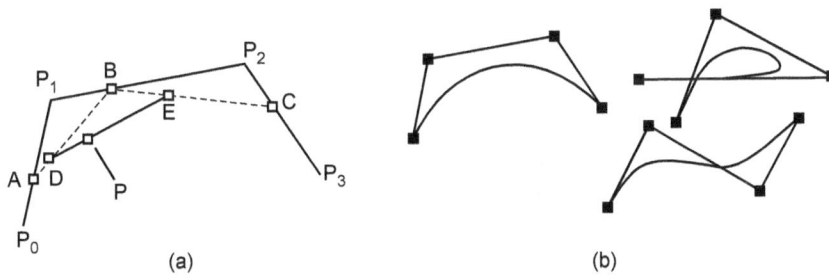

Fig. 13.37 de Casteljau algorithm applied to points P_0, P_1, P_2, and P_3

For a given value of t, point A is placed fraction t of the way from P_0 to P_1, and similarly for points B and C. Then D is placed fraction t of the way from A to B, and similarly for point E. Finally, the desired point P is located fraction t of the way from D to E. If this is done for every t between 0 and 1, the curve $P(t)$ starts at P_0, is attracted toward P_1 and P_2, and ends at P_3. It is the Bezier curve determined by the four points.

The Bezier curve based on four points has the parametric form

$$P(t) = P_0(1-t)^3 + P_1\,3(1-t)^2\,t + P_2\,3(1-t)t^2 + P_3\,t^3 \qquad\qquad ...(13.7)$$

Each control point P_i is weighted by a cubic polynomial, and the weighted terms are added.

The terms involved here are known as Bernstein polynomials.

Bernstein polynomials

Bernstein polynomials, restricted to the interval [0, 1], became important in the form of Bezier curves. A numerically stable way to evaluate polynomials in Bernstein form is de Casteljau's algorithm.

A linear combination of Bernstein basis polynomials is called a Bernstein polynomial of degree n.

The Bernstein polynomials are

$$B_0^3 = (1-t)^3$$
$$B_1^3 = 3(1-t)^2\,t$$
$$B_2^3 = 3(1-t)^2\,t^2$$
$$B_3^3 = t^3$$

These cubic Bernstein polynomials are easily remembered as the terms one gets by the raised expression $a(t) = (1 - t - t)$, which is simply 1 for all values of t to the third power.

Consequently, $P(t)$ is an affine combination of points, and thus a legitimate point.

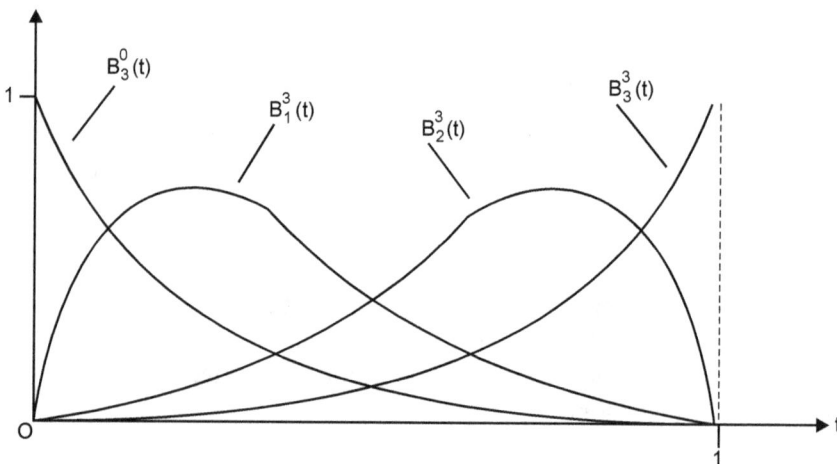

Fig. 13.38 The Bernstein polynomial of degree 3

Fig. 13.38 is the shape of the four Bernstein polynomials of degree 3 as t varies between 0 and 1.

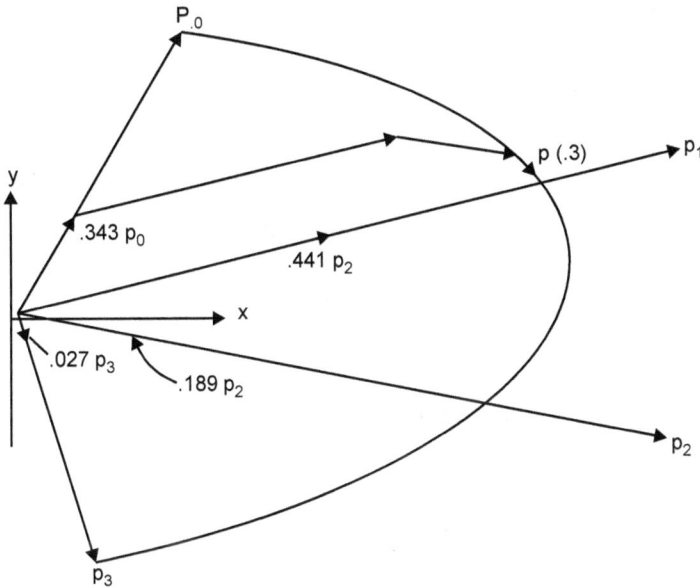

Fig. 13.39 Blending four vectors with Bernstein polynomials

Fig. 13.39 illustrates geometrically how the four points $p_0, \ldots \ldots p_3$ in Eq. (13.7) are blended together to form $P(t)$. View the points as vectors bound to the origin (so we write P_0 as p_0, and so on) and let $t = 0.3$. Then equation becomes

$$p(0.3) = 0.343\,p_0 + 0.441\,p_1 + 0.189\,p_2 + 0.027\,p_3$$

In Fig. 13.39 the four vectors are weighted and the results are added using the parallelogram rule to form the vector $p(0.3)$.

Extending the de Casteljau algorithm to any number of points

In the previous section we saw how the de Casteljau algorithm uses tweening to produce quadratic parametric representations when three points are used and cubic representations when four points are used.

For each value of t, a succession of generations are built up, each by tweening adjacent points produced in the previous generation (superscript for P is the generation number):

$$P^4i(t) = (1-t)P^3i(t) + t\,P^3i+1(t)$$

. . . .

$$P^L i(t) = (1-t)P^{L-1}i(t) + tP^{L-1}i + 1(t)$$

$$\text{for } i = 0,1,\ldots\ldots\ldots L$$

The superscript k in $Pki(t)$ denotes the generation. The process starts with $P_i^0(t) = P_i$ and ends with the final Bezier curve $P(t) = P_i^L(t)$.

The resulting Bezier is

$$P(t) = \sum_{K=0}^{L} P_k B_k^L(t)$$

...(13.8)

where k^{th} Bernstein polynomial of degree L is defined as

$$B_k^L(t) = \binom{L}{K}(1-t)^{L-k} t^k$$

where $\binom{L}{K}$ is the binomial coefficient function given by

$$\binom{L}{K} = \frac{L!}{K!(L-K)!} \quad \text{for} \quad L <= k$$

The value of this term is 0 if $L < k$. Each of the Bernstein polynomials is seen to be degree L. As before, the Bernstein polynomials are the terms one gets when expanding $[(1-t)+t]\,L$, so we are assured that

$$\sum_{k=0}^{L} B_k^L(t) = 1 \quad \text{for all } t$$

and $P(t)$ is a legitimate affine combination of points.

Bezier curves in openGL

1. OpenGL supports Beziers through mechanisms called *evaluators,* used to compute the blending functions of any degree.

2. Evaluators are general mechanisms for working with Bernstein polynomials.

3. Smooth curves and surfaces are drawn by approximating them with a large number of small line segments or polygons. They are described mathematically by a small number of parameters such as control points.

4. An evaluator is a way to compute points on a curve or surface using only control points. They do not require uniform spacing of u. Bezier curves can then be rendered at any precision.

5. 1D Bezier curves can also be used to define paths in time for animation.

1D Evaluators

```
GLfloat ctrlpoints[4][3] = {...};
void init(void) {
    glMap1f(GL_MAP1_VERTEX_3, 0.0, 1.0,
            3, 4, &ctrlpoints[0][0]);
}
void display(void) {
    glBegin(GL_LINE_STRIP);
for(i=0;i<=30;i++)
    glEvalCoord1f((GLfloat)i/30.0);
glEnd();
}
```

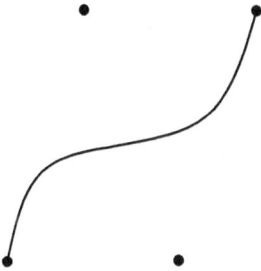

Fig. 13.40

Defining a 1D Evaluator

glMap1(target(type), u1, u2, stride, order, points_to_array);

- *target:* tells what the control points represent
- *u1,u2:* the range of variable *u*
- *stride:* the number of floating-point values to advance in the data between one control point and the next
- *order:* the degree plus one, which it should agree with the number of control points
- *points:* pointer to the first coordinate of the first control point

Evaluating a 1D Evaluator

```
glEvalCoord1(u);
glEvalCoord1v(*u);
```

- Causes evaluation of the enabled maps
- u: the value of the domain coordinate (need not be equally spaced)
- More than one evaluator can be defined and evaluated at a time
  - (ex) GL_MAP1_VERTEX_3 and GL_MAP1_COLOR_4
  - In this case, calls to glEvalCoord1() generates both a position and a color

Example: /* define and enable 1D evaluator for Bezier cubic curve */

point ctrlpts[ ] = { .... } ;

glMap1f (GL_MAP1_VERTEX_3, 0.0, 1.0, 3, 4, ctrlpts);
glEnable (GL_MAP1_VERTEX_3);

/* GL_MAP1_VERTEX_3 specifies data type for ctrlpts,
range of u = [0.0, 1.0], 3 is the number of values between control
points, (order = degree +1) = 4   */

/* With evaluator enabled, draw line segments for Bezier curve */

glBegin (GL_LINE_STRIP);
      for (i = 0; i <= 30; i ++)
           glEvalCoord1f ((Glfloat) i/30.0);
glEnd ( );

Equally Spaced Points

Rather than using a loop, we can set up an equally spaced mesh (grid) and then evaluate it with one function call:

glMapGrid(100, 0.0, 1.0);

sets up 100 equally-spaced points on (0,1)

glEvalMesh1(GL_LINE, 0, 99);

renders lines between adjacent evaluated points from point 0 to point 99

2D Evaluators

Everything is similar to the 1D case, except that all the commands must take two parameters, *u* and *v*, into account.

1. Define evaluators with *glMap2**()

2. Enable them with *glEnable*()

3. Invoke them by calling *glEvalCoord2*() between a *glBegin*() and *glEnd*() or by specifying and applying a mesh with *glMapGrid2*() and *glEvalMesh2*()

To define and evaluate:
glMap2f(target, u1, u2, ustride, uorder, v1, v2, vstride, vorder, points);
glEvalCoord2f(u, v);

Example 4

point data[4][4] = {.........};
glMap2f(GL_MAP_VERTEX_3, 0.0, 1.0, 3, 4, 0.0, 1.0, 13, 4, data);
Note that in the *v* direction data points are separated by 13 floats since array data is stored by rows.

13.5.3 THE B-SPLINE BASIS FUNCTION

In numerical analysis, a B-spline, or basis spline, is a spline function that has minimal support with respect to a given degree, smoothness, and domain partition. Any spline function of a given degree can be expressed as a linear combination of the B-spline of that degree. Cardinal B-splines have knots that are equidistant from each other. B-splines can be used for curve fitting and numerical differentiation of experimental data. CAD and computer graphics, spline functions are constructed as linear combinations of B-splines with a set of control points.

The term "B-spline" is short for basis spline. A spline function is a piecewise polynomial function of degree $<k$ in a variable x. The places where the pieces meet are known as knots. The number of internal knots must be equal to or greater than $k-1$. Thus the spline function has limited support. The key property of spline functions is that they are continuous at the knots. Some derivatives of the spline function may also be continuous, depending on whether the knots are distinct or not. A fundamental theorem states that every spline function of a given degree, smoothness, and domain partition can be uniquely represented as a linear combination of B-splines of that same degree and smoothness, and over that same partition.

Although the literature offers many different approaches to formulating B-splines, there is a single formula that defines all B-spline functions of any order. It is recursive relation that is easy to implement in a program and is numerically well behaved.

Each B-spline function is based on polynomials of a certain order, m. These are the two most important cases, although the formulation allows us to construct B-spline of any order.

Before going ahead let us first discuss knot vectors.

The Knot Vector

The knot vector can, by its definition, be any sequence of numbers, provided that each one is greater than or equal to the preceding one. Some types of knot vectors are more useful than others. Knot vectors are generally placed into one of three categories:

1. Uniform

2. Open uniform

3. Non-uniform

Uniform

These are knot vectors for which

$$t_i + 1 - t_i = \text{constant, for all } i$$

For example:

$$[1, 2, 3, 4, 5, 6, 7, 8, 9]$$
$$[0, 1, 2, 3, 4, 5]$$
$$[0, 0.25, 0.5, 0.75, 1.0]$$
$$[-2.5, -1.4, -0.3, 0.8, 1.9, 3.0]$$

Open Uniform

These are uniform knot vectors which have k equal knot values at each end:

$$
\begin{aligned}
t_i &= t_1, & i &<= k \\
t_i + 1 - t_i &= \text{constant}, & k &<= i < n + 2 \\
t_i &= t_k + (n + 1) & i &>= n + 2
\end{aligned}
$$

For example:

$[0,0,0, 0, 1, 2, 3, 4, 4, 4, 4]$	$(k = 4)$
$[1,1,1,2,3,4,5,6,6,6]$	$(k = 3)$
$[0.1,0.1, 0.1, 0.1, 0.1, 0.3, 0.5, 0.7, 0.7, 0.7, 0.7, 0.7]$	$(k = 5)$

Non-uniform

This is the general case, the only constraint being the standard

$$t_i <= t_i + 1, \text{ for all } i$$

For example:

$$[1, 3, 4, 22, 23, 23, 49, 50, 50]$$
$$[1, 1, 1, 2, 2, 3, 4, 5, 6, 6, 6, 7, 7, 7]$$
$$[0.2, 0.7, 0.7, 0.7, 1.2, 1.2, 2.9, 3.6]$$

NOTE: The shapes of the B-spline functions are determined entirely by the relative spacing between the knots.

Definition of B-Spline Functions

A B-spline is a piecewise polynomial function of degree $<n$ in a variable x. It is defined over a domain $t_0 \leq x \leq t_m$, $m = n$. The points where $x = t_j$ are known as knots or break-points. The number of internal knots is equal to the degree of the polynomial if there are no knot multiplicities. The knots must be in ascending order. The number of knots is the minimum for the degree of B-spline, which has a non-zero value only in the range between the first and last knots. Each piece of the function is a polynomial of degree $<n$ between and including adjacent knots. A B-spline is a continuous function at the knots. When all internal knots are distinct, its derivatives are also continuous up to the derivative of degree $n-1$. If internal knots are coincident at a given value of x, the continuity of derivative order is reduced by 1 for each additional knot.

It is useful to make the order of a B-spline function explicit in the notation, and so instead of saying simply $R_k(t)$ (B-spline blending function), we denote the kth B-spline blending function of order m by $N_{k,m}(t)$. Consider:

$$P(t) = \sum_{k=0}^{L} P_k N_{k,m}$$

We have

- a knot vector $T = (t_0, t_1, t_2, \ldots\ldots)$
- $(L + 1)$ control points P_k
- order m of the B-spline functions

$$N_{k,m}(t) = \left(\frac{t - t_k}{t_{k+m-1} - t_k} \right) N_{k,m-1}(t) + \left(\frac{t_{k+m} - t}{t_{k+m} - t_{k+1}} \right) N_{k+1,m-1}(t)$$

For $k = 0, 1, \ldots\ldots, L$.

This is recursive definition, specifying how to construct the mth-order function from two B-spline functions of order $(m - 1)$. To get things started, the first-order function must be defined. It is simply the constant function 1 within its span:

$$N_{k,1}(t) = \begin{cases} 1 & \text{if } t_k < t \leq t_{k+1} \\ 0 & \text{otherwise} \end{cases}$$

Note that this set of functions automatically sums to one at every t, so it is legitimate to use them in forming combinations of points.

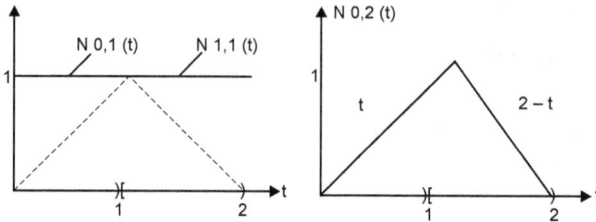

Fig. 13.41 Construction of linear B-splines

Computing B-spline blending functions

```
float bSpline (int k, int m, float t, float knot[])
{
        float denom1, denom2, sum = 0.0;
        if(m==1)
return (t >= knot[k] && t < knot[k+1]); //Basic condition
        denom1 = knot[k+m-1] - knot[k];
if(denom != 0.0)
        sum = (t - knot[k]) * bSpline(k, m-1, t, knot);
        denom2 = knot[k+m] - knot[k+1];
if(denom != 0.0)
        sum += ( knot[k+m] - t) * bSpline(k+1, m-1, t, knot);
}
```

How to use multiple knots in the knot vector

We have used only B-splines based on equi-spaced knots. By varying the spacing between knots, the curve acquires much greater control of the shape of the final curve.

Now, consider an example when two knots are set very close to each other. $T = (0, 1, 2, 3, 3 + \varepsilon, 4 + \varepsilon \ldots \ldots \ldots)$, where ε is a small positive number. Fig. 13.42 shows the situation of knot vector:

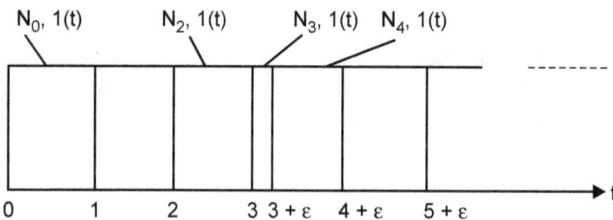

Fig. 13.42 Moving knots close together

The piece of each polynomial lying in the interval $[3, 3 + \varepsilon]$ becomes squeezed into a very narrow span. The blending functions will clearly no longer be translations of one another. If ε is set to zero, this span will vanish altogether, and a multiple knot will occur at $t = 3$. This knot is said to have a "multiplicity of 2."

Fig. 13.43 shows the resulting blending functions. In Fig. 13.43(b) two of the linear B-spline shapes are discontinuous. Figure 13.43(c) has quadratic shapes with discontinuous derivative at $t = 3$. In general, an i-smooth curve is reduced to an $(i - 1)$ smooth curve at multiple knots. Fig. 13.43(d) is a cubic B-splines curve that has 1-smooth everywhere, but not 2-smooth at $t = 3$. We can notice in Fig. 13.43(c) that if quadratic B-splines are used, the curve will interpolate control point P_2, because the blending function $N_{2,3}(t)$ reaches 1 at $t = 3$, and all other blending functions are zero there. In general, when t approaches a knot of multiplicity greater than 1, there is a stronger attraction to the governing control point.

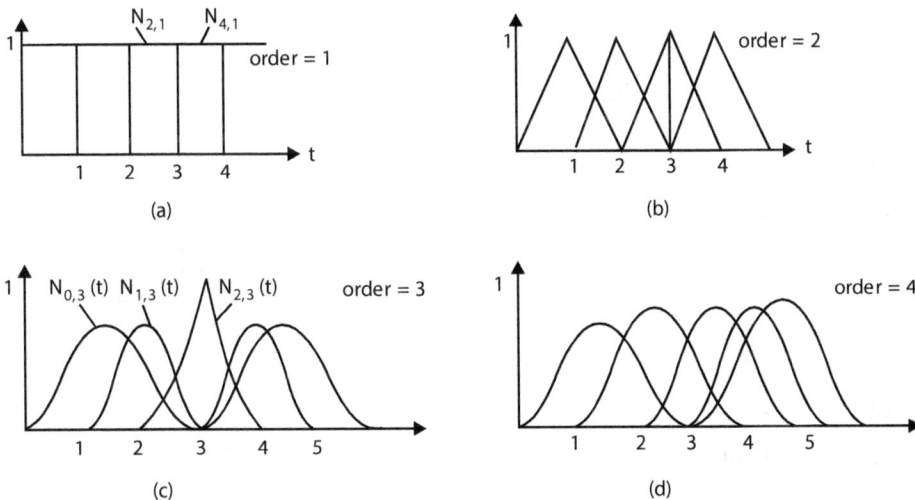

Fig. 13.43 B-spline shapes near a knot of multiplicity 2

Quadratic splines become discontinuous near a knot of multiplicity 3. Cubic splines exhibit a discontinuous derivative near a knot of multiplicity 3, but they also interpolate one of the control points. By adjusting the multiplicity of each knot, the designer can therefore change the shape of the curve in a predictable fashion.

Knots with positive multiplicity

If a knot vector contains knots with positive multiplicity, we will encounter the case of $\frac{0}{0}$. It is necessary to define $\frac{0}{0}$ before calculation. Therefore we shall define $\frac{0}{0}$ to be 0. Fortunately, this is only for manual calculation. For computer implementation, there is an efficient algorithm.

If t_i is a knot of multiplicity k (i.e., $t_i = t_i + 1 = \ldots\ldots\ldots= t_i + k - 1$), then knot spans $[t_i, t_i + 1)$, $[t_i + 1, t_i + 2)$, ..., $[t_i + k - 2, t_i + k - 1)$ do not exist, and as a result, $N_{i,0}(u), N_{i+1,0}(u),..., N_{i+k-1,0}(u))$ are all zero functions.

Consider a knot vector $T = \{0, 0, 0, 0.3, 0.5, 0.5, 0.6, 1, 1, 1\}$. Thus, 0 and 1 are of multiplicity 3 (i.e., 0(3) and 1(3)) and 0.5 is of multiplicity 2 (i.e., 0.5(2)).

As a result, $m = 9$ and the knot assignments are

u_0	u_1	u_2	u_3	u_4	u_5	u_6	u_7	u_8	u_9
0	0	0	0.3	0.5	0.5	0.6	1	1	1

Let us compute $N_{i,0}(u)$'s. Since $m = 9$ and $p = 0$ (degree of basis functions), we have $n = m - p - 1 = 8$. As the following table shows, there are only four non-zero basis functions of degree 0: $N_{2,0}(u)$, $N_{3,0}(u)$, $N_{5,0}(u)$, and $N_{6,0}(u)$.

Basis function	Range	Equation	Comment
$N_{0,0}(u)$	All u	0	since [u0, u1) = [0,0) does not exist
$N_{1,0}(u)$	All u	0	since [u1, u2) = [0,0) does not exist
$N_{2,0}(u)$	[0, 0.3)	1	
$N_{3,0}(u)$	[0.3, 0.5)	1	
$N_{4,0}(u)$	All u	0	since [u4, u5) = [0.5,0.5) does not exist
$N_{5,0}(u)$	[0.5, 0.6)	1	
$N_{6,0}(u)$	[0.6, 1)	1	
$N_{7,0}(u)$	All u	0	since [u7, u8) = [1,1) does not exist
$N_{8,0}(u)$	All u	0	since [u8, u9) = [1,1) does not exist

Now, we proceed to basis functions of degree 1. Since p is 1, $n = m - p - 1 = 7$. The following table shows the results:

Basis function	Range	Equation
$N_{0,1}(u)$	all u	0
$N_{1,1}(u)$	$[0, 0.3)$	$1 - \left(\dfrac{10}{3}\right)u$
$N_{2,1}(u)$	$[0, 0.3)$	$\left(\dfrac{10}{3}\right)u$
	$[0.3, 0.5)$	$2.5(1 - 2u)$
$N_{3,1}(u)$	$[0.3, 0.5)$	$5u - 1.5$
$N_{4,1}(u)$	$[0.5, 0.6)$	$6 - 10u$
$N_{5,1}(u)$	$[0.5, 0.6)$	$10u - 5$
	$[0.6, 1)$	$[0.6, 1)$
$N_{6,1}(u)$	$[0.6, 1)$	$2.5u - 1.5$
$N_{7,1}(u)$	all u	0

Fig. 13.44 shows the graphs of these basis functions.

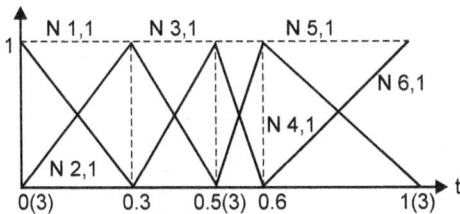

Fig. 13.44 Graphs of basis functions

Let us take a look at a particular computation, say $N_{1,1}(u)$.

$$N_{1,1}(t) = \left(\frac{t - t_1}{t_2 - t_1}\right)N_{1,0}(t) + \left(\frac{t_3 - t}{t_3 - t_2}\right)N_{2,0}(t)$$

Put $t_1 = t_2 = 0$ and $t_3 = 0.3$ into the above equation:

$$N_{1,1}(t) = \left(\frac{t}{0}\right)N_{1,0}(t) + \left(1 - \frac{10}{3}t\right)N_{2,0}(t)$$

Since $N_{1,0}(t)$ is zero everywhere, the first term becomes $\dfrac{0}{0}$ and is defined to be zero. Therefore, only the second term has an impact on the result. Since $N_{2,0}(t)$ is 1 on [0,0.3), $N_{1,0}(t)$ is $1-\left(\dfrac{10}{3}\right)u$ on [0,0.3).

Next, let us compute all $N_{i,2}(t)$'s. Since $p = 2$, we have $n = m - p - 1 = 6$. The following table contains all $N_{i,2}(t)$'s:

Basis function	Range	Equation
$N_{0,2}(u)$	[0, 0.3)	$\left(1-\left(\dfrac{10}{3}\right)u\right)^2$
$N_{1,2}(u)$	[0, 0.3)	$\left(\dfrac{20}{3}\right)\left(u-\left(\dfrac{8}{3}\right)u^2\right)$
	[0.3, 0.5)	$2.5(1-2u)^2$
$N_{2,2}(u)$	[0, 0.3)	$\left(\dfrac{20}{3}\right)u^2$
	[0.3, 0.5)	$-3.75+25u-35u^2$
$N_{3,2}(u)$	[0.3, 0.5)	$(5u-1.5)^2$
	[0.5, 0.6)	$(6-10u)^2$
$N_{4,2}(u)$	[0.5, 0.6)	$20(-2+7u-6u^2)$
	[0.6, 1)	$5(1-u)^2$
$N_{5,2}(u)$	[0.5, 0.6)	$13.5(2u-1)^2$
	[0.6, 1)	$2.5(-4+11.5u-7.5u^2)$
$N_{6,2}(u)$	[0.6, 1)	$2.5(9-30u+25u^2)$

Fig. 13.45 shows all basis functions of degree 2.

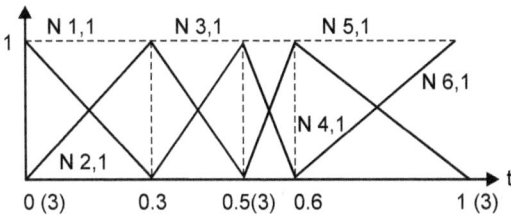

Fig. 13.45 All basis functions of degree 2.

Let us pick a typical computation as an example, say $N_{3,2}(u)$.

$$N_{3,2}(t) = \left(\frac{t-t_3}{t_5-t_3}\right)N_{3,1}(t) + \left(\frac{t_6-t}{t_6-t_4}\right)N_{4,1}(t)$$

Put $t_3 = 0.3$, $t_4 = t_5 = 0.5$ and $t_6 = 0.6$ into the above equation, and we get

$$N_{3,2}(t) = (5t - 1.5)N_{3,1}(t) + (6 - 10t)N_{4,1}(t)$$

Since $N_{3,1}(t)$ is non-zero on $[0.3, 0.5]$ and is equal to $5t - 1.5$, $(5t - 1.5)^2$ is the non-zero part of $N_{3,2}(t)$ on $[0.3, 0.5]$. Since $N_{4,1}(t)$ is non-zero on $[0.5, 0.6]$ and is equal to $6 - 10t$, $(6 - 10t)^2$ is the non-zero part of $N_{3,2}(t)$ on $[0.5, 0.6]$.

Let us investigate the continuity issues at knot 0.5(2). Since its multiplicity is 2 and the degree of these basis functions is 2, $N_{3,2}(t)$ is C^0 continuous at 0.5(2). This is why $N_{3,2}(t)$ has a sharp angle at 0.5(2). For knots not at the two ends, say 0.3, C^1 continuity is maintained since all of them are simple knots.

Standard knot vectors

If the knot vector does not have any particular structure, the generated curve will not touch the first and last legs of the control polyline. This type of B-spline curve is called an open B-spline curve. If the first and last knots are not a multiple of m, the curve will not be tangent to the first and last legs at the first and last control points, respectively. One special choice of knot vector has become a standard for curve design. With this arrangement, the designer interpolates the first and last control points, thus better able to predict where the computed curve lies.

The standard knot vector for a B-spline of order m begins and ends with a knot of multiplicity m and uses unit spacing for the remaining knots. Let us start with an example and then see how it arises. Suppose there are eight control points and we want to use cubic ($m = 4$) B-splines. The standard knot vector turns out to be

$$T = (0, 0, 0, 0, 1, 2, 3, 4, 5, 5, 5, 5)$$

The eight blending functions, $N_{0,4}(t), \ldots, N_{7,4}(t)$, defined on those knots are shown in Fig. 13.46(a). $N_{0,4}(t)$ and $N_{7,4}(t)$ are discontinuous and have a support of only one unit span. Only $N_{3,4}(t)$ and $N_{4,4}(t)$ have the usual span of four points. The remaining blending functions have two or three unit spans, and their shapes become more distorted as they approach the first and last knots.

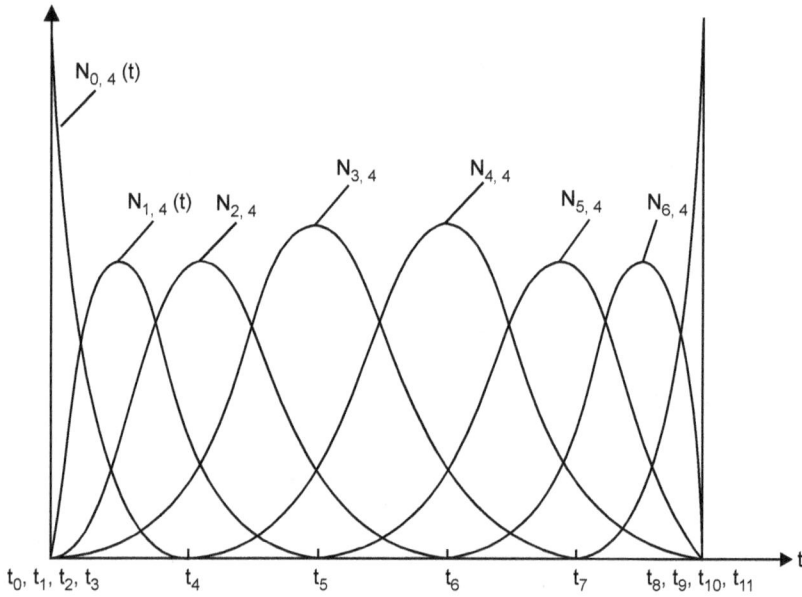

(a)

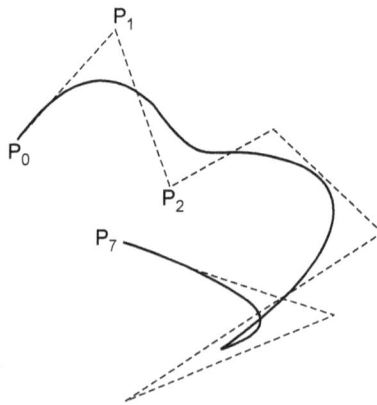

(b)

Fig. 13.46 (a) Eight cubic B-spline blending functions defined on the standard knot vector. (b) The resulting curve based on 8 control points

When we take all the blending functions together, this set of functions always ensures interpolation of the first and last control points. At $t = 0$, all blending functions are zero except for $N_{0,4}(t)$, which equals 1.

Fig. 13.46(b) shows an example of a curve based on eight control points. Clearly the first and last points are interpolated and the curve directions at these points are as promised.

The standard knot vector for $(L + 1)$ control points and order-m B-splines is described as follows:

1. There are $L + m + 1$ knots all together, denoted by $t_0, \ldots, t_{L+m}$.

2. The first m knots, $t_0, \ldots, t_{m-1}$, all shares\ the value 0. (The first m blending functions start at $t = 0$.)

3. Knots $t_m, \ldots, t_m$ increase in increments of 1, from value 1 through value $L - m + 1$. (The final blending function, $N_{L,m}(t)$, begins at $t_L = L - m + 1$ and has a support of width 1.)

4. The final m knots, $t_{L+1}, \ldots, t_{L+m}$, all equal $L - m + 2$.

See the implementation of above points in programming language. It generates the standard knot vector for the given values of m and L.

```
Void buildKnots(int m, int L, double knot[])
{
        //build the standard knot vector for L+1 control points
          and B-spline of //order m
        int i;
        if(L < (m-1))
        return;
        for(i = 0; i <= L+m; i++)
        {
              if(i < m)
        knot[i] = 0.0;
        else if(i <= L)
        knot[i] = i - m + 1;//i is at least m here
              else
                knot[i] = L-m+2;
        }
}
```

Constraint: The order m can't exceed the number of control points ($L+1$).

Bezier Curves Are B-Spline Curves

We may want to clamp the curve so that it is tangent to the first and last legs at the first and last control points, respectively, as a Bezier curve does. To do so, the first knot and the last knot must be of multiplicity m. This is called a clamped B-spline curve. Bezier curves are a special case of B-spline curve. This is so because the B-spline blending functions defined on the standard knot vector are in fact Bernstein polynomials when $m = L + 1$!

That is, $N_{k, L+1}(t) = B_k^L(t)$ for $k = 0, \ldots \ldots \ldots, L$.

Spline in OpenGL

- OpenGL provides functions for both Bezier (GL) and B-spline (GLU) curves and surfaces.

- These functions can be used to interpolate vertices, normals, colors, and textures.

GLU B-spline curves

- These functions are actually NURBS (non-uniform rational B-splines) but they can be used to generate uniform splines that are not rational.

- You have to create a NURBS object:

    *GLUnurbsObj * curveName;*

    curveName = gluNewNurbsRenderer();

- Then you can assign the curve properties:

    gluBeginCurve(curveName);

    *gluNurbsCurve(curveName, nKnots, *knotVector, stride, *ctrlPoints degParam, GL_ MAP1_VERTEX_3);*

    gluEndCurve(curveName);

- When done with the curve you can delete it:

    gluDeleteNurbsRenderer(curveName);

- You can also assign properties to the curves with

    gluNurbsProperty(splineName, property, value);

B-spline surfaces work similarly except you use *gluNurbs* surface which has parameters for both dimensions.

13.5.4 Interpolation Technique

When polynomial sections are fitted so that the curve passes through each control point, the resulting curve is said to interpolate the set of control points. Interpolating curves are commonly used to digitize drawings or to specify animation paths. Cubic polylines are often a reasonable compromise between flexibility and speed of computation. Compared to higher-order polynomials, cubic splines require less calculation and memory and they are more stable. Compared to lower-order polynomials, cubic splines are more flexible for modeling arbitrary curve shapes.

Linear interpolation is the simplest interpolation method. Applying linear interpolation to a sequence of points results in a polygonal line where each straight line segment connects two consecutive points of the sequence. Therefore, every segment (P,Q) is interpolated independently as follows:

$$P(t) = (1 - t) \cdot P + t \cdot Q$$

where t belongs to $[0,1]$. By varying t from 0 to 1 we get all the intermediate points between P and Q.

Interpolation using piecewise cubic polynomial

Cubic interpolation splines are obtained by fitting the input points with a piecewise cubic polynomial curve that passes through every control point. Suppose we have $n + 1$ control points specified with coordinates:

$$p_k = (x_k, y_k, z_k), k = 0, 1, 2, \ldots\ldots, n$$

A cubic interpolation fit of these points is illustrated in Fig. 13.47.

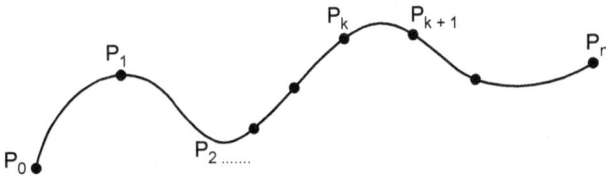

Fig. 13.47 A piecewise continuous cubic-spline interpolation of n+1 control points

We can describe the parametric cubic polynomial that is to be fitted between each pair of control points with the following set of equations:

$$x(t) = a_x t^3 + b_x t^2 + c_x t + d_x$$
$$y(t) = a_y t^3 + b_y t^2 + c_y t + d_y$$
$$z(t) = a_z t^3 + b_z t^2 + c_z t + d_z$$

where ($0 \leq u \leq 1$). We need to determine the values of four coefficients a, b, c, and d in the polynomial representation for each of the n curve sections between $n + 1$ control points. We do this by setting enough boundary conditions at the "joints" between the curve sections so that we can obtain numerical values for all the coefficients. The next section discusses common methods for setting the boundary conditions for cubic interpolation spline.

Hermite interpolation

The kth cubic segment of the curve is given by

$$y_k(t) = a_k t^3 + b_k t^2 + c_k t + d_k k = 0, 1, \ldots\ldots, L, \text{ for } t \text{ in } [0, 1]$$

We denote the value of its derivatives by s_k (i.e. $y_k'(0) = s_k$). In some cases the values s_k are given by the user as input, and in others they are computed from other required properties of the curve.

We develop conditions on the coefficients a_k, b_k, c_k, and d_k so that each segment interpolates the given values y_k at $t = 0$ and the value y_{k+1} at $t = 1$:

At $t = 0$: $d_k = y_k$

At $t = 1$: $a_k + b_k + c_k + d_k = y(k + 1)$ for $k = 0, \ldots\ldots, L - 1$

This provides $2L$ conditions. We will force the derivatives of $y_k(t)$ to equal the given values s_k and s_{k+1} at $t = 0$ and $t = 1$, respectively. Since the derivative is $y_k'(t) = 3 a_k t^2 + 2b_k t + c_k$, this gives the condition:

At $t = 0 : c_k = s_k$

At $t = 1$: $3a_k + 2b_k + c_k = s_{k+1}$ for $k = 0, \ldots\ldots, L - 1$. This provides another $2L$ condition, so we have a total of $4L$ conditions on the $4L$ unknown coefficients. Notice that setting the derivatives to the given slope values in this fashion automatically forces the slope to be continuous at the joints, so the curve is 1-smooth.

The Natural Cubic Spline

This interpolation curve is a mathematical representation of the original drafting spline. We formulate a natural cubic spline by requiring that two adjacent curve sections have the same first and second parametric derivatives at their common boundary.

If we have $n + 1$ control points, then we have n curve sections with a total of $4n$ polynomial coefficients to be determined. At each of the $n-1$ interior control points, we have four boundary conditions. The two curve sections on either side of the control point must have the same first and second parametric derivatives at that control point, and each curve must pass through that control point. This gives $4n-4$ equations to be satisfied by the $4n$ polynomial coefficient. We get an additional equation from the first control points p_0, the position of the beginning of the curve, and another condition from control point p_n, which must be the last point on the curve. We will still need two more conditions to be able to determine values of all coefficients. One method for obtaining the two additional conditions is to set the second derivatives at p_0 and p_n to zero. Another approach is to add two extra "dummy" control points, one at each end of the original control point sequence. That is, we add a control point p_{-1} and a control point p_{n+1}. Then all of the original control points are interior points, and we have the necessary $4n$ boundary conditions.

The natural cubic spline has a major disadvantage: if the position of any control point is altered, the entire curve is affected. Thus, natural cubic splines allow for no "local control" so that we cannot restructure part of the curve without specifying an entirely new set of control points.

SUMMARY

In this section, first we described the way to represent curve, either in parametric or nonparametric form: parametric cubic curves, a major type of curve, are hermit curves defined by two endpoints and tangent vectors, Bezier curves defined by two endpoints and two other points that control the endpoints tangent vectors, and spline curves. All the Bezier curves, hermite curves, and B-splines are translation and rotation invariant. The distinction between curves that interpolate the points and those that only approximate the points was emphasized. In either case the small set of control points, along with an algorithm, produce an infinite set of points along the curve, one for each value of the parameter t.

The Bezier curve is the simplest one. In a Bezier curve the de Casteljau algorithm can compute any point on the curve in a few iterations. The complication of the Bezier curve is that the degree of the Bezier curve depends on the number of control points. The Bezier curve lacks local control. Changing the position of one control point affects the entire curve.

We therefore examine a richer class of blending functions based on spline, which are piecewise polynomials that piece together in such a way that various order of derivatives are everywhere continuous. The B-spline can generate any spline and is the most concentrated of such shapes. It allows local control of shapes. It is more complex than a Bezier curve. The degree of curve is independent of the number of control points.

Then we discussed interpolation where, instead of being attracted towards the control point, the algorithm is forced to interpolate the given control points. We focused on piecewise polynomial curves, and developed conditions on various coefficients so that the curve not only interpolates the points but also has a prescribed velocity at each point.

Finally we discussed the curve design technique to design of different families of surfaces, including ruled surfaces and surface of revolution.

EXERCISES

1. Define OpenGL. Explain it with some examples.
2. Explain briefly at least six graphical functions of OpenGL.
3. List the open GL operations. Explain any four in detail.
4. What are the advantages of OpenGL?
5. How does OpenGL work? Explain the OpenGL rendering pipeline.

OBJECTIVE QUESTIONS

13.1. The technique used to produce a transformation of one object into another is known as
    (*a*) morphing   (*b*) betweening
    (*c*) blindfolding   (*d*) cutaway

13.2. A phosphor with low persistence is useful for
    (*a*) animation   (*b*) image processing
    (*c*) CAD method   (*d*) presentation

13.3. A system designed for some training applications is a
    (*a*) GUI   (*b*) simulator
    (*c*) CAD   (*d*) process monitor

13.4. A transformation used for dragging in computer graphics is
    (*a*) translation   (*b*) rotation
    (*c*) scaling   (*d*) reflection

13.5. At which part of the OpenGL graphics pipeline is illumination performed?
    (*a*) before the MODELVIEW transformation
    (*b*) between the MODELVIEW transformation and PROJECTION transformation
    (*c*) between the PROJECTION transformation and viewport transformation
    (*d*) between the viewport transformation and rasterization

13.6. What is the purpose of the reshape callback in OpenGL?
    (*a*) to change the shape of the model
    (*b*) to change the shape of the viewport
    (*c*) to re-calculate the camera properties when the window is resized or reshaped
    (*d*) to re-calculate the modeling transformation when the window is reshaped

13.7. When the sides of rectangles are aligned with the coordinate axes then the rectangles are called

(*a*) overlapping rectangles   (*b*) aligned rectangles

(*c*) symmetric rectangles   (*d*) equivalent rectangles

13.8. What does *glut* stands for?

(*a*) OpenGL Utility Toolkit   (*b*) Graphic Language Utility

(*c*) Graphic Language Utility Toolkit   (*d*) General Language Utility

13.9. What is the meaning of Vertex2i in command *glVertex2i*()?

(*a*) Command takes 2 arguments of integer types representing pixel information of vertices

(*b*) Command takes 2 vertices in argument and represent them in integer format

(*c*) Command initializes the vertices as value equals to 2 in integer

(*d*) Command allows the vertices value differ by integer 2

13.10. The data type supported by the *GLint() OpenGL* is

(*a*) 16-bit integer   (*b*) 32-bit integer

(*c*) 8-bit integer   (*d*) 64-bit integer

13.11. The value for the aspect ratio of a golden rectangle is

(*a*) 1.6085   (*b*) 1.618034

(*c*) 1.628876   (*d*) 1.652151

13.12. What is the trivial acceptance condition in the Cohen-Sutherland line clipping algorithm?

(*a*) FFFF   (*b*) FTTT

(*c*) TTTT   (*d*) FFFT

13.13. What is the aspect ratio?

(*a*) width/height   (*b*) height/width

(*c*) width/width   (*d*) height/height

13.14. Which syntax of *OpenGL* is used for setting the world window in 2D graphics?

(*a*) *gluOrtho2D*()   (*b*) *glViewport*()

(*c*) *glLoadIdentity*()   (*d*) *glMatrixMode*( )

13.15. What is the format of the data type used to save in OpenGL?

(*a*) stack   (*b*) queue

(*c*) matrix   (*d*) file

13.16. Which function of *OpenGL* is used to plot a point in 2D space?

(*a*) *glVertex2f(x,y)*   (*b*) *glBegin(GL_LINES)*

(*c*) *gluOrtho2D*( )   (*d*) *glViewport*()

13.17. Which one is a v–contour generated curve?
   (*a*) v varies while holding u is constant.
   (*b*) u varies while holding v is constant.
   (*c*) u and v both vary same time.
   (*d*) none of the above

13.18. A Bezier curve is a polynomial of degree _____ the number of control points used
   (*a*) one more than   (*b*) one less than
   (*c*) two less than   (*d*) none of these

13.19. Clamped B-spline curve P(t) passes through
   (*a*) two middle control points   (*b*) two end control points
   (*c*) both (*a*) and (*b*)   (*d*) neither (*a*) nor (*b*)

13.20. Changing the position of control point P_i only affects the curve $P(u)$ on interval
   (*a*) $[\,u_i, u_{i+p+1})$ (*b*) $[u_{i-1}, u_{i+p+1})$
   (*c*) $[u_i, u_{i+1})$ (*d*) $[u_i, u_{i+p})$

13.21. Which of the following is a type of parametric curves and surfaces?
   (*a*) Bezier and rational Bezier   (*b*) B-spline
   (*c*) NURBS   (*d*) all of the above

ANSWERS

13.1 (*a*)	**13.2** (*a*)	**13.3** (*b*)	**13.4** (*a*)
13.5 (*b*)	**13.6** (*d*)	**13.7** (*b*)	**13.8** (*a*)
13.9 (*a*)	**13.10** (*b*)	**13.11** (*b*)	**13.12** (*a*)
13.13 (*a*)	**13.14** (*b*)	**13.15** (*c*)	**13.16** (*a*)
13.17 (*b*)	**13.18** (*b*)	**13.19** (*b*)	**13.20** (*a*)
13.21 (*d*)			

INDEX

www.ingramcontent.com/pod-product-compliance
Lightning Source LLC
Chambersburg PA
CBHW080654220326
41598CB00033B/5201